'With *Pompeii*, Ray Laurence (a disting[uished] writer Alex Butterworth have done som[ething] is the fullest and most readable account I know ... a splendid panorama of both a provincial city and a wider political and cultural world ... Perhaps the most impressive feature is the sheer detail, and the lightness of touch in presenting it ... A third of the city still lies buried and one very much hopes that Laurence and Butterworth will be there as it is opened up'
Peter Jones, *Sunday Telegraph*

'By using the very latest archaeological and historical research, *Pompeii* offers a vivid portrait of a lost city during the 25 years leading up to the eruption that destroyed it ... We find a world rich in wine, ritual, sex, political scandal and over-the-top partying. This book is a wonderfully accessible introduction to the social history of the Roman Empire as a whole'   *Daily Express*

'Butterworth and Laurence have produced something imaginative and new. Evocative, precise, kaleidoscopic and enormously vivid ... a significant and innovative work of historical imagination. It deserves to reach a wide readership'   Professor Andrew Wallace-Hadrill

'One turns eagerly to Alex Butterworth and Ray Laurence's wonderfully vivid and detailed account of Pompeian social history, *Pompeii* ... They tell their story with a confident authority, blending descriptions of Pompeian society into a consecutive narrative that artfully combines local and Imperial history from the accession of Nero in AD 54 to the volcanic eruption in 79. It is an ambitious project based on an impressively encyclopaedic knowledge of the literary and archaeological evidence, and it offers a great deal of information not found in any other book on Pompeii ... this is a bold, vigorous and original book. Readers will learn a lot from it ... Alex Butterworth and Ray Laurence's exuberant tour de force'   T. P. Wiseman, *Times Literary Supplement*

'This book attempts to restore meaning to the dusty ruins, with notable success ... It is the great achievement of this book that we feel we know these people, and their tragedy moves us. The life and death of Pompeii is evoked with verve and authority'   Jane Stevenson, *Observer*

'With an excellent bibliography, notes and index, *Pompeii: The Living City* fulfils every requirement of an erudite historical exposition, while achieving something far greater through its entertaining and well-written text'
Nick West, *Tribune*

'An immensely evocative, well-written and powerful portrait of what life was really like in Pompeii. Read it!'   Tom Holland, author of *Rubicon*

'It takes a real act of imagination to recreate the life that once filled the city's streets. Ray Laurence is well qualified to make the attempt ... Now he has

teamed up with Alex Butterworth, a writer and dramatist, to bring the city to life in a more readily accessible and attractive fashion. What the authors have done is to attempt to tell the story of the last twenty-five years of Pompeii's existence in something of the style of a novel. The book is stuffed with information: how to get married, how to stand for the town council, where to get sex at a price, the problems of owning slaves, how to make a living in shipping, how to conduct a Roman funeral, with attractions of exotic religions ... a splendid piece of imaginative reconstruction ... reading *Pompeii: The Living City* is about the best preparation I can think of for a visit to the city'
Jeremy Paterson, *Literary Review*

'Butterworth and Laurence paint a rich, multi-layered and utterly memorable picture of Pompeii and their book is a thumping good read'   *Irish Examiner*

'This heavily researched but readable book, which is also splendidly illus-trated'
Jane Gardam, *Spectator*

'In a very lucid and entertaining style, *Pompeii: The Living City* pulls together all the recent scholarship on the buried town and turns it into a compelling and yet highly detailed narrative. I only wish it had been available when I was researching my novel'
Robert Harris

'Brings Pompeii startlingly alive once more'   *History Today*

'An original and vivid recreation of unfolding events in the doomed city ... The whole is written in a lively style, with nice touches of humour ... a good read'   *British Archaeology*

'A vivid portrait of place and people before the cataclysms of AD 62 and 79'
Church Times

'Accessible, wide-ranging and evocative and makes surprisingly compelling reading'
Ben Jarman, *Catholic Times*

'For those looking to be transported back to the living city, it will be hard to resist'
Oxford Times

Alex Butterworth is a writer and dramatist, who holds degrees from the University of Oxford and the Royal College of Art. This is his first book.

Ray Laurence is a Research Fellow in the Institute of Archaeology and Antiquity at the University of Birmingham. He has published seven academic books on Roman archaeology and history.

Pompeii is the winner of the 2006 Longman–*History Today* New Gen-eration Book of the Year award.

Pompeii

THE LIVING CITY

Alex Butterworth &
Ray Laurence

PHOENIX

A PHOENIX PAPERBACK

First published in Great Britain in 2005
by Weidenfeld & Nicolson
This paperback edition published in 2006
by Phoenix,
an imprint of Orion Books Ltd,
Orion House, 5 Upper St Martin's Lane,
London WC2H 9EA

An Hachette UK company

7 9 10 8

Copyright © Alex Butterworth and Ray Laurence 2005

A CIP catalogue record for this book
is available from the British Library.

ISBN 978-0-7538-2076-6

Typeset by Butler and Tanner Ltd, Frome and London
Printed and bound by CPI Group
(UK) Ltd, Croydon, CR0 4YY

The Orion Publishing Group's policy is to use papers that
are natural, renewable and recyclable products and made
from wood grown in sustainable forests. The logging and
manufacturing processes are expected to conform to the
environmental regulations of the country of origin.

www.orionbooks.co.uk

CONTENTS

LIST OF ILLUSTRATIONS

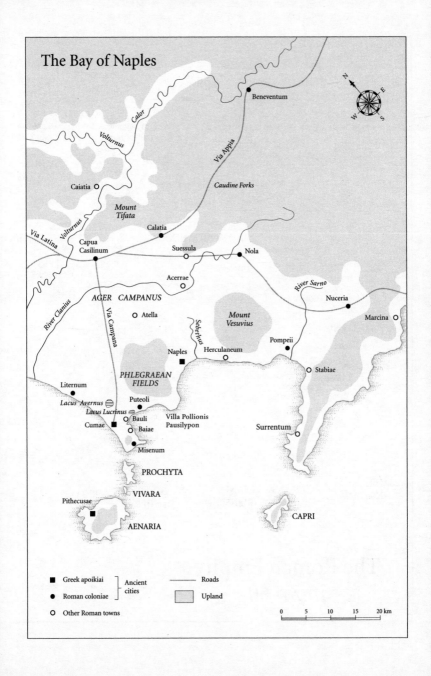

The Bay of Naples

Beneventum

Calor

Volturnus

Via Appia

Caudine Forks

Caiatia ○

Mount Tifata

Via Latina

Volturnus

Calatia ●

Capua Casilinum ●

Suessula ○

Nola ●

River Sarno

Acerrae ○

River Clanius

Via Campana

AGER CAMPANUS

Atella ○

Mount Vesuvius

Nuceria ●

Marcina ○

Sebethus

Naples ■

Herculaneum ●

Pompeii ●

PHLEGRAEAN FIELDS

Liternum ●

Lacus Avernus

Puteoli ○

Villa Pollionis Pausilypon

Stabiae ○

Lacus Lucrinus

Bauli ○

Cumae ■

Baiae ○

Surrentum ○

Misenum ●

PROCHYTA

VIVARA

Pithecusae ■

CAPRI

AENARIA

■ Greek apoikiai ⎤
           ⎬ Ancient cities
● Roman coloniae ⎦

—— Roads

○ Other Roman towns

Upland

0 5 10 15 20 km

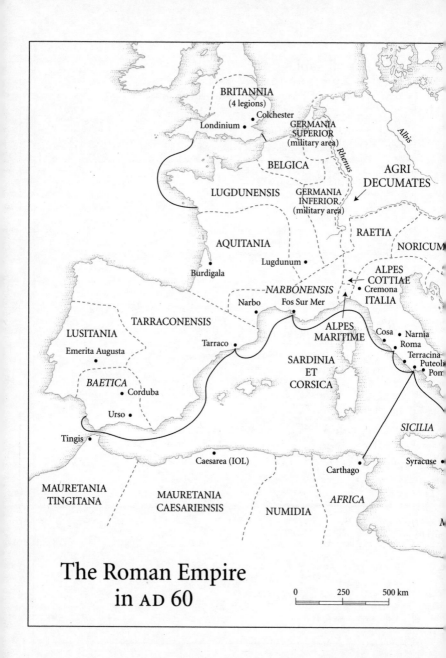

The Roman Empire
in AD 60

0   250   500 km

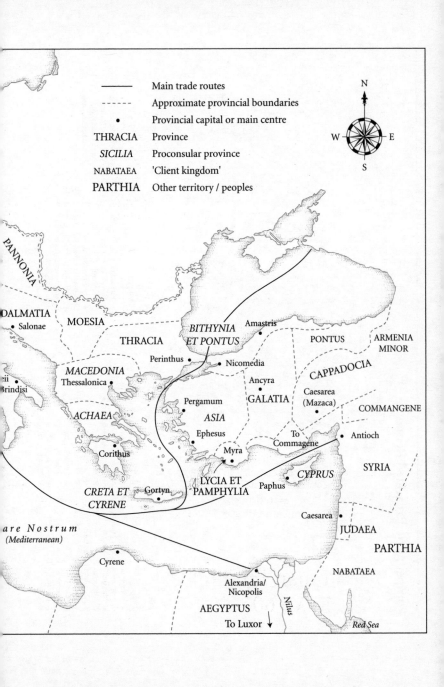

Main trade routes
Approximate provincial boundaries
Provincial capital or main centre

THRACIA   Province
SICILIA   Proconsular province
NABATAEA   'Client kingdom'
PARTHIA   Other territory / peoples

N
W   E
S

PANNONIA

DALMATIA
• Salonae

MOESIA

THRACIA

*BITHYNIA
ET PONTUS*   Amastris •   PONTUS   ARMENIA
MINOR

MACEDONIA   Perinthus •   • Nicomedia

Thessalonica •   CAPPADOCIA

Ancyra •

Pergamum •   GALATIA   Caesarea
(Mazaca) •

ACHAEA   *ASIA*   COMMANGENE

• Ephesus   To
Commagene   • Antioch

Corithus •   Myra

*CRETA ET
CYRENE*   Gortyn •   LYCIA ET
PAMPHYLIA   Paphus •   *CYPRUS*   SYRIA

...ii •
...rindisi •

Caesarea •

are Nostrum
(Mediterranean)   JUDAEA

PARTHIA

• Cyrene   NABATAEA

Alexandria/
Nicopolis

AEGYPTUS   *Nilus*

To Luxor ↓   *Red Sea*

Pompeii: The Excavated Remains

Herculaneum Gate

Vesuvius Gate

Nola Gate

Sarno Gate

Nuceria Gate

Stabian Gate

Marine Gate

Unexcavated

0   50 100 150 200

Metres

N
E
S
W

KEY

A Forum
B Temple of Apollo
C Capitoline Temple of Jupiter
D Eumachia Building
E Macellum
F Temple of Public Lares
G Comitium
H Curia
I Temple of Venus
J Theatre
K Odeon

L Theatre Palaestra/Gladiator Barracks
M Isis Temple
N Triangular Forum
O Temple of Aesclupianus
P Sarno Baths
Q Stabian Baths
R Central Baths
S Amphitheatre
T Palaestra
U Suburban Baths
V Temple of Fortuna Augusta

Houses

1 Fabius Rufus
2 Umbricius Scaurus
3 The Vettii
4 The Faun (Satrii)
5 Dioscuri (NigidiusVacula)
6 Citherista (L.Popidius Ampliatus)
7 Marine Venus (Lucretius Valens)
8 Julius Polybius
9 Menander (Poppaei)
10 Amorini Dorati (Poppaei)
11 Villa of the Mysteries
12 Praedia Julia Felix
13 Marcus Epidius Sabinus
14 Sailor

Nothing can last for ever;
Though the sun shines gold
It must plunge into the sea.
The moon has also disappeared
Which but now so brightly gleamed.

Graffito from Pompeii

The Far End of the Journey

October AD 79

It was the hour before dawn and the sky above Luxor was already showing the same sickly yellow hue that had tinted it every day for the past month. Not far from the towering statue of King Memnon a small group of men stamped and shivered against the unnatural cold, their cloaks gathered about them. Once in a while they would glance towards the statue's vast stone feet, between which their master sat, a solitary figure, awaiting first light, when the ancient king would utter his famed greeting.

So still did Suedius Clemens, the Prefect of the Camps in Egypt, hold himself that, as the minutes passed, the dust that filled the air began to settle on his clothes and skin, covering them in a dark film. He had travelled far to arrive here, across the deserts of sand and the deserts within himself, and now was a moment for contemplation. Word of the disaster in far-off Campania had reached Alexandria while he had been finalising the preparations for his last tour of inspection. The first traders to hurry their ships back to Egypt, in flight from the plummeting fire and surging waves, had quickly filled Alexandria with tales of an apocalypse – of how the mountain of Vesuvius had exploded into flames, breathing fire over the cities in its shadow and raining down stone.

Although Clemens had known Pompeii well, from his days spent there as the Emperor Vespasian's sacred judge, when his advisors suggested that the planned expedition to the Egyptian interior be cancelled, he had overruled them without hesitation. But as the days had passed, he had come to regret his decision. With each step he took, memories of Pompeii drew ever closer.

Heading east from the Nile, the Prefect had counted the caravans crossing the land that thirsts; had watched them approach from one horizon and disappear over the other with their precious freight, and known that they might be heading for Pompeii. He had pressed on, far into the eastern desert, until he came to Mons Porphyrites, where rain fell only once every decade in a single torrential burst. There he had witnessed the terrible mines, and the men who quarried the bright stone without cease, lit at night by the flames from high-stoked pyres and watched over by the round towers of the garrison fortress. But in his mind's eye it was the rare purple-flagged porphyry floors of Pompeii that he saw.

Looping back to the Nile, he had been thrown back into the world of Roman rule. To ears for so long assailed by orders barked out in rough soldier's Latin, the mellifluous Greek he heard in the towns and villages through which they passed was captivating, and the babble of the Egyptian boatman a balm to his mind. But he had forgotten how time had passed, that November had come, and he was caught unawares by the chants of Isis worshippers as they celebrated her lover's rebirth along the banks of the river. The slender ibises puncturing the water with their curved beaks and the crocodiles sliding into the Nile from their mud shoals were all too familiar from the painted walls of Pompeii.

At last, Clemens had reached Luxor and, with it, the end of his journey. In a few days he would return to Alexandria and then take ship to Italy. Would Pompeii still be there for him to see? – the city he had judged so freely, yet which only now, perhaps too late, he had come to appreciate. Could anyone from Pompeii possibly have survived?

INTRODUCTION

In July 1738, workmen digging the foundations of a summer palace for Charles of Bourbon, the King of Naples, discovered the first hard evidence of the cities that had been buried by Vesuvius in AD 79. Statues and other fragments from antiquity had been coming to light in the area for centuries but it was only then that a new professionalism was brought to bear on the process of investigating what lay beneath the fertile fields of Campania. Passages were tunnelled down to the theatre of Herculaneum and occasional honoured visitors allowed to explore by torchlight, while treasures were added to the private Bourbon collections by the cartload. But the King's excitement was tinged with frustration.

Although funding for the work in the area was unstinting, the great discrepancy between the present-day and ancient ground levels impeded progress. When, in 1755, the construction of the Sarno Canal revealed further remains a few miles away, this time only a few metres underground, it was hoped that the new site might allow far more rapid exploration. Working outwards from what was subsequently revealed to have been a complex of bars, baths and rental property belonging to a woman called Julia Felix, it soon became clear that an extensive lost world did indeed lie within reach. But what was this place that stood on a small escarpment that was still known in local folklore as 'Civita', or 'the City'? The reticence in the classical sources on the subject of the eruption testifies to the depth of the shock that was felt at the time: all they offered to the King was a simple list of places that had been destroyed. Only when a dedicatory inscription came to light, was the truth revealed. The ancient city was Pompeii.

News spread fast by the standards of the day: a city was being

3

unearthed on the Bay of Naples that still breathed with the life of ancient times. Amongst the educated classes of Europe, for whom the classical world was still a very present ideal, the chance to travel back in time was a marvel not to be missed. Pompeii, less than a hundred and fifty miles south of Rome, quickly became an indispensable destination on the Grand Tour. Goethe, the greatest poet of the age, visited and watched the excavation of a house that was named in his honour; William Hamilton, the British Ambassador to Naples, sent samples of volcanic materials to the Royal Academy, whilst his wife, Emma, became famous for adopting classical poses, or 'attitudes'; others were to translate the aesthetic of Pompeii into Wedgwood pottery and Adam interiors; Mozart visited the newly uncovered Temple of Isis in 1769 and the memories of its mysterious precinct remained with him vividly enough to inspire the composition of *The Magic Flute* almost twenty years later[1] (Plate 26). In the nineteenth century, the novelist Stendhal was inspired to write, 'The strangest thing I saw on my travels was Pompeii, where you feel as if you have been transported back into the ancient world; even if you normally believe only proven facts, here you feel as if, just by being there, you know more about the place than any scholar.'

Two and a half centuries later, the modern visitor no longer clambers down, awestruck, into the Pompeii excavations, but pays his entrance fee and walks up the steep slope towards the Marine Gate in the company of a fraction of the two million and more tourists who pass through the turnstiles each year. Yet the initial experience remains overwhelming: more than three square kilometres of buildings – houses, hovels, temples, markets, baths and theatres – stand exposed to view, at least where the vigilant custodians and barred streets allow it. Walking Pompeii's streets at the dawn of the third millennium, it is impossible not to feel something of Stendhal's intimation that there, history is almost alive. But such an impression can be deceptive.

At the end of the eighteenth century and during the excavations of the nineteenth, artists recorded the pristine quality of the buildings as they came to light: the pigments luminous in the recently unearthed wall paintings, the graffiti-covered plasterwork, though cracked, still clinging to the walls. Only at the height of four metres or more, where the last layers of ash had settled, were the buildings cut short; below, it was as if the ancient residents had only just departed. Except that, tragically, many of them remained. Trapped within the compacted volcanic debris were the skeletons of hundreds of the city's inhabitants, clutching their belongings and clinging to loved ones in air pockets that bore the impression of each body's final agonies. The curious tourist of the 1860s and later, wandering the excavations, might even have witnessed the reappearance of these ancient citizens – seen plaster poured into the moulds left in the ash and the hardened casts of the dead gently lifted free.

Theirs is an experience that we can only envy. Today, the two thirds of the city that has been excavated is rapidly deteriorating. Plaster and paint flake off walls, mosaics are scuffed and *tesserae* scattered, while the walls that were once loud with graffiti now stand bare and silent.[2] Most of the major artworks have been removed for preservation – those, at least, that have not been stolen to order for private collectors, hacked out from the site itself. With their departure, and the fading under the effects of sun and rain of most of what remains, the colour of the city has gone. No longer does the casual visitor have the information needed to imagine the city in its full glory, or bring to life, in the mind's eye, those who inhabited it: the slaves who arrived in Campania, from Africa or the cold north, and were driven to market in Pompeii; Caecilius Jucundus, the city's steady but aspiring auctioneer, who kept a meticulous account of his sales, including a sideline in human cargo; the political clique of Julius Polybius, with his finger in so many pies; or the elusive Grosphus, who failed to keep the peace during his term in office as a senior magistrate.

Rather than the ancient graffiti and political posters that once covered the walls and summoned the flavour of the lost world, the most resonant graffiti still visible in Pompeii today is perhaps that in the toilets of the cafeteria: 'If I'd wanted ruins I could have gone to Kabul.'

And yet the means to bring the bleak walls back to life does exist, hidden away in the great tomes that transcribe the graffiti originally written by self-selecting loudmouths, and the thousands of appeals to voters that were written on Pompeii's walls on behalf of candidates standing for election to public office, or else encoded in artwork from the walls and floors of the city that now lies in museum vaults; information that was locked up in the bones of the eruption's victims, or sits on bookshelves, waiting to be extracted from the literary texts of the time. From work carried out on these sources, it is now possible to refute the dystopian versions of the city promulgated by nineteenth-century Christian moralists, and revise the more errant academic interpretations of later years. Such knowledge is hard won.

Pompeii contains probably the greatest density of data of any ancient archaeological site in the world, but that only augments the challenge facing contemporary scholars. The sheer volume of material that can be drawn upon, along with the shortcomings in technique and record-keeping of many of those who have worked on the site in the past, make the task of bringing all the disparate evidence into some meaningful relationship especially difficult. The state of almost all the skeletal remains from the site is symptomatic: having been disarticulated in the nineteenth century by students of eugenics and race who were interested only in skulls, the bones now lie in charnel houses, piled according to type. Where they were found is not documented. The records for many of the artefacts retrieved from buildings is little better: hundreds of Day Books that record the daily activities and finds of the site's earlier excavators lie gathering dust, and now themselves need to be 'excavated'. While those whose endeavours are catalogued in them required strong muscles and physical endurance to shift the hundreds of thousands of tonnes of *lapilli* – the tiny pellets of volcanic material – that buried the city, the historians and archaeologists of the last thirty years have required equivalent amounts of patience, persistence and restraint to make sense of what was left behind.

The product of their intellectual efforts is astonishing, with seemingly random facts marshalled into embryonic accounts of human lives. Records of the height at which bodies were found has been cross-referenced with studies of volcanic eruptions to better understand the victims' final hours; the layering of political writing on walls has been used to create a chronology of political life and to reconstruct networks of allegiance in the city during the preceding decades; and careful investigation below the ground level of AD 79 has revealed the heritage with which those citizens lived. The extension of plaster-cast techniques from bodies to the space left by incinerated plant roots has made it possible to recreate the fauna of gardens and farms and has made sense of agricultural techniques, while the discovery in 1982 of a great many new skeletons from Herculaneum has allowed the kind of analysis of disease and physical condition that was previously impossible. Even with a virtual moratorium on any new archaeological work in the unexcavated areas of the ancient city, the re-examination of existing evidence has prompted new interpretations of how domestic buildings were used by their inhabitants and of the distinct character of different areas of the city.

The primary intention of this book is to bring together this wealth of information, together with certain original insights, in a story of life as it was lived, in all its strangeness, during the troublesome twenty-five years leading up to Pompeii's destruction. The cities of Vesuvius have regularly been used as a lens through which to view an era that they are supposed to typify: an age when the wealth of Roman Italy reached unprecedented heights, levels of slavery burgeoned, and a rigidly structured society had to confront these changes. Yet it is a mere quirk of fate that the place which most defines our understanding of society in the Roman Empire is a small section of coastal plane, the lower slopes of a volcanic mountain, and the local port and commercial centre, situated in a farming and resort area about a hundred and fifty miles south of Rome. This is the micro-history of that place and its ill-fortuned inhabitants, as the days of ease were left behind and the Pompeians confronted a series of grave threats, whose origins were both human and divine. It is a portrait of a society oblivious to the tragic destiny that awaited it.

Insofar as it considers the larger Roman world, this was a period dominated by Nero's infamous reign. His influence was felt across his empire, and especially so in Pompeii, where through his second wife the Emperor had a particular personal interest. But just as the accounts of Nero's career are open to varied interpretation – with the precise chronology of events possibly manipulated by ancient historians to achieve particular effects, and an ideological agenda always in play – it is still more difficult to be certain, from a distance of two thousand years, precisely when certain events in a small town took place. Even the exact date of the earthquake that devastated Pompeii in AD 62 (or was it AD 63?) cannot be pinned down, and the dates when particular individuals held public office still less so. About the sequence of events, however, it is possible to be more confident, and within that framework we know the extent to which the rhythms of life were shaped by a rigid calendar of festivals and markets.

It is almost certain that, in decades to come, aspects of how we understand Pompeii will change fundamentally. Even the excavation of a single new building could overturn our preconceptions: the discovery of a dedicatory inscription that fitted a temple facade could change the god's name by which it is known; some electoral postings could elevate a minor political figure to new heights in our estimation; another cache of wax tablets might add a whole new dimension to our understanding of the city's economy. After all, an entire third of the city still lies buried, and only a few yards behind the facades on the north side of the main street – whose occupants' names we sometimes know but which are otherwise unexplored – dazzling data might reside. Thanks to improved research methods, three of the most recent buildings to be investigated – the House of the Chaste Lovers, the House of Julius Polybius, and that of Fabius Rufus – have furnished a wealth of extraordinary new insights. And it is little wonder that some want to delve deeper into the Villa of the Papyri outside Herculaneum and its library of scrolls. For the moment, though, we believe that what follows is accurate insofar as it is possible to be so; for those who wish to explore the subjects touched upon further, an extensive bibliography has been provided.

The exception is those sections printed in italics, which are straightforward fictional reconstructions. Whilst it would be foolish to imagine that one might enter into the mind of another human being at such a distance of time and across so many subtle and not-so-subtle cultural differences, these interludes propose ways of seeing the experience of certain Pompeians in relationship to their world and their fellows. In some cases they are men and women about whom something is known; where this is the case, a consistency has been maintained between the fictional portrayal and discussions of the evidence concerning them. In other cases, especially those of women and slaves – groups who are almost entirely absent from the documentary record – an even greater degree of licence has been called for. The accounts of all their lives should be treated as firmly grounded conjecture, but conjecture nevertheless. From the woman dying in the arms of her gladiator-lover, to the 'prostitutes' endorsing embarrassed candidates for election, there are already more than enough myths about the ancient people of Pompeii.

Opening his history of a period that overlaps with ours, Tacitus remarked, 'The history on which I am entering is that of a period rich in disasters, terrible in battles, torn by civil struggles, horrible even in peace.' In its basic lineaments, the relevance of the period spanning the first centuries BC and AD to our own times appears unmistakable, and has been much remarked upon in recent years. Ours is an age when the wealth of the rich and the poverty of the global underclass is as great as ever it was in Rome; when the trade that feeds the untrammelled consumption of luxuries and natural resources at the heart of empire mimics the extortion of tribute from vassal states in ancient times; and when the ageing, shrinking population of the West again requires that the youthful replenishment of its stock by immigrant labour be well managed to avoid destabilising society. And whilst the eruption of Vesuvius was a catastrophe to challenge the confidence of even the most powerful empire – and one which was looked for, and long prophesied, by Rome's enemies in what is now the Middle East – explicit contemporary parallels will be eschewed.

It should never be forgotten, that the archaeology of Pompeii is primarily that of a disaster zone. Only because of its tragic end, and the powerful preserving effect of burial in volcanic debris and mud, has Pompeii generated such a wealth of material and sustained so much interest for so long. Yet amazingly, whilst it is necessary to grub around for even the smallest hint of the life of a female slave in the city – an inscription on a ring, perhaps, or a child's headstone that is no more conspicuous than that of a pet – a unique record has been found, far away, of one man who had been in Pompeii shortly before the eruption.

The name of Titus Suedius Clemens is still visible where he carved it into the colossal foot of King Memnon's statue outside Luxor, along with his rank as Prefect of the Camps in Egypt. Even then the monument would have been in ruins. Although Memnon and his companion a few metres away had once reached a height of over twenty metres, by the time Clemens saw them they were already in a state of truncated semi-ruination. Nevertheless, the stone figures were still capable of inducing such awe that they found their way onto the itinerary of even the most jaded Roman tourist in Egypt. For here was evidence that sophisticated societies could pass from memory, made more striking still by the belief that one of the statues represented the Ethiopian king who had fought beside Rome's own founding father, Aeneas, in defence of Troy. That the statue whispered strange sounds at dawn – a greeting to Memnon's mother, some said – only increased its mystique.

The phenomenon was easily explained: the seismic activity that had so badly damaged the statue's twin had opened a chamber inside Memnon, which amplified the vibrations created when the dawn air was warmed by the sun. But whilst the acoustics of the statue were unknown to Suedius Clemens, he knew well enough the strange effects that seismic disturbances could have: on men and society. In around AD 75, he had been dispatched on a mission to Pompeii, a city that thirteen years earlier had been plunged into chaos by a devastating earthquake. There he had acted as an imperial judge, tasked with solving the city's most pressing problems. And it is there, in the city beneath Vesuvius, that the only other inscriptions to mention him have been found, commemorating his contribution to the city.

It was late AD 79 when Suedius Clemens found himself in Luxor, and there would have been much on his mind. Only weeks earlier, on 24 August, the single greatest catastrophe to strike the Roman world had destroyed Pompeii.[3] But our story of that city begins twenty-five years earlier, when the unexpected elevation to the imperial throne of a vibrant young man seemed to herald a bright new dawn. A papyrus document discovered in Egypt, bearing the date 17 November AD 54 captures the excitement of the moment: 'The expectation and hope of all the world has been proclaimed Emperor; the good genius of the world and the beginning of all great and good things, Nero, has been proclaimed Caesar.'[4]

CHAPTER I

Death of a Roman Knight

November AD 54

Decimus Lucretius Valens stretched out his frail body on the couch that his servants had positioned in the summer dining room at his request. From there he watched the last of the weak sunlight retreat behind the roofline of the courtyard, and felt the room grow cold. From the nearby street the sounds of the city could be heard as it went about its business: men returning home from the baths to prepare for dinner, shopkeepers sliding in the wooden slats to shut up their premises for the day, empty wagons trundling back out to the farms having delivered their produce.

On his own country estate, not far beyond the city walls, Valens's slaves would be finishing their outdoor jobs for the day, scattering a last cartload of dung around the olive trees before going inside to charge the oil lamps. Afterwards they would begin their evening work of sharpening stakes and poles for the vines, repairing their tools and building hives for the bees. He wondered whether his own bees had supplied the wax from which his death mask had been sculpted the day before; he hoped so.

Valens was resolved that the coming night would see his release. Like the gladiators in the troupe that the Lucretius family owned, he would approach death unflinchingly. He had lived for more than sixty years and was reconciled to his end. When younger he had visited Lake Avernus, beyond Puteoli and the steaming Phlegraean Fields, where it was said the mouth of Hades opened. He remembered that it had not been far to travel, only a long day's journey there and back.

His generation was nearly all gone now. How many were left in Pompeii who could remember the solemn procession that had carried the body of the great Emperor Augustus, founding father of the Empire, on its journey back from Nola to the capital? How many who had honoured its sacred freight during the hot hours of the day, when it had rested in the marble halls of the towns through which it passed? He remembered it well: the corpse of an old man, worn out by the strains of long service in public life; a body like his own.

No children of his blood still lived, but the Lucretius family name would continue. He had seen to that by adopting an eager young man from the Satrius family. The Satrii had been only too willing to forge a relationship with an ancient family of knights who had strong links with the imperial court. And his new son had already shown his qualities. He would do well, Valens was sure of that.

It was dark now and he felt tired. With his own passing and that of his contemporaries, the Pompeians would begin to forget the Divine Augustus and the austere ideals on which his Empire had been built. But it was too late for such thoughts. Valens was departing and Pompeii would have to find its way without him.

As soon as the Roman Knight Decimus Lucretius Valens passed on, the procedures for celebrating his life swung smoothly into operation: the executors of his will were summoned, the authorities notified, meetings of the appropriate official bodies convened. Their task was to prepare a pageant of public mourning. Valens's wife, whose name we do not know, would have suppressed her grief in accordance with Roman society's prohibition on the expression of private sentiment; to all appearances she would have accepted the whims of the goddess Fortuna without complaint. Her husband had provided for her needs, but her status now, with no surviving children, was far from secure: much would depend on the adopted heir.[1]

As the widow donned her dark robes of mourning, she might have worried about the young man from the Satrius family who had taken her husband's name. Was he slightly too willing to take risks? A year or two earlier this Decimus Satrius Lucretius Valens had made a bold statement of his political allegiances by becoming Pompeii's priest of Nero: his *flamen*. It was now November. Some would have thought him foolhardy; others prescient. The young prince's mother, Agrippina, aided by her allies – and in particular the boy's tutors, the millionaire philosopher Seneca and the bluff soldier Burrus – had done everything possible to position him as the Emperor Claudius's successor. An image of precocious maturity had been sculpted and Nero's assumption of the *toga virilis* (marking the transition to adulthood), had been fast-tracked. This emphasis on the adulthood of the teenager was a key component of a strategy to sideline Claudius's natural son, the young Britannicus. The two stepbrothers, divided by only a couple of years in age, had appeared side by side in public – their respective styles of dress designating one a man, the other a mere boy – and Nero had capitalised further on his adult status by marrying Brittanicus's elder sister, his own stepsister, Octavia. It was a clever move, since it not only cemented Nero's position within Claudius's immediate family, but also symbolised the political union of two families who had contested the imperial throne for half a century.

In late AD 54 the years of preparation paid off. When, in October, Claudius died – at a suspiciously early age, with poisonous mushrooms the suspected cause, and rumour rife about how they had escaped detection by his food taster – the sixteen-year-old Nero was immediately proclaimed the inheritor of the imperial mantle. Britannicus was still alive, but with bribes securing the loyalty of the legions, Nero seemed unassailable. Yet, for all his apparent ascendancy, even in provincial Pompeii no one would have needed reminding how quickly the fortunes of those at the imperial court could change. After all, who could know what powerful supporters Brittanicus might eventually rally to his cause?[2] And if Nero faltered in the coming months, the young Decimus Satrius Lucretius Valens, now known to everyone as Nero's *flamen*, would be dragged down with him and the family name tarnished.

The home of Decimus Lucretius Valens has been identified, with some reliability, just inside the eastern wall of the city in a surprisingly unostentatious location near the Sarno Gate. Situated on the city's main thoroughfare – now known as the via dell'Abbondanza – and close to the amphitheatre where the Lucretii are known to have sponsored games involving their own gladiators, the family house is almost as far as it could be from the commercial and political heart of Pompeii in and around the forum (see Plate 9).

There, the rebuilding during the great Augustan age at the end of the first century BC had created a grand public space with porticos, temples, administrative buildings and market facilities. Although a little narrow relative to its length, as a result of the constraints of older buildings on either side, it conformed almost exactly to the ideal laid down by the architectural writer Vitruvius. It would seem reasonable to expect the houses of the city's leading figures to have congregated around such a space but, for the Lucretii and others like them, the hubbub of the city was only one part of their existence.

A recent excavation in Scafati, the suburb of modern Pompeii close to which the ancient city lies, has revealed that the Lucretii also owned a substantial country villa, and it holds the key to why Valens needed to adopt an heir. Sixty metres from the main structure, in a magnificent garden laid out to evoke the idyllic landscape of Elysium, the Roman Paradise, stands the family tomb: a small house itself, complete with doors, a roof and an altar. Inside the enclosure, a series of stones carved in the shape of human heads and bearing inscriptions mark the position of the funeral urns, beside which are small funnels that allowed libations to be poured down to sustain the deceased below. Known as *columellae*, these stones offer an insight into the lives and fates of four generations of the Lucretius family, including Valens's two known children, a son and a daughter, who died in childhood.[3]

Perhaps, on his regular visits to the forum, the grieving Valens had watched with envy as Satrius and his healthy sons carried out their business before retiring to their grand house – the largest within the city's walls – that was set just one block to the north of the Temple of Jupiter. Now called the House of the Faun after an especially fine bronze statue of a dancing satyr that was discovered on a pedestal in the atrium hall, and that may have been intended as a visual pun on the name 'Satrius', it is a conspicuously impressive building. Like many Pompeian houses, it has shops on either side, but nothing detracts from the elegance of the pilasters that flank the high, wide jaws of the entrance, as though alerting the visitor to stand tall. Once inside, two consecutive peristyle courtyards can be seen stretching off into the distance, offering a pleasing play of perspective into the private depths of the house, that could have been concealed by screens and curtains as the occasion required.

This was the home of a family who had commanded the respect of the community for a long time, even before Roman rule, and were accustomed to holding important civic positions. With its fine decoration and exquisite mosaics that had been carefully restored, rather than simply replaced, on a number of occasions since they were first installed, the building oozed the values of old money. But at the beginning of the first century BC, conflict with Rome had shaken the assured outlook of its indigenous Oscan-speaking inhabitants and many old families had never quite recovered their prestige.

The watershed for the Satrii and their like had come in 80 BC when the troops of the Roman dictator Lucius Cornelius Sulla had entered the territories of the cities supposedly allied to Rome to quell their rebellious demands for more equal rights with their dominant neighbour. Even then, the Oscan-speaking city was past its heyday, but the inhabitants were proud of their heritage. The greatest houses had been built during the second century BC and their spectacular architecture was a reminder of the Greek civilisation that had once ruled Campania, while the traditions of the Samnite race were also strong in the area. When all the cities in the region had succumbed to Sulla's army, Pompeii was left as the sole irritant, holding out against siege. Following their final defeat, Pompeii's citizens were to pay heavily for their pride. Sulla had to make good on the promise he had made to his troops, by rewarding them with land and property to which they could retire and begin their civilian lives. And what better way to find it than by ousting from their homes those who had dared answer back to Rome? Pompeii's transformation into Sulla's 'Colony of Venus' – the *Colonia Cornelia Veneria Pompeianorum* – saw the imposition on the region of an entire legion of probably four to five thousand men, all of whom demanded at least enough land to yield a living, and far more for the higher ranks. In some cases they even brought families with them, and the city found itself flooded with new inhabitants.

It was a traumatic period for the natives. The Roman veterans presented a profound culture shock: battle-hardened by long years of service, the old soldiers were better entertained by a gladiator's dance of death than by the refined pleasures of the theatre. The imposition of their political traditions caused even greater resentment, according to Cicero. And that was before they embarked on their building programme: a capacious amphitheatre, a redesigned forum and a second small theatre for music or rhetoric competitions, all of which were paid for by incomers whose vast funds had most likely been expropriated from their new neighbours.[4]

It is difficult to trace the fortunes of the native families during this period, some of whom were clearly reduced from wealth to destitution without leaving any tangible trace of their fall. However, whilst relatively few of these earlier family names appear in the records of political life in the city's latter years, this does not necessarily mean that their descendants were not active. It seems that many families changed their names in order to ingratiate themselves with their new rulers. The Satrii were known throughout Campania as the Suttii before this time, and there are numerous other examples of such Romanisation: Numistreii becoming Numistrii; Luccaeia, Luccia; Lassaei, Lassii. The differences seem subtle, but to contemporaries these were bold statements that appear to have brought clear advantages. In those families with two branches, the one that opted to camouflage itself with a more Romanised name is consistently seen to have been the more successful.[5]

As the initial impact of the changes diminished, however, even those native families less inclined to seek a rapprochement might have been able to claw their way back up the social ladder, parleying their native know-how into profit and buying land back on the cheap from veterans who found a farmer's life too much like hard work. As their wealth returned to them, so did their political power. In an inscription on the seating of the amphitheatre, the unmistakably native name of Istacidius Cilix is listed as a town magistrate alongside his Roman colleagues. Elsewhere there is evidence of intermarriage between native and Roman families: Lassii marrying Clodii, Epidii marrying Lucretii. From the moment the colony was established, all children born in Pompeii would have been citizens of Rome merely as members of the Menenia tribe, the archaic and now administrative grouping that encompassed most Campanians.

For all the deficits experienced by the native population, there was also a dawning sense of belonging within the Roman state, with all the privileges and guarantees of protection that entailed.

By the time the young man from the Satrius family was adopted by Decimus Lucretius Valens, his family home would have received an addition to its grand entrance: a mosaic that offered a welcome not in Oscan but in Latin: 'HAVE'. It was a sign of how far things had come in a century: the young man who could claim an ancestry that was deeply rooted in the soil of Campania would have had no trouble in declaring himself a Roman. But some things mattered even more than being a citizen of the greatest empire in the known world. For whatever national allegiance Satrius Valens professed, it was the very particular character of the ground beneath his feet in Pompeii that would ultimately have the most profound influence on his life.

When the first inhabitants of Pompeii chose to build their settlement on the strategic escarpment at the mouth of the River Sarno, during the Bronze Age at the latest, it would not have occurred to them that the escarpment on which they stood had been created long before by a fiery outpouring of lava from the seemingly benign mountain that loomed above. Vesuvius and the surrounding area had been one of the most important agricultural centres of the Italian peninsula for centuries before AD 54: famously fertile and verdant, the slopes of the mountain itself were planted with vines and olive groves and said to be a favourite haunt of the god of wine, Bacchus. But for the attentive etymologist, the fiery origins of Pompeii were hidden in the city's name. In summing up the folk-lore of the area some centuries later, the writer Servius would describe how the word 'Pompeii' celebrated the triumphant procession or *pumpe* of Herakles after he had driven out the giants from Campania.[6]

According to legend, the last of Herakles' Ten Labours required the hero to steal the red cattle of the monstrous winged giant Geryon, and drive them back to Greece. Tradition placed Geryon's abode in what is now Spain, while Campania was the place where Herakles was forced to break his return journey and lock up the cattle while he attended to more pressing business. For amidst a landscape wracked by fire, the race of giants ('sons of the earth, by reason of the vast bulk of their bodies', according to the geographer Strabo) were waging war on the gods, and the giants held the upper hand. Only by his personal intervention could Herakles turn the tables and force the Giants back into their fiery vaults underground.[7]

Herakles gave his own name to Heraklein, or Herculaneum, the town that would be twinned for ever with Pompeii in its tragic destiny. Nearby, the coastal resort of Baiae, where the Roman rich holidayed alongside the imperial family and enjoyed the healing waters, was said by some to derive its name from the Greek for cattle-pen. North of Baiae were the Phlegraean Fields, a lunar landscape pitted with vast craters, where the volcanic activity beneath had caused sections of land to collapse. Strabo dramatically warned his readers that these blazing lands 'full of sulphur and fire and hot springs' were 'the thunderbolt-wounds of the fallen giants that give out such streams of fire and water'.[8]

The Romans lived in a world suffused with myth and ritual that had evolved over centuries. The gods that the citizens of Pompeii worshipped with regular sacrifices were conceived of as being not intrinsically different from the men and women who attended the ceremonies. Having once existed on the familiar physical plane, alongside the generation of men that preceded the heroes who fought in the Trojan War, these super-beings of a bygone age now dwelt somewhere apart from humankind but were still amenable to its bribes and entreaties. References to them abound throughout Pompeii, both in decorative form, in the wall paintings of houses, and in the passionate imprecations or curses that can be read in graffiti on the walls of the city. How earnestly the citizens of Pompeii invested in the power of the gods – how truly they believed that the fabric of their own reality was interwoven with the threads of destiny or divine caprice – it is impossible to know. But the pervasive presence in Pompeii of shrines at which to honour or placate deities, or to ask for intercession, suggests that the gods informed every aspect of the existence of its inhabitants.

To modern eyes, the full strangeness of this worldview is hard to fathom, especially for those more familiar with a monotheistic or even secular culture. Everything from the threshold of a building to the different stages of childbirth was ritualised with its own presiding god, while the spirits of such abstractions as family and place were also accorded a significance unimaginable to a mind unaccustomed to animistic modes of thought. Patterns of bird flight and the composition of an animal's internal organs held secret meanings that could only be interpreted by enlightened specialists. Like a society in the collective grip of some obsessive-compulsive disorder, afraid of stepping on the cracks in the pavement, every point of contact with the divine was governed by precise and immutable rules.

When Romulus had founded Rome – or so the story went – he had yoked a bull and a cow to a plough fitted with a bronze blade and drawn a deep furrow around the space that the city was to occupy, raising the ploughshare from the ground to mark each gate. From then on, Rome and later her colonies were defined by the *pomerium*: the sacred buffer zone that encircled the controlled urban environment with a barrier against all malign and anarchic forces, particularly the spirits of the dead. With even the emperors buried in great mausolea beyond the *pomerium* of Rome, there could be no exceptions: the dead were kept alive within the city through commemoration in public statues and domestic shrines, but the active presence of their spirits was definitely undesirable.[9]

Diogenes had known that something like this would come up just when he had half a dozen other burials and a slave crucifixion already backed up. The funeral of a big man, a knight no less, a high-profile personage. The messenger who was sent out of the city by the executors of Decimus Lucretius Valens made no apologies: the law laid down that, in a case like this, the undertaker must drop everything. For every other order missed, he'd be obliged to pay double his own quoted price for someone else to step in and finish the job. But did they care?

As he and his assistants trudged the path around the northern walls of the city, the caps of their trade set squarely on their heads, Diogenes felt little but weary resentment. Why must he take this circuitous route rather than the shortest path to Lucretius's house, the one that led through the paved streets of the city? The Romans made little sense to him. Their foolish rules forced him to live outside the walls as if his mere presence could pollute their dreams. He was even forced to bathe in the cold morning water, with only the crippled and diseased for company. It was many years since he had arrived from Asia Minor as a slave and he had since won his freedom, but still such pettiness infuriated him.

On his arrival at the Valens household, Diogenes found the heavy doors closed and bushy sprigs of pine already nailed to them to declare the presence of the dead. Mournful music filled the scented gloom of the atrium, where the floor was piled with baskets of fruits and wreaths of flowers. Diogenes directed his men to arrange the decorative tributes around the couch on which the dead man rested. The honoured Valens would have to lie here for the next day or two while his friends and clients visited to pay their respects. Diogenes applied all the tricks at his disposal to keep the body supple and delay the onset of necrosis. Before he had finished his work, the atrium began to fill with members of the household. Among them was a row of slaves due to be freed under the dead man's will, their hats designating their new status. They would hold a vigil over the body for as long as it remained in the house.

Before long, a young man appeared, bearing himself with a slight swagger: Decimus Satrius Lucretius Valens. With a performance of piety before the family he would soon lead, the dead man's heir opened a series of cupboards to reveal in each the weird semblance of a face. These uncannily lifelike replicas of dead ancestors were sculpted in a yellow-skinned wax that had been stained to still greater strangeness by the thick smoke of the oil lamps, in which they had been steeped over the years. Though the undertaker had witnessed such masks many times before, they still unnerved him: he was instructed that his task was to dispose of the dead safely beyond the walls, yet at moments like this it was as though they had returned.

The elite of the Roman world was unique among ancient cultures in preserving vivid likenesses of those members of their family who had achieved political office. Yet much about these ancestor masks remains uncertain: whether they were made when the individual portrayed first won political office, whether they were updated to mark later achievements, and when they joined those older masks of antecedents as a focus of domestic pride. It seems likely though that they were kept at home. In the atrium, probably in small cupboards such as are depicted in carvings on certain tombs, and from which they could be removed at important junctures in the life of the family – to be closer, for example, to the infant newly born into the family, or to the young man celebrating his entry to adulthood, or to the body of the dead descendant whose spirit was soon to join them. It seems too that the artists who created them strove for a high degree of verisimilitude so that the appearance of past generations at the key rites of passage in an individual's life would make a very immediate and startling impression.

The physical evidence for perishable wax masks is inevitably elusive, but a wax bust with glass eyes from the city of Cumae, fifty or so miles to the north of Pompeii, though not itself an ancestor mask of this type, demonstrates the lifelike results that the sculptural technique could produce.[10] Pliny the Elder even goes so far as to insist that these masks were the most characteristic form of portraiture in Roman culture. Such likenesses of noble men in whose faces was written a strength of moral character would challenge future generations to live up to their standards. Pliny regretted that, by the time he was writing, shortly before the eruption of Vesuvius, the tradition of the wax mask was beginning to wane, usurped by alternative modes of commemoration from Greece. He was probably referring to the kind of bronze or marble busts that did withstand the heat of Vesuvius, and still survive as a vivid record of many Pompeian faces, sadly in most cases now nameless.

Nothing was more important to a member of the Roman elite than to possess a family name whose noble lineage was publicly acknowledged and which would be perpetuated through worthy children. From the grandiloquent family tombs that lauded the inhabitants' achievements, to the inscriptions on public buildings that stood as a memorial to their benefactors' generosity, or the public statues like that which was erected to Decimus Lucretius Valens in celebration of his status as a Roman knight or *eques*: all served to advertise a family's past achievements and to recollect the traditional virtues to which they would be expected to adhere. It was by such custom and ritual that a fundamentally conservative society controlled and limited change. Yet in one key respect Roman society was also strikingly dynamic: in the freeing of slaves to become citizens.

The Roman Empire is alone among all the slave societies that have existed, in that significant numbers of those it imported in chains would eventually earn their freedom and become citizens. Although slaves were denied all rights, including over their own bodies, they could nevertheless aspire ultimately to be freed and to establish a family. They might, in due course, take pride in their own lineage in just the same way as their masters had.

On being freed, a slave took the first two parts of his master's three names as his own. We know, for example, of a Decimus Lucretius Stephanicus, who had almost certainly been a slave of Decimus Lucretius Valens known merely as Stephanicus before being freed.[11] It was the freed slave's continued identification with their master and his family, along with the opportunity both to borrow funds and share in a network of contacts, which provided them with the platform to become such a formidable force within the economy. However, a family would have freed only their most dutiful, loyal and reliable slaves. It would have been inconceivable to let men and women who bore the precious family name loose in the world unless there was considerable confidence that they would not bring it into disrepute. The names of successful families were the Roman equivalent of commercial 'brands' and were guarded as jealously as the image rights of contemporary celebrities.[12]

Concerns over the effect of mass manumission, and the erosion of traditional values that the influx of a new alien component in society might bring about, had been expressed since at least the time of Cicero, a century before the accession of Nero as emperor. Displays of liberality in releasing large numbers of slaves had come to be seen as self-indulgent, a kind of *luxuria* to be ranked alongside gluttony and effeminacy. With this in mind, in 2 BC, as part of the all-encompassing programme of national renewal to which he devoted his life, Augustus had enacted legislation to impose strict limits on the number of slaves who could be freed in a will, both in absolute terms and as a proportion of the entire slave household, along with guidance about the suitability of candidates. The floodgates were to be kept firmly shut while even the steady stream that was allowed to flow was carefully monitored. Augustus also introduced measures to provide an incentive to good behaviour and make the world of freedmen to some extent self-policing.

With the death of the Emperor Claudius, the freedmen of Pompeii would have been concerned that difficult times lay ahead. Claudius had been notoriously reliant on freedmen advisors and his powerful wife Agrippina had gone so far as to trick his favourite freedman, Narcissus, into exile with promises of a cure for gout. On the death of her husband, she had quickly ensured that Narcissus would never return by sending troops to his Campanian retreat to demand that he commit suicide. His untimely death would have struck a worrying chord with imperial freedmen such as Julius Phillipus or Claudius Verus, who had settled in Pompeii, as well as with those such as Quintus Coelius Caltilius Iustus, who was the son of a freedman new to Pompeii and had been adopted by a member of the elite to erase the taint of his birth.

Their fears, however, were unfounded. Despite proposed legislation that freed slaves should wear a special uniform and be re-enslaved if they showed insufficient respect for their masters, the following fifteen years of Nero's reign would show that freedmen probably had less cause for anxiety than the aristocracy. The needs of both the economy and the body politic for fresh blood ensured that there were many opportunities available to them, while the treasury also benefited from the handsome fees paid by freedmen on their admission into those official associations that afforded them status. Although a freedman was barred from being elected to the town council, nothing prevented his son from standing and so, from the moment of a slave's manumission, the slow but steady process began of his integration into Roman society as a citizen.

This social fluidity seems surprising, given the Romans' core ideal of continuity through a family line, as symbolised by the pervasive cult of ancestors. Yet it is explained by a number of simple factors: the financial qualifications necessary to stand for public office, which the struggling elite sometimes failed to meet; Roman laws of inheritance that stipulated the equal division of property between all children, male and female alike; and high levels of infant mortality. The impossibility of balancing these considerations, so unpredictable and so stringent, led to an unexpectedly high rate of adoption, as was the case amongst the elite of Pompeii.

Aiming for the ideal of one surviving male child who could inherit an estate in its entirety, the elite limited the size of their families; but in so doing they risked the loss of all of their children from the diseases of infancy, to which the high number of child tombs around Pompeii and other Roman cities bears painful testimony. It was precisely this issue that caught out Decimus Lucretius Valens. He was not alone in his dilemma – alongside the twenty or more sons of freedmen who held places on the hundred-strong town council of decurions during the years before the eruption of Vesuvius we are also aware of more than twenty adoptive sons who helped to fill the seats.

Three days had passed since Licinius Romanus had received news of the death of Decimus Lucretius Valens. But now, as he headed to the forum for a meeting of the city council, he was ashamed to find himself musing not on the great man's past, as he should during the period of mourning, but on his own future. Sometimes he felt awed simply to be allowed to attend, listening to his elders, learning the form. But then he watched his companions – young men from backgrounds not unlike his own, sons of freedmen quite new to the city; confident men like Julius Polybius and Claudius Verus – they showed respect but no fear. Even for those not yet allowed to speak there was no doubt that public office would beckon before long.

Romanus had arrived early, some time before the third hour, when the council was due to begin its extraordinary session, at which it would vote an official donation towards the cost of Decimus Lucretius Valens's funeral and memorial. Romanus's knowledge of families like the Lucretii was already well developed: wandering in the forum, he had often read the inscriptions beneath the statues of equestrian figures that declared the eminence of members of the Lucretii as Roman knights. Men who could claim such status boasted a personal wealth at least four times greater than the hundred thousand sesterces that he had managed to scrape together to qualify for admission to the council chamber.

But while it sometimes seemed to him that he would never join the true elite of Pompeii, some men offered a more encouraging vision of what was possible. Gnaeus Alleius Nigidius Maius, for example, who had been adopted as an adult into the wealthy trading family of Alleius Nobilis. Unlike the Lucretii, the Alleii might not be old money, but Maius had forged a political career at least as impressive as the adoptive son of Decimus Lucretius Valens.

As Romanus pondered the careers of the two men, a rainstorm swept towards Pompeii from the range of mountains a few miles inland. Beneath the downpour the streets cleared of citizens. As the council members crowded under the portico outside the curia building where they were to hold their meeting, Romanus stayed close to Quintus Coelius Caltilius Iustus. Although the son of a freedman new to Pompeii, Iustus had been adopted by an important family, and the previous year he had served as a senior magistrate. A good role model, perhaps he might give Romanus some advice.

Elsewhere in the city the society of freedmen named the Augustales had decided to erect a statue to Valens's memory, while another group had agreed to fund a set of bas-reliefs for the tomb, engraved with symbols of his position.

To those who passed the Lucretii house early on the morning of the funeral, a strange cacophony would have been audible: the mingled sounds of musicians testing their instruments, paid wailers warming up their vocal chords to the requisite pitch of grief, dancers practising their moves, and actors – recruited from friends, family and the professional stage – running through their last rehearsals of the ticks and idiosyncracies of the family ancestors whom they were to impersonate.[13]

For the sleepy neighbour, stretching outside his front door, forgetful of the day's significance, the first appearance of the funeral party from the entrance of the house would have caused a sudden jolt into wakefulness. Foremost among the wax masks worn by the actors was that of Decimus himself, to all appearances alive again and accompanying his corpse on its last journey. Behind the actors, the household would have lined up, the newly manumitted slaves appearing for the first time as free citizens to advertise Decimus's generosity with their expressions of grief-stricken gratitude. And then at last, the appearance of Decimus's corpse, and the procession could begin its slow passage west down the long *decumanus major* towards the forum.

Custom dictated that the body of Decimus be exposed to view for the duration of the procession, formally dressed and arranged by the undertaker's craft in an elegant and lifelike pose. Perhaps it was made to recline on one elbow as though for dining – as is sometimes depicted on tomb carvings – or else was propped in a seated position ready to receive the encomiums that would be declaimed in front of the assembled mourners when the cortège finally reached the forum. The funeral of such a distinguished man was sure to have drawn crowds – those attracted by the spectacle as well as the many clients who owed a debt of gratitude to Valens for the generosity he had shown them during his life. Responsibility for them would now fall to his heir.

Those who lived in the west of the city would most likely have made directly for the forum to await the arrival of the procession, but the route taken would have allowed the majority of mourners to fall in along the way without making any great detour from their homes, tributary trickles of citizens flowing from the side streets that emerged between the blocks of buildings at intervals of forty or fifty metres. In Pompeii, there was none of the clustering of elite dwellings that was to be found in Rome a century earlier – nor any evidence of the kind of gated communities into which the fearful elite of the twenty-first prefer to retreat – but rather shops and taverns and workshops, wrapped in the skirts of grandiose town houses with tiny apartments nestling above. And so, at every point where the procession swelled, it would have been with a mixture of faces from all social ranks, from the highest to the very lowest, though hierarchy would quickly have asserted itself as the mourners took up their proper places in the parade.

First to join the procession would have been the household of Decimus's heir, who, following his adoption, had taken up residence in a house across the street from the Lucretii family, of which he was now head. Tenant farmers and villa owners from beyond the eastern Sarno gate would have come early too, gathering at the point of departure, together with those who lived in the easternmost corner of the city near the amphitheatre and the huge exercise ground known as the *palaestrum grande*. Lucretius's gladiators might also have congregated here, had they been lodging in the tavern down by the Nuceria gate that they were known to frequent, rather than the barracks behind the theatre in the west of the city where they were housed at the time of the eruption. They would have known to hang back in the rightful place for *infames* – those deemed unsavoury by polite society.

Next, from houses on the right-hand side of the street, the families of two future magistrates might have appeared: first, that of Trebius Valens, at this time no more than a child led by the hand; then the family of Julii freedmen, the young Julius Polybius, accompanied by Julius Phillipus, who was either his father or elder brother. From the streets to the left, the households of the grand families, the Ceii and the Poppaei would have trooped out, their houses set one block back from the main street. And then a little further on, from a doorway on the left that led to what was, at that time, a modest house with a single courtyard, Lucius Popidius Ampliatus might have emerged, though for all we know he might not even have taken up residence in the property yet. Over the next few years, he would expand it into something truly palatial.[14]

Having walked about a quarter of a mile, the cortège would have arrived at a breakwater where the main street was crossed by the other great thoroughfare, today known as the via di Stabia. It traversed the city on a perpendicular axis between what are now known as the Vesuvius and Stabian Gates.[15] On the far side of the high kerbstones designed to block the route to wheeled vehicles, an imposing structure rose, the nature of which is still debated. Known as the Arch of Holconius after the man whose statue was set up next to it, the structure was probably built by him to commemorate an action of the Emperor Augustus.[16] However, expert technical opinion now considers the four piers that remain to be too thin to have supported arches big enough to span the distance between them. Arch or not, the monument marked the beginning of the ceremonial area that, a hundred metres further on, opened out into the forum; between here and there no bars were found and the private houses, belonging to such esteemed families as the Epidii and Cornelii, possessed a greater grandeur.

Decimus Satrius Lucretius Valens would have had much to ponder as he took his place in the forum, facing the crowds who had come to honour the man he had acknowledged as father for such a short time but all of whose hopes now rested on his shoulders. It is not possible to be sure of his age at that moment, though to gauge by the date when his own son stood for election to the lower magistracy, he was probably already in his late twenties.

To be the *flamen* of Nero at such a time would surely have seemed to most in Pompeii like an enviable position. Nero had marked his accession by declaring that he intended to rule by the same principles as had guided his great great-grandfather Augustus, who had demanded *pietas* – a respect for the proper order of things, both within this world and between man and the gods. To many, the beginning of Nero's reign heralded a possible return to a lost Golden Age.

Like Nero, Augustus had been extraordinarily precocious in his political ascent. Only twenty-one (and still known as Octavian) when he had avenged the murder of his adoptive father, Julius Caesar, at the battle of Philippi, he was barely thirty-two when he defeated his erstwhile comrade-in-arms Mark Antony, and his Eastern consort Cleopatra, and claimed Egypt for a unified Roman Empire. Assuming unprecedented power after decades of social disruption, Octavian's determined project to restore Rome's greatness had been underwritten by a fiercely conservative ideology of moral austerity and dutiful devotion: to the state, and ultimately to the emperor. And that figurehead, the embodiment of the high ideals, was Octavian himself, recast in 27 BC as something more than a man and bearing the name Augustus, that had previously been an epithet applied only to the gods (Plate 5a).

But, while the buildings of the forum that surrounded the mourners at Valens's funeral would have been charged with the ideology of Augustus – the shining marble and painted gold of their facades proclaiming the enduring theme of moral and religious renewal, the endless shrines and statues celebrating his divinity –

the heart of the city also held warnings of how quickly hope could sour.

Had Valens craned his neck to check the time on the sundial in the courtyard of Apollo's temple, he might have remembered that its donor had been an associate of the same Marcus Holconius Rufus whose statue stood next to the 'arch'. This Rufus, along with an ancestor of Valens's adoptive family called Decidianus Lucretius Rufus, had been one of the torchbearers for Augustus's reforms in Pompeii; together with Gaius Egnatius Postumus, he had remodelled the entire precinct of Apollo at his own expense as well as refurbishing the city's main theatre. Pompeii owed him much and it paid its dues. In addition to the statues it erected, it ensured that his son inherited the position of Augustus's *flamen* on his death. But when the leader of the Holconii family in the following generation chose badly and associated himself too closely with the Emperor Caligula, the reaction was ruthless. Following Caligula's fall, no member of the Holconii family would hold office for almost forty years.

The parallels between the early reign of Caligula and the situation in AD 54 were uncomfortably close, though perhaps more apparent with the benefit of hindsight. Caligula had been Nero's uncle, and his accession had also been met with the acclaim of the masses; like Nero, Caligula had been a young man who could rely for his early popularity on the Roman enthusiasm for glittering youth. For all Nero's fine words now, who could yet say whether he would ultimately follow in the footsteps of Augustus or Caligula?

It was a good day for a funeral. The rain had cleared and the forum was freshly festooned with garlands for the forthcoming festival of Jupiter, behind whose temple rose the mountain of Vesuvius. Surveying the crowds of mourners, Decimus Satrius Lucretius Valens was confident that his time had truly come. The temples and market halls on the west side of the forum reminded him of Rome, their very shape and function inspired by the buildings in the great forum of the capital, their shrines and altars so often devoted to Augustus and his descendants. And now, Valens was the representative of Rome in Pompeii; the new emperor's most favoured figure.

He was proud of the funeral arrangements. No expense had been spared. Two thousand sesterces had been donated towards the perfumes alone, almost all of which would have gone up to the heavens in sweet smoke by the time the ninth day was over. Unlike the simple tastes of his own Satrii ancestors, and of those other old families of the city who took pride in their modest burial plots, this Lucretius would lie under the finest marble. His tomb would be tasteful, though, unlike the ludicrous palaces that freedmen were now erecting for the afterlife. There had been sumptuary laws passed to curtail such excess, but they were having little effect. Perhaps Nero would enforce a new austerity to match that of Augustus.

Other magistrates had spoken and now the moment had come for the eulogy. A wave of stillness spread over the forum. The impersonated ancestors stopped their tomfoolery and sat motionless in their ivory curule chairs. When Decimus Satrius Lucretius Valens stepped forward he suddenly felt the piercing gaze of their eyes – the eyes not of the actors, but of the men whose line he was pledged to continue. Not until the masks had been returned to their cupboards, the family had been purged with fire and water, and the house finally swept and purified with roasted salt and spelt, would he be free of their judgement. Bracing himself, he began to speak.

I

During the four hundred years between the beginning of the second century BC and end of the second century AD, sea-borne trade in the Mediterranean reached a peak of activity that would not be seen again for more than a millennium. And the exuberant years of the early Roman Empire placed those living in Campania firmly at the centre of one of the greatest economic booms the world has ever seen. The piracy that had plagued the previous century had been extirpated and the sea lanes were clear; any appetite, however exotic, could it seemed be satisfied. As the contemporary scholar Pliny the Elder wrote, 'Everyone is aware that as a result of the world being united under the majesty of Roman rule, life has improved thanks to trade and the shared blessings of peace,' while Juvenal robustly asserted that it seemed as though, during his lifetime, there were more men to be found aboard ship than on dry land. To those enjoying the fruits of empire, Juvenal's satirical observation would hardly have seemed an overstatement.

When Augustus died in AD 14, the greatest prize in the Hellenic East had been firmly in Rome's possession for forty years. The acquisition of Egypt, with its vast expanses of cereal cultivation and wealth of natural resources, was the culmination of the ambition that had powered Rome since its first emergence as a Mediterranean power, three hundred years previously. In the intervening centuries, Rome had ruthlessly engaged its rivals, one after another, defeating them in battle, usurping their trading satellites and lesser allies, and assimilating their culture and religion to its own. The defining victory in its early years of expansion – that which made the other Mediterranean powers recognise the threat to their position – had been over Carthage:

Hannibal's home and the pre-eminent maritime power in the western Mediterranean.

Beaten repeatedly in a series of life-or-death struggles with a resilient Rome in the following sixty years, Carthage's final defeat in 146 BC saw the city of Queen Dido razed cruelly to the ground, only to be rebuilt by its conquerors a century later as a trading partner – early Rome clearly recognised where her real interests lay. By Nero's day, Carthage's vanquished military might was best commemorated in the elephants – Hannibal's weapon of terror – that were now kept for ceremonial purposes by Rome's emperors (see Plate 5e).

Barely pausing for breath, Rome had moved next to confront and occupy Macedonia, with whom wars had flared up intermittently in the preceding decades. No longer the power it had once been under Alexander, the territories he had conquered, including Egypt, had long since been dispersed between his generals' heirs and their successors. Yet Rome's wholesale plunder of the country's wealth allowed the lifting of almost all taxes on its own citizens. It was a privilege that would be maintained for centuries, and attentively guarded by its beneficiaries, as the Roman Republic's expansion continued relentlessly. By the mid-second century BC, further success in the southern Balkans, following the defeat of Corinth, offered up the great civilisation of Greece as the victor's spoils. By now there could be no doubt that Rome was both insatiable and irresistible.

Yet while military adventurism had played an essential part in expanding Rome's territorial holdings, by the first century AD it was the nation's mercantile and technological enterprise that best characterised its empire. The occasional conquest of new territories would continue to bring a windfall of booty and slaves, but it was increasingly clear that only by exercising administrative control over trade could Rome sustain her dominance and satisfy the expectations of those lucky enough to call themselves its citizens.

To meet Rome's costs, tax was levied on everything in Egypt from baths to dykes, from salt and oil to the sale of animals. Land taxes and poll taxes raised millions of sesterces every year for the coffers of the Roman treasury, while the larger part of the revenue was paid directly in kind from the abundant wheat fields of the Nile. It was a bonanza that held out the promise of an end to shortages in Rome, and of what had been endemic popular unrest, always assuming that the logistical challenge of the wheat's transportation could be mastered. But nothing was beyond the ingenuity and commitment of the nation that now referred to the Mediterranean possessively as *mare nostrum* – 'our sea'.

Enormous freighters were built, known as 'firs' and 'pines' after the great trees that were lopped down to make keels and masts. Their hulls were coated in a coloured encaustic sealant to keep the water out but also to help them slip through the water.[1] Even so, the journey of between fifty and seventy days from Alexandria to Puteoli in the teeth of powerful winds was a long slog for the grain fleet, while the smaller ships that valued the security offered by their larger cousins strained to keep up with the convoy. On the return leg, though, with the wind behind them, the skippers were said to 'drive [their ships] like racehorses'. Seized with the competitive spirit, a thousand nautical miles could be covered in nine days, at speeds averaging over four and a half knots; a hard life for those manning the rigging.[2]

However, the risks were great, with the seas declared impassable from the eleventh of November to the tenth of March and dangerous for almost two months on either side. Wise heads advised against investment in trade. But for many, the profits that might be accrued were impossible to resist. The appetite for wealth that drove men to hazard their lives and investment on the uncertain seas had made Campania, and in particular the great port of Puteoli – only a few miles north of Pompeii around the sparkling Bay of Naples – a powerhouse of the Roman economy.

From the second century BC onwards, Roman construction techniques had been revolutionised by the discovery of the special properties of the volcanic ash known as *pozzolana*, or 'Puteoli sand'. Turning his attention briefly from the layout of cities and design of buildings to the nitty-gritty of practical construction, the architectural theorist Vitruvius had enthused, 'There is a naturally occurring powder that produces remarkable results. It is found ... in the territories of the municipalities that surround Mount Vesuvius.

When mixed with lime and gravel it produces a strong building material, especially useful for piers built out to sea, as the mixture hardens even under water.'

The superlative results that could be achieved with the magical cement can be seen on the exquisite spherical glass flasks that were blown in Puteoli for sale as souvenirs to travellers returning home to distant lands. Etched with panoramas of the quayside, they show a series of monumental moles that formed a breakwater through which ships passed to safe harbourage.[3] Though found only in Central Italy, the *pozzolana* was easily transported as ballast in ships for use all around the Mediterranean; wherever it was used, the merchant's life was made easier and more efficient, and the risk to his ships in harbour reduced.

The bloated sacks of grain that burly stevedores stooped to carry from the holds of the Alexandrian fleet, down gangplanks onto the quays and then on into the warehouses of Campania, had under-written the credibility of Augustus as he progressed his plans. And they also kept his successors largely untroubled by the popular unrest that had unsettled the Republic before. By the time of Nero, Rome's legions and traders were firmly established around the entire Mediterranean, with the conquered lands administered, for the most part, as provinces under the authority of a governor who was appointed centrally by the senate or Emperor.

In many respects, though, the real power rested with the communities who managed the routine aspects of business and shipping on a day-to-day basis. Trade was the binding force of the Empire, but it was the small cities of that Empire – those, alike, in Libya or Spain or provincial Italy but especially those on the coastlines – that provided the building blocks. In each, a city council enforced the law and kept order within their own communities. But whilst the authority was Roman, the language, culture and religion were at least as likely to be Greek.

From the islands and mainland of Greece itself, through Asia Minor to Egypt, Sicily and the south of Italy, the vestiges of the older civilisation still permeated everyday life. But they were not simply the mute remains of a dead culture that had once thrived on the shores of the Italian peninsula, and left behind settlements such as Paestum in the region just to the south of Pompeii known as Magna Graecia. Greece continued to be a living influence. Sculptures and paintings that were looted from the palaces of Greece provided the model for endless reproductions and set the agenda for Roman art far into the future, while her gods had long ago become those of Rome under other names.

Arriving off the coast of Campania, the master of a ship from far afield could have navigated by reference to places whose names were suffused with the maritime folklore of the ancient Hellenic Mediterranean: the island of Capri, where the Sirens sang out their fateful song; Baiae, which was said – by those who rejected the tale of Herakles leaving the bounty of his raid on Geryon in its 'cattle pens' – to take its name from a member of Odysseus's crew. Yet for the Roman of the first century AD, it would have been quintessentially Roman imagery drawn from Virgil's epic the *Aeneid* that now dominated; the ubiquity of scenes from this piece of Augustan propaganda that were painted on Pompeii's walls shows just how engrained in the Roman psyche it had become. Now, when bringing his ship into harbour, the mariner could have looked for the great naval port of Misenum, at the very northern tip of the Bay of Naples, where Aeneas's eponymous trumpeter was supposedly buried.

Augustus's determination to fuse the social revolution he had wrought and the very idea of empire into the Roman sense of identity had prompted Publius Vergilius Maro to rewrite Rome's origins in the form of an epic foundation myth. His long poem the *Aeneid* drew together the disparate strands of Roman mythology for the first time, to demonstrate how, in the person of Augustus, a golden age of empire had dawned that was predestined from the moment Aeneas fled the sack of Troy, bearing his father Anchises on his shoulders. The message of the *Aeneid* was unmistakable. All the testing times of Rome's history had been mere preparation for the moment when Augustus, who could claim a direct line of ancestry to Aeneas and his divine mother Venus, ascended the imperial throne. Virgil's improbable tale was seized upon enthusiastically by those hungry to believe that, finally, times were changing for the better.

CHAPTER 2

Seven Weeks from Egypt

March AD 56

The mariners of the Europa *cried out in delight as they rounded the headland of the Sorrentine peninsula. At long last the great mountain of Vesuvius hove into view and the end of their journey was in prospect. For the first fortnight, the stars had guided them on their solitary journey across the Mediterranean from Egypt; the rest of the way they had stayed within sight of land, hugging the shoreline for safety. There were many who thought their master Tryphon a fool for attempting a winter crossing, risking their lives to bring spoilt city dwellers the out-of-season luxuries they craved. But this time they had been lucky.*

As Tryphon set a course through the straights between the island of Capri and the mainland, the great, glittering Bay of Naples spread out before them, filled with vessels of every kind. Out towards the open water on their port side, the three hundred strong crew of a quadrime tested its speed, its oars and timbers groaning in the distance; this would be the boat's first outing of the year from the dry hangars of Misenum where the navy's ships were hauled up to overwinter. Nearer to hand, insolent fishing boats bobbed in the spring sun, ready to run for home at the first sign of a squall. And as far as the eye could see, villas dotted the coastline, their elegant jetties thrusting out into the water.

Drawing closer to land, the crew fixed their sights on a gaggle of skiffs and lighters that spilled out from the mouth of the Sarno estuary. Behind them, the height of the shoreline rose and the buildings solidified into an unbroken mass: the city of Pompeii. Most prominent of all was the Temple of Venus, luminous in the sunlight.

'Venus the Saviour' declared a Greek inscription on a wall in

Pompeii, above a painting of the goddess helming a boat being blown along with full sails.[1] The statue of Venus in Pompeii's temple to the goddess would have mirrored this pose. Holding a great bronze rudder, she looked out to sea from her magnificent temple built in the early years of the colony, on land that had been cleared of houses for the purpose.[2] It was the act of a city proud of the status bestowed on it by Sulla after he had claimed Pompeii for Rome and renamed it the 'Colony of Venus', in honour of the favours that the dictator felt she had shown to him. But when Augustus came to the throne, the people of Pompeii had even greater reason to cherish their protectress, since she was now claimed as the mother of Rome's founding father, Aeneas, and fountainhead of the Julian bloodline.

The mythical daughter of Jupiter by the wife of Vulcan, Venus's original incarnation in Italy had been as a fertility deity; only in the third century BC had she become identified with the Greek goddess of love, Aphrodite. The territory of Pompeii had been steeped in this older tradition of worship since long before Sulla had added the name of his protectress to the new colony. An inscription in Oscan from what was then the home of Venus's priestess, Mamia, refers to the feast of Mefitis, the earlier name by which the goddess would have been known locally. Often in the images depicting her that proliferate around the city she appears in familiar form: as the sexy nude in a scant bikini of filigree gold of one statue, or the conventional flaxen-haired nymph rising from a shell with which Decimus Satrius Lucretius Valens chose to decorate his home (Plate 16). But she is also often shown crowned and regaled in a celestial gown covered in astrological symbols, resplendent in a chariot drawn by four elephants; a feisty goddess with a flavour of the mystical East.

For the crew of any ship foolhardy enough to chance a February crossing of the Mediterranean, it was Venus's role as protector of mariners and shaper of fate that demanded their gratitude. 'Venus is the weaver of webs,' one landlocked lover scratched onto a wall. 'From the moment that she sets out to attack my dearest, she will lay temptations along his path. He must hope for a good voyage, which is also the wish of his Ario.'[3] Sailors departing on a journey would have implored her mercy in the courtyard of the temple, and

dedicated gifts to her when their vessels returned home safely laden
with foreign goods: paintings of storms, for example, that their ship
had survived. That Venus' temple was positioned to jut out towards
the sea, even at the cost of the fine private houses that had previously
occupied this prime location, was a strong statement: Pompeii was
looking ever outwards for its future prosperity.

Pompeii had always been an important staging post for goods transported down the River Sarno. When the geographer Strabo referred
to Pompeii's port in the last quarter of the first century BC, he
described the service it provided for Nola, Nuceria and Acerra,
three sizeable inland cities that were almost as close to Puteoli as
Pompeii, but preferred the latter.[4] From these cities woollen goods,
wine and oil would have arrived on barges of shallow draught to
be transferred onto seaworthy vessels, along with Pompeii's own
produce, for shipment to almost anywhere in the Empire. Containers of wine produced by the Lassius and Eumachius families
have been found in Gaul, now southern France, while in the depths
of Egypt, at the mines at Mons Claudianus close to the Red Sea,
the discovery of the quartermaster's records has revealed the lengths
to which the Empire's defenders would go to secure luxury goods.
Olive oil, wine and fish sauce were all imported, but most of those
stationed there could only afford them by setting the cost against
future earnings; yet they were ready to borrow and borrow again to
buy some brief reminder that they were Romans.[5]

When the sailing season was in full swing, Pompeii's quayside
would have heaved with activity, as merchants loading local goods
competed for space with sailors who had just arrived on the same
route along which their colleagues were about to depart. A ship of
average size, like that wrecked off the isle of Elba in around AD 60,
could carry five thousand or so amphorae of fish sauce, and wedging
them securely into place with brushwood took time; but men who
had spent long days at sea and were eager to enjoy the delights of
dry land would have shown little patience with anyone blocking
their path.[6] And whilst few perishables were imported, exotic fruit
being the one exception, a ship's master would have wanted any
animal cargoes disembarked as quickly as possible. Strange ravening

creatures could have been seen as they were wheeled up the hill to the city in their cages: perhaps lions and tigers destined for the amphitheatre or even occasional curiosities that had no Roman name, but are known to us now as giraffes, and hippopotami.[7] There would have been the spectacle of humans in chains too, mostly men and women who had passed through the great slave market in Ephesus and would soon be put up for sale again.[8]

Against the reek of sweat-soaked bodies that had spent too long aboard ship, sweet relief would have seeped from other cargoes that came from still further afield. The silks from China, the gold and the gemstones, would have passed unnoticed, but with them came wafting fragrances of unimagined beauty. From the east coast of Africa there were spices that had been shipped across the Erythraean Sea – which blurred the Indian Ocean and Arabian Gulf into a single vast expanse of water – to be unloaded at the ports of Barbarikon or Barijgaza at the mouth of the Indus. There they had joined packets of bdellium gum from the interior of the subcontinent, and costus root from the high Himalayas, to travel north over land, passing, perhaps, through the great desert oasis of Palmyra, or the port of Muza on the Red Sea, from which thousands of small vessels picked up their perfumed freight for the onward journey. Then in Egypt, once the 25 per cent tariff imposed by the Roman authorities had been grudgingly paid, the bundles of cassia and cinnamon, cardamom, cloves, ginger and sandalwood would be marked with the seal 'Spices of Caesar' and allowed to progress. Now, finally, having been landed in Campania, they would find their way in varying, perfectly judged proportions, into the pretty flasks that lined the counters of the perfume dealers' shops.

With the caravan routes from Aelana, Leukos Limen and Berenice carrying a steady flow of goods to be collected in the East, the trading concerns that did business out of Pompeii would have resented any delay in turnaround. But one letter, written on papyrus by a sailor in the grain fleet during the second century AD, suggests that even though it could take a fortnight to unload a ship in Italy and have its cargo checked, it could sometimes take as long again before permission was given by the authorities to put back to sea.[9]

*

The position of Venus's temple outside the city walls and near the harbour is a clue in the vexed problem of identifying where Pompeii's port was situated. The ruined city now lies almost two kilometres distant from the sea and nearly one kilometre north of the River Sarno. Whilst the areas of the walled city that overlooked the sea and the river have been excavated, exploration of the lower-lying areas outside the walls, at the foot of its escarpment, has been so partial that many basic questions about Pompeii's identity as a port remain unanswered. Some work was carried out in the nineteenth century, but in most places modern housing developments now block further research. To locate the docks requires an understanding of how the coastal landscape has altered over the last two millennia.

A region like Campania, that has been so defined by seismic and volcanic activity, is very likely to be subject to the dramatic geological phenomenon known as Bradyseism, by which land levels can rise or fall by several metres in the space of only a few years, or even months, as a result of activity thousands of metres below the earth's surface. Behind the modern seafront in Puteoli, the shells of ancient molluscs can still be seen clinging to the marble columns of the Roman market hall – often referred to, mistakenly, as the Temple of Serapis – up to a height of three metres, from a period when they were submerged by water. In the sixteenth century the ground on which this building stands rose by six metres before falling back four, while in the early 1980s it gained a further two metres, coinciding with a major earthquake. Overall, these findings appear to corroborate the evidence from nearby Torre del Greco that sea level during the Roman period was at least four metres *below* that of today. However, since Bradyseism can occur quite inconsistently, even over a relatively short distance, the geological results cannot necessarily be taken at face value. The wave-like 'folding' created in the landscape by these seismic movements could well have left even the harbour facilities at the foot of the Pompeian escarpment high and dry.

Amongst those watching the arrival of the *Europa* from the quayside may have been a sea-trader known as Cellius Africanus, whose name alone suggests exotic origins with commercial interests to match. Africanus is known to us from a converted domestic property in the south-eastern part of the town not far from the Nuceria Gate, where stacks of imported amphorae were found that indicate a wholesaling business that conducted trade with Africa and the Orient. The property has been called the House of the Ship Europa, after the fully rigged vessel trailing a dinghy that was drawn on the wall with such an eye for detail that it could only have been produced by a sailor or someone familiar with the ship (Plate 3). The proximity of this building to the southern wall of the city strongly suggests a port just beyond in which the merchandise could have been landed. Ease of access through what are now known as the Marine, Stabian and Nuceria Gates to waterside facilities would have been an important consideration for Africanus in deciding where to site his business.

In light of evidence such as this, and the implication in Pliny's use of the word *adluo* that the River Sarno flowed directly past the city, it seems plausible that the holes drilled along a row of seventeen blocks of limestone below the Marine Gate, even though ten metres higher than modern sea level, could represent the mooring rings of a quayside.[10] Certainly they resemble such provision found in other Roman ports, and until recently many assumed that this was indeed their intended use. However, the total absence of archaeological evidence of marine life anywhere nearby, revealed by recent excavations, has reopened the debate.[11] Is it really plausible that Pompeii's harbour could have been situated on a bay at the mouth of the River Sarno, even though the sea now lies at some distance?

Rivers famously wander, constantly changing course as human generations and their memories pass away. Today the Sarno is now a mere trickle compared to the river it once was.[12] It is also quite possible that it followed a significantly different course. Three miles out of Pompeii, on dry land, the remains of thirty-eight ancient cypress trees have been found, often planted along river banks in classical times, together with a rustic shrine erected by a member of a prominent family of wine producers. For the wine producers of Campania the river was crucial, providing a means of transporting the produce of their vineyards to port, and they would have had good reason to give thanks for its steady flow. Upstream, the remains of villas have been discovered that trace a line parallel to the current river but about a mile to the north and it seems safe to imagine that the ancient course of the river was closer to Pompeii than it is today. We also know from geological analysis that the river spread into a delta at its mouth.

A promising scenario for the Roman era, then, would see the river flowing about half a mile south of the city before splitting around a delta, bringing its northern channel to within a few hundred yards of the Marine Gate. But if this was the case, what was the harbour itself like? Were boats simply beached for unloading, as vessels of up to one hundred tons could be in the tideless Mediterranean? Or were the merchants of Pompeii more ambitious for their port?

The landscape paintings that decorate the walls of Pompeii and the smaller towns around Vesuvius are often considered to be un-reliable in their representation of topography and architecture: the tottering wedding-cake elevations of maritime villas in self-consciously pastoral paintings certainly seem to show a considerable degree of artistic licence (Plate 2). Yet very often the archaeological evidence supports their seemingly fantastical visions. And when a wall painting such as that found in Stabiae, a few miles south of Pompeii, depicts a small port, it too is likely to contain more than a semblance of reality. The harbour shown lies opposite a small island, where boats are moored and from which fishermen cast their lines, but the natural shelter afforded by it is supplemented by two small artificial moles. It is a perfectly plausible vision of Pompeii in the early years of Nero's reign, painted by an artist who may well have travelled out from Pompeii for the purpose. And to comple-ment his visual testimony, there are other reasons to suppose that the Pompeian waterfront may have been highly developed.

Twenty years of archaeological fieldwork at the end of the nine-teenth century uncovered evidence of a density of building outside the walls of Pompeii towards the coast and river that suggests extensive suburbs.[13] A colonnade of shops was excavated in the area now known as Bottaro whose contents – including anchors, weights for nets and medicinal phials – strongly suggest chandleries and pharmacies whose customers were mariners and shipowners. In the vicinity, two villas were found – one of them belonging to Cellius Africanus – along with a housing block and other independent establishments, some of which appear to have been warehouses.

The theory that there were extensive suburbs outside the walls of Pompeii has been given further weight by the discovery of tombs belonging to local officials in the *pagus Augustus Felix suburbanus*. *Pagus* was the Roman administrative term for a settlement outside a town, which would have held its own festivals and boasted its own officials who, in contrast to the city magistrates, were allowed to be freedmen. The remains of the officials from the Pompeian *pagus* were buried in the necropolis outside the Nuceria Gate on the southern side of the city. Tombs bearing their names have also been found outside the Herculaneum gate that leads out north along the coastline. This would be consistent with a suburban sprawl that followed the walls of Pompeii where they faced the water, extending along the banks of the Sarno and north along the shore of the bay.

The prominence of references to the officials and their assistants (*magistri* and *ministri*) of the *pagus Augustus Felix suburbanus*, compared to those of other areas of the city and outlying territory, suggests that the *pagus* was a centre of wealth creation in Pompeii during the early imperial period. Its officials were clearly affluent enough to patronise the arts, funding the erection of a sizeable segment of seats in the amphitheatre and placing a statue of the highly popular turn-of-the century actor Norbanus Sorix in the Basilica of Eumachia in the forum.[14] If these luxuries could be afforded, those who made their money from the port and the businesses associated with it would certainly have been eager to invest in developing the infrastructure on which their commercial success was founded. With this in mind, and the necessary building material near at hand in the form of the magical *pozzolana* concrete that had transformed Puteoli, it seems plausible that the quayside at Pompeii may have been relatively sophisticated.

The tugboats that had towed the Europa *towards the mooring posts that marked the shallower water were unhitching their lines and pulling away; already flat-bottomed lighters had punted alongside to begin the unload-*

ing. Umbricius Scaurus watched with satisfaction from the balcony of his villa as the boatmen in the lighters raised their poles high into the air and plunged them into the water to find purchase on the sandy bottom below. It was still almost three months before the grain ships from Alexandria would arrive at Puteoli. Pompeii had seized the initiative, and Scaurus would see a healthy return on his share of the Europa's cargo.

However, his satisfaction turned to dismay when he noticed the melee of vessels at the mouth of the Sarno. There was a logjam of barges carrying local produce from the agricultural estates upstream, their bows still trailing long strands of the vegetation that grew thick on the river's sedgy banks. Scaurus could see the accident coming but knew that a shout of warning from high on the city walls would go unheard.

A lighter that had loaded its fill from the Europa edged towards shore between two bulbous coast-hugging ships at anchor. Unexpectedly, the pair lurched, a sudden gust of wind swinging their prows together. Even at a distance, the sharp crack of timbers made Scaurus flinch. The lighter was holed. Water poured in through the breached boards, drenching the bundled cargo and dragging the boat down. Stevedores who had been wading into the water to carry goods onto dry land swam to save what they could, but it was clear that there was little they could do. On his balcony, Scaurus turned away, his mind already teeming with calculations of loss and liability.

Many of Pompeii's elite inhabited the grand houses that looked out over the sea and the river. They were built on an extravagant scale, with great picture windows that punctured the city's old defensive walls. A particularly fine example is the house of Umbricius Scaurus.[15] His expansive home had once belonged to Maras Spurnius, unsuccessful commander of the defenders of Pompeii during the siege of Sulla, but under the ownership of the Umbricius family it was extended and made far more luxurious. Built on split levels and set into the edge of the tufa escarpment, no fewer than three reception halls, or atria, along with a grand peristyle courtyard were found at street level, while the accommodation on the lower floors included a private bath suite.

Not far away, in a similar location on the western edge of the escarpment, was the elegant house of Fabius Rufus, where, in order to provide the clearest possible view of the sea, the impressive row of dining rooms had virtually no fourth wall. Between the rooms, narrow passages facilitated the inconspicuous movement of slaves, who could thus cause minimal distraction while providing refreshments to those gazing out. The suite of dining rooms evokes days spent in languid leisure; one can almost imagine a visitor being offered a similar artifice to the home-buyer in Roman Sicily who thrilled at the prospect of owning a property that overlooked scenes of fishermen with their nets, only to discover, on completing the purchase, that their endeavours had been staged for his benefit.[16] A quote from the poet Lucretius, scratched into a wall of the house of Fabius Rufus – a site rich in graffiti – suggests the cynical calculation that underlay the kind of wealth creation needed to support such a household. Limited to the words 'Pleasant it is over the great sea', it is discreetly elliptical. The full and accurate quotation that is being alluded to runs: 'Pleasant it is, when over the great sea the winds trouble the waters, to gaze from shore to shore upon another's great tribulation: not because any man's troubles are a delectable joy, but to perceive what ills you are free from is pleasant.'[17]

Ungenerous as the attitude may have been, such *schadenfreude* was understandable. As men with mercantile interests, Fabius Rufus and his neighbours would have observed from their picture windows the fluctuation in their own fortunes as well as those of others connected to them. In the extant business records from Pompeii the names of Rufus's freedmen – Fabius Secundus, Fabius Agathinus and others – occur with some frequency and their success or otherwise would have had a direct bearing on Rufus. Many in the elite preferred to conduct their entrepreneurial activities at arm's length, setting up the best of their freed slaves in businesses which they furnished with capital investment and the guarantee of a patron's protection, while standing back to cream off the profits. This arrangement can be explained by the interplay of many different motivations, but foremost was the aristocratic disdain towards trade that Cicero had eloquently expressed in the previous century.[18] The elite deemed it beneath their dignity to dirty their hands with the practicalities of business. And why should they when there was no lack of willing proxies?

Even Cicero, though, made allowances. 'Commerce,' he wrote, 'if on a small scale, is to be considered mean. But if it is on a large scale, importing a great deal from various sources and distributing it widely and honestly, then it is not to be censured very greatly. Indeed, if such people become satiated, or rather I should say content, with their profits, and after many arrivals in port finally arrive on a landed estate, then we owe them the highest respect.' The undercurrent of hypocrisy is unmistakable. As a mosaic from the house of Vedius Siricus, who was to become one of Pompeii's foremost public figures, bluntly put it, 'Profit is Joy!'

One man who made the transition to full respectability was Gnaeus Alleius Nigidius Maius.[19] Like Decimus Satrius Lucretius Valens, Maius had been adopted in adulthood but, in contrast to Valens, the background of his adoptive parents was not of the first order. Clearly, though, they had succeeded in bettering themselves, as the ashes of Maius's adoptive mother, Pomponia Decharcis, were placed in the tomb of Eumachia, a famous priestess and dignitary of an earlier age.[20] Their presence there, beside members of the important wine-exporting Lassius family, suggests that Pomponia had found herself a patron in the great Eumachia. This grand matriarch had paid to build a basilica in the city's forum in the early years of the first century, and had clearly wielded considerable influence. The dedication on her building reads: 'To Augustan harmony and respect', but this monument to *pietas* would also have served to glorify her own name, and that of her son, Marcus Numistrius Fronto.

A marble statue of the great lady herself, paid for by the fullers of the city, was found in the furthest recesses of the building, its location a gesture of self-effacement that would have fooled nobody. From her posture to the style of her hair and the gown pulled over her head in matronly modesty, Eumachia was represented as the very image of Augustus's own virtuous wife, Livia, who had contributed from her own purse to the cost of refurbishing Rome's forum. It was no accident that Eumachia chose to be associated with this paragon: when the basilica was completed, Livia's son Tiberius had just succeeded Augustus as emperor, and doubtless Eumachia hoped that her own son would achieve comparable success on the local political stage.

There is no evidence that Numistrius Fronto did make it to the most senior magistracy in the city – to become *quinquennalis duumvir* – or even that he stood for office at all; perhaps the information has been lost, or maybe he died before his time came. But it was an honour that did not elude Maius a few decades later. Perhaps benefiting from the late Eumachia's reflected glory through adoption, he appears to have reached the pinnacle of public office in Pompeii at a relatively early age.[21]

Quite how a member of the elite began a career in local politics is unclear, though it is likely that to maintain numbers in the council, the most promising youths attended as observers before full admission. Rhetoric competitions would have allowed them to distinguish themselves in the eyes of their elders, some of whom might have been on the lookout for men to adopt and carry forward their family name. By the time these men were in their mid-twenties, the two positions of junior magistrate, or *aedile*, would have been open to them. Standing for election at the same time were candidates to be one of the two senior magistrates, or *duumviri*, who would already have held the junior office some years earlier.

The elections took place every March and the term of service was one year, but every fifth year, as in AD 56, the senior office became that of *duumvir quinquennalis*, the magistrate responsible for the census carried out at this time. The men who held this office wielded real power and helped ensure continuity in society by setting the longer-term agenda of the civic government; they also had both the right and obligation to enquire into the lives of their fellow Pompeians in intimate detail. The marital status and procreative intentions of private individuals, the composition of their households, even their business interests, were open to examination, and the privileged knowledge this afforded the magistrate was surely open to abuse. It was not a charge that could be levelled at Gnaeus Alleius Nigidius Maius, however, who appears to have been a model of probity and highly conscientious as a guardian of the community for years after his term had expired.

Even if he was not familiar with Pompeii's producers and merchants before assuming office, there was one towering figure Maius could definitely not have overlooked, though even he might have marvelled to learn the full extent of Umbricius Scaurus's empire.

Like Maius, Umbricius Scaurus was a 'new man' – that is to say, from a family with no track record in public service – but it did not stop him from rising to a position where he could command the respect of the city council and own a truly palatial dwelling. Manufacturer and consummate businessman, Scaurus was the city's leading exporter of salted fish products, especially the salty fermented fish sauce called *garum* – a cousin of Vietnamese *nuoc mam* – that had made Pompeii famous during the previous half-century. Both a staple of the Roman diet and a luxury, according to grade, *garum* was used as a flavour enhancement in everything from pear and honey souffle to boiled veal to steamed mussels, while the solid dregs of the production process were sold to the poor as *allec*, a flavoursome paste. Referred to by its alternative name of *liquamen*, *garum* actually appears in the majority of recipes in Apicius's famous cookery book, and together with honey and wine is one element in the sweet-and-sour combinations that characterised Roman cuisine.

Pliny once remarked of *garum* that scarcely any other liquid except unguents had come to be more highly valued, and the marketing of the fermented fish sauce drew on this comparison: after excellent, first-rate and best qualities, came 'the flower of' and even 'the flower of the flower of'. The phrase 'Pompeian' was usually only added as an extra commendation on those vessels destined for export, though an exception might have been made for tourist souvenirs offered at a mark-up to gullible games-goers, while the 'best filtered *liquamen*' was kept under the counter for the true connoisseurs. Seneca, who dismissed the luxury as 'an expensive bloody mass of fish which consumes the stomach with its salted rottenness', was not among them.[22] But for those who could stomach the smell of sun-rotted fish intestines, and had the ambition to claim a share of the market, there was undoubtedly money to be made.

Scaurus had no qualms about publicising the origins of his fortune: the centrepiece of the middle atrium in his house was a mosaic depicting four *urceii* – elegantly elongated jugs – three of which bore his business stamp. It was a stamp that would have been immediately recognisable to everyone in Pompeii and was embossed onto more than a quarter of all such vessels in the kitchens and inns of the city. Indeed Scaurus's *urceii* have also been found as far afield as Fos-sur-Mer in what was ancient Gaul.

Given the size and influence of Umbricius Scaurus's business, it is curious that none of the vats and tanks required for the sauces's preparation have been found within the walls of Pompeii (although a number of improbable possibilities have been proposed). Similarly surprising is the paucity of references in the graffiti and painted notices that cover the city's walls to the *salsamentarii*, the workers who produced the sauce for Scaurus and his many competitors. Perhaps, like the missing harbour facilities of Pompeii, the *garum* sauce factories lay outside the city walls, now hidden under modern conurbations.

Although the Roman port of Cosa, further up the coast, was losing its importance in the first century AD, having failed to establish a viable urban community to balance the large, self-sufficient villas that dominated its hinterland, it nevertheless offers some evidence to support this idea. For two hundred years its port had been a successful entrepôt, known, like Pompeii, for its export of wine and salted-fish products. Excavation in the surrounding area has revealed that the factories for *garum*, along with wine-pressing plants and potteries for the manufacture of amphorae, were set back only a short distance from the docks. At the height of Cosa's commercial success, this artisanal zone would have been a hive of activity: the lagoon behind the port was even developed as a commercial fishery.

Pompeii did not possess such a natural feature, and the workshops of the Pompeian *pagus* may be lost to us, but we do know of another extramural resource that would have attracted the attention of a man looking to make his fortune in fish sauce: salt pans.

In pre-Roman times, the port on the Sarno had been known as the *veru Sarinu*, or 'Salt Port', because of its association with the nearby marshes where salt from trapped seawater could be dried and harvested. A 'salt road' into the city is also recorded in Oscan inscriptions.[23] One can imagine Umbricius Scaurus travelling out of Pompeii by the 'Salt Gate', now known as the Herculaneum Gate, to survey the salt pans to the north of the city, perhaps with a view to bidding for a five-year contract to exploit them in the auction of city-owned rental properties that it would have been Maius's responsibility to oversee during the census year. It certainly seems more than chance that a plot outside this gate was allocated by the town council for the family tomb of the Umbricius family, within easy reach of their town house. Some speculation has even suggested that an open area between the two, just on the town side of the gate, was a market where the crusty lumps of crystal would have been available wholesale. Its position would have been most convenient for Scaurus to either sell or buy salt, especially if his factory was situated outside the walls nearby.

When it came to the local sale of the end product, Scaurus ran one shop himself and granted franchises for two others to bear the famous family stamp. These franchises went to his freedmen Umbricius Abascantus and Umbricius Agathopus. This was a convenient way of doing business: ultimate authority remained with the patron, while those to whom power was delegated received the honour of being known as 'friends' of the great man, in the euphemistic back-slapping corporate-speak of the day.[24] It was their reward for taking a share in the risk. As long as they all remained amicable, and fortune shone on them, everybody was a winner. A 'friend', Umbricius Ampriocus, was also involved in the overseas trade, but while he only exported to Spain, another of Scaurus's traders, Marcus Valerius Euphemus, brought Spanish *garum* to Italy as well as exporting it. Perhaps the astute Scaurus recognised that offering consumers choice could bolster profits.[25]

Whatever the detail of the complex world of Roman business relationships – of *publicani*, *mancipes* and *mercatores*, with their indecipherable roles – there can be no doubt of the crucial part played by the *negotiatores*. These were the financiers who arranged the loans that underwrote the physical end of the business: the hiring or purchase of boats, the acquisition of cargoes and the significant cost of warehousing the goods. Of the two major collections of wax tablets discovered in Pompeii, one records the transactions of just such a group of financiers, known collectively as the Sulpicii. The wax, of course, melted in the fierce heat of the Vesuvian eruption, but the charred wooden backing remained and often the indentation of the stylus with which the writer inscribed the wax left a mark on the wood behind. Through painstaking work, archaeologists have been able to piece together an extraordinary picture of financial and mercantile life in Campania.

The company operated by these intriguing characters specialised in supporting various aspects of the trade with Alexandria that operated out of Puteoli. It appears to have comprised a dynasty of freedmen, perhaps originally slaves of the ancient family of the Sulpicii Galbae, who had long before owned warehouses in the Tiber docks of Rome. They were a well-connected group, counting prominent senators and men from the imperial court among their investors, and some of the sums of money involved were far from insignificant: in one instance it seems that they were able to raise from their own private resources a hundred and thirty thousand sesterces, equivalent to the annual salary of one hundred and fifty legionaries. If such an amount had belonged to any one of them alone, and had he not been debarred as a freed slave, the lucky man would comfortably have qualified for entry to the town council of Pompeii.

Quite how the Sulpicii archive ended up in Pompeii rather than Puteoli presents a particularly tantalising mystery. There is evidence of the presence of members of the Sulpicii association in Pompeii, but the traces are faint: the name is scrawled in graffiti in the forum basilica where trade was conducted and elsewhere near a roadside bar, while a Gaius Sulpicius Phosphorus is listed among the witnesses to a sale by the auctioneer Caecilius Jucundus, whose records constitute the other major archive of tablets from the city. A further link is provided through an occasional intermediary used by Umbricius Scaurus, Euphemus, the trader with Spain who figures three times in deals brokered by the Sulpicii. Sadly there is nothing to indicate whether any of the main figures in the business lived in Pompeii, or whether they perhaps retired there, preferring to be away from the hustle and bustle of Puteoli. Such had been the case with a man called Marcus Marius in the previous century, whose disinclination for public life we are familiar with from the letters written by his friend Cicero.[26]

The building in which the archive was discovered is now known rather inaccurately as the Murecine Inn, after the area of modern Pompeii in which it was found. In fact, evidence suggests that, rather than being an inn, it was more likely to have been some sort of clubhouse for the officials and other important men of the *pagus Augustus Felix suburbanus*. Finds excavated on the site have included a small painted terracotta statue of a paunchy figure that is recognisable as such an official from his *toga praetexta*, and a wall painting of a sacrificial procession featuring many similarly dressed figures of more athletic build and elegant demeanour (Plate 10). If their local allegiances were in doubt, the figure of the river god Sarno is painted on the walls, his long hair hanging bedraggled like someone just emerged from the marshes. His presence would have been a fitting tribute to the source of the local trade on which the city's mercantile wealth was first founded.

With its five dining rooms, each equipped with built-in stone couches, the building would have furnished ideal facilities for convivial eating, and it would go on to play an important part in the strange drama of the Neronian years. But by the time of the eruption in AD 79 it had, for some reason, become little more than a storeroom for assorted junk. Were the documents secreted there because of their importance, or rather dumped there because they were no longer relevant? Was this place chosen as inconspicuous since it was, by then, shunned by those who remembered its old associations? Or was it, rather, those very associations that somehow made it a fitting site for such a cache? Perhaps, in the final analysis, the tablets' location was simply an accidental consequence of the panicked flight of their owner as Vesuvius exploded.

The high-rolling life of freedmen merchants, greedy financiers and their *arriviste* associates in the ports of the Bay of Naples is brilliantly captured in the *Satyricon*, said to be the first 'novel' ever written. Composed by Petronius, who was almost certainly the same man as served as Nero's advisor on cultural matters and impresario for his private entertainments, it offers a scabrous account of the misadventures of a couple of ne'er-do-wells in a world that has lost its moral moorings and is adrift in cruelty, excess and shallow ostentation. Of the fragmentary book that has survived, much of the most memorable action takes place in a port city that commentators have identified as Puteoli, though certain physical details – such as the 'Beware of the Dog' mosaics at the entrance to houses – are also familiar from Pompeii. For men like the Sulpicii, who appear to have somehow straddled the societies of the large and smaller ports, it would have been hard not to recognise something of themselves and their clients in the fictional characters.

One section of the book revolves around a dinner party, and at its heart stands the monstrous figure of the host, Trimalchio, a freedman whose shameless ascent to the financial heights is based on bold speculation on sea voyages and a steady nerve: undeterred at having lost three ships during his first season of trading, he gambles again and wins. Now in a position to invest his own money in other people's ventures, he delights in bullying and browbeating all those less successful than himself. Stripped of its more outlandish exaggerations, the *Satyricon* provides an unparalleled window into the milieu of the most fascinating yet elusive group in mid-first-century Roman society: into the pressures they created within the existing order, and how these were accommodated.

Yet, far from making uncomfortable reading for the models of its fictional characters, it is quite possible that the real freedmen on whom the satire was based would have revelled in the recognition that it gave them, since self-effacement and sensitivity have never been the hallmark of the successful entrepreneur. The Umbricii and Fabii freedmen of Pompeii, and at one remove the money-lending Sulpicii of Puteoli, would clearly have taken pride in the personal qualities of daring and acumen that underpinned their flourishing ventures, since a life at the mercy of the sea and storms would have been full of enough vexations to test even the most phlegmatic merchant. And having taken the risks, they would have wanted the full rewards. To such self-made men, exclusion from the higher reaches of public life on the nonnegotiable basis that they had once been slaves must have been especially galling.

The Romans suffered from an obsessive *philotimia* – a love of status as conceived in very particular terms: the status conferred by wealth but, more importantly, by the elected public offices for which only a free-born man could stand. A freed slave would have to wait until his children came to adulthood and assumed full rights of citizenship before he could see them able to compete for coveted places on the city council.[27] The chance to hold office in certain limited areas such as the *pagus* would have been seen as a privilege by some, but was scorned by others. However, for those freedmen on whom fortune had truly smiled, and who had stayed in favour with their ex-masters, there was one means to effectively buy their way to status. Known indulgently as the 'second town council' – though their function was almost entirely ceremonial – the society known as the Augustales enjoyed privileges just a notch below that of the *decurions*, as the members of the main council were known, including priority at public events such as religious ceremonies and theatre performances.

This society, named after the Emperor Augustus and established during his reign, probably arose first in Campania at the subtle prompting of the Emperor, who, with characteristic foresight, saw it as a necessary pillar to support social stability. So popular did it prove, and so prestigious that, by the mid-first century AD, any stigma of association with ex-slaves had been lost, and even the free-born were queuing up to join. Admission to the local Augustales lay in the gift of the decurions, thus ensuring loyalty to the established elite among the *arrivistes* eager for status. Additionally, on joining, a hefty fee had to be paid into the public coffers. Alleius Eros and Alleius Stephanus – who are associated with their patron and probable ex-master, Alleius Nigidius Maius, as witnesses in a business transaction recorded in the Jucundus tablets – exemplify the kind of loyal freedmen cultivated by the elite households to propagate their vision of society.

Sadly, fewer than a dozen other Pompeian Augustales have been identified, usually on the basis of individual inscriptions, compared to over a hundred in Herculaneum, where a full membership list has been discovered as well as the impressive building that served as their lodge.[28] There is no reason to suppose, however, that the club was any less popular in Pompeii. Certainly, the few Augustales we do know of in Pompeii appear to have played prominent roles during the final, tragic decades of the city. It is in Trimalchio himself that we find the sole literary representation of the association, and it is hard not to see his obsession with his reputation after death echoed in the intriguing circumstances of an Augustalis from Pompeii by the name of Munatius Faustus.

Like Trimalchio, Munatius Faustus was known as a merchant, and was just as obsessed as his satirical counterpart with the absurdly grandiose mausoleum in which his remains would be placed after his death. On application, the town council allocated a prime plot outside the gate as the final resting place for Faustus, his wife Naevoleia Tyche and members of their family. But the story does not end there. Following Munatius Faustus's death, and presumably having laid hands on his wealth, his widow arranged for the construction of a far more magnificent tomb on the other side of the city, outside the Herculaneum Gate. More than four metres high, and elegantly carved with a bas-relief of a ship at sea – part commemoration of his renown as a seafarer, part evocation of the barque that would carry him across the River of Death – its inscription boasted of the double-sized, plump-cushioned seat in the theatre that Faustus had been accorded as a member of the Augustales. There was also a scene of the great freedman with his entourage engaged in action. Above the tomb inscription, overlooking it all was the small carving of a woman: Naevoleia Tyche herself.[29]

Perhaps it is not so surprising that in death Naevoleia surpassed her husband; having outlived him, she chose to occupy this new tomb herself, alongside their freed slaves: the operators of their business, whose skill had ensured her continued financial well-being. Other freedmen who may well have aspired to such heights but were not so single-minded in their ambition fared better in death. One freedman of the prominent Cuspius Pansa family, Cuspius Cyrus, did become a magistrate of the *pagus Augustus Felix* yet retained enough affection to be buried in a companionable tomb amongst his family, friends and fellow Cuspii freedmen.

Cuspius Cyrus stood in a huddle with the representatives of shareholders in the Europa's cargo. Voices were raised over what to do about the damaged goods. The boatman of the wrecked lighter insisted that the greatest loss was his; that compensation must be paid. But Umbricius's man pointed towards the drenched packages that lay on the quayside. For among the sacks of spoiled grain lay smaller bags of muddy powder, precious spices from lands far beyond Egypt that would never now make their full value at market. And, most heartrending of all, the remains of an exquisite table of filigreed ivory, once supported on legs carved as sinuous dancing ladies, now lay shattered into a dozen pieces.

Tryphon, the Alexandrian captain, wanted a speedy conclusion, concerned that the case might delay his return journey and cost him a whole trip over the season. But all the parties were exhausted and despondent – no solution would be reached today. It was the fifth of March, the festival of Isis Navigidium and no one wanted to miss the evening procession down to the sea. And so it was agreed that they would refer the matter up to their patrons, to be resolved if possible through their good offices. Failing that, it would go before a judge in court and that was in no one's interest.

Distant music drifted down from the Temple of Isis, where the festivities were beginning. Lured by the sound towards the sacred precinct, Cyrus pushed his way through crowds of worshippers, some true devotees, others drawn by the spectacle and the promise of generous feasting and merriment that would follow. The atmosphere was thick with the East, as the smoke of incense and other spices mingled in the evening air with the voices of the male and female choirs, lined up on either side of the temple steps. Shaven-headed priests dressed in white gowns that bared their torsos to just below the nipple tinkled their sistrums in knowing syncopation.

Cyrus was not surprised to recognise so many faces in the throng; after all, this was an occasion with particular resonance for those who made their living from the sea. There were Popidius Natalis, the client of Cyrus's own patron, Cuspius Pansa, and Popidius Ampliatus, who had once been Natalis's companion in slavery; and wasn't that one of the Lucretii just to the right of the swarthy faces of the Europa's crew?

What drew them all here, Cyrus wondered. Isis had always attracted slaves and freedmen who looked for something to call their own. Also a fair share of women from all ranks: a goddess who had suffered loss and humiliation, a merciful woman who promised absolution in life and rebirth after death. It was no longer just about that, though. Not unless the successful men of the town had suddenly discovered their vulnerable side. Perhaps the touches of familiarity made the exotic palatable. After all, wasn't the rudder that the priests were bearing as a symbol of Isis like that of Venus? Weren't both goddesses the friends of seafarers?

Cyrus felt his wife touch his arm; as he turned to greet her, the boat appeared, borne on the shoulders of worshippers from the recesses of the temple. The painted vessel was like a great bowl spilling over with fruits and other offerings, into which the crowd thrust scraps of papyri scrawled with their prayers. Thinking of the sunken boat, of the hazards endured by the Europa, of his own unborn child, he wished that he too had brought a prayer. And then he understood. What Isis offered was hope.

The cult of Isis had originated in Egypt and much of the imagery associated with it evoked the Nile, but as with so much else, it arrived in Italy mixed with strong Greek influences (Plate 4). With this kind of ethnic profile it would have been eagerly received in a region like Campania. In ancient Naples there were more Greek surnames than Roman, while the evidence from Pompeii also suggests a strong presence of Greek immigrants, at least in the lower ranks of society. Analysis of skeletons found in Herculaneum has revealed genetic diversity on a scale that more than confirms the region's reputation as a melting pot of peoples, while the records of sailors enrolled in the imperial fleet at Misenum suggest that native Italians accounted for no larger a proportion of the crews than were provided by Mauretania, while more than forty times as many men were recruited from a combination of Thrace, Egypt and modern Turkey.

Whether the cult of Isis was simply another example of Roman culture absorbing and reshaping external influences or a much more radical challenge to the collective ethos of traditional religion is much debated. In AD 19, the Emperor Tiberius had reacted with disproportionate anger to a sexual misdemeanour on the part of a priest of Isis and demolished an Isis temple as punishment, suggesting that the religion undermined state authority. But there can be little doubt that by the mid-first century there were many Isis worshippers in Italy. With the emphasis on individual responsibility that was encapsulated in its programme of initiation, purgation and redemption, the Isis religion foreshadowed the other Eastern cults that would gain popular followings in the centuries to come, most familiarly that of Jesus, the self-declared Judaean Christ. Hymns to Isis from the following century make clear the revolutionary ambitions of her followers: she encompassed all other gods and could be worshipped in their name, offering a vision of equality between the sexes that must have been very appealing to women.[30] But whilst women, including members of the elite, were early adopters, the cult's appeal soon permeated a society that felt increasingly at home with the cultural influences of an East that had once seemed alien and threatening.

To some, however, rather than familiarity assuaging their fears, the impact of the East came to represent everything that was wrong with Rome. The exotic goods that flowed unceasingly into the port of Puteoli, and on to the capital – a proportion spilling out to cities along the way – encouraged a love of sensual Oriental luxury that the empire's moralists abhorred. Pliny echoed the complaints of a hundred years earlier when he bemoaned how the flow of Rome's hard-won wealth eastwards, with a generous cut disappearing into the pockets of merchants along the way, weakened the Empire to the benefit of her enemies. In 22 BC the furore had resulted in laws to limit the amount of money that could be spent on dinners, festivals and other luxuries, but they had proved to be of little effect. Roman ladies still hungrily adopted the fashions of the East, wore its perfumes, and paid through the nose for the privilege. And Roman men were not exempt from the fever of conspicuous consumption, craving as they did the extortionately expensive purple *murex* dye produced from the shells of mussels to colour the trim of their prized *toga praetexta*, the clothing of the elite. The gravestone of one Augustalis from the Bay of Naples records him as a *murex* dealer. Ten thousand mussel shells were needed to colour a single toga; no wonder he could afford admission to the club.[31]

Coins of this era, stamped with the face of Nero, have been found as far away as Sri Lanka; Pliny describes how his lifetime had witnessed the first appearance of giant clams from the Indian Ocean, up to four foot long and called *tridacna* by the wits of the period because they took three bites to eat.[32] The remains of two specimens have been found in Pompeii, as well as six pearl oysters from a similar source. With far-flung trade flourishing and a sturdy infrastructure developing to support it, it is not surprising that religious imagery from far afield made its way into the homes of Pompeians. In AD 40, traders from the Red Sea kingdom of Nabataea had established a community in Puteoli: they were the kinsmen of intermediaries on the greatest caravan route to the Far East that passed through their capital, Petra. Sometime around the middle of the first century AD, such a caravan transported a carved ivory tripod table on the first stage of its journey from Satavahana in the northern Indian kingdom of Deccan to Pompeii, where it would end up in fragments. All that remains of it today is a section of one leg that was found in the House of the Four Styles: a caryatid in the shapely form of the goddess Lakshmi, two tiny acolytes by her side, posed in a manner that bears an uncanny resemblance to statues of the equivalent Roman goddess, Venus.

Down on the quayside, Tryphon was now alone. On the far side of the harbour he could see the vanguard of the Isis procession reach the waterline, their lanterns glittering off the ripples. He waited until the sacred boat with its overflowing cargo of wishful thinking and goodwill had been brought forward before he set off up the hill. He was too dog-tired to face their jollity. It would only make him homesick for his friends in Alexandria.

Today should have been a proud one, and a time for him to thank Isis for her care of the Europa *on its reckless venture. And then the accident had happened. They'd have to sort that out between themselves. He certainly wasn't going to bear the cost but he'd still suffer the inconvenience. It wouldn't be the first time he'd been stuck here longer than he intended; one year he'd squeezed a second trip into the season but had been caught out by bad weather and forced to overwinter in Campania. At least if the merchants and their patrons dragged their feet over deciding the share of responsibility for the damaged goods, there were old acquaintances he could look up.*

Filthy as he was from weeks at sea, he walked straight past the baths beneath the Sea Gate – it was too late for that tonight – mentally stowing away the message scrawled beside the bench there: 'Anyone who sits here should read this before anything else: if you want a fuck, ask for Attica. Costs sixteen asses.' He had the cash and the desire but not the energy. In any case, he'd still be in town for the festival of Liberalia – for the honey-soaked cakes, foul-mouthed conversation and general frolicking. By the seventeenth he'd be feeling more himself.

The town didn't look so big from offshore, but Tryphon was quickly lost in its streets. He barely remembered the way to the hostel he'd stayed in on his last visit. Why had they never thought to number the houses here like they did in Alexandria? And why no street lights? Tripping on the kerb he cursed himself for forgetting to bring a lantern. Then, through the gloom he saw a familiar sight: the sign of an elephant; and below it an open door, from which a smoky light spilled out in welcome. Inside the inn the figure of a woman, her head bound in a Greek kerchief, swayed to the sound of castanets.

'Why stay outside, weary with dust, when you could recline on a couch of grass?' her voice seduced. 'There are garden nooks and arbours, mixing cups, roses, flutes, lyres, and cool bowers ... There's fresh wine too, just drawn from the jar and a watery murmur of a brook to ease your troubles away. And little cheeses dried in a basket of rushes, and waxen plums and sweetly blushing apples ...' Tryphon needed no further invitation.

—— II ——

When, in the spring of AD 58, Nero led the exodus of the aristocracy from Rome to the resorts of Campania, he would have been justified in feeling that his vacation was well deserved. The honeymoon period of his reign was over but the new Emperor's achievements were already proving him to be a leader of real substance.

The past three years had seen an impressive juggling of domestic and foreign policy initiatives. In Rome, the transformation of the Campus Martius into the site of public baths and a great wooden amphitheatre had secured popular support. Abroad, two new provinces had been added to the Empire through a combination of skilful diplomacy and well-weighted military pressure: the Cottian Alps to the north, created on the death of King Cottius, and Pontus in the East, ceded to Rome by King Polemon. Trade was flourishing, and blueprints for a series of great new engineering projects were under commission. Fifty years later, and with the benefit of hindsight, even the Emperor Trajan would describe the first five years of the Neronian age as a model of good governance.

April was Nero's favourite month in Campania, a time of warm sun and fresh breezes when the winter growing season had brought nature into full bloom. The adulation showered upon Nero by the happy citizens of the towns and cities of the region would have made his visit sweeter still: men like his *flamen* Decimus Satrius Lucretius Valens, or the freedmen of the Helvii and Salarius Crocus who were ministers of the Fortuna Augusta Temple in Pompeii. An embassy from the town council would recently have informed Nero of the dedications made, as a matter of course, to celebrate his reign.

For most of the Romans who made the two- or three-day journey to Campania, though, perhaps staying overnight at villas they owned for the purpose along the way, the petty concerns of the locals would have held little interest. To them, the Bay of Naples was a place of pleasure, pure and simple, whether it came from immersion in the hot springs for which the area was first famed, or in the dissolute life for which the seaside town of Baiae in particular had long been notorious: the orgies, drunken beach parties, extravagant dinners and languid boating trips that Cicero had catalogued a century earlier.

Above all, it was the Hellenism embodied by the Greek city of Naples – Neapolis – that they craved: a chance to set aside the starched formality of Rome, put behind them the stinking streets and filthy mob, and indulge in a culture that valued pleasure and encouraged an appreciation of art for art's sake. Even the dictator Sulla was said to have let his hair down here and was rumoured to have draped himself in the Greek style *chlamys*. Setting aside the more lavish entertainments that were available, Campania could also offer theatre, sophisticated conversation and a relaxation of sexual morals. Once sampled, the sweet fruits of the Bay of Naples appear to have been instantly addictive to Rome's repressed elite.

Nero had acquired the taste for such pleasures in childhood and, far from abandoning his passion for performance on becoming emperor, he indulged in it all the more. There were risks for him in doing so: whilst on one side of the family tree his lineage stretched back, through adoption, to Augustus, on the other it showed that the blood of Mark Antony flowed in his veins. A man swayed from duty by the temptations of the Hellenic East, nearly a century after his suicide, Antony was still held up by the history books as the epitome of moral villainy, whose birthday was marked in the calendars as a day unfit for festivals. For Nero to be seen as favouring the ways of Antony over those of Augustus might jeopardise his reign. Yet even the fierce opposition of his mother, Agrippina, had failed to deter him from hiring a professional *citharoedus* to teach him the lyre-like instrument that he believed it was his destiny to play: four years on, his proficiency was approaching the level where he would feel confident performing for a public audience.

In the meantime, there was no shortage of fine villas in Campania, including those owned by the imperial estate, where Nero could practise. The home of Calpurnius Piso, who could claim a pedigree to rival that of the emperors themselves, was available to him and could offer sympathetic company: the elder Piso was known as a 'singer of tragic parts', while his son was a contemporary of Nero. But it was more likely to have been the villa of Domitia Lepidia, his paternal aunt and guardian during some of his formative years, in which Nero now stayed. If so, it was a bold statement of allegiance. Throughout his life, Nero would always be the focus of bitter power struggles between different court factions. In the spring of AD 58, one such campaign had recently come to a head and the poisonous mood surrounding it had not yet dissipated.

Much of the credit for the early successes of Nero's reign must be given to his advisors, Seneca and Burrus, yet they fought a constant war of attrition with an envious Agrippina to maintain their influence over her son. In AD 55 she had nearly seen off the pair, but the following year Domitia had acted against her on their prompting. Targeting Nero's soft spot, she had persuaded the popular actor Paris, a personal favourite and close companion of the Emperor, to level charges of conspiracy against Agrippina in an attempt to drag her down. It was a close call, but, rather than Agrippina's political demise, the following year had seen an imperial edict issued, banishing pantomime actors from the whole of Italy; this was too convenient to be anything other than a result of Agrippina's machinations. And with each dramatic shift between accusation and counter-accusation the stakes were being raised.

Being a creature of appetite, and missing his favourite entertainment, Nero quickly saw to it that the actors were recalled. An adept in the ways of the court, Paris returned but was wise enough to shun the metropolitan limelight and play the provinces until the storm had passed. Perhaps with the notion of being close enough to entertain the Emperor on demand, in AD 58 it seems he was performing on the stage in Pompeii, and writing sycophantic messages to its civic leaders on the walls of the fine House of the Dioscuri, where he may have lodged with a relative of Alleius Nigidius Maius.[1] It would be interesting to know how Paris reacted during his sojourn there when he encountered Pompeii's own priestess of Agrippina, an elite lady by the name of Vibia Sabina.

Amidst all this turmoil, it was little wonder that Domitia's villa, with its elegant pools of farmed fish, seemed so attractive to the Emperor. Immured in this world of luxury, Nero would barely have noticed the reality of life on the land around them: the poverty in which the smaller farmers lived despite the natural abundance of their fields and orchards, the inhuman misery of the chain-gangs of slaves who worked the estates, their bodies riddled with arthritis or distorted by hard physical labour.

However, if any of Nero's close associates had troubled to ask after the history of the many villas around the bay that had now ended up in the hands of the Emperor, they might have paused to wonder who was more cursed. For while life was short and hard for those who toiled the land and scraped by on a diet of wheat and pulses, ultimately fortune could be almost as unforgiving to those who feasted on turbot and oysters. Within a few years every one of those political operators who swarmed round Nero in AD 58 would have met a violent end.

CHAPTER 3

Slaves and the Territory

April AD 58

It was still dark when Simulus woke, stretched, and pulled a goatskin around his shoulders against the chill air of the hovel. Last night's fire was nearly dead in the hearth and his first task – today, as every day – was to tempt some small flame out of it. After what seemed an age, the wood started to kindle: he would soon need to gather more from the forest over towards Herculaneum.

For a brief moment he allowed his muscles to warm. Next door, his slave was stirring on her creaky pallet: when she heard him start to turn the millstone she would emerge to sieve the flour and prepare the bread that would see them through the day. The rats and weevils were as hungry as either of them, and it made no sense to grind the wheat down before it was needed, only to see it squandered on vermin. Still, the local stone offered a good rough surface on which to break the grain, and the cracked husk and lighter powder soon formed thick piles.

When Simulus stepped out of his hut into the crisp dawn, the morning sun was rising over the mountains behind Vesuvius. To the south, he could see the walls of Pompeii through the low mist, with the temples of the forum standing proud above them: in between, the landscape was crowded with farms, villas and plantations of all sizes. Simulus tore bunches of parsley, rue and coriander from the herb garden beside his house, and carried them in for Scyphale to grind in a pestle with garlic, hard cheese, oil and vinegar – the ingredients for a relish that would add flavour to their coarse bread.

Hunger was a constant fear. But there were others who lived on far less than he: the slaves who worked on the imperial estate nearby, or on the far side of the boundary stone that marked the end of his own property. The land beyond belonged to the rich man Fannius Synistor and was well tended and fruitful. But Simulus would not have wished to change places with Receptus, a tall, pale slave from the north who had been made overseer by Synistor and now faced the daily loathing of the other slaves he managed.

Simulus might be poor, but he was a free man with his own small piece of land: a fifteen iugera *plot that had been in the family for half a dozen generations. There weren't too many of them left now, smallholders like him, descendants of Sulla's veterans not even of the native farming stock. Many had sold up and moved out, their land swallowed by the big estates. Those who remained, tiny islands in an ocean of grand villas, looked out for one another; no one could afford a wine press for themselves alone and an ox was beyond their means, but by pulling together most things were possible. He even ate meat once in a while, a bit of mutton stew when a sheep was slaughtered for sale, a water-fowl trapped in the Sarno marshes.*

The biggest blessing of all was the soil itself, so rich and light and fertile, easy to plough and generous in its yield. It needed to be if he were to make ends meet. Yet he often remembered the words of Horace that his father had recited to him as a child: 'Happy indeed is the man who remains, as our pure-hearted ancestors, far from the world of business, and who cultivates the family farm.' Living in the foothills of Vesuvius, the farmers had many reasons to give thanks to the goddess Ceres, and Simulus had vowed to attend her annual festival on the fifth of the month. He might even stay to watch the ceremonies in the theatre, but he would have his work cut out to afford a day away from the farm.

Classical writers are united in their praise of the natural advantages of Campania, especially the slopes of Vesuvius, which were covered in beautiful villas and farmland almost to its pockmarked summit (Plate 15). 'Nowhere is the climate gentler ... nowhere is the soil richer ... Liber and Ceres outdo one another,' trills Florus in his *Brief History*, invoking the goddesses of wine and wheat, while Strabo marvels that, 'in the course of one year, some of the plains are seeded twice with spelt, a third time with millet, and others still a fourth time with vegetables!' Pliny too claims that the trees bear fruit three times a year and waxes anthropomorphic about how Nature excels herself in an effort to meet man's appetite for gastronomic pleasure. He is also more specific about the causes of the abundance, citing soil mechanics that facilitate good drainage while retaining water at lower levels. Modern soil analysis can add that the presence of high levels of phosphorous and nitrogen, complemented by a slightly acidic pH level of 5.6 from the sulphur that today still leaches from the volcanic rocks below, creates highly effective growing conditions. The seven hundred or so railway trucks that now leave the area every year filled with fruit and vegetables for export to northern Europe confirm the land's fertility. In ancient times, much of the abundance would have been consumed locally, as transportation over any distance by land was exorbitantly expensive.[1]

Although Pompeii was ringed with walls, the city's jurisdiction extended far out into the surrounding territory. Officially, the political administration of the city would have covered around a hundred square miles, but the effective total was probably at least double that. All of this area lay within the zone that had been repeatedly fertilised by deposits of ash spread by Vesuvius's ancient and long-forgotten eruptions. And within this band lay the opulent maritime villas on the coast where rich Romans holidayed during the summer months. The fashion for such properties had begun at least a century and a half earlier, when piracy no longer threatened the shoreline, and as yet it showed no signs of abating. Pompey the Great had owned such a pleasure palace, while the ruins of Pollio's grand villa, 'Pausilypon', still stand on a headland near Naples. As a result of routine imperial arm-twisting, it was left in a bequest to Augustus, the same emperor as had famously punished its late owner for his exceptional cruelty in throwing a slave into a pool of lampreys for a petty offence.

Sadly, the dispersed nature of the buildings in the Pompeian territory, and the sprawl of modern suburbs that now cover it, have made recent excavation of villa sites quite unusual. To date, approximately four to five hundred of the larger townhouses have been excavated inside the walls, a figure that would probably increase by almost a third if those areas that remain buried were accessible. The wealth of architectural and social information that they provide only emphasises how little we know in comparison about the outlying territory. There, the bulk of villas and farms were investigated during the nineteenth century, and were recorded to the less rigorous standards of the time. In many cases they have since been reburied. Recently, however, pioneering work in such scientific fields as the analysis of the area's flora and fauna, has greatly augmented our understanding of life outside the city's walls.

Some of the richest information concerning the farms of the Pompeian territory comes from a village on the foothills of Vesuvius that was partially excavated and now goes by the name of Boscoreale, after the royal hunting forests that grew there until the sixteenth century. The clusters of villas and farm buildings that have so far been revealed give the impression of an area of great wealth, leading some to propose this as an alternative candidate to the harbour for the ancient title of *pagus Augustus Felix suburbanus*.

Graffiti, signs and especially electoral notices offer clues as to the ownership of particular dwellings within the city walls, but in the villas outside the city evidence is usually in the form of rings with name-stamps that were left there by freedmen who were most probably their bailiffs. In the case of two villas in this area, it seems likely that the Emperor himself was the owner.

In the smaller of the two, excavation led to the discovery of an exceptional hoard of beautifully embossed drinking cups and a thousand gold coins, worth over a hundred thousand sesterces, twenty times the value of the next largest monetary find in Pompeii. The circumstances under which this sum came to be deposited here are not known and may well reflect the chaos immediately prior to the cataclysm of AD 79. However, to put the find into perspective, this sum could have supported a family of six for almost a thousand years – even if the speculators of Pompeii's later years had hiked the price of wheat as high as it could go – or alternatively bought fifty highly skilled or exotically beautiful men and women at the slave market.

The second imperial villa, in the neighbouring hamlet of Boscotrecase, was built about eighty years before the eruption, probably by Marcus Vipsanius Agrippa, Augustus's most loyal supporter since their school days together. He was a proven military commander, project manager for the transformation of Rome into an imperial capital of luminous marble, and a mainstay of the new administration. Agrippa played along with the etiquette of the new regime and bequeathed everything he had to Augustus on his death, only so that Augustus could then decline to accept the legacy in a flourish of imperial largesse. But such forebearance was shortlived: when Agrippa's son Postumus foolishly overreached himself, he was summarily banished and his property declared forfeit. In the following decades, the villa would have haunted the thoughts of at least one other emperor: it was almost certainly here that Claudius's son, Drusus, died by asphyxiation in a bizarre accident when a pear, thrown into the air and caught in his mouth, went on to lodge in his gullet.[2]

With such a tragic history, it is likely that by Nero's reign the villa was little frequented by the imperial family, yet it continued to be run as a commercial enterprise on the Emperor's behalf, as many such villas were. When Vesuvius erupted twenty years later, the estate was being administered by an imperial freedman, whose name appears on two seals found in the remains of a cupboard. The nature of his ruthless management is unmistakable in the stocks kept for the punishment of slaves and the eighteen tiny cells in which they would have slept, crushed together.

Although owned by the imperial family, there is no reason to suppose that these two villas operated any differently from other farm holdings, which would have been equally careless of their slaves' welfare. It is thought that the population of the Pompeian territory exceeded by two to one the ten or twelve thousand people living within the city walls, and a large proportion of these inhabitants would have been slaves. The hundreds of farms dotting the area would have needed staffing at a rate of at least a dozen slave workers for every hundred *iugera* – just over sixty acres – and ideally double that; but with slaves imported into Campania by the shipload, such labour would not have been hard to come by.

With the burgeoning slave population – probably representing one third of the entire head count in Italy and one fifth throughout the Empire – the gulf between rich and poor in the Roman world was extreme. Its closest modern equivalent would have been the slave societies of Brazil or the United States at the beginning of the nineteenth century, though both were far shorter-lived. As in those societies, the welfare of most slaves, particularly those bought up in bulk as fodder for the agro-industries, was of little concern or interest to the elite. As a consequence their lives have left barely a trace, either in literature or the material remains of the Roman world: only the elite's perception of their 'walking tools' is recorded by history. Their first impression of those who would in some cases live alongside them for many years, and become as intimate as their immediate family, was usually when assessing them at market. It is impossible to imagine the maelstrom of emotion – the fear and humiliation and fury and so much else – that the captives would have felt as they stood in Pompeii's forum being groped, prodded and mocked by prospective bidders, whose language few of them would have understood.

Each city had its own venue for the trading of slaves and in Pompeii the raised platforms recessed into the facade of the Eumachia building and the Macellum have been proposed as likely auction blocks.[3] Here the pathetic huddles of hominids would have been paraded for inspection, the feet of some whitened with chalk as a sign that they were freshly imported, all with boards hung round their necks to tout their less conspicuous virtues or cagily admit their faults: whether they loitered on errands, were diseased or infertile; whether they had ever been runaways or criminals, or if they had attempted suicide.[4] Alongside the old lags, many of those present would still be in a state of shock, having been torn from their homes and transported in miserable conditions by sea, or else driven on a forced march halfway across the continent.

Where whole family groups had been captured, they were often sold together, although they could not count on this: the parents of children who were fitter and more useful than they could only plead with their eyes not to be parted from them. Others who were up for sale had been kidnapped by slave traders or simply collected by them from the exposure sites outside the city walls where unwanted infants were abandoned.[5] Then there were those being sold on by owners who no longer had use for them, some of whom might even have been reared within the household. The home-bred slave was such a desirable commodity that time off work was held up as a

74

reward for slaves who bore three children, and freedom a vague prospect for those who hit the ultimate productivity target of four.[6] From the blocks, all would disappear onto farms or into the dark back corridors of elite houses, the vast majority to be overlooked thenceforth, or perhaps admired and misused for their beauty, or else, just possibly, valued for the practical talents they could bring to their new masters' households.

It is possible to catch occasional glimpses of the careless brutality with which slaves were treated in the gruesome remains of those who died in the AD 79 eruption. In one shocking discovery, the remains of a chain gang were unearthed outside the walls of Pompeii, their skeletons still shackled together as fire and brimstone fell from the heavens. According to Columella, ten was the ideal number for such work parties, since 'this system will induce them to compete with one another, and also identify those who are lazy'. In another excavation, the body of a single, presumably domestic, slave was found still manacled as he and his master attempted to flee the eruption. Yet the slaves' owners would have felt no shame: after all, Cato explicitly advised farmers to dispose of old and tired slaves in the same breath as he discussed discarding worn-out farm implements.[7] And worn out they would have been, after only a few years of the pitiless regime of labour to which agricultural slaves in particular were subject. Scientific analysis of bones from Herculaneum and Pompeii reveals that a proportion of the bodies that plausibly equates to the slave population were riddled with arthritis or distorted by repetitive overwork.

Two skeletons, found close together and both males of around forty-six years of age, clearly underline the cruel differences in physique that different lifestyles could create. One is a fine figure of a man, well nourished, with strong, thick bones and the musculature of an amateur athlete, his only peculiarity being a birth defect that left one arm disproportionately long. The other is a spindly specimen who stands ten centimetres shorter than his social superior, his muscles worn out from grinding labour on a poor diet, the vertebrae in his lower back fused as a result of Forestier's disease. The mouth of the former was in good condition, that of the latter a vile wreck of abcesses, one so large that it was draining into his sinuses. So clear are the distinctions that it is painfully unsurprising to read that the elite looked on their slaves as though they belonged to another, lower species.

What is perhaps more surprising is that female slaves who suffered similar disadvantages so often passed muster as sex objects in the eyes of their masters, who might exploit them personally or make them available at a price to fellow slaves. More permanent relationships between slaves were a possible reward for loyalty or good service, or else as a breeding arrangement. Whatever the circumstances of conception may have been, the pregnant body of one sixteen-year-old slave girl who died in the eruption exhibits the consequences of the maltreatment she endured. The slow growth of her bones and pelvis, her small stature and undernourished condition, plus the fact that four of her vertebrae were fused together as a result of the crippling weights she had been required to heave around while her body was still developing, show that her early demise spared her an agonising and doomed labour as she struggled in vain to give birth, her anatomy making it impossible. It was quite possibly a blessing for her unborn child that it never saw the light of day. Children reared on slave farms were expected to earn back the cost of their maintenance, and one way to ensure their financial viability was to bind parts of their growing bodies to produce deformities. 'Freaks', such as pinheads and dwarves, commanded a high premium at auction and were considered a pleasing ornament to a household.

But for all the small privileges he was allowed, perhaps the most soul-destroying role among the slave population fell to the *vilicus*, or agricultural foreman. A slave himself, the *vilicus* was responsible for the day-to-day management of rural estates and their slave population – including the organisation of the chain gangs – in the absence of the master. Although there is a marked absence of material evidence about the lives of such men, they appear in the literature of the period, though the elite writers are more preoccupied with their imagined faults than with the difficulties they must have faced in wielding power over their fellow captives. Indeed, farm owners were obsessively mistrustful of their *vilici* and the laws that governed the lives of even the most privileged could be hugely oppressive, forbidding them ever to break bread with others or have close associates. The trips into town on business that were part of the remit of the *vilicus* would only have intensified his sense of frustration; any brief pleasures he allowed himself there could be severely punished. Even attendance at a festival such as that of Ceres was unacceptable without specific permission, whilst in the market gardens he passed on the way he would have watched with envy how freed slaves cultivated the land loaned to them by their patrons.

The rules concerning the conduct of the *vilicus* were intended to remove any temptation to corrupt dealing, but their effect was to isolate him and ensure that he could never develop the reciprocal relationships that might ultimately make life as a freedman viable. Unlike the slaves who ran the town houses of the elite and had the opportunity to become close to their masters, such was the distrust of the *vilicus* that in most cases manumission was only a faint prospect. The estate was a place of hopeless exile for domestic slaves in disgrace, where the status of the servile was truly sub-human.

It was not until two years earlier, when Receptus had been promoted to vilicus *at Fannius Synistor's farm, that he had grasped the full misery that the master's arrival could provoke. For eleven months out of twelve, Receptus's word was law on the estate and he was loathed for it by every slave and hired hand who worked under him. It was he who saved money by cutting the rations to the sick; he who set a day-labourer adrift the instant they'd got their feet under the table; he who drove the slaves out in the face of storms and hailstones to dig pits for manure or scrub the farmstead clean, and who ordered the beatings of those who slackened at the task.*

Having been one himself, he knew how the slaves cursed him in the confused whispers of a dozen different tongues when alone at night, their voices animated but their limbs quite still, knowing that the slightest movement would tug the shackles and chafe the ankles and wrists of everyone along the line. 'Isn't he a slave like us? Didn't he once work alongside us?' But they weren't in his place when the twelfth month came round and the master arrived from Rome on his annual visit of inspection.

From the moment Fannius Synistor had set foot on the farm in late March, things had started to go awry. With barely a nod to the household gods, he had marched off to look over the farm, brandishing the little he had learnt from a desultory reading of Cato and Varro. At every step there was new criticism. Why had the brambles been allowed to grow too high? Why were the slaves' tunics torn? Where was the scythe he had loaned to his neighbour? Why had the debts not been collected? And what was Receptus doing, allowing the labourers a second break in their sixteen-hour day? Any explanation that Receptus offered was coldly rebutted. Having given Receptus authority over his property, Synistor seemed unable to trust that he would not exploit it to his own advantage.

And now, at dawn on the fourth day of his master's visit, Receptus found himself at the Vesuvian Gate of Pompeii, dispatched to hire day-labourers from where they gathered beside the muleteers' inn just inside the walls: specialists to graft the vines, even though he knew that the stems weren't ready for it and wouldn't be for another week at least.

Maximus was desperate for work, but Receptus ignored him – the graffiti down the street explained why: 'Veneria has sucked the cock of Maximus throughout the vintage, leaving both her holes empty and only her mouth full.'

Knowing that even the best men would fail to win Synistor's approval, Receptus chose carefully but quickly; better not to give his master time to scrutinise the slave gangs' performance without him there to drive them on, or to intimidate the young slave girl Chloe, who had been nervous for weeks since hearing that she was to meet her master for the first time. Synistor had not yet broken the news that he had decided to take her back to Rome with him as a gift for a friend.

One of the most interesting discoveries in Boscoreale was the spectacular villa-farm of Fannius Synistor – a man otherwise unknown to history but whose distinctly un-Roman last name hints that his own family may in an earlier generation have tasted the wretchedness of slavery. It seems unlikely that the farm provided his primary source of income – the generously proportioned rooms and beautiful wall paintings suggest a mere dabbler in the agricultural sphere, yet one who could afford the very best location and accessories for his hobby. It is an impression seemingly borne out by Synistor's preference for romantically fustian wine-production methods over more cost-effective techniques: special treading vats were used rather than the usual presses, in order to avoid bruising the grapes.

The agricultural writer Columella described three basic types of country house: the *villa urbana*, the *villa rustica* and the *villa fructuaria*. The first was a bolt-hole for those based in a nearby town or city and its agricultural functions were negligible; the second a working farm, devoted to the production of crops for sale; the third, a self-supporting entity that would feed the labourers and provision the owner's main household but also doubled as a pleasant country retreat with all the necessary amenities for leisure. Fannius Synistor's villa appears to belong to the last category, a place that was more about recreating a pastoral idyll than earning a living. Indeed, Columella even went so far as to identify an additional category of property, termed *pastio villatica*, where such extravagances as peacocks, cranes and game were reared. The archaeological evidence of vases made with internal pottery tunnels for the rearing of dormice demonstrates that the farming of such delicacies was more than satirical fiction. But in many cases the function of this type of livestock was mainly decorative. Such country seats might have been worth a fortune as real estate, but their commercial value was questionable at best: to most of their owners, they must have seemed more like bottomless money-pits.[8]

In this they mirrored the luxurious maritime villas on the coast, where aristocrats vied with each other to create ever more ostentatious constructions. When Varro – the prolific scholar of the turn of the previous century, who was perhaps best known for his horticultural writings – castigated his contemporaries over their competitive architectural ambitions, he surely had one eye on these seaside follies. For some, there was money to be made from fish-farming, and Roman engineering allowed the construction of large tanks in which the oxygen and saline content could be maintained at fixed levels and the continuous circulation of water ensured. From these it might have been possible to harvest up to one hundred and fifty tonnes of fish each year; Pliny writes of the yield from a certain Lucullus's ponds being worth four million sesterces.[9] But for the most part such extravagance could only lead to ruin, unless the canny owner financed his excesses through wise investment.[10]

Domitia Lepidia, Nero's aunt, may have farmed luxury fish in the extensive ponds of her villa at Baiae but, tacitly at least, she seems to have recognised that her *piscinae* scheme was more a charming artifice than a sound business proposition. At least she was not reliant on them for income. Evidence of her ownership of warehouse buildings and a working property in Puteoli suggests that she had an interest in trade and, presumably, if the commercial life of a rowdy seaport were deemed an acceptable source of cash for the Emperor's aunt, she would also have had interests in the more genteel sphere of local agriculture.

A century earlier, Cicero had observed that the decadent party set were eagerly snapping up profitable farms on the Campanian plain to underwrite their indulgences down on the coast; by the AD 50s, the same principle still pertained. With ideal growing conditions, good transportation by land and sea, together with ample provision of slave labour, it seems that the Pompeian territory provided a perfect opportunity for those who wished to see a healthy return on an investment. Landowners who also had shipping interests might even have procured their own slaves, thus avoiding having to pay a middleman. However, with slave-trading seen as a rather distasteful business, they would usually have kept such economies to themselves.

Boscoreale provides a vivid example of a profitable working farm, or *villa rustica*, as Columella would have termed it. Here, a single rectangular compound houses both simple living accommodation and the equipment needed to process the farm's crops: presses to extract the juices of grapes and olives, a large open-air yard with dozens of large *dolia* set into the ground for the fermentation of wine, a barn with an earthen floor beaten hard for the threshing of corn. All are established in accordance with the best practice recommended by agricultural experts of the day. And along the corridor off which the fermentation area is accessed, small rooms are arranged to house the slave labourers, keeping them apart from anything that could possibly offer a distraction from their agricultural tasks.

There is little in this villa to suggest any interest in the picturesque. The kitchen, dining room and some of the smaller rooms that would have provided sleeping space are placed around a yard, alongside which lie a domestic bakery and stables. And whilst there is a small bathhouse, any echoes of the peristyle of leisured life are very faint. It is known that oxen were kept in even the grandest town houses of Pompeii – two skeletons were found in the House of the Faun – but not where they would have impinged on the everyday life of the occupants; here, the mules would have been brought out into the farmyard through the kitchen. Everything is in clear contrast to those country retreats where the entire layout was conceived to provide diners with the most panoramic view possible. Other local farms, including that known as the Villa Regina, made marginally more concessions to elegance in the form of colonnaded courtyards or the occasional stretch of painted wall, but their focus was similarly on productivity: of vines and wheat, as well as almonds, walnuts, cherries and apricots. Admittedly, even in the more modest Boscoreale farm, the sumptuous figs for which Pompeii was renowned were grown, little luxuries destined for the best tables in the city.

By the hard logic of agrarian society, enormous power lay in the hands of those who owned and successfully operated large estates. Not only was their land a potential source of income, it could also be exploited to buy up political credit, particularly in times when food was short. From the middle of the first century BC onwards, the inhabitants of Rome had received a grain dole from the Emperor that provided two-fifths of a family's dietary needs. The cost to the state was a sixth of its total revenue, but the plebs were not to be palmed off with anything less. In Pompeii, though, the responsibility for such welfare measures fell to private citizens, whether doing their duty by needy clients and dependents according to the age-old conventions of patronage, or buying public favour during service as a city magistrate or in the run-up to the elections.[11]

Among the likely landowners in the Pompeian territory were those who had moved into the area from elsewhere and, through buying up land, had bought their way to political prominence. One such local migrant was Lucius Albucius Celsus, who had arrived twenty years before with enough cash to buy the second biggest house in Pompeii – known now as the House of the Silver Wedding – and who had risen rapidly to political office alongside Decimus Lucretius Valens. His son, Lucius Albucius Iustus, was probably one of the senior magistrates elected in March AD 58 alongside Veranius Hypsaeus.[12]

Another recent arrival, who would play a less benign part in the looming crises to confront Pompeii, was a member of the Grosphus family which originated in Sicily. The island at the heel of Italy had been the first province of Rome, and remained a great centre of wheat production, ranking only just behind Egypt, but it was notorious for its political corruption.[13] Having had himself adopted into the Gavius family some time in the previous few years in order to secure a presence on the Pompeian town council, it seems likely that Gnaeus Pompeius Grosphus set about applying his talents in both agricultural money-making and shady dealing. He made common cause with Livineius Regulus, a man who had been banished from Rome by Claudius a decade or so earlier. It was something of a standing joke in the capital that the supposedly harsh punishment of exile to beyond the hundredth milestone from Rome placed miscreants squarely on the sun-drenched beaches of the bay.[14] It also placed them in the midst of some of the most successful and ambitious freedmen, whose businesses appear to have been booming on the Bay of Naples at this time.

It seems likely that these freedmen would have looked to convert their wealth into farms, thereby joining the country gentry for whom the possession of such estates was a token of permanence in the social hierarchy. It was certainly an aspiration of their grotesque fictional representative, Trimalchio, from the *Satyricon*. Around Pompeii the names of freedmen have been associated with a number of villas through the discovery of name-seals, though in what capacity is not clear.[15] But most prominent of all in Pompeii during this period, as presumably elsewhere, were the children of imperial slaves who had been manumitted from the household of the Julio-Claudian dynasty and who bore this mark of distinction in their *nomen*, the middle of the three names that was passed down from father to son. Of these, the family we know most about, from the relatively recent excavation of their home, is that of Gaius Julius Phillipus and Julius Polybius.

What we can gauge of Julius Polybius's personal background and the social networks he cultivated in Pompeii suggests a man of unusual wealth and charisma. Even his Greek third name – a name given by parental preference – points to a certain swagger on the part of Polybius's father, since statistical analysis has shown that even where both parents carried Greek names, almost half chose to disguise their offspring's ethnicity and settle for a solid Roman alternative. More particularly, Julius Polybius shares this most personal part of his name with one of the most famous imperial freedmen of his father's generation, a Polybius who served as *ab studiis*, or literary advisor to the Emperor Claudius and who was warmly remembered in an inscription by a free born woman, Perelia Gemella, only a few miles up the Campanian coast. To suggest a family connection would be to go too far, but even if the young Polybius's name was chosen merely by way of a tribute to this excellent role model, it once again celebrated origins that a more precarious family might have sought to conceal.

The Julii had good cause to be confident. Julius Polybius and Julius Phillipus, his father or possibly just his brother, stood at the centre of what was destined to become perhaps the city's most powerful network of political movers and shakers during the AD 60s and into the AD 70s. In the previous quarter-century, Pompeii had become a favoured venue for a large number of other freedmen from a similar background who were looking to establish families in their own right. Men with an imperial pedigree such as Tiberius Claudius Claudianus and Claudius Verus, along with other newcomers like Rustius Verus and Licinius Romanus, found common cause and offered one another reciprocal support as they climbed the greasy pole of local politics, while freedmen of major Pompeian families like the Popidii were pleased to be associated with them. What is more, the presence of branches of these families in Rome, Puteoli or Delos implies that their commercial and trading activities may have had a long reach.

That the respect accorded to Julius Polybius rested on the

financial resources he could command is strongly suggested by the four great strongboxes that stood in the public area of his house. Whilst his associates were more liberal in expressing their wealth through the kind of luxuriously appointed homes that characterised the age – private baths and a nyphaeum, or fountain area complete with statues, in Rustius Verus's home, for example – Polybius himself was content to project a more steady and civic-minded persona. This sent out the signal that he and his descendants were men who embraced the sober traditions of the society that they had joined. Situated a short distance down the main street from the Arch of Holconius, the house boasted the only monumental *vestibulum* in the whole of Pompeii: a galleried entrance area that had been preserved unchanged since the early part of the previous century and offered reassuringly conservative echoes of grand public architecture.

In the April of AD 58, Julius Polybius was likely to have been one of the two young men then approaching the end of their term as junior magistrate or *aedile*.[16] With a home on the main street, which the funeral cortège of Decimus Lucretius Valens had processed past four years earlier, Polybius was to prove an influential presence in the city, and it seems probable that his success was to some extent rooted in the soil of the territory. When, in later notices urging his election to the senior magistracy, a number of supporters praised him for his 'good bread', they were not referring to his skills as a baker but to his generous distribution of a bread dole – a strong recommendation in a candidate for public office.[17] If, like others in Pompeii's political elite, he owned a granary, or operated a bakery through slaves, freedmen or clients, it would simply have been so that he could maintain control over the whole cycle of food production. After all, why let a tradesman take any of the credit merely for handling the fruit of the land? A painting from the walls of the city shows just such a dignified, togate figure standing behind a bakery stall in the forum, dealing out loaves into the outstretched hands of the masses. A modern politician would recognise it instantly as the perfect photo opportunity.

Bread, made from wheat alone or mixed with the autumn crop of spelt, was the staple food of the Roman diet and would have been consumed by the poor in quantity. To meet demand, and not-withstanding the supplement provided by the great Egyptian grain *annona*, up to three-quarters of all agricultural land in Italy would have needed to be planted with cereal crops. Analysis of the skeletal remains from Julius Polybius's own house in the city has assumed a daily calorific intake for each person equivalent to 9.4 kilograms of wheat, or ten loaves of bread. Of course, for the more sophisticated palates of the elite who could afford it, bulk would have been replaced by more refined and nutritionally beneficial fare. Meat, wine, cheese, fruit, vegetables and olive oil were all part of the Pompeian diet. Olive oil worked out at three times the cost of wheat for the same number of calories, and Cato limited his workers to an allowance of only half a litre a month. But in the household of Julius Polybius, there would have been little economic need for such restraint, at least for the moment.

Most of the Pompeian elite would have sustained their urban household through the cultivation of arable land within easy access of the city, supplemented in some cases by the produce from market gardens, sometimes even found within the walls. For the city's most important men, being seen to own productive land demonstrated their ability to meet the basic needs of the people, and that meant owning conspicuous estates in the vicinity. Those who were struggling with the weighty financial requirements necessary to remain eligible for the town council might well have had to be more circumspect, opting to own either a main residence in town with purely functional farming land outside, or else a luxurious but productive country estate along with only a modest town house.

In the absence of Pompeii's own bronze tablets of law, which we know were recast during the AD 60s but of which no trace has been found, the most reliable reference point for issues of Pompeii's civic governance is the colonial charter of Urso in Spain, that was found near present day Osuna in the late nineteenth century.[18] Engraved onto four tablets in around the 40s BC, the text records one hundred and thirty-four points of reference, along with the marginalia and amendments made during the drafting process, and there is no reason to suppose that provisions for Italy a hundred years later were significantly different. An earlier charter from

Tarentum states that all who wish to stand for public office must own a house roofed with at least fifteen hundred tiles within one mile of the city's boundary; it may be no coincidence that, based on those so far discovered, the probable number of villas within a similar distance from Pompeii amounts to roughly one hundred, the same as the number of seats in the council of *decurions*.

It is from a cache of wax tablets discovered under collapsed masonry in the upper storey of a Pompeian house that historians have managed to glean their most comprehensive understanding of the business arrangements and social hierarchy of Pompeian society. Caecilius Jucundus combined the roles of auctioneer and banker to act as an *argentarius* for the businessmen of Pompeii. Whether arranging the exchange of goods and commercial rights, or offering short-term credit and deposit facilities, he and his colleagues were essential to the smooth running of most transactions.

Born around the end of Augustus's reign, by AD 27 Jucundus may already have joined his freedman father, Felix, in the profession for which he would remain famous two thousand years later. By AD 58 he would have been in his mid-fifties, firmly established and enjoying the respect of the most important men in Pompeii, who entrusted him with their business and willingly acted as witnesses when he oversaw the dealings of others. The bronze bust of his father that was found in Jucundus's house suggests a man of sober demeanour and keen mind, not so much at ease with himself that his clients might wonder whether he needed his percentage cut of their sales, but straight-dealing and discrete. Jucundus had competitors in Pompeii, but it is tempting to imagine that during the AD 50s it was he who set the professional standard as an *argentarius* to which others in the small world of Pompeii aspired. His sons would go on to stand for political office, having finally shed the lingering taint of Felix's servile background.

The business was not large, but Jucundus's associates were reliable. His offices were probably somewhere around the large *macellum*, or food market, in the forum, or else in the front section of his house nearby. The names in the one hundred and fifty-three documents evoke a frenetic world of scuttling underlings, sweaty-palmed colleagues checking the progress of a difficult deal, and sniffy *decurions* who had to be welcomed with due deference before they would condescend to make their mark. Certain duties were delegated to freedmen – Phoebus, Communis and Chryseros – while Jucundus's slaves, Philadelphus, Menippus and Dionysus, are all named at different times as making payments on his behalf. In addition, half a dozen or so probable associates in the business, including a freedman of the Helvii called Apollonaris, appear frequently in the list of seven or so signatories who witnessed each exchange and were clearly on hand to make up numbers when needed.

Jucundus could also call in favours from the elite. The venerable ex-magistrate Quintus Appuleius Severus, who heads the list in ten of the surviving tablets, and appears another five times in second place, seems to have been in the auctioneer's pocket; maybe some kind of sweetener was offered for his attentiveness and the kudos his name carried. But he was not alone in indulging Jucundus: the names of the city's past and future grandees also crop up – along with Julius Polybius, there are Claudius Verus, Marcus Obellius Firmus and others – their relative status charted exactly by their shifting place in the order of witness names.

It is one of the peculiarities of Roman society that its obsession with status was such that any two Pompeians who happened upon one another in the forum would have been able to establish who held precedence almost instantly, as though some complex computation of prestige was constantly ticking over in any social situation. Where the ordering of witnesses in Jucundus's tablets is inconsistent, it almost certainly demonstrates not an error, but a genuine shift in the respective status of the individuals concerned. Moreover, social position was not only a matter of concern to the elite, who could cite public office or family pedigree in their cause. In one case we can see the petty squabbling of Publius Minicius Atticus and Aulus Veius Nympha, both infinitesimally inconspicuous to the eyes of posterity, over who should come seventh and who eighth in a list of witnesses, to the point where the scribe was even forced to delete and re-enter their names in the order that was finally agreed.[19]

Like everyone else, Jucundus would have known his own place: a man doubtless welcomed for dinner by those on whose behalf he acted for as long as he was useful to them, but merely a small-time banker by the standards of the Sulpicii of Puteoli, whom he would have known by repute if not by personal acquaintance. The sums he handled were sizeable for Pompeii, but decidedly modest by the standards of international trade: the occasional sale in excess of thirty thousand sesterces, a handful worth less than one thousand, but most settling at around the four to five thousand sesterces mark, or the cost at auction of enough wheat to keep a medium-sized bakery supplied for the best part of a year. His commission as broker was a mere one or two per cent of the total,[20] and the jobs were varied – where one month Jucundus might have been negotiating the lease of some big public contract, the next he could have been involved in the more mundane business of selling off furniture to simplify the division of spoils between testators in a will. When his more illustrious clients required, it seems that Jucundus was even prepared to travel on slave-dealing business, as evidenced by a deal he did in neighbouring Nuceria for the wealthy Publius Alfenus Varus, who wished to resell some slaves he had bought at auction.[21]

As a senior centurion in the Praetorian Guard, Publius Alfenus Varus enjoyed considerable prestige in Nuceria in AD 58. In the previous year, Nero had begun settling a large contingent of army veterans there to bolster the local population, and these men would have particularly appreciated the significance of Varus's military rank. Varus's father, a *decurion* on Nuceria's town council, certainly took pride in his son's achievements and both put their names to the slave contract brokered by Jucundus.

Jucundus may not have derived quite so much pleasure from his role. He would have reached Nuceria by crossing the Sarno bridge and travelling on through Pompeian territory until the familiar orientation of the fields on a north-east to south-east grid gave way to the Nucerian system of alignment with the points of the compass. But the sense of crossing into foreign lands may have gone deeper than that; on top of the inconvenience and the embarrassment of having a hand in the slave trade, Nuceria was not always the most hospitable place for Pompeians. There was a deep-seated rivalry between the two towns that, before long, would boil over into violence.

The spring festivities had begun in the ancient sanctuary of the fertility gods, beyond the Nuceria cemetery, where the Sarno broadened out towards the sea. Crowds from the city and countryside had come to offer sacrifices in the name of Ceres, the earth mother who brought rebirth after winter. Fannius Synistor and a handful of other landowners who were only occasional visitors to the region stood mingled with the local elite, but humble tenant farmers were there too, and peasants clad in little more than animal skins. All were eager to propitiate the goddess for a successful growing season, and the priestess Alleia, daughter of the esteemed decurion Alleius Nigidius Maius, was present to act as their intermediary.

Synistor watched as the first stage of the ceremony concluded and the statue of the goddess was raised and carried off in procession, up towards the city and the theatre, where the rites would continue. The sacrificial meat was left sizzling on a fire, the appetising smell a reminder to those who would later return to dine.

When Synistor and his companions reached the corridor that formed the lower entrance to the theatre, several of the highly favoured freedmen from the Augustales association were there already. Together they awaited the moment when they could enter to claim their seats in the front rows. From inside and above, the excited chatter of the humbler spectators echoed against the narrow walls as unseen women, freedmen and slaves hurried round the perimeter of the theatre complex, clambering up to the rim of the semi-circular auditorium from which they could swarm down to claim their seats in the appointed areas. Expectations were high.

Synistor knew all about the actor Paris from his exploits in Rome, but his presence here was something of a novelty. The man beside him volunteered that talk in the bars and at dinner parties had been of nothing else for weeks. Even now, when the performance was about to begin, the touts were still asking astronomical prices for the tiles shaped like rings and plucked chickens that granted admission. With Paris on the stage, and Poppaea, Nero's mistress, in the audience, for one short day it felt almost as though Pompeii were the centre of the world.

III

The power of the court factions, whose intrigues had dogged Nero since long before he became Emperor, was still finely balanced at the end of AD 58. On one side, the Emperor's advisors Seneca and Burrus fought to hold Nero to the political programme that he had adopted on his accession; on the other, Agrippina constantly schemed to sway his judgement against them and reclaim for herself the role of puppeteer that she had always intended. With coins from the early years of Nero's reign that bore her profile stamped alongside that of her son still untarnished, no one could doubt the power she had wielded (Plate 5c).

Until recently, the growing enmity between Agrippina and the men she had personally selected as her creatures at court only a few years earlier had been played out through a series of proxies. In the process, most of them had been carelessly destroyed, but as long as the leading actors remained standing, there could be no lasting resolution. Now the stakes were raised. The ferocity of Agrippina's attacks had shown no signs of abating – quite the opposite – and the Emperor's counsellors were forced to conclude that they had no choice but to act decisively, to save not only their policies, but even their own skins. Having failed with the actor Paris, the chosen instrument of their campaign was now to be a cherished daughter of Pompeii, a young woman who had quickly established a strong enough place in Nero's heart to challenge the supremacy of his mother.

Ambition was in Poppaea Sabina's blood as much as it was in Agrippina's. Even the name she bore, that of a maternal grand-father who had given distinguished service as a consul and general, had been taken out of necessity, to disguise the identity of an overreaching father. When still a young man, her father Titus Ollius had made the grave error of accepting the friendship of Sejanus, the Praetorian Prefect who had gone on to outrage the Roman aristocracy with his despotic ways during the prolonged withdrawal from public life of the Emperor Tiberius. When Sejanus was caught plotting to seize the throne, and executed, Ollius had been plunged into disgrace and had struggled to regain his footing; his daughter clearly preferred not to be tainted by association.

But if the unsentimental Poppaea had inherited a taste for power from her father, it was from a mother who had been praised as the most beautiful woman of her day that she derived the means to achieve it. Charming and witty, Poppaea knew how to exploit her most personal assets in Nero's Rome: a world of theatrical illusion and flirtatious game-playing. Already married twice, her second husband being the Emperor's boyhood friend Otho, the clever seductress made sure she always maintained a modest demeanour in public. But acerbic commentators noted that her veil tantalised even as it concealed. It was whispered that, in private, she could be perfectly wanton in pleasing her various lovers.

Little is known about Poppaea's life before her appearance in her early twenties as a glittering addition to Rome's smart set; it is likely, though, that at least some of her childhood was spent in or around Pompeii, where evidence has been found that suggests the presence of both the maternal and paternal sides of her family. If so, the House of Menander is a promising candidate for her home. As so often in Pompeii, the identification of the building's owners is uncertain, but a ring bearing the name Quintus Poppaeus Eros was found on the body of a man who died in the adjoining bailiff's house. Also found in the main residence, stored away in the bathhouse, was a great cache of silver plate and jewellery.

Wealth is no sure indicator of status, but the large gold men's rings that were part of the collection point firmly towards this being the home of a very affluent aristocratic family. In the course of the preceding hundred years the property had expanded into the neighbouring buildings of the block and could boast a suite of five reception rooms fit for hosting the grandest of occasions. That Italy's dictator Mussolini chose it, nearly two millennia later, as the venue for an extravagant lunch party for visiting dignitaries, testifies to its opulence.

Other traces are found within Pompeii of the family of the local girl who was destined for great things. A second branch of Poppaea's family appears to have lived in the House of the Golden Cupids. Like the House of Menander, this was an unusually grand building – even for a city not lacking in domestic grandeur – with finely decorated rooms and a beautiful peristyle garden. Already in the AD 50s it was surrounded by thriving shops and other businesses, built into the fabric of the block containing the house, that would have been run by dependents of the aristocratic owners. At some point, Poppaea herself owned a pottery in the suburbs of the city: a wax tablet discovered in Herculaneum records the sale of a slave girl whose new owner was to collect her from the factory.[1]

As AD 59 dawned, a seething knot of sexual jealousy was electrifying the already stormy atmosphere around the Emperor, and in the eye of that storm stood Poppaea. Quite how and at what point Nero and Poppaea began their affair is unclear. The accounts contradict themselves, claiming both that the marriage to Otho was a sham from the beginning – a front conceived to conceal the Emperor's existing dalliance from his wife Octavia and mother, Agrippina – and that their adultery was unintentionally prompted by Otho boasting to Nero of his wife's beauty. Either way, it is impossible not to suspect that Poppaea was actively involved in the affair's inception, probably with the connivance of Seneca and Burrus. Certainly they would waste no time in exploiting the couple's passion to drive a wedge between Nero and Agrippina, who considered Octavia to be an essential ally, as the daughter of Claudius and one solid guarantee of Nero's legitimacy as emperor.

Agrippina, once so adept at trading on her female wiles, found that she had lost her touch just when she needed it most. Instantly smitten with Poppaea, Nero found the continued presence in Rome of her husband Otho intolerable, regardless of how co-operative the behaviour of his old friend might have been. Seneca's trusted counsel deflected Nero from his decision to execute Otho. Instead, the cuckolded husband was made governor of Lusitania on the distant Atlantic seaboard, a role for which he had no demonstrable aptitude. At that point, Agrippina knew the game was up. A last-ditch bid to win back Nero through incestuous seduction failed, with her son refusing even to grant her a private audience, and she withdrew to her country estates.

Freed from her grip, Nero turned on his mother with a vengeance: litigators stepped forward to hound her through the courts on the slimmest of pretexts, while murderous measures only failed because a lifetime spent gulping down antidotes had left her immune to the effects of poison. Even a plan to collapse a bedroom ceiling onto her while she slept failed because of intelligence leaked by insiders who remained loyal to her. But once set on matricide, the Emperor was not to be so easily thwarted. Poppaea steeled his resolve with demands that she be allowed to return to her husband unless the Emperor intended to make a decent woman of her. The prospect of losing her was unbearable.

Installed in the villa of Calpurnius Piso for the March AD 59 senatorial recess, Nero plotted with renewed ingenuity. Only a few miles away, Pompeii was immersed in preparations for its annual elections at the end of the month, and the five-day-long Festival of Minerva when the city's artisans were entitled to down tools and celebrate. But Nero would have given little thought to local politics or plebeian holidays as he paced the rooms of the palatial building. Beside the great pool at the heart of the villa, surrounded by fine statuary, he may have found reassurance for this most unnatural of crimes in an extraordinary bronze that stood there: one of the most impressive pieces of workmanship to have survived the eruption. Rendered in explicit and transgressive detail, a goat in the throes of ecstasy is ravished by the lascivious god, Pan.

Perhaps it was when he turned to gaze out over the bay from the villa's long balcony that inspiration struck. Sending a letter to his mother, Nero invited her to join him in Campania to celebrate the Festival of Minerva at a dinner near Baiae. Rightly cautious, her suspicions were probably raised further by her son's excessive attentiveness, personally greeting her on the beach when she disembarked and escorting her to the villa. Agrippina insisted on the precaution of being carried to dinner in a sedan chair, but by the time the meal was over and Agrippina found herself standing on the shore with her son kissing her breasts in farewell, she had foolishly dropped her guard.

Once out into the deep waters of the bay, the lavishly furnished ship supplied by Nero to ferry her back to her residence sprang its surprises: while Agrippina pondered her son's surprising change of heart, the canopy above her crashed down with the full weight of the lead piled above, its fall broken only by the high sides of the couch on which she lay. Seeing that she had survived, the sailors quickly capsized the ship and Agrippina was only able to swim to the safety of a nearby vessel thanks to the self-sacrifice of her attendant, Acerronia Pollia, who distracted the sailors with claims that it was, in fact, she who was the Emperor's mother. Taking the servant at her word, they bludgeoned her to death with an oar.

On shore, Nero and his conspirators reconvened with a feverish determination to ensure that Agrippina did not escape. A messenger sent to Nero by his mother had a sword dropped at his feet to frame him as an assassin: furnished with the pretext they needed for summary justice, the Emperor's advisors acted swiftly. The vow taken by the Praetorian Guard to protect the whole family of the Caesars prevented them from delivering the *coup de grâce*, but no such prohibition bound the navy. Anictetus, the freedman admiral who had contrived the collapsing canopy on the boat, now threw a cordon of marines around Agrippina's villa to exclude any possible witnesses, while he and his men stormed in, hunting their prey down to her bedroom.

Years earlier Agrippina was said to have replied to an astrologer who told her that her son would rule but would also murder his mother, 'Let him kill as long as he rules.' Now, already injured, exhausted and terrified, Agrippina 'presented her womb to the stabbing swords' of her assassins and the prophecy was fulfilled.

CHAPTER 4

A Worthy Man, Vote for Him

March AD 59

Decimus Satrius Lucretius Valens was relishing a brief moment of repose in the late-afternoon sun, when the sound of hammering shattered the peace of his courtyard garden. After a day of onerous official duties and hours of negotiations on behalf of his clients, his nerves were frayed. But his irritation lasted only a moment, before he remembered that the sound was that of laurel branches being nailed to his door in honour of his position as Nero's priest. It was only a gesture, traditionally made by the town council on the first of March to mark the beginning of the Festival of Mars, but it bolstered his spirits.

Thoughts of the morning's ceremonies weighed heavy on his mind. When the senior magistrate Albucius Iustus had gazed up at the flight of birds up above and seen in them signs of a calm and steady year ahead, instead of nodding his agreement as he usually did, the augur who stood beside him in purple robes had whispered in his ear. Iustus had again turned his face skywards. The skittering flight of the starlings presaged hard months ahead, he now warned. And the augur concurred.

Valens knew how these things worked. Skilled though they might be at reading signs of the gods' intentions, the augurs were not immune to the mood of unease that was carried in with the news from Rome. There, the monstrous birth of a serpent from a woman's womb and the many bolts of lightning that had struck targets across the city, including a married couple who were felled as they embraced, gave credence to the rumours of discord in the imperial family. The sun itself had been briefly extinguished. If there were clouds on the horizon, then the augurs of Pompeii were not going to risk their reputations merely to oblige a local magistrate who wanted his term of office to end on an optimistic note. Since becoming flamen of Nero,

Valens had basked in the reflected glory of the dynamic young Emperor. There was no doubting the popularity of an emperor who trailed the good times in his wake. Stories of his nocturnal shenanigans in the back streets of Rome had been easily laughed off as high spirits. But Valens knew how fast the public mood might turn if Nero became tainted with bad luck. Already he had heard that there were those in Rome questioning the direction that the Emperor's reign was taking, and before long those murmurings of dissent might be heard in Pompeii too.

With the arrival of March, the time had come to confirm the final selection of those who would stand for election as senior and junior magistrates. It was crucial that they choose the right men. Valens himself was backing the Sicilian, Pompeius Grosphus; he was a relatively new face around town but showed application. And Valens felt an affinity to Gavianus, or Gaius Publius Gavius, as he had been known before Grosphus had adopted him to be his heir, and who was now the latter's running mate. The two planned to stand on a family ticket, allowing them to pool campaign resources. Valens admired their audacity. But would other members of the council feel the same?

When asked to help advance the political career in Rome of a friend's stepson, Cicero had offered the wry observation, 'At Rome if you want it you shall have it; at Pompeii it would be difficult.'[1] Read in the light of the three thousand and more professionally sign-painted endorsements of political candidates that have been found on the walls of Pompeii, it would be easy to think of the city as a flourishing grassroots democracy with little room for nepotism. Much of the evidence appears to point to fiercely contested elections, with intense popular engagement in the process as candidates campaigned to mobilise every last vote. However, the reality of political representation was rather different, with political life increasingly stage-managed by the powerful families of the city.

The *curia*, or *tribus*, was the crucial voting unit in the Pompeian electoral system, with different groupings within the city conducting primary elections to determine their preferred candidate. As in Rome, it appears that these groups in Pompeii usually derived their names from particular neighbourhoods, such as the forum or various gates to the city, and records of the Forenses, Campanienses,

Salinienses and Urbulanenses support this. But the names of important local families also seem to have been attached to such groups, as in the case of the 'Poppaeenses', who derived their name from the family of Poppaea, implying that leading families could have considerable influence over the votes of their clients and dependents.[2]

By Nero's reign, Pompeii was seeing a small number of prominent families almost monopolising the most important positions in the city's governance. Of the annually changing posts, only the lower magistracies – the aedileships – were actually contested, while the senior magistrates – the *duumviri* – were selected by some other means and then merely rubber-stamped into office by the electorate. According to the constitutional charter of Urso, it was the elder of the senior magistrates who oversaw the election of their successors.[3] Presumably the same was true of Pompeii.

Patronage ran right through Roman society. The emperor governed through officials who comprised a civil service, but there was no sprawling bureaucratic system: 'small government' was favoured, with responsibility for decision-making devolved as far as possible. The cities and provinces that made up the Empire did not necessarily have a direct representative in government. Unlike the city of Como in the north of Italy, for example, no one from Pompeii sat in Rome's senate. Nevertheless, contact with Rome was mediated by certain favoured individuals, who consequently stood at the head of their local pyramid of power; for those who wanted their pleas or opinions to be heard, the patronage of such a figure was essential. Where one pyramid had its base, several others would have reached their apex, with the *paterfamilias* of a major Pompeian family being able to deliver the votes not only of his family members, but of all those in direct receipt of his support or protection. With the number of free adult males eligible to vote in Pompeii numbering at most four to five thousand, and around one hundred *decurions* sitting on the council, it is perfectly possible that almost everyone was the client of a small number of influential opinion-makers who could consequently help swing an election.

The potential of a candidate standing for the office of magistrate in Pompeii was reckoned as the sum of three essential qualities: the personal abilities and educational achievements that would make him a capable administrator; the number of clients who turned to him as their voice in public or legal matters; and the depth of his pockets. In a world where the cost of education was met privately, and where the income of the elite would be intimately linked to the breadth of their clients' interests, the first two qualities were, to a great degree, encapsulated in the third. The costs of public service were far from negligible. The records from elsewhere of a senior magistrate's expenditure itemise for his year in office: '6,000 sesterces as fixed fee. For the supply of the legions: 3,450 sesterces. For the rebuilding of the Temple of Diana: 6,200 sesterces. For the victory games of Augustus Caesar: 7,750 sesterces.'[4]

It was expected that a junior magistrate would go on to become a senior one, and that he would finally aspire to the ultimate honour of becoming one of the *duumviri quinquennales*, for the census. At this rate, had he held office on only two occasions, he would already have spent almost half of the hundred thousand sesterces that had originally qualified him for membership of the council of *decurions*. He would receive little financial reward: the entourage of secretaries, musicians and bearers of official insignia that each magistrate was assigned was more than subsidised by his own fixed contribution to public funds on assuming office. Not for him the perks of administrators in the provinces, where private profit was accepted as legitimate recompense for a number of years spent away from civilisation. Public office in Pompeii was simply not an option for those who only just made the cut.

A major source of expenditure for the magistrate would have been the funding of public building work. Augustus had encouraged prominent citizens everywhere to put their shoulders to the wheel of change and pay for the refurbishment of old public buildings or the construction of new ones. Throughout Pompeii, buildings would have trumpeted the generosity of their benefactors with bold inscriptions. Now a visitor must squint up at the entablatures to discern the names carved on the discoloured marble, but then the carved letters would have been filled with grey lead or glistening bronze. Inscriptions were everywhere: on the grand buildings of the forum, on the vast marble basin with the exquisitely shallow profile that still rests on its pedestal in the Forum Baths.[5] Had the marble that recorded such acts of generosity not proved so tempting to post-eruption looters, it is likely that many other similar gifts would have come to light. A fragment of a marble inscription referring to a junior magistrate was even found at a villa in Oplontis to which it had, for some reason, been removed before the eruption.[6]

By the mid-first century, there appears to have been a general decline in the private funding of public buildings throughout Campania, though entertainment and leisure facilities were still being erected. Perhaps years of generosity had limited the opportunities for further improvement in the physical condition of Pompeii. But the candidates for public office did not lack for alternative ways of impressing the people. Free bathing was one inducement for citizens to support a particular candidate, and legal sources made it clear that buildings similar to the Stabian Baths in Pompeii were leased annually to junior magistrates for this purpose.[7] The stomachs of the poor could never be overfilled with free bread. And if all else failed, one gesture was certain to be well received: Pompeii's amphitheatre had been attracting the crowds for longer than any other still standing, and the city had not escaped the increasingly feverish appetite for gladiatorial games that was sweeping the Empire.

Augustus had stipulated that any displays of civic patronage should be affordable and the moralistic writers of the first century allude to excessive expenditure on public works, grouping it together with other forms of *luxuria*. It was an attitude that was clearly articulated by the historian Cassius Dio, writing with the benefit of hindsight from the third century. He puts the following words into the mouth of Maecenas, a political fixer and literary patron of the Augustan age:

> Cities should not indulge themselves with commissioning too many public buildings on too large a scale, nor should they squander their resources on a large number or a variety of public games, in case they exhaust themselves with futile projects or arouse irrational rivalries that make them quarrel amongst themselves.

They should certainly stage their festivals and spectacles ... but not to the extent that the public treasury or the estates of private citizens are ruined as a result, or that any resident stranger need contribute to their expense ...[8]

The candidates of AD 59 would have done well to take heed, since it was never advisable for a politician to be in hock to an outsider like Grosphus, or his likely sponsor, Livineius Regulus.

The threat of bankruptcy was a very real one for some magistrates. It was as a precaution against this that potential candidates were obliged to make a deposit to the treasury to prove that they could cover future expenditure. Nevertheless it is tempting to imagine that Pompeian families such as the Rusicelii and Terentii, who are known to have held a magisterial post only once, disappeared from view precisely because their finances were ruinously depleted by the cost of office. Few of the elite who won the prized magistracies saw their sons follow in their footsteps, while still fewer *decurions* could expect their grandchildren to achieve a similar status. The Senate in Rome also saw a turnover in its membership that was dramatically rapid, with a full three-quarters of those families that could meet the financial qualifications in one generation failing in the next. Doubtless it was the anxieties arising from this state of affairs that prompted the call in AD 56 for restrictions on the number of freedmen and their sons. Unsurprisingly, there were occasional shortages of willing candidates for election to civic posts. To ensure a supply, some constitutions went so far as to include provision for those eligible to be publicly listed on the order of the city council, and the reasons for their reluctance held up to public scrutiny. Elite life was conducted within a shame culture and public office was a primary civic duty.[9]

Before dawn broke, the morning air filled with tempting smells of baking bread and the snorting of donkeys, which walked an endless round to keep the bakers' grindstones turning. The streets of Pompeii were already bustling with activity, as the mass of lesser citizens hurried to attend the daily salutatio *of their patron. Outside the doors of each of the major houses, small crowds assembled to await admission by the night doorkeeper* whose oil lamp guttered behind the grille. Even in the side streets, clients were congregating outside less ostentatious houses. The luckier visitors enjoyed their place on one of the stone or wooden benches provided for the purpose; the less fortunate rubbed sleepy eyes and grumbled.

The noise of expectant chatter in the street outside echoed round the atrium of Gnaeus Alleius Nigidius Maius's home. He had instructed his seneschal to delay admitting the crowd so that their presence might be noticed; with elections coming up, it was helpful to remind the city of his prestige. Maius knew that Nero's flamen, Valens, was backing the double ticket of Grosphus and Gavianus, but Maius was not alone in thinking that the pair seemed dangerously close to Livineius Regulus. Disgraced under the Emperor Claudius, the senator had lived out the previous decade of his exile near Pompeii. But who really knew where an enemy of the divine Claudius stood, now that the late emperor's wife and adopted son were at each other's throats? To many minds, Regulus could only spell trouble.

Maius drained a cup of water by way of breakfast, then headed out into the colonnade that surrounded his garden. Ahead of him he could see the throng as they jostled in the atrium, waiting for admittance to the room where he would shortly hold his audience. Taking a seat beside his money chest, he watched the nomenclator scan the assembled crowd of petitioners as they settled down to respectful silence, mentally sorting them by precedence. Some came to request his support in a trade dispute, or a word in the right ear about a loan, but most attended simply to claim their sportula – the financial handout that he so generously provided. Maius knew them all well, and how to manipulate their individual vanities and weaknesses: when to shame them with a slighting comment, and when to put them at their ease with friendly greetings; how to make it seem as if the coins slipped into their hand as they left were a mere token of esteem.

Today, though, the face that confronted him from the head of the queue was not that of a regular visitor. The young Licinius Romanus, upon whose initiative he had often remarked, appeared awkward as he waited. Maius could remember how it had felt to be standing for election for the first time, supplicating the great men of his own earlier years for their support. He decided at that moment to take Romanus up as a protégé. Valens had the senior magistracies sewn up, but the injection of a little competition into the campaign for the junior posts could be no bad thing.

As soon as the heavy doors of the patron's house swung open, the true theatricality of the daily *salutatio* in the grand houses of Pompeii became obvious.[10] Through a narrow entranceway off the street lay the atrium in all its archaic splendour, and in its centre the rectangular pool of the *impluvium*, open to the sky above and catching its light. The tall, broad screens usually used to keep out the cold or block off other rooms were deliberately pulled back. Now not only did the vast, high space of the atrium confront visitors, but beyond it a carefully framed vista of rooms and gardens. First, the *tablinum*, the transitional space where their patron would receive them beside the strongboxes that contained an archive of documents attesting to the political careers and honours of the *paterfamilias*'s forebears, alongside the monetary wealth that was the other essential guarantee of continuity in elite life.

Behind him, his clients would have caught sight of the evenly spaced columns of the peristyle courtyard, planted with box hedges and flowers, adorned with statues, allowing a glimpse into the leisured private life of the household that certain guests might be invited to join. Painted panels, showing scenes from mythology, led the eye into the depths of the courtyard beyond the columns, creating a feeling of opulence. And if the courtyard itself were not capacious enough to contain the fountains, statues and bird-covered shrubbery that furnished the ideal town garden, then *trompe-l'oeil* paintings on the wall to the rear could create the illusion of such a space (Plate 17). Everything conspired to create a perfect backdrop to the performance of power and largesse that was about to take place: the handing out of the *sportula*.[11]

Later in the first century, when Juvenal turned his acerbic wit on the relationship between client and patron in his *Satires*, he offered a vision of a society that had lost its dignity while still clinging to the empty gestures of a previous age: 'Clients were guests in those days, but now Roman citizens are reduced to scrambling for a little basket of scraps on their patron's doorstep.'[12] Originally, the *sportula* had been the mechanism by which the aristocracy rewarded their clients' loyalty with a daily share of the produce from their agricultural lands: first in the form of dinner taken with the patron, later with an allowance of food to take away, and finally with a cash donation. It was a ritual that embodied the natural rights of citizens to share in the bounty of the community whilst allowing the elite to maintain their dominance by an insistent reminder of their dependents' obligation to them.

One might read the graffito from the exterior wall of a Pompeian house that declares, 'A benevolent god lives here', in the light of such a relationship. But other graffiti from the basilica and elsewhere hint at a state of affairs that was closer to the degeneracy described by Juvenal. Meal invitations are pleaded for – 'Let anyone who invites me to dinner prosper!' – and, on one very conspicuous wall, Lucius Istacidius is pilloried for his parsimony in failing to issue any such offers. Any carelessness in the personal relations between client and patron that formed the spine of Roman ideology could only have signalled a fraying of the unspoken contract that saw largesse dispensed in return for political affiliation.

Leaving the *salutatio*, the patron class of the city converged on the forum to conduct their business, accompanied by a select group of retainers, and importuned along the way by those wanting favours. One painted panel in the atrium of the *praedia* (mixed rental property) of Julia Felix depicts just such an entourage parading into the forum. Others from the same series show the sights that would have greeted them there: men begging charity as fine ladies swept past; pots and other tools and utensils laid out on the ground for sale; all the everyday activities of a provincial city (Plate 13).

In the school that was held under one of the porticos, one father might even have noticed his son being summoned to the front of class for misbehaviour, and stretched over the back of another pupil to receive a beating. Corporal punishment was used liberally and even in later life the nostalgia many Romans felt for the halcyon days of childhood was poisoned by the memories of the horrific floggings they had received.[13] In this case it was perhaps administered in the establishment of a certain Sema, who in later years would lead his class in endorsing a candidate standing for election.[14] And whilst he might have struggled to command attention for other subjects, there would have been real interest amongst the boys in the electoral campaigning that was about to begin: many of the older ones, who were about to move on to the next stage of education, would have envisaged themselves as future candidates.

For girls and younger male children, the earliest years of their education would have taken place at home where, once the master of the house had left for the day, the atrium became the domain of their mothers and female associates. Although it was generally perceived to be a female role, some fathers took responsibility for infant pedagogy more seriously than others: Cato the Elder abandoned all work except pressing state business to teach his son a curriculum that dealt with reading and law but also encompassed fighting in armour, boxing, horse-riding, 'but also to endure both hot and cold, and to swim strongly through the eddies and currents of a river.'[15] But following the rite of passage from *infantia* at the age of seven, by which point the child was expected to have shed their milk teeth, any boy destined for public life embarked on his initiation into the public world, and his training in the skills needed for him to thrive there.[16] Accompanied by a slave, he would have set out early, greeted his teacher with a kiss, and settled down to smooth out his wax tablet in preparation for the writing and dictation lessons that would follow. The presence of his slave at the back, waiting for the morning's classes to finish, should have acted as a warning for the pupil to be diligent: the cleverer slaves who performed this role would have listened in intently, and some went on to scale far greater intellectual heights than their young charges.

It is likely that the education of the time, in Campania especially, bore a strongly Greek complexion. According to Strabo, half a century earlier, Naples had been particularly famed for its tutors, who favoured it for the familiarity of its Greek style of living and the peace and quiet in which they could indulge their taste for learning. In AD 59 one of the most esteemed teachers of the age, the father of the poet Statius, ran a school there that attracted students from across Campania; even the great families of Rome occasionally enrolled their sons and it could count generals and provincial governors among its better-known alumni.[17] Some of the heirs to Pompeii's wealthier families might conceivably have attended Statius's school or another similar establishment in Naples;

pupils certainly travelled from Sorrento, which was half as far again from Naples as Pompeii, and lodged in the city. There, or in Pompeii's forum, the range of subjects taught was similar, and is listed in one notice on a Pompeian wall: 'reading and writing and rhetoric'.[18]

Rote learning was at the core of the initial stages of education. Literary texts were chanted, with Virgil a particular favourite: when we read crude misquotations in Pompeian graffiti – '*Veni, vidi, futui*': 'I came, I saw, I fucked' – it may be these schoolboy tests that were to blame.[19] Other rote learning tasks paid greater dividends: the recital of multiplication tables would have been an invaluable preparation for calculating interest rates, as Horace had once remarked, and a certain level of literacy was required to fulfil ones duties as a citizen.[20] Some, though, got by well enough without too much schooling. As the character of Trimalchio boasts in the *Satyricon*, with the self-made man's bluff disdain for formal education: 'I did not learn geometry and literary criticism and useless nonsense like that. I learned how to read the letters on public inscriptions, I learned how to divide things into one hundredths and work out percentages, and I know weights, measures and currency too.'[21]

Trimalchio was clearly blind to the educational refinements on which he had missed out. Despite all the sycophancy shown by the elite guests at his fictional dinner party, to them his shortcomings would have been immediately apparent. One omission in his education were the *colloquia*: a key part of the more advanced curriculum that involved older male children in linguistic exercises concerning everyday life. Addressing such issues as the right and wrong way to wield authority over slaves, dependents and the great mass of citizens who were one's inferiors, the *colloquia* reinforced lessons that would have been learnt through observation in the elite family home. Discourtesy and the unjust exercise of power, at which Trimalchio showed himself to be so adept, were the stigma of bad breeding. However, more significantly, he had also never received the kind of training that prepared the sons of the elite for public office. Not that the grotesque freedman would have had any real call for the knowledge of grammatical theory or the rhetorical skills that would have been on full display from his social superiors at the opening of the election campaign.

The *professio* was held every March in the *comitium* building that stood in the south-east corner of Pompeii's forum, between the administrative buildings and the entrance from the main street. Convoked by the incumbent magistrates, the citizens would assemble to witness a public declaration of intent by those who sought office in the forthcoming election: women as well as men would be present, and could later voice their opinions, even though they could not vote. Many in the crowd already knew where their allegiances lay, whether it was with a patron's relative, a neighbour, or a candidate who could command the support of some club or group to which they belonged. Others would have been undecided, and for the candidates to the junior magistracies it was an opportunity to demonstrate their panache as orators and win some converts to their cause. But when flamboyance threatened to run away with them, they would have done best to remember the advice of Cato: 'Keep to the subject and the words will follow.'[22]

As soon as the candidates had officially announced their intention to stand, the arrangements for the election were posted on the narrow roll of notices that, according to another of the paintings from Julia Felix's property, was stretched for several metres across and between the pediments of the equestrian statues in the forum. But it was not enough for candidates simply to notify the electorate, or to announce their own claims, even for those magistracies that were uncontested. In order to raise their prestige within the community, they needed to make visible the level of support that they enjoyed. Nearly every wall in the city was used for the painted proclamations of political allegiance that would have remained for years until eventually painted over or whitewashed out. The early excavators of Pompeii found such notices right across the city, and although they have now crumbled away or been removed, a detailed catalogue does exist (Plate 25). Candidates who came from less prominent families and could therefore not rely on the existing family 'brand' or automatic backing from family dependents, appear to have had a particular need for such visual displays of popularity.

They would have pounded the streets, canvassing among the myriad trade associations and clubs, hoping these *collegia* would offer their official support and thus the backing of all their members.[23] The walls of Pompeii carry expressions of allegiance from groups as diverse as theatre-goers and ball-players to poultry-sellers, garlic-dealers, tenant farmers, farmhands, fishermen, hauliers and fullers in all their specialised forms. Everyone, it seemed, wanted to make their preferences heard.[24]

We know of a number of professional signwriters in Pompeii from the signatures they often left on their work. It is understandable that they were proud enough of their calligraphy to put their name to it: compared with the untrained hands that scribbled graffiti, the elongated red or black capital letters executed by the *scriptores* were elegance embodied. The agglomeration of signatures around a workshop on a back street south of the via dell'Abbondanza, and a couple of blocks along from the Temple of Isis, suggests that the signwriters 'Astylus' and 'Papilio' had their base there.[25] They would have had no scruples about daubing their proclamations over the existing decorations on a wall. But what would the householder have felt when an expensive mural was embellished in this way? Would a declaration of political allegiance have seemed more important? In some cases supposedly sacrosanct tombs were painted upon. Could the families of the deceased have been so carried away with political enthusiasm that they sanctioned the desecration of a family mausoleum, or was it simple overenthusiasm on the part of the painters?

The work of the *scriptores* continued late into the night when the streets were less crowded and the walls more accessible, and it may be that the cover of darkness inspired a degree of licence. In some of the electoral endorsements, the individual personality of the *scriptor* shines through: a note to thank the owner of a bar for the loan of a chair to stand on, an aside to the torch-carrying assistant to hold the ladder still, or some implied mockery of a competitor. Mostly, however, the message was simple and direct: the candidate's name and the office for which he was standing, the identity of the endorser, together with one of a limited repertoire of abbreviated phrases of praise: VB, DRP, OVF.[26] A good man. Reflecting the dignity of the republic. I beg you to elect him. The directing hand of the organising families and their *amici* is unmistakable in the uniformity with which the virtues of particular candidates were promoted from one corner of Pompeii to the other. As Seneca once dryly observed, 'We call all candidates honourable men.' But times were changing. Later slogans would praise candidates for the more specific benefits that they could offer to the community; perhaps by then the currency of 'honour' had been devalued and the citizens of Pompeii were seeking more material evidence of vote-worthiness.

In the darkness all the child could hear was the hiss of the smouldering fire and, somewhere distant, a sound like thunder. He was bent double, his skin raked by the heat, his eyes smarting. He cried for help and pushed in vain at whatever it was that had fallen over his head to trap him. Then, suddenly, as he felt close to suffocating, his world was flooded with sunlight and he was back in the fullery courtyard, surrounded by laughing workers.

The usually vile air, filled with the fumes of burning sulphur that were used to bleach the cloth, now seemed as clear as the breeze from the sea. All around, the other workers had stopped what they were doing to laugh at him, following the rumbling baritone of his master Ululitremulus. In his giant hand, his master held aloft the bright white dome of a drying frame wrapped in a damp toga. It was this that had been his prison. Gasping for breath, the boy thought it wise to join in the laughter and was rewarded with a fierce slap on the back from the master's free hand.

Fabius Ululitremulus knew how to play a practical joke, but he liked to think he knew how to take one too. Was he not happy to let all and sundry tease him about his nickname, 'The Owl'? If he took exception when children followed him down the street hooting, it was only understandable. And what if he had laid out that traveller who had refused to have his cloak cleaned by a man he said carried bad luck like the 'owl' he was? How else should he react to someone who impugned the symbol of the fuller's protective goddess, Minerva, just because the bird took its name from the ululating lament of mourners.

No, Ululitremulus was a fair boss. His slaves and employees might be labouring in the treading vats and soaking basins of his laundry business on the first morning of the five-day Festival of Minerva, but they would be allowed their leisure later. Far better to have the last batch of togas ready for the election than to come back to work in five days and have to rush to complete them in time. Making sure the big men were smartly turned out was not a job to be taken lightly. After all, weren't the candidates so called precisely because they were so candida – *so brilliantly white. If that meant a few extra hours bleaching their togas over the sulphur fires, scrubbing in the fullers' earth, and polishing the surface of the cloth, then so be it.*

As Ululitremulus led his party through the streets to join the parade, he had the feeling that the whole city was prepared. The previous evening, the fullers had met and agreed on whom to support for the junior magistracies. He was satisfied with their decision. Now, as they turned off towards the Temple of Minerva in the city's old ceremonial space beside the theatre, he could see the preparations for the elections in the forum. The posts and cords from the cattle market were set out to create channels through which the different groups of voters would pass, and at one end were caskets into which they would throw their marked slates.

He did not know that, in later years, he would remember this short walk as the calm before the storm. When he woke the next morning, his head sore from the wine he had drunk at the fullers' feast, the streets were abuzz with news that the Emperor's mother, Agrippina, was dead – murdered, it seemed, though by whom, and why, were questions on which no one was yet prepared to risk an opinion.

—— IV ——

The aftermath of Agrippina's murder was handled with greater efficiency than its messy, if determined, execution. Before leaving Campania, Nero gave a pitch-perfect performance of filial devotion, briefly mourning his mother even while those around him publicised her death as a justified strike against a deadly conspirator. So mixed were the messages being sent out that, in Pompeii, the priestess Vibia Sabina may well have offered sacrifices in Agrippina's memory, and the city council was probably wrong-footed into sending their condolences to the Emperor. But by the time Nero returned to Rome, only shortly afterwards, the senate and the people of the capital were joined in ecstatically welcoming his survival of the supposed plot.

His salvation was celebrated with a 'Great Games', and the outpouring of popular support appears to have been genuine. It must have seemed to Nero as though, finally, he could become his own man. As if to mark the transition, he arranged a second, private celebration on the occasion of the first shaving of his beard, the *iuvenalia* rite, which was a key moment in any Roman man's life. During the festivities, citizens of all ranks willingly participated in the theatrical performances; one lady of eighty is said to have danced a pantomime (Plate 8). There was no sign yet of the coercion that would characterise the years to come, although the event did see the first appearance of the youth club, the *Iuvenes*, better known as the *Augustiani*, who would become such important supporters of the Neronian regime. But the happiness on display was not universal. Burrus is said to have shed a tear at the shameful spectacle of his emperor performing: perhaps he knew Nero well enough to see where it was all likely to lead.

Amongst the fine collection of statues in the garden of Poppaea Sabina's villa at Oplontis, two figures that once stood beside one another would have caught the eye: one a princely youth of Julio-Claudian appearance, the other a lady some years his senior, whose upper lip juts out petulantly, and on whose hair remnants of a reddish paint can still be seen today. The age difference is roughly that between the amber-haired Poppaea and her married lover, Nero, and it is hard not to see in the pair an image of their relationship in AD 59, when the Emperor's wife Octavia still stood in their way. For all the recent improvements in his life, there were still many personal problems for Nero to dwell upon. There were also many political issues for his advisors to remind him of. Prominent among these was the growing unease in Campania, caused by the threat of major changes in Rome's management of its import routes, and the economic impact they might have. The situation called for careful planning and management, yet rather than mitigate the effects, it appears that the policies that were adopted only exacerbated them.

It had been the Emperor Claudius who had commissioned plans for the creation of a great new port at the mouth of the River Tiber, but with the most unpromising location of a sandy beach to work with, the practicalities of the design had taxed even the most ingenious of the Emperor's engineers. Not until the late AD 50s was the solution they decided upon finally taking shape. The approach chosen involved *pozzolana*, and entailed an extreme demonstration of the miraculous cement's potential to transform a coastline. One entire arm of the embrasure needed for the vast harbour was cast from a single mould, which was nothing other than the hull of the huge freight ship that had once carried the obelisk that now stands in the Vatican from Egypt to Rome. When the cast had set, the ship's timbers were prized away to reveal the results.

It would be another generation or more before Puteoli finally ceded its pre-eminence as the imperial grain harbour and foremost port facility in Italy to the young pretender, following the completion of the latter's inner basin. By AD 59, though, the great new port, known simply and boldly as Portus, was already starting to steal trade, and discontent in the old engine room of Roman trade was rife. Only the previous year, the streets of Puteoli had rever-berated with ugly scenes of mob violence that had to be suppressed by military intervention. In the weeks before the debacle, the senate in Rome had been bombarded with rival petitions from the port city. On one side, the common people claimed that the city's magis-trates were extorting rapacious taxes while, on the other, the council of *decurions* appealed for help in quelling a situation where stone-throwing and threats of arson were spiralling into outright insur-rection. The senate's response was measured but decisive: a cohort of the Praetorian Guard was dispatched, who targeted a handful of the ringleaders for elimination and so frightened their followers into submission. Order was restored but the root causes of the trouble remained unresolved.

Over the coming decade, Nero would pursue three separate policies with a bearing on the problems in Campania. The most grandiose called for the construction of a canal to stretch between Puteoli and Rome and so mitigate or even reverse the advantages of Portus. Rather than risking shipwreck on the last hundred miles of coastline, or in the incomplete harbour area of Portus (where several hundred ships would sink at anchor during a storm in the early AD 60s), the grain fleet could either dock at Puteoli and transfer their load or else continue their voyage in calm, protected waters. In its desire to pit the resources of the empire against the Herculean task of canal construction, of all the three schemes it was the one that bears the clearest sign of Nero's personal authorship.

The second – that was in fact attempted before the canal stumbled off the drawing board – involved the universal lifting of taxation on imported goods, though even with the help of such a document to draw on as the stone tablet concerning tariffs that was found recently in Ephesus, quite what this meant in practice remains obscure. This move was smeared by later commentators as fiscal irresponsibility and an early indication of Nero's hopeless profligacy, allowing con-sumers to buy at reduced cost the luxuries they already purchased with such relish, and importers to increase their profit margins. However, it could also be seen as a considered policy to stimulate trade and increase personal wealth that would then be circulated back into the economy. Even if tax-collectors were less venal than they had been before Augustus checked their abuses of power, their increased accountability had not entirely eliminated corruption. The popularity of the move would have been clear to Nero. But it was surely the economically astute mind of Seneca that foresaw the benefits of placing additional capital in the hands of the Empire's dynamic merchants, thereby encouraging them to be ever bolder in their entrepreneurialism. As a man who had huge investments in Rome's overseas provinces, on which returns and repayments were sluggish, he quite possibly also had a personal interest in creating a short-term boom.

It was the third measure, though, that would have the greatest impact on the lives of the inhabitants of Campania: the foundation – or in Pompeii's case the retrenchment – of a series of colonies to serve as settlements for army veterans. A steady stream of old soldiers were always in need of homes and a living on their retirement, and in the second half of the AD 50s there is likely to have been a particularly large influx of demobilised legionaries.

Rome's ancient, smouldering enmity with Parthia – in what is now the region occupied by Iran and Iraq – was again flaring up, and Corbulo, the Roman commander in the East, was determined to retake Armenia. However, the campaign he planned would involve marching and fighting at altitude. The legions based in Cappadocia and Galatia, in modern Turkey, that were at his disposal had gone to seed during the prolonged peace and were filled with soldiers who were inadequate to the task and would need paying off. A plot of land to farm in the best region of the fatherland seemed only a fair exchange for risking one's life in battle against barbarians, as every veteran would inevitably claim he had. What was more, the need to woo the military to Nero's cause was clearly on the minds of his advisors at this time. AD 59 saw the second occasion on which a payout was made to soldiers to secure their support; the first, on his accession, had cost a total of forty-five million *denarii*. Giving away other people's land, particularly in depopulated areas, through the declaration of a veteran's colony was a more economical solution to the problem.

Nuceria had been the first to receive its consignment of demobbed soldiers. The arrival of men of energy, eager to contribute to the community of their new home town, would have been welcomed by the resident population, even if Corbulo's rejects were not quite the chiselled heroes that the women of Nuceria might have hoped for. It is possible to guess at the appearance of these hoary veterans from the skeleton of one soldier who died on the beach at Herculaneum when Vesuvius erupted. Even had he not been wearing a bronze belt of military style at the time, his personal history would have been hard to mistake: tall and muscular, he did not carry his thirty-seven years lightly; too much time spent astride a horse had left him with a rolling gait that was made clumsier still by the wound from a sword stabbed deep into his thigh in some past battle; the three teeth knocked from his jaw in that or some other encounter had been joined by three others to give his face a lopsided grin or, more likely in the circumstances, a grimace.

In the future, the people of Pompeii would always make a point of excluding their neighbour Nuceria from lists of 'the true Neronian colonies', as one graffito in the city pointedly expressed it. They would have good cause for being so curmudgeonly. Almost immediately, a move that was intended to stabilise the cities of Campania had precisely the opposite effect.

CHAPTER 5

No Place for Idlers

July AD 59

From daybreak on the first day of July AD 59, the whole of Pompeii was on the move. It was the end of one rental year and the beginning of the next, and across the city those moving house or taking up occupancy of new business premises struggled to get the heavy work done before the full heat of the midsummer sun began to beat down. Mules with towers of furniture strapped to their backs picked a path over the flagstones; carts snapped their axles under the strain of carrying a family's worldly goods. Life-sized statues and precious objets d'art that had been crammed in alongside the paraphernalia of domestic life spilled into the slurry that covered the streets.

For Pherusa, clinging to the legs of Nero's statue in the forum as she struggled to keep her balance on the narrow pedestal, anything that drew the gawping crowds away was a welcome relief. It was three nights since she had failed in her escape from the household into which she had been sold as a slave. Together, she and Polycarpus had made for the nearest city gate under cover of darkness and had hidden on a roof nearby, ready for the moment when the great doors were swung open and they could slip out amongst the early morning crowd of day-labourers. Once outside the walls, the marshes of the Sarno would have provided a hiding place until the inevitable pursuit cooled and they could take ship for whatever distant destination first offered itself.

All that had come to nothing. As she had jumped down from the roof, Pherusa had twisted her ankle: she cursed her master, who must have paid to have spells cast in order to stop his slaves from leaving the limits of the city. But she had been determined that her companion should not suffer with her and, after much persuasion, Polycarpus had agreed to leave her *behind. He had urged her to return home before their absence was noticed, but Pherusa had planned ahead and hobbled instead to the nearest statue of the Emperor, to claim sanctuary as any slave was entitled to do.*

Now she would have to wait to discover her fate. Two officials had arrived with some ceremony on the afternoon of her first day there, accompanied by a gaggle of assistants. But even though she could understand little of what they said, it was clear from their demeanour that they considered her predicament an amusing diversion. And then this morning she had understood. In a building on the other side of the forum she had seen the same group of flunkies with two different officials, who were clearly new to the job. Perhaps with this change of personnel she could hope for a better hearing.

The details of why it was considered necessary to compress the starting date for all property rentals in Pompeii into a single day are uncertain, but this was not the only example of how Pompeian society held very specific ideas about the appropriate time or place for particular activities. A number of calendars have been found in Pompeii and other cities that illuminate the rhythms of commercial, religious and judicial life in the ancient city. With almost a third of the year given over to religious celebrations, and restrictions of one kind or another imposed on most other days, it was important for everyone to keep track. Other records, found elsewhere in Italy, include additional information on the festivals that would have shaped the Pompeian year: from notes on the temples involved, to speculation on the origins and meaning of the rituals by antiquarian experts.

About forty festivals appear almost consistently in all documents and can be assumed to have been the key points in the year. Woven into this tapestry of religious observance were hearings of legal cases by judges selected from the ranks of the council members. Individual days in the calendar are divided into three categories to denote their suitability for judicial hearings: on the *dies fasti*, cases could be conducted at any time, on those marked with 'EN' the court session could last only between the time when a sacrifice was first made and the moment when the entrails were offered up, whilst on the *dies nefasti* no judge was allowed to sit. They were conventions that may well have frustrated the hope of speedy justice for people like Pherusa.

Market days in the forum were also carefully organised. A list written outside a shop on the main street lists Saturday as market day in Pompeii and Sunday in Nuceria, with the traders moving on to Atella, Nola, Cumae and Puteoli, before ending up on the Friday in either Rome or the regional centre of Capua.[1] Other documents – most notably from Praeneste, just outside Rome, and Nola – show the conversion charts that enabled magistrates to reset the dates on which markets could be held in exceptional circumstances, and such was the case in July.

The first Pompeii market in July was always particularly busy. On the nineteenth, the year's second great Parade of Knights would take place in Rome, when up to five thousand of Italy's richest men rode through the capital on horses provided by the state, garlanded as though victors in battle, in commemoration of the help given to the Romans by the twin gods Castor and Pollux in an ancient battle. The culmination of the event was the Festival of Apollo, but it was preceded by five days of markets. Pompeian traders might well have been tempted to pack in two weeks' worth of business in Campania at the beginning of the month and then haul their goods north to Rome for the festival. Local knights such as the young *flamen* of Nero, Decimus Satrius Lucretius Valens, would also have been eager to join the flow of visitors to the capital once Pompeii's own major festivities were over.

But the beginning of July was also a busy time in the political calendar. The inauguration of Pompeii's magistrates on 1 July of each year was probably handled in a similar manner to that recorded for the city of Urso, where the incoming officials took an oath at a public assembly on market day in which they swore to keep correct accounts and to preserve public money, presumably along with undertakings of diligence in other duties. In AD 59 the senior magistrates were Grosphus and Gavianus, and Licinius Romanus may well have been one of their junior partners.

Much of the responsibility for financial issues fell to the senior magistrates, who could draw on the experience of at least one previous term served in a junior capacity and possibly also prior service in their current position. But for political neophytes like Romanus, who were only in their mid-twenties, stepping into their posts as junior magistrates for the first time, the range of responsibilities that faced them must have seemed daunting in the extreme. Confronted with such problems as a slave girl demanding sanctuary at the feet of the Emperor's statue, or the chance of popular protest spreading from Puteoli, the early weeks of July AD 59 would have represented a steep learning curve. At least the young men would have been aided by a large retinue of slaves who provided services as diverse as herald, soothsayer, flute-player and messenger. And when the junior magistrates felt the need for assistance, four slaves were constantly on hand, who assisted at public sacrifices and to whom responsibility for basic law enforcement was delegated.[2]

The magistrates administered their affairs from the three *curia* buildings in the forum. Between the ruins of the central and western *curia* buildings, the modern visitor will find a narrow passageway that runs south, through a small doorway into what appears to be a private house and out towards a terrace that hangs at the edge of the escarpment. With a fine view of the river and harbour, a newly installed junior magistrate such as Licinius Romanus might have sought a few minutes' reprieve from the pressures of his office, but it would have been in vain. The sight below of boats ferrying passengers across a river in which the water level was worryingly low, the sound of traffic on the streets and the scant dribble of water from the fountain nearby were a clear reminder that his priorities were necessarily more mundane. The regulation of passenger vessels was within his remit, as was the city's water supply, and the use of the city's streets. And beyond that, the unfamiliar underbelly of his birthplace and all its vices awaited exploration.

The job description of the junior magistrate focused on his duty to ensure both the moral and physical health of the city, and the practical scope of this brief was almost unmanageably wide. It encompassed roles that are now shared between the vice squad, public health inspectorate, licensing bodies and other authorities. The young men of genteel upbringing, who had donned shining white togas to contest the honour of becoming magistrates, spent the vast majority of their year of service immersed in the less salubrious side of life. Each day, their minds would have been filled with filth and squalor, from the literal problems of blocked sewers and vermin-infested cookshops, through the sordid legal issues that surrounded slave-trading, prostitution and grotesque gluttony, to the administration of gladiatorial games, and the bathetically petty squabbles of market-stall holders.[3]

Market days were particularly busy for the young magistrates. It was down to them to ensure fair and well-ordered trading, and that each stallholder was in his proper place. July was an especially busy month: the tablets of Caecilius Jucundus record that, with the grain harvest recently completed, agricultural sales reached their first peak of the year at the end of June. Everyone from landowner to day-labourer was flush with funds. Muleteers would have tethered their beasts on the outskirts of the town in the care of a paid *stationarius* and made for the thronged forum, and the owners of warehouses would have opened their cellars to discharge the goods stored below for sale. The forum paintings from the *praedia* of Julia Felix show all manner of small-time merchants hawking their wares from small wooden stalls or straight from the pavement on which they spread out coloured cloths to better display their pots and pans and metal tools (Plate 13). On the west side of the forum, just outside the entrance to the temple of Apollo, the bawdy nicknames of Verecunnus and Pudens are written on the wall to mark their pitch: the former a pun on the Latin for female genitalia, perhaps a corruption of Vecilius Verecundus, who had a house in Pompeii and a felt-making business on the main street.[4]

Yet the image of a freewheeling bazaar that this evokes is only partially correct, as Pompeii had followed Rome's example in its clean-up of public spaces. In its early years, the forum in Rome had been slippery with the overspill from the stalls of butchers and fishmongers, but Augustus's reign had seen these trades moved on and their places taken by money-lenders and auctioneers. In Pompeii, the erection of a vast *macellum*, or market hall, at the mouth of the forum near the Capitoline Temple allowed the removal of the messier trades into their own specialised building, the walls of which were decorated with colourful murals of the produce on offer. It was also specially equipped with a shaded tank for live fish to be kept in optimum conditions. Together with its neighbouring temples, the *macellum* was one of the buildings that blocked off the industrial zone that lay behind: at a stroke, the newly marbled forum became not only pure in appearance but comparatively odourless too, its bright colonnades rising serenely above the less salubrious aspects of Pompeian life.

Anecdotal evidence from the period suggests that enforcement of the laws that maintained order in the market could be heavy-handed. Literary sources record irate officials toppling the stalls of fishmongers who sold luxurious species at inflated prices, and vessels for oil or wine that were smaller than the declared size being smashed on the flagstones.[5] Had Licinius Romanus needed to test the reliability of a vessel's size on an early tour of inspection, he could have referred to the ancient stone table positioned close to the wall where Pudens and Verecunnus had made their marks. Sunk into its surface were holes of a volume equivalent to the most common measures of quantity, recalibrated in the previous century when Roman rather than Oscan standards had come into force.

Notices had gone up around the city declaring that Polycarpus had fled and the slave hunters were out in force to track him down. No one could be in any doubt of the punishment for harbouring such a runaway and, in the heat of July, any attempt he might make to cover the brand on his face would only draw attention. He could not get away and his recapture would provide the senior magistrates Grosphus and Gavianus with something to boast about at the games they were due to host shortly.

Nevertheless, Licinius Romanus stood frozen with fury on the steps of the curia *building as he looked over at the pathetic, filthy figure on the Emperor's statue. Still she refused to move from her perch at the Emperor's feet, whining and snivelling in pain. Even assurances of her safety had failed to lure the slave girl down. As far as he was concerned, she could stay there until she dropped, but the spectacle was most unsettling. In the homes of Pompeii, everyone was looking at their slaves and wondering where dissent or even danger might be lurking. Something would have to be done.*

The creature's owners were arguing that she had been sold fraudulently, with no declaration of an earlier attempt to kill herself. Confronting them was Zabda, the dealer who had first brought her to Pompeii, and was currently back in town on business. Foreseeing a compensation claim he was insistent that the aedile's annual edict had been obeyed to the letter, and that if there were loopholes in that document, they were not his concern. Now he had taken to haranguing the slave girl where she languished, demanding that she corroborate his claims.

It was time to put a stop to this nonsense. Directing two of his assistants to bring her down by force, Romanus left the forum and headed out along the main street towards the Stabian Baths. At least there he could expect a warmer welcome. With the help of his sponsor, Alleius Nigidius Maius, he had taken a lease on the bath complex for certain days when admission would be free to a grateful public; an election promise that was guaranteed to win his supporters' continued favour.

Pausing opposite the baths, he watched as slaves carried in the stumps of trees, uprooted, according to custom, by the light of the waning July moon, to stoke the blazing furnace that heated the building. Outside the main entrance, those who were waiting for the waters to warm, pored over notices announcing the programme for the Festival of Apollo that was about to start and that would culminate in games on the thirteenth of the month. Everyone was relieved that the Emperor had not extended his ban on provincial governors giving games to the cities of Italy. This month's games in particular aroused high passions, commemorating as they did Hannibal's unsuccessful invasion of Campania nearly three hundred years before.

But as Romanus moved on, through the baths and towards the door at the back that opened onto a very different part of the city, the possible reasons for the Emperor's move gnawed at his mind.

The rear entrance to the Stabian Baths, in stark contrast to its facade on the pedestrianised stretch of the *decumanus maximus*, gave onto a dog-leg of a street that remains to this day one of the most notorious in the city. Only twenty or so metres deeper into the warren of narrow streets, over which the balconied upper storeys of buildings projected to obscure all but a sliver of sky, stood the largest brothel in Pompeii. The same distance again would have brought Romanus to a small triangle of ground at the side of the road, backed by a wall on which the denizens of this dark area had scratched venomous threats against erstwhile friends in what seems like a jealous vendetta. Round every kinked corner were bars and bakeries, tanneries and fulleries, together with all manner of other trades, interspersed with walled market gardens and the tiny curtained cubicles where street whores offered their services. The bustle of activity in this maze swung to the sound of artisans singing their favourite songs – 'I drink the wine, both young and old; both young and old cure all my ills' – learnt at the theatre or in the tavern.[6]

Although even important private residences did accommodate commercial and manufacturing premises within their structure, there was still a marked preference for keeping the city's less savoury trades as occluded as possible, and the elite wanted their magistrates to see to it that they stayed that way. This area at the very centre of Pompeii was consciously moulded to provide just such a hidden zone. It was these streets that the temple and *macellum* of the forum had been so cleverly designed to conceal, blocking off streets that had once emerged from the area, and leaving only narrow service passageways. In front was the polished face of civic majesty, behind the territory that in one contemporary writer's memorable words, 'feared the *aedile*'.[7]

In this heavily plebeian and proto-industrial zone, as throughout the entire area surrounding the forum, the streets follow a markedly haphazard course as if conforming to some ghostly and wayward ground plan. In this, the area is quite distinct from the rest of Pompeii, most of which is laid out according to a clear grid pattern, albeit sheered and slightly irregular, with two or three major streets crossing the city in both directions. Within this larger grid, two-thirds or more of the city is subdivided into roughly regular blocks containing multiple business and domestic units, but in the south-western corner around the forum nothing is so straightforward.

This distinction in the layout of different parts of the city has led archaeologists to postulate a theory of an *altstädt* or 'old town', according to which Pompeii had originally occupied a much smaller area spreading back from the Marine Gate, as the city of the first century AD does, but extending barely half as far to the north. Such a vision of the city's development sees the crush of narrow streets around the forum as a consequence of planners diverting their path to avoid older buildings that nevertheless gradually disappeared, though not before having left their trace on the map. The supposed later expansion into previously unoccupied space would then explain the less compromised and more formal planning, though such a theory is difficult to tally with the evidence for prolonged occupation of the entire site within the walls that more recent examination of the lower levels of Pompeii's pre-eruption archaeology has brought to light.

In their different ways, both the haphazard streets to either side of the forum and the almost uniform blocks of buildings elsewhere surely confounded many an ancient visitor, for Pompeii was a city without street names and numbers. Traders who entered Pompeii on market day may have found their way by means of the stone plaques representing the symbols of different trades – two men carrying amphorae close to an electoral posting by the stevedores, a quadrant and hammer for a construction company, a goat of uncertain meaning – that were set into walls above head height. Similar plaques with geometric designs may have had some symbolic meaning along with pictures representing erect phalluses, which have been taken as signposts to the red-light districts, but are more likely to have been intended to ward off the evil eye.

The only evidence of anything resembling official signage dates from the weeks in the early part of the first century BC when Sulla had Pompeii under siege. Written in the old Oscan language – and known as the *eituns* notices, from a word that recurs – they were situated near street corners and indicated muster points for the city's defenders.[8] There is only one recorded instance of an inscription concerning a city street, and it celebrates the generous resurfacing carried out by a pair of junior magistrates.[9]

A visitor seeking directions from a passer-by received not an itinerary of street names but a list of urban landmarks such as markets or arches or bathhouses, together with physical descriptions of the roads – long, broad, straight. With the number of individual properties in the city probably numbering several thousand, arrival at one's destination clearly relied on further advice being sought along the way. Even the Almighty had to rely on this clumsy procedure, as we know from the Acts of the Apostles, where the best instructions available for a divinely ordained rendezvous in Roman Damascus were: 'Go into the street which is called Straight and inquire at the house of Judas.'[10] This approximate style is echoed in a graffito from a necropolis outside Pompeii: 'At Nuceria ask for Volvellia Primigenia in the Vicus Venerius by the Rome Gate.'[11] In this case, the destination was profane: Primigenia, according to other graffiti, was an especially desirable prostitute. Clearly she was well known in her local 'Venus District', even though its name suggests that she was far from being the only representative of her trade to be found there.[12]

The circulation of traffic in Pompeii appears to have been tightly controlled. Recent comparisons of the depth of the ruts worn into the city's streets by the passage of wheels over the course of many decades indicates that a rigid traffic system was in operation. This system appears to have stipulated a single direction in which certain corners could be taken and probably limited access to particular streets, perhaps according to the time of day. As so often, aspects of Pompeian life appear surprisingly modern, making the demands on the time of Pompeii's law-enforcement agents even greater. And in addition to controlling the traffic, the junior magistrates also had to ensure that the roads, with their deep gullies and high pavements and stepping stones, did not become blocked with the slurry of animal and human excrement that accumulated there.

When Pompeii's young magistrates felt the need for a reminder of the unpopularity they would accrue for any failure in this area, they need only have thought of the humiliation that Caligula had heaped on one lackadaisical magistrate. By AD 59, the young Vespasian was rising dizzyingly through the ranks of the army with a great future in prospect. However, back when Caligula sat on the throne, he had been serving as an *aedile* in Rome and his future had looked considerably less certain. When the Emperor took exception to the state of the streets, he personally instructed the Praetorian Guard to stretch out the folds of Vespasian's toga and fill them with the filth he had overlooked.[13] Yet Caligula's nostrils were perhaps particularly attuned to offending smells and Romanus may have got away with far less diligence in Pompeii. Levels of tolerance to the stench that pervaded every area of urban existence were generally high and the noses of ancient Pompeians were to a great extent desensitised to the kind of olfactory shocks that would send any twenty-first-century Westerner reeling.

It was a process that doubtless began with shortcomings in certain areas of personal and, in particular, dental hygiene. The skeletons of those trapped in Pompeii at the time of the eruption show plaque thickly calcified onto teeth from which, to make matters worse, the enamel had often been worn away: the result of chewing on bread containing gritty fragments that had flaked off the basalt millstones in which the flour was ground. Tooth decay and stinking abscesses caused by overindulgence in sweet luxuries were a hazard too, as the skeleton of one young girl pitifully testifies. But while toothache might have made for a testy population, it was at least one that barely noticed the clouds of bad breath emanating from those around them. Perhaps only the newest slaves, freshly extracted from a rural existence, retched at the prospect of attending on their finely dressed but foul-smelling superiors. The scented lozenges that some sucked would have done little to disguise the stench. Before long, sorties into the fetid back streets of the town on one errand or another would have blunted even the most delicate of senses.

In some areas of the city where workshops abounded, the smells would have been a curious mixture of the foul and the fragrant. Only a short distance apart along side streets, *garum* sauce and sweet-smelling essences of rose and violet were decanted into their respective flasks, each of a similarly dainty size. One building on the main street, close to the amphitheatre and still a private residence in AD 59, would in later years be converted into a small distribution centre for *garum*.[14] Even then, its walls still bore the brightly painted images of peacocks and vegetation that had been commissioned by the original owners of the house, and customers must have felt that they were entering a rather exclusive boutique. The staff of perhaps four or five, who lived on the premises, also enjoyed an unusually pleasant working environment. In the peristyle courtyard were facilities for only small-scale production: six pottery barrels, or *dolia*, one of which had once contained wine. Into these would have been placed herbs collected from the bushes that grew around the edges of the courtyard's central garden, and anchovies, the bones of which were discovered by twentieth-century archaeologists in the dregs of *allec* that still smelled of fish. On quiet afternoons when trade was slow, the workers could have lazed under the shade of the fig tree whose branches spread wide and whose large, soft leaves stroked the ground. For those using the latrine nearby, the leaves also provided a convenient ancient equivalent of toilet paper.

There was ample provision in Pompeii for those who found themselves in urgent need of somewhere to urinate. In the forum, a large latrine with seating for more than twenty was available for public use. Elsewhere in the city, enterprising fullers like Fabius Ululitremulus slung pots from roadside walls for the purpose, since one man's waste was, to another, a valuable commodity: a source of ammonia with industrial uses which, in slightly over a decade, would start to be taxed by the Emperor. Malefactors who failed to take advantage of these facilities had no excuse, whether they were ignoring the prohibitions written on private walls or the more euphemistic warnings advising them that they were in 'no place for idlers'.[15]

Competition for the golden liquid was intense: tanners, gold and silversmiths, and dye-makers all used it in their work. It was even stored in quantity by fruit-growers until it had staled and could be used to feed their trees and so sweeten their produce. Such was the demand for ammonia of the correct alkalinity – excessive drinking rendered the resulting urine worthless to fullers – that other sources were also plundered. Fine specimens of wood pigeon and scrawnier examples of their drab domestic cousins are widely represented in wall paintings from the area, and the guano from the forum and the dovecots of private houses would have been eagerly scraped up for recycling.[16]

It is not surprising that the fulleries were considered to be repugnant places and the fullers themselves notoriously crude and dishonest (Plate 6). It is one of the paradoxes of the ancient world that the appearance of cleanliness was produced by its opposite. Though clothes were bleached bright white and sharp folds created by the

1. Vesuvius looms over the streets of Pompeii.

2. The Coastal Strip. Maritime villas along the coast, from the House of Marcus Lucretius Fronto.

3. A representation of the Ship Europa under sail, a crew member spotting land from the crow's nest. Graffito from the House of the Ship Europa.

4. Nilotic scene of a type popular in Pompeii with its strong links to Egypt, showing pygmies at play among the hippopotami and crocodiles.

5. (left to right, in rows)

a) Emperor Augustus
b) Emperor Nero (2:3 scale)
c) Nero and Agrippina

d) Nero as Apollo The Citherode (2:3 scale)
e) Nero in an elephant-drawn chariot
f) Emperor Vespasian (2:3 scale)

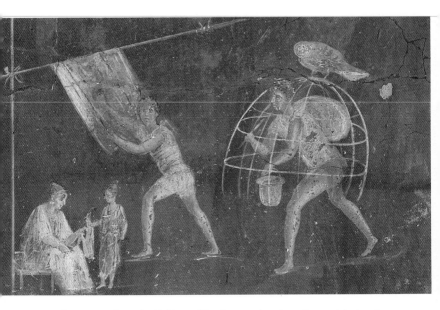

6. Fullery scene from the Fullery of Stephanus, showing a hooped drying frame on top of which perches an owl, the symbol of Minerva.

7. Scene of cherubs making and sampling wine, from the House of the Vettii.

8. Actors prepare for the performance in a mosaic from the House of the Tragic Poet.

9. The Riot of AD 59, in which the Nucerians were vanquished and for which the Pompeians bore the blame. A trivial incident led to a serious fight between the inhabitants of the colonies of Nuceria and Pompeii at a gladiatorial show. As a result many Nucerians were carried, maimed, to Rome. Note the awning to provide shade and the name of Decimus Satrius Lucretius Valens on the wall of the *palaestra* to the right, one of two rival dedications.

11. (right) Sacrifice from the altar of the Temple of the Genius of Augustus, showing the covered head of the priest and *victimarius* with hammer, stripped to the waist. The flute player to the rear would have ensured that no inauspicious sounds were heard.

10. Procession of magistrates wearing the purple-trimmed *toga praetexta*, with sacrificial bull and sheep, from the Murecine building or 'Inn'.

12. This bas relief, one of two from the altar in the atrium of the House of Caecilius Jucundus, represents the very moment of the earthquake of 5 February AD 62. The two sacrificial animals, the bull and the startled pig, are appropriate to a double festival day: the Pompeian Lares and the anniversary of Augustus. The Temple of Jupiter and the entrance to the forum lean precipitously, and the equestrian statues are jarred from their mounts.

13. One of a series of scenes of forum life from the atrium of the Praedia Julia Felix that were painted at least a decade after the earthquake, when repairs to this part of this city were still in progress. Others in the series depict togate figures reading a scroll of notices hung between the statue pedestals, and a lady and her servant being importuned by a beggar.

14. The second bas relief from the House of Caecilius Jucundus shows the efforts to restore the city in the immediate aftermath of the earthquake. An ox-drawn cart carries stone to repair the city wall, where the Vesuvius Gate and *castellum aquae* are seriously damaged. The scene at the right may depict offerings being made to Hercules in the grove dedicated to his cult, outside the city.

large wooden presses that stood at the entrance to fulleries, the smell of sulphur and ammonia would have lingered on them, mingled in some cases with the odour of shellfish from the purple murex dye. Yet a respectable member of the Roman elite with an unblemished record of public service could still be called *lautus*, or well-washed, in admiring tones: the reek of urine and rotten fish was ambient to Pompeii and must have passed all but unnoticed.

The heavy key to the building remained in the possession of the doorkeeper down below, but that did nothing to diminish the thrill that Phileros felt on being first admitted to his new home, with business premises alongside. It was only a modest town house with a tiny atrium, a couple of shops with counters facing onto the street and the small fullery next door. But he couldn't have afforded it without the help of his old mistress Vesonia, who had lent him half the surety, and the contribution of his trusted business partner, Marcus Orfellius Faustus.

As Phileros's furniture and effects were put in place, their owner listened with pleasure to the footsteps and voices that could be heard in the neighbouring buildings as the equipment in the fullery was rearranged according to the instructions of the foreman he and his partner had hired. He could even hear the poor specimens of humanity he now counted among his labourers, wheezing about as they struggled for the little air their lungs could gulp in after years spent immersed in sulphur and ammonia fumes, their skin cracked and scabrous, their hands unable to resist the urge to scratch for more than a few moments. But for all their infirmities, to Phileros they meant profit of a kind he could never have aspired to had he stayed in the fruit-and-vegetable line.

He wondered how long it would take him to integrate himself into the community. His old home lay halfway across town and the people around here were strangers. He had secured an unwritten agreement with the baths to tap their water supply, a crucial resource in this season of dry riverbeds and water rationing, but for such things to go smoothly he would need the local official to put in a good word for him with the magistrates. He had noticed the man this morning, when passing the crossroads shrine, and he didn't look like such a hard man to persuade: a freedman, like Phileros himself.

Later on, Phileros thought, perhaps he would make some small sacrifice to the Augustus and the local lares too, joining the queue behind the recent bride offering a coin to the god of the marriage bed, and the various travellers lodging in the area. It would be a chance to meet his neighbours and get a sense of the place – maybe find whether there was the same unease here as in his old area. For recently he had had the distinct impression that some conspiracy was afoot.

Although Roman society had become more stable since the later years of the Republic, even in the second half of the first century AD the fear of revolution from below remained strong in the minds of the elite. On 23 July each year, the Festival of Concordia commemorated the reconciliation that had been effected between the patrician class and the plebs four hundred years earlier, following a period of particularly intense confrontation. More recently, though, it had been the slave population and their descendants who were perceived to pose the greatest challenge to internal order. At the turn of the first century BC, one dangerous slave rising had centred on Capua and Nuceria, but the rebellion that would have lingered in folk memory in Pompeii was that led by the gladiator Spartacus in 73 BC, whose name appears in old graffiti there. His army of slaves, one hundred thousand strong according to some accounts, had encamped in the crater of Vesuvius before defeating five legions sent to quell them and marching unsuccessfully on Rome.[17]

When Augustus came to power, weeding out sedition and reaching a permanent settlement of the slave and freedman problem would have been high on his agenda. But such a complex challenge required a skilful and multi-faceted solution. At the top end of the social scale, Augustus's creation or encouragement of the association of Augustales dealt very effectively with the frustrations of those affluent freedmen who had hit the glass ceiling of social respectability. However, such opportunities were too distant to seem a realistic goal for the vast majority; what was more, having less to lose than their wealthier colleagues, it was precisely this underclass who were most likely to revolt against the status quo. Cicero records just such a case of insurrection, describing how, '... a levy of slaves was held on the front of the Tribunal of Aurelius, on the pretext of forming clubs men were enlisted *vicus* by *vicus*, formed into squads, and incited to force, deeds of violence, murder and robbery . . .[18] It was reform of the two features of social life that Cicero had mentioned – the clubs and the *vici*, or neighbourhood organisations – that would comprise the twin points of Augustus's policy.

In 7 BC, Augustus had subdivided the city into two hundred and sixty-five *vici*, in place of whatever obscure organisation of neighbourhoods had previously existed. In addition, he had refocused their activities on the street-side shrines that were a long-established feature of the urban landscape, and where the potent *lares*, or guardian spirits, of the local crossroads (*compitales*) were worshipped. As always, it was a carefully designed move to extract the maximum benefit for the larger programme of social renewal that was, wherever possible, identified with his own 'august' persona. The cult of the crossroads was an archaic tradition and deep-rooted in the Roman psyche; long before they had conferred their protection on cities, the *lares compitales* had been agricultural gods of boundaries and fertility, to be found at the intersection of farming estates. Now even these most ancient deities were co-opted to the cause of the founding father of the Empire. The privilege of tending the shrines fell to the neighbourhood officials, who also served as priests at the *compitales* ceremony.[19]

Unlike the members of the city council, or the elected *duumviri* and *aediles*, these 'magistrates' could be drawn from the ranks of freed slaves, while unlike the members of the Augustales club, their assistants could even still be slaves. This parallel world of officialdom was conceived to give real prestige to those second-class citizens who stuck to the straight and narrow and respected the Roman way of life. As well as the conduct of worship, there were real responsibilities to be shouldered: tasks such as firefighting, census-taking and the day-to-day supervision of hygiene. With *vici* shrines placed in close proximity to communal water fountains, officials were also assiduous in their duty to prevent pollution of the supply.[20] In return, they received the honour of being permitted to wear the *toga praetexta* on ceremonial occasions, when formal dress was the order of the day. With its purple trim, such finery was otherwise the preserve of the city's elected magistrates and the most promising young men who had not yet reached adulthood (Plate 10).[21]

In theory, anyone from the neighbourhood who put their name forward for the posts stood an equal chance, since selection was by lot. In practice, though, freedmen and slaves who bore the name of important families figure prominently in the only list of district officials to have survived in Pompeii. Once again, patronage had a part to play alongside random fate. It is another example of how elite control of the social machinery rewarded obedience and good behaviour by slaves with their gradual absorption into a higher class. Even the lowly slave 'ministers', who assisted the main local officials, could look forward to a brighter future as a result of their good fortune. One such Pompeian fathered a family that would rise to take its place among the *decurion* class within a couple of generations.

The second prong of Augustus's assault on sedition involved the policing of all the *collegia*, or clubs and societies, to which Roman citizens could belong. The writing on the walls attests that there were many such associations in Pompeii, and for the most part they were entirely innocent groups that devoted their time to providing solidarity in trade issues, boozy companionship, and reassurance that the cost of members' burials would be covered from their pooled funds. Nevertheless, they would not have been exempt from strict municipal laws such as that which insisted: 'No one is to take part in an illegal gathering within the city's jurisdiction or hold a meeting of a society or *collegium* for that purpose or conspire that it be held or act in any way to encourage the above.' Roman law was more ferocious still, going so far as to consider the creation of an unregistered *collegium* to be the equivalent of occupying a public building with armed men, and punishable accordingly, while even those legal clubs who admitted a slave without the knowledge of his owner were liable to a fine of ten thousand sesterces.[22] If the chance to become a local official was the carrot, this was unquestionably a stick and perhaps hints at the somewhat oppressive experience of living under the imperial regime.

The implementation of such restrictive legislation, along with the early detection of civil unrest, depended on the vigilance of men such as the officials, who could report any suspicions they might have about individuals in their neighbourhood. But it must also have required the maintenance of extensive police records, which were probably kept in the *curia* building in the forum, where the junior magistrates were based. The ease with which certain professions, such as teachers or philosophers, along with members of specific ethnic groups, could be expelled quickly and en masse from Italy at the whim of the government strongly suggests that such records were kept. So too does the existence of a sizeable underclass who were officially designated as *infames*, a classification that included actors, undertakers, bankrupts, gladiators, deserters, rent boys, prostitutes and pimps. In certain circumstances they were not even extended the normal protection of the law, as it was applied to the respectable majority.

When, in July AD 59, Licinius Romanus, in his capacity as junior magistrate, followed up on rumours that had reached him concerning possible disturbances in the city, it was probably to the illegal *collegia* that he looked, and specifically to those involving the less reputable members of society. If so, he might well have been looking in the wrong place. Trouble was brewing of a most serious nature, and when an inquiry into the causes of the catastrophe was later conducted at senatorial level, illegal *collegia* were apportioned only a part of the blame.

The sole surviving documentary record offers only a bare outline of what occurred on that dark day for Pompeii in AD 59, along with a summary of the punishments meted out in its aftermath.[23] Yet taking this information, together with that contained in a painting of the incident that decorated a wall in the house of the actor Actius Anicetus near the amphitheatre, it is possible to recreate the story of what happened.

Pompeii and its neighbour Nuceria had been long-standing rivals, and there is a tone of reasonably good-natured banter in the few examples of graffiti that concern their relationship. Although they were a good half-day's walk apart, it is clear that the relationship between their populations went beyond Pompeii's mere usefulness as a port for Nuceria's produce. Nuceria might have been less steadfast than Pompeii in the previous century's war against

Rome, but otherwise they shared similar histories: both were old colonies and both possessed early examples of amphitheatres. The Pompeians probably liked to think of their own as superior: built by the landowner Gaius Quinctius Valgus and the wine exporter Marcus Porcius, who had made their fortunes by profiteering from Sulla's settlement of the city, it was certainly venerable. It predated Rome's first amphitheatre by half a century and had already been giving good service for years when Vitruvius wrote his advice that cities should design their forums so that they could be adapted to accommodate games. By AD 59, though, its design may have started to seem rather dated, with no space under the arena for scenic machinery and only two entrances.[24] The Nucerians were in the habit of scrawling advertisements for their own gladiatorial games in the necropolis outside the gate that led back home, and it may be that there was an element of taunting in this reminder of their more up-to-date facilities.

Perhaps, as they watched their rivals pour into the city to attend the Games of Apollo that July, the Pompeians no longer felt so confident of their superiority in other ways too. After all, Nero had recently granted Nuceria a new colonial charter, resulting in an influx of army veterans to bolster the town's resources and erect new public buildings. Whether the Nucerian visitors of July AD 59 were already geared towards aggression when they arrived in Pompeii, or whether the violence was the result of provocation they encountered there, will never be known, but amongst those who made the fifteen-mile journey from the other side of the Sarno was a large contingent of veterans – men in their mid-forties with more than twenty years of service behind them and an urge to assert their loyalty to their new home town. It may be that the young aristocrats, or *iuvenes*, of Pompeii felt they had something to prove against these middle-aged legionaries: after all, before he had shaved his beard and entered manhood, the Emperor Nero himself had seen nothing wrong with joining gangs of elite youths in inciting brawls in the theatre, and carrying out muggings at night. Even now, he was contemplating making them the basis for his theatrical claque.[25]

As the Nucerian veterans made their way up to the main street and its many bars and shops, or fanned out into the side streets in search of a quieter place to drink, they would certainly have presented an intimidating sight: shopkeepers on their route must have cursed them for damaging their trade. On the day of gladiatorial games, as country-dwellers converged on the amphitheatre from Pompeii's various gates, businesses across the city looked to benefit from passing custom. For weeks before, Pompeii's craftsmen had been busy bottling and packaging their goods ready for sale to those paying a rare visit to the city. Some producers – such as those in the *garum* sauce trade – feverishly hawked their wares on street corners, urging the games-goers to turn aside and visit their workshops. Endless wagons, atop which whole stitched cowhides swelled with new local wine, had been swaggering along the streets to the city's bars, the foamy liquid inside being siphoned off through one of the dead beast's feet into *dolia*, as required. But it would have been the perfume-dealers who were the envy of all – or at least those among them who had been lucky enough to win a contract to supply *sparsiones* to the arena. When the heat of the July afternoon became unbearable, what was better than a cool haze of scented water sprayed onto the crowd by a special attendant?

With an affluent backer like Livineius Regulus underwriting the munificent spectacle that they were laying on, the senior magistrates Grosphus and Gavianus would have been able to allude to many added extras in the posters they put up to advertise their games: refreshing perfumes, apples to moisten mouths dry from shouting out encouragement to the desperate gladiators, an awning hauled out over the banked seating on long poles with ropes and pulleys rigged by some retired sailor from the Misenum fleet.[26]

In the house of Decimus Satrius Lucretius Valens, just a single block away from the amphitheatre, the chants of the gladiators' supporters would have been audible as they approached in both directions down the main street: perhaps the family even heard the names of fighters from their own troupe. The family gladiators would doubtless have been used in the games staged by Valens a couple of months earlier and the long exterior walls of the *palaestra*, the city's walled sports field, were covered with paintings of gladiatorial scenes with his patronage remembered in large letters (Plate 9).

As Pompeians and Nucerians jostled their way through the narrow entrances to the arena, they traded taunts and insults, specks of spittle flying too, and enraging their targets. It was not until the water-organ began to churn out its tune that there was a lull in the barracking, and for a while, when the gladiators began their fights, attention was focused on the games.

The sand had twice been stained a darkening crimson before the spectators resumed their own sport. At first it was only a matter of more insults being hurled, along with the odd cushion. But, quite unexpectedly, the tone of the exchanges changed. At first, only a few people noticed the blood that spouted from a broken nose clutched behind shaking hands, or the figure slumped unconscious from a blow to the head. It was when a stone hit the costumed figure of Death's boatman, Charon, busy overseeing the removal of a gladiator's corpse, that the crowd took notice. After that things quickly degenerated.

Spectators were leaping out of the audience and onto the sand to take the place of the gladiators, who beat a welcome retreat. Screaming women and children huddled together in the banks of seats as their husbands and fathers climbed over them to join in the melee. When anyone tried to escape the throng on the sand and return to the seating, they were hauled back down. Then, suddenly, there was the flash of steel, and the cries of pain took on a different pitch: from somewhere, somehow, weapons had been produced. There was no time to wonder whether the armoury had been broken into, or where else the swords might have come from. That it was a preplanned ambush was only too clear. And panic spread.

The Pompeians enjoyed a home advantage: familiarity with the terrain and greater numbers. Around the rim of the amphitheatre ran a parapet, topped with railings to protect spectators from the thirty-foot drop on the other side. Many now tripped on it as they risked the plunge to escape: crumpled on the ground below, they were picked off as soon as they landed. Pressed by attacks from all sides, the men of Nuceria who were still trapped inside fought for the exits, but the ancient amphitheatre had not been designed with ease of escape in mind and their reaction had been anticipated. Where the tight entrances funnelled the Nucerians out in small numbers, gangs were ready and waiting.

Before long, the routes to the gates of the city were littered with bodies that lay hacked and bleeding, and trails of fresh blood followed those lucky *enough to get away. As the adrenaline began to subside, there was a strange silence amid the carnage, broken only by the cries of the dying. At that moment no one was in any doubt that there would be a heavy price to pay.*

By far the greater loss was on the Nucerian side. The ambassadors who carried Nuceria's complaints to Rome probably exaggerated in their claims that there was not a family in the city that had not lost a father or a son. They did, however, take with them an impressive collection of the injured, whose suppurating wounds reinforced their case. Yet no one in the capital wanted to take responsibility for passing judgement: the buck passed from Nero to the senate and then to the consuls before landing back with the senate, which finally handed down harsh sentences. Perhaps there was the feeling that these illegal *collegia* enjoyed some special favour with the Emperor. Could the sons of Pompeii's elite be somehow implicated?

But it was the organisers who took the bulk of the blame. Livineius Regulus, an exile once already, was sent into exile again. Grosphus, who had grafted so hard to inveigle his way into Pompeian society, was stripped of his magistracy, together with Gavianus, and both were most likely exiled too.[27] Those clubs that had been formed illegally were disbanded. Two pieces of graffiti may have a bearing on the question of who belonged to these clubs. The first mentions the 'Pompeian youths of Venus'.[28] The other, adjacent to it, seems to provide a stronger clue: 'Campanians in one victory you perished with the Nucerians.'[29] It was the inhabitants of the territory outside Pompeii who referred to themselves as 'Campani' or Campanians. But most intriguing of all was where these graffiti were found: in the house of the Popidii, one of whom was to become a prominent Augustianus, Nero's newly formed club of claquers. Quite what this all adds up to is impossible to say, but the disruption might have been only a foretaste of what was to come, in more insidious forms, during the following decade.

Whoever it was that provoked the fight, and whatever they hoped to gain, in the end it was the whole of Pompeii that lost. The cost to the city of the riot was a ten-year ban on all gladiatorial spectacles: for that time its vaunted arena would lie empty or host only some pallid alternative involving athletes or wild animals. Whether the junior magistrate Licinius Romanus was punished is not known, nor even whether he survived: if anyone was in the thick of the fighting on that ignominious day, striving to calm a situation that should never have been allowed to get out of hand, it would have been him.

— V —

When the festival of Janus ushered in AD 61, Nero's reign was fast approaching its mid-point. Seven years had passed and scarcely seven more remained before it would reach its brutal conclusion. As the New Year auguries of AD 61 were taken in the forum of Pompeii to determine the direction that the city should follow in the coming twelve months, there was no opportunity to ask for a second opinion. Ancient lore laid down that it was only the message written in the flight of the very first birds to be seen on the first day of January that mattered. The news they conveyed cannot have been good. Yet in the private houses and temples, where a fragrant and comforting smoke rose from the saffron scattered on the fires that even Campania needed in the colder months of the year, the citizens of Pompeii gathered around in search of warmth and hoped in vain for the best.[1]

The festival of Janus was traditionally a moment for taking stock: as the two-faced god looked both forward and back, so his worshippers were expected to reflect on what had gone before, learning the lessons of the previous year as they planned for what was to come. In the recent past lay the shame of the riot and its humiliating repercussions but, for much of the population, the hope engendered by the early years of Nero's reign and his infatuation with Poppaea lingered on. 'Happily to the judgements of the Augustus, father of the country, and to Poppaea, the Augusta,' proclaims one graffito, while another grovels: 'With you both safe, we are happy for ever.' As time passed, however, their protestations of loyalty would begin to sound hollow.[2]

Since the murder of Agrippina, Nero had pursued, ever more assiduously, his own taste for activities that offended the traditional

Roman sense of decorum. What had begun as an exuberantly child-ish reaction to the sudden lifting of all the prohibitions imposed by a strict mother – the Emperor toying first with chariot-racing, then mild debauchery, before graduating to hardcore amateur dra-matics – was already degenerating into something altogether more extreme and sinister. No longer were all his subjects prepared to turn a blind eye. There was still a long way for the Emperor to fall, but the glow of hopeful expectation that had surrounded him was rapidly fading. And the political and financial corruption practised by those around him only made matters worse.

For all the good sense with which he seems to have guided the first years of Nero's reign, Seneca was a hypocrite of the first order. In advice written to the Emperor, he condemned the quest for pleasure, on the grounds that it 'made the soul effeminate'. Yet he was immensely wealthy, with a highly developed taste for luxury and a notorious weakness for what was then deemed transgressive sex with youths who had already passed the threshold into manhood. His greatest fault, however, was his willingness to exploit his priv-ileged position at the heart of government to engage in what can most kindly be described as morally dubious business dealings. Chief among these was the vicious practice of foisting loans on Rome's provinces at crippling rates of interest, with the stipulation that the natives would then use the money to buy into Roman civilisation through the Empire's merchants, and so emulate the ways of their conquerors.

His latest victims were the recently occupied Britons, who had been running up debts for their new cities, temples and togas at such an extravagant rate of interest that their initial debts were doubling every two years. When it became clear that the expected repayments were not going to be forthcoming, Seneca abruptly foreclosed. But the extraction of upwards of forty million sesterces from a people who were not used to a fully developed, monetary economy could not be effected without considerable pain. In January, AD 61, the doors of Janus's temple, open for the last one hundred and eleven years to signify that the Empire was at war, were about to swing still wider, in recognition that another war was afoot. Provoked beyond endurance, the British tribes, under Queen

Boudicca, had finally taken up arms against the rapacity of an occupying Roman force intent on reclaiming Seneca's capital investment.

When Boudicca mocked the troops who opposed her for their effeminacy, compared to the bristling masculinity of the Britons under her banner, she unknowingly pinpointed the sorest spot on the Roman psyche. Since its very foundation, Rome had prided itself on being the epitome of a warrior state, founded on the premise that virtue and virility were all but synonymous, as their shared Latin root (*vir*: man) makes plain. Throughout the Republic, all adult men under the age of forty-six – or at times even sixty – had been liable to serve for sixteen years in the infantry of the legions, or ten in the cavalry; the majority of the male population would have been conscripted for some period of their life and, at any time, one in seven would have been in uniform. Even since the reforms made in the time of Augustus, that had turned the army into a professional rather than a purely citizen body, up to a fifth of all the young men in cities like Pompeii had to be recruited, each on a twenty-year commission, to maintain the numbers required to garrison the expanding Empire.

An accusation of effeminacy was not one that any self-respecting Roman – soldier or civilian – would have felt able to laugh off: even the reputations of Julius Caesar and Mark Antony had been sullied by the stories of youthful indiscretions with older men that dogged their later life. So when a barbarian woman implied that Rome's finest young men might be the passive party in acts of sexual penetration, it was deeply wounding to the national pride. It was also a very astute observation.

The example being set by the Emperor and his coterie must have led the citizens of places such as Pompeii to suspect that a larger cultural revolution was indeed underway, and to wonder how their lives might be changed by it. For what the powerful voices of Roman conservatism spoke of as a crisis of 'effeminacy', may have been seized upon by others as an opportunity to revisit society's hypocritically prescriptive sexual morality, as well as other long-standing taboos such as the glass ceiling that limited the careers of those who were not born free. If the Emperor could get away with murder, then surely a little loosening of the restrictions on who could hold public office was not out of the question for a rich freedman, or even a brief affair with a slave for a *decurion*'s wife? It would not have taken much for the rules that had shaped society for centuries to come tumbling down.

CHAPTER 6

Yours for Two Coins

January AD 61

For the last half-hour Lollius Synhodus had tried everything he could think of to quell his nerves. Yet nothing could distract him from the rhythmical groans that echoed from the depths of the house. Pacing the atrium, he struggled to drown out other thoughts. But even here, as slaves arranged kindling on the formal hearth, ready to be lit once the baby was born, he could not escape his torment. For he knew that the quandary in which he now found himself was entirely of his own making. The child now forcing its way into the world was not his, but that of his patron Julius Polybius. It was he who had connived to bring Polybius and his own wife, Clodia, together, pimping her for the sake of a paltry loan.

Lollius feared for Clodia: that the creature inside her would be too big and prove unable to escape the womb, or that the effort would break her heart, or that infection would enter the space vacated and eat her from within. As he had left his wife to her fate, squatting with her back against the low birth chair, panting, Lollius had seen in her parting glance that she shared his fear. A sickness gripped him. His own mother had died bringing his sister into the world, and too many of his friends had lost relatives the same way.

From the time of their marriage they had sworn never to have children, flying in the face of every expectation. How then had it come to this: Clodia risking her life with the assistance of a slave midwife who barely spoke the language and was only available because she was good for nothing else? So strange to her were the customs of Pompeii that a cousin of Clodia's had needed to prompt her to let down his wife's hair so that her womb entrance could relax. What good would she be when it came to the delivery?

With every minute that passed, he half-hoped, half-feared to hear the cry go out for the surgeon. It would mean the baby's head was impacted and a danger to its mother. Well then, it would have to be removed. Suddenly Lollius was seized by a feverish inspiration. Should he burst in now and insist that they follow this course? He knew the routine from hearsay: the instruments hurriedly laid out on their rolled-leather case, a long fine saw deftly manipulated to slice the cranium open and then dice it into fragments for ease of removal. One moment of decisiveness was all it would take.

But then he heard the first, gasping cry of the newborn creature. Instinct took hold and suddenly Lollius found himself offering Vaticanus a sacrifice for the care the god had shown in this, his sole duty. His slaves smiled and nodded their congratulations, and a flame was set to the kindling and sparked the symbolic fire that would be kept alight through the first hazardous days of this child's life. The sight of his wife, alive and well, erased all anger and jealousy in an instant and, as the midwife was nudged forward with the baby and bent to place it on the ground before him, his paternal instincts surged to the fore.

Now the invocations of the attendant gods poured thick and fast from his lips: first of Ops, as the baby boy lay supine and vulnerable, then of Levana as he scooped the wailing bundle up, formally accepting him into the family. Honey and spelt were pledged to Cumina for her guardianship of the cradle, and to Rumina for her care in the baby's feeding. Around him, the room was a blur of movement. But Lollius was already planning for the future. No more than four years on the wet nurse's breast so that the child's jaw did not become too pronounced. Tight swaddling so that only the right arm was free and the boy would surely become an orator. But he was getting ahead of himself. For now, his priority was to hang another doll outside the house to signal the addition to the family.

The beginning of Pompeii's year saw the annual festival of *Compitalia*. Bursts of colour exploded beside the city's thoroughfares as the shrines administered by the neighbourhood officials were made ready for the ceremony. In a niche behind each shrine, the statuette of Augustus was decked with garlands of flowers, along with those of the *lares* that flanked him, and up to a dozen other accompanying deities. Honey cakes baked by every household in the neighbourhood were brought as offerings, and in the street outside their homes families hung dolls and balls to represent each of their members: the former for citizens, the latter for slaves. In AD 61 the year of the census had come round and such visible tallying of household members helped the magistrates to count the population.

But the census was far more than simply a head-count. Citizens were assessed in relation to everything, from their choice of a wife, to their intentions to beget children, to the everyday arrangement of their lives – and the questions they might have to endure could include details as intimate as the style in which they chose to entertain friends, and their sexual proclivities. On such subjects, the dolls and balls hung outside their homes were mute.

When it came to assessing how well a wife was fulfilling her role within the family into which she had married, the criteria were simple. The very term for marriage – *matrimonium* – made clear the very least that was expected of a bride: that she should become a *mater*, or mother, and should do so in short order. With most grooms twice as old as the girls they married, there was pressure for heirs to be born quickly so that they could reach maturity while the *paterfamilias* was still alive to promote their careers. The state was unambiguous about its impatience to see children produced: at the census, husbands were required to swear on oath that conception was their earnest intention. Repeated failure to conceive would see pressure being brought to bear for a divorce, while any suspicion of adultery on the part of a wife – which might draw into question the legitimacy of whatever children were born – would be punished harshly.

When, on the evening before her wedding, a young bride-to-be dedicated her toys to Venus and set aside the dress that signified her immaturity, she must have known that, at a stroke, her childhood had been brought to an end, and with it any idle dreams of future freedom. Already, since she had first begun her monthly bleeding, the world around her would have quickly constricted, with a chaperone appointed to guard her virginity, and the visitors she was allowed to receive carefully monitored. Even her diet was adjusted to remove meat and reduce the intake of animal fats – the misguided regime recommended by medical experts as a healthy preparation for pregnancy. It was to be hoped that her parents had taken equal notice of the medical advice to wait until after her fifteenth birthday before marrying her off.[1]

Of her future husband, she is likely to have known little – less, in all likelihood, than the slaves who had been in attendance while the more senior women of the family had weighed up the candidates and decided on a match for her. Up to that point, suitors may have ventured on the first stage of courtship, with formal letters, and possibly gifts too. These would have been delivered to the girl's house, to be sifted by the girl's mother and her friends, and either passed on to the object of desire or returned with a curt dismissal.[2] But even if the bride-to-be had been allowed to read the letters, the text would have offered only formulaic protestations. Not unless she had paid attention to the city's graffiti while still free to wander about, or eavesdropped on her elders, would a girl have been better informed about the real nature of the exchange into which she was about to enter. One Zosimus is clear about the bargain he wants to strike with a certain Victoria: 'I ask you to become the support of my old age. If you don't believe I have money, don't love me.' Elsewhere, it is the greedy instructions issued by a coven of match-makers that is alluded to: 'The doorkeeper must stay awake for those bearing gifts; but, when the hand that knocks is empty, he can play deaf and sleep against the lock.'

Romantic love was generally considered to have no place in the marriage game, or even to be positively pernicious as the basis for a lifelong partnership: Pompeians like the *decurion* Bruttius Balbus – whose professions of devotion to his wife Fortunata are written on the walls of his house – might well have been condemned by some of his contemporaries as foolish and uxorious. Certainly the impression conveyed by the elite male writers whose words have come down to us is often of an excessively functional attitude to marital sex: in the not-so-distant past, even married couples in the capital had been punished for displaying affection in public. Yet to judge from the numerous expostulations and invocations of Venus on Pompeii's walls, romantic love was still a potent force in at least some people's lives. Vignettes of jealous needling or flirtatious wheedling capture moments of passion that leavened their subjects' hard lives, as in the case of two weavers from nearby workshops, Successus and Severus, who traded barbed comments on the walls of a bar. 'Successus the weaver loves a barmaid named Iris who does not care about him. And the more he begs, the less she cares,' writes one rival, only to be swiftly rebuffed in what develops into an increasingly ill-tempered exchange. Innumerable other couples flirt and bicker, their tortured emoting the only mark they left on history.[3]

In the course of the previous hundred years, the preferred form of marriage had actually been altered to accommodate women who insisted on maintaining some financial independence from their husbands. Now they could choose to remain, officially, a member of their father's household or that of a male blood relative, but there were disadvantages in this arrangement too, since it rendered the institution of marriage less stable as well as more flexible. And with the law continuously weighted against women, how much it really empowered wives is far from clear. For most young women fresh from the marriage ceremony, the best they could hope for was that they might eventually come to feel some affection for the old men whose lives they would share, or else that they might be widowed early enough to be an attractive proposition for remarriage (Plate 18).

Because of the nature of society at the time, there are relatively meagre documentary traces of the lives of Pompeii's women. Much of what we know about them concerns their bodies and appearance, since it was by these attributes, rather than for their emotional and intellectual qualities, that their society judged them. From mythical scenes of goddesses, to everyday visions of ladies attended by maid-servants at their toilet, the walls of Pompeii abound with idealised images of femininity. Everywhere, these paragons of their sex appear almost uniformly self-possessed, with wide, dark eyes that gaze either uncompromisingly into the middle distance or directly out at the viewer, regardless of whether they are captured by the painter in the throes of willing passion or in the process of warding off a sexual assault. Judging by the skeletons of the more wealthy women from Herculaneum, the upper class wives of Pompeii would have shared the willowy figures and noble features of their pictorial counterparts.

It seems probable that the complexions of such women were equally delicate and refined. The contrast between the flesh tones of the men and women depicted in the fantasy world of Pompeii's erotic paintings is more pronounced than occurs naturally: the men bronzed and the women pale as alabaster. Women of higher rank – or those high-class courtesans who emulated them for the gratification of their clients – may have demonstrated that they could afford a life of leisure by cultivating a pallor that would only have been possible for those who need not venture outdoors during the hottest hours of the day, or who could rely on slaves to ensure that they were shaded if they did. And, if such measures were not feasible, they could always turn to cosmetics. While pigments were applied to define the crimson of lips and to colour the cheeks, they were also used to emphasise the pellucid purity of the skin by highlighting in blue the veins that ran beneath.

Body hair was also removed to create smooth contours, and eyebrows plucked to pencil-line arches. Among the many instruments of beautification that have been found in Pompeii are numerous tweezers and forceps too small to be of any use to a surgeon. Depilation, including that of the pubic region, was widespread. However, those women beautifying themselves solely with the purpose of keeping their men might have found it instructive to read a graffito by one self-appointed expert, who believed, 'It is much better to fuck a hairy cunt than a smooth one: it both retains the warmth and stimulates the organ.'[4]

When it came to hair on the head, styles passed into and out of vogue faster than the imperial throne changed hands. In AD 61, few women were still wearing their hair parted in the centre – the favoured style during the days of Claudius – instead they were tending towards a more elaborate curling of the hair where it fringed the brow with the rest pulled back and woven into plaits at the nape of the neck. Hair extensions would come into fashion in the course of the next decade, as high proto-pompadours became the order of the day. One professional coiffeur with a shop in Pompeii offered the kind of elaborate hairdressing that handmaids might have struggled to accomplish at home.[5]

In all respects, the beauty industry was big business in Pompeii.

Affluent women struggled to emulate the idealised femininity of the frescoes on their walls, who stared into polished bronze or silver mirrors with justified self-regard, their dressing tables bare of any artificial means of enhancement. Yet the great range of ingeniously wrought bottles that have been found testifies to the lengths to which some women in the real world would go to preserve or improve their looks. For those who could afford it, the craftsmanship in the city could furnish customers with a variety of styles of necklace, rings, earrings and arm rings in any metal and embellished with pearls, emeralds, cornelians, agate or jasper. Even the less accomplished pieces could only have been made in a society in which labour was cheap: tiny images of birds or animals are meticulously carved into the surfaces of gemstones no larger than a child's fingernail, earrings like golden berries are stitched together from dozens of individually curled balls of metal.

Despite this, less than one in ten of the women of Pompeii whose bodies have been found were wearing or carrying jewellery, and of them only a fraction would have owned a complete set. In this provincial town, to be adorned in gold from head to toe was a sign of the very highest status and almost all the jewellery that has been discovered would have belonged to the wives of members of the town council. That ownership of such objects was relatively restricted, even in an age of conspicuous expenditure on luxuries, puts Pompeii's place in the larger scheme of things into some perspective.

Those who took such trouble to make themselves alluring must have been all too aware of the contradiction between the conservative ideals of womanhood and the everyday reality of their lives. There was intense pressure on a new wife to live up to the example of such women as a Roman mother who was praised by her son for 'modesty, probity, chastity, obedience, wool-working, diligence and fertility'. At the same time, when the wives of elite men were left endless hours of leisure with little to do except anxiously time their own reproductive cycles, it is little wonder if they were tempted to infidelity. While most of the ubiquitous erotica in the city was directed primarily at men, the sheer variety of the imagery would have allowed women to find something within it that spoke to their own sexuality. Explicit images of sex in every imaginable position and permutation – with orgies and bestiality commonplace – abounded on the walls of public and private rooms alike. Pigmies copulated by the dozen, simpering women bent over to offer themselves to their lovers with pleas to 'put it in slowly', representations of sex between men made a regular appearance, and barely literate boasts detailed elaborate sexual encounters in every next piece of graffiti a citizen chanced to read.

For contemporary Westerners burdened with – or enlightened by – two thousand years of Judaeo-Christian religious teaching, the process of understanding Roman sexuality and the erotica that covers Pompeii's walls might require some preconceived ideas to be set aside (Plate 20). Many of the site's earlier excavators saw the erotica as evidence that life in Pompeii was a sexual free-for-all. But a society's sexual mores often lie deeply buried, and it is notoriously difficult to see past the lies and posturing of those who are eager to volunteer stories of their sexual escapades. In the case of Pompeii, those offering us their opinions are the men, and occasionally the women, who took the time to scratch their thoughts into the plaster of the walls. However, a wealth of other literary, artistic and archaeological sources can give a broader insight into the cultural context of the time. If the threshold of acceptability in sexual matters really was so high, what were the taboos that were being broken to cause the reign of Nero to be characterised by contemporaries as one of sexual excess and debauchery?

The answer lies in the rigid demarcation of sexual roles for different groups in society and the sex acts that were appropriate to them. And especially – in this most phallocentric of cultures – it lies in the closely guarded right to sexually penetrate another person, and the social and psychic debasement implicit in being the person penetrated. It was the fear of somehow losing control in this area, rather than any more generous acknowledgement of female desire, that shaped the way that women's sexuality was presented in art and literature. Overtly sexual women were deemed suspect and ripe for demonisation. In the *Satyricon*, for example, Petronius cannot resist telling the story of an elite woman with a taste for rough trade, whose maid acted as her procuress. Similarly, the scenes from the life of Pasiphae that appear on the walls of the House of the Vettii and elsewhere allude to a woman – the queen of Crete, no less – whose actions were driven by lust, with terrible consequences. According to the myth, Daedalus would never have been called upon to design his famous labyrinth had he not earlier contrived a wooden cow in which Pasiphae could conceal herself and receive a bestial servicing from a bull (Plate 19). And when it came to women's assertive attitudes during Nero's reign, Seneca had been happy to bear witness that, 'They feed the most outlandish sexual appetites, and among men they act the part of men.'[6]

His claim could be taken at face value, just as the advice offered by one graffito to the traveller on his way into Pompeii might be seen as a balanced appraisal of a society where free love was blossoming: 'If anyone's looking for tender embraces in this town, he should know that here all the girls are available.' It is more likely, though, that this was the embittered comment of someone who felt that all womankind was abandoning those attributes of fidelity and maternal devotion that had justified whatever status they were traditionally accorded. Far easier to castigate women for their lusts than address their legitimate aspirations, both inside and outside the sexual realm.[7]

Nevertheless, other graffiti from Pompeii do hold out one tantalising and very surprising possibility for the indulgence of women's sexual needs: services are advertised that offer cunnilingus, an activity that was perceived as very demeaning for men to perform. 'Glyco licks cunts for two asses,' seems like a bargain compared to Maritimus, who charges four but does add, 'Virgins accepted.' Are these plausible signs of male prostitution being on offer to women, or merely sexual insults? The detail of one comment, which appears to express female preference, points to the former. 'Satyrus, don't lick cunt inside the opening but outside the opening.' Is it possible that when there was no risk of conception, it was condoned for wives, perhaps even those of the elite, to buy their non-penetrative pleasure?[8]

It is not possible to know the answer: probably it would have depended on the nuanced issue of whether it was pleasure or penetration that constituted infidelity. In a world in which romantic love had so little respect, the key point may be a practical one. Penetrative sex between a woman and a man other than her husband threatened not only his reputation, but also the legitimacy of his heirs; in so doing, it undermined the sanctity of family ancestry on which an elite man's whole belief system and authority were based. Little wonder, then, that in normal times, Roman society imposed such fierce sanctions – legal and moral – on those who transgressed. Indeed, so strong was the fear of a woman's ability to manipulate a man's emotions that the use of magic to cause someone to fall in love was punishable by death.

The impotent anger that men felt at the facility with which female sexuality could challenge their authority perhaps found unconscious expression in art, where passive female figures are frequently to be seen being subjected to sexual violence and humiliation at the hands of male aggressors. The scene from the House of Menander showing the aristocratic ladies of Troy being raped and carried away by the Greeks as their defeated soldiers look on, powerless to intervene, is especially resonant. In a world where virtue in sex meant simply to take one's pleasure in the most assertive way possible, there was deemed to be a kind of perverse praiseworthiness in sexual violence. For an adult Pompeian man to eschew the sexually dominant role was to render himself effeminate and ridiculous, and to risk being classed for ever among those whose body had been used like that of a woman. On this hung all other niceties of interpretation. Neither the sex of the recipient nor the type of penetration was of any relevance: only the thrusting conquest. So clear-cut was the issue that vaginal, anal and oral sex were each described by two different verbs, one denoting the active role and one the passive: to be the kind of man who did one set of things (*futuere*, *pedicare* and *irrumare*) would see you welcomed in the politest society, but to do the other (*crisare*, *cevere* and *fellare*) was to risk becoming a legal outcast.

To be the subject of sexual assault was the most humiliating punishment possible for an adult male citizen: when the threat was made by a god, it was wise to take notice. Priapus was perhaps the most ostensibly primal figure in the Roman pantheon and although his statues were almost ubiquitous, they were not meant to pass unnoticed, even amidst the vegetation where they were often sited. Frequently painted bright red to enhance their fearsome aspect, it was not the colour of the images but the prodigious size of Priapus's penis that declared his purpose most clearly. Adapted by the Romans from a Greek god with similar physical attributes, he was at once a bringer of luck to those who worshipped him and the fierce protector of gardens against anyone who stole the crops. And the terrible punishment that he threatened? Rape. 'I warn you, woman, you will be fucked; boy, you will be buggered; and as for the bearded man, he can give me his mouth,' asserts the god in the *Songs of Priapus*. Another extract is more visceral still: 'This rod shall enter the thief's guts as far as the hair and hilt of my balls.'[9]

Curiously, it was the same punishment that a cuckolded husband was legally entitled to inflict on his wife's lover – forced sodomy – though in one of the strangest images to be conjured by a writer of the period, Juvenal describes a wronged husband opting to carry out the punishment using an expensive fish rather than his own member. Although a piece of grotesque satire, it is hard to imagine that the law would have intervened in such a case: in almost every respect it not only accommodated any form of vengeance that a wronged husband might demand, but positively insisted upon it. At its mildest, the law made punishment for an adulterous wife mandatory – exile from her home and exclusion from the family tomb – and held her husband culpable as a pimp if he failed to report her crime. When a woman's father was shamed by having his daughter caught in flagrante with her lover in either his own home or that of a husband, he was entitled to kill them both: only the requirement that they both suffer the same fate acted as a restraining hand. A husband was granted similar rights, as long as his wife's lover was one of his own slaves or freedmen, or an *infamis* such as a gladiator or actor. The jealous image of wives who liked to 'kiss the tracks of the whip' appears to have been one that many husbands could not get out of their minds.[10]

Such draconian legislation would not, of course, have been easily enforceable, and a more humane attitude probably prevailed to prevent most cases reaching court. Indeed, in images from the walls of private homes in Pompeii it appears almost as though attitudes towards the unpredictability of passion were tolerant, in an echo of Ovid's liberal opinion that 'the man's a boor who's too offended by his wife's affairs'. One example from the House of the Capitals depicts a bearded old man stooping to inspect a cramped cage in which he holds a group of winged Cupids under lock and key, only to discover that two have escaped. The viewer can immediately see what he cannot: that they have made straight for the figure of his attractive young wife, who leans against a nearby wall, one of the little messengers of love hurrying behind her skirts while the other offers two crowns, presumably in token of the kingdom of love that she will soon rule with her clandestine consort. It is impossible not to see in this a mockery of what seemed to many by Nero's reign to be an archaic and unenlightened repression of natural impulses.[11]

It is clear that, by this time, bastard children were often allowed to remain within the family: in their wills, many fathers of the period explicitly excluded children born to their wives by other men, on the grounds of illegitimacy, calling them 'the person who is not my son', 'the brigand', 'the gladiator', or 'the one born of an adulterer'. The language is harsh, but it is worth remembering that, although excluded from inheritance, they could just as easily have been exposed at birth, and their mothers denounced as adulteresses. Perhaps they had only half-accepted the chastening and heartfelt pronouncement from a graffito in the House of Caecilius Jucundus: 'May those who love prosper; let them perish who cannot love; let them perish twice over who veto love.'[12]

There may be another reason for this fierce resentment of the illegitimate interloper by the betrayed husband. Childbearing entailed huge risks for the mother, and many of those illegitimate children who survived to be later spurned by their nominal fathers might, in the course of their birth, have cost him a wife. The availability of relatively advanced obstetrical instruments – such as specula, made to a design that would not be improved until the late nineteenth century – helped little with a difficult delivery in circumstances where infection was rife.

Taking the risks of childbirth together with the financial implications for large families of the division of inherited wealth, no family of good standing would want to chance the life of its *mater-familias* in unnecessary pregnancy. Anatomical analysis of the female skeletons preserved in nearby Herculaneum suggests that the desire to manage the fertility of its elite women may have been a key factor in shaping the sexual morality of the time.[13] The average number of children born to these women, even those already past their reproductive years at the time they died, was significantly less than two: nowhere near enough to sustain population levels. The scientific findings support anecdotal evidence from Rome at this time that small families or indeed childlessness were becoming common. It was a sure sign of a society shifting away from a civic-minded concern with the provision of manpower for armies and commerce, towards a greater emphasis on the individual's personal wishes. At its insensitive extreme, the attitude is encapsulated in one Pompeian graffito that reads: 'I don't care about your pregnancy, Salvilla; I despise it.' The question is, how did the writer expect Salvilla to have avoided her predicament?[14]

For those content to follow old wives' recommendations, there were any number of forms of contraception available, of varying degrees of efficacy or absurdity: from barrier methods involving elephant dung, to magical preventatives, to a simple post-coital routine of squatting and sneezing. Then, if these failed, there were many different ways to poison or traumatise the body to induce an abortion before it was necessary to have recourse to surgery. The only reliable way to avoid conception, though, was to avoid sex – or at least vaginal sex – altogether. It was perhaps in this spirit that one man described his bashful satisfaction in a couplet of poetry found in the Villa of the Mysteries just outside the Herculaneum gate of Pompeii: 'Here I have penetrated my lady's open buttocks; but it was vulgar of me to write these verses.'[15]

Fellatio was another practical alternative and the elite owners of grand houses could have read brief accounts of its practice on their own walls: Fabius Rufus would have learned that 'Romula sucks her man here and everywhere', while in the House of the Silver Wedding, Sabina was 'sucking it, but not doing it right'. However, in a culture that prized eloquence and public oratory so highly, and in which it was customary for those of similar rank to exchange kisses in greeting, no aristocratic wife could have been expected to sully her mouth by such a practice. The erotic pictures of women fellatrices often show their heads being forced down by the recipients of their attentions: if they were ladies of the elite, it is no surprise that they squirmed in an attempt to avoid becoming orally impure. If alternative sexual practices were what an elite man craved – or, for that matter, if it was simply anxiety-free straight sex he wanted – there was no shortage of either professional or amateur practitioners in the city to whom he could turn.[16]

The men of Pompeii hardly needed a pretext for their hypocrisy in matters of sexual morality, yet concern for their wives' health would have provided one in abundance. Adultery by women might be punished in the most draconian manner possible but, as long as he was not caught with the wife or daughter of a man of equal or higher status, a philanderer was effectively, if not legally, immune to prosecution or complaint. Even better if a man paid his lover for her services or she was otherwise under his control.

Stoics such as Musonius may have believed that it was 'immoderate' to have sex with slaves, but then he and his associates held that any sex that did not take place within marriage and for the strict purpose of procreation was wrong. The right-thinking majority unsurprisingly perceived him and his sympathisers as moral radicals. Indeed, it was widely felt that the fastidious should be persuaded to overcome their scruples for the common good: 'When you're hungry,' wrote Horace, 'you don't turn your nose up at anything except peacock and turbot, do you? When your crotch is throbbing and there is a slave girl or homebred slave boy at hand, whom you could fuck straight off, you don't prefer to let your engorged member burst, do you? I certainly don't. I like sex that is easy and obtainable.'[17]

But how did a *paterfamilias* feel when he, or one of his male relatives or guests, took advantage of the household's 'walking tools' to relieve their sexual needs? In light of the physical gulf between the free-born and their slaves – though there were certainly beautiful and expensive exceptions, sometimes bought expressly for the purpose – did it somehow seem akin to miscegenation or bestiality? Or was it simply like prostitution in the comfort of one's home and with no bill to pay at the end? Might there sometimes have been an emotional exchange, or was it always and inevitably a purely functional event? And, most difficult of all to contemplate, how must it have been for the recipient of these attentions, or those of his or her fellow slaves with whom they had an emotional bond yet who were obliged to look on helpless? To know that all the dangers of pregnancy that the lady of the house wished to avoid were instead being piled on an uncomprehending slave, who may well have been too young to bear them as well?[18] A ring found in the likely harbour area of Murecine is engraved with the words 'To his *ancilla*': a statement of enduring affection for his slave lover from the man represented by a statuette of a portly figure in a toga that was found nearby, or a gold band to symbolise sexual ownership?

The temptation for any female slave to insinuate her way into the master's heart must have been strong and sexual relations not always as unwelcome as the disparity in power might suggest, at least once her spirit was broken, as Cato advised doing as a matter of course soon after a slave was first bought. Only a handful of female slaves and up to scores of men might have shared the same dingy slave quarters, and their master was fully within his rights not only to take a girl for his own pleasure but to decide on who her slave partners should be and when they were to have access to her: they could even be charged for the privilege. Indeed, so absolute was the *droit de seigneur* that it really only made sense for slaves to look for some arrangement with their master that worked to their advantage.[19]

If for some male owners there were racial differences to reckon with when entering into a relationship with a slave, others clearly relished the exoticism of it all. Africans, Asians and northern Europeans were all equally alien and mocked for the fact, but black slaves were in the minority and considered most aesthetically admirable. One lascivious graffito salivated, 'He who loves a dark-skinned girl burns on black coals; when I see a dark girl I gladly eat blackberries.'

For those looking outside the home, finding a prostitute would have posed few challenges in Pompeii, though quite how widespread the sex trade was remains an open question. Even conservative estimates put the number of brothels at around ten, of which the most famous example is the *lupanar* that lies close to the forum, amidst the huddle of streets where many less salubrious manufacturing trades also found a home. Here, in the tiny rooms of the wedge-shaped building that sits on an acute corner, clients like Fenbus or Agathus – whose work in the perfume industry doubtless bought them favour with the girls – could pick their pleasures and positions from paintings above each room's low entrance or from a placard paraded around the building by one of the prostitutes. To one side of the entrance, a second door leads to the upper storey, where five extra rooms could be thrown open when business was brisk, when sailors poured off a ship newly arrived in the harbour, for example, or when crowds were brought in by theatrical or gladiatorial shows. At these times, the overspill could count themselves lucky to have avoided the short solid masonry bed and pillow with which the downstairs rooms were furnished.

Pompeii catered for a whole spectrum of tastes, from clients who liked the luxurious to those who preferred the rough and ready. Clusters of licentious graffiti mark out the territory of the city's street-walkers, in which those with particular specialisms declared what distinguished them from the competition. In the north of the city, Aphrodite, Veneria, Spendusa, Nymphe and Timele hung out on the street that led directly between the *macellum* and the Temple of Jupiter up towards a dead end in front of one of the towers in the city wall. The last of these women advertised herself as a skilled fellatrix but, since Nymphe was a rival in that department, she made it known that she also enjoyed anal sex. They touted for business barely a stone's throw from some of the most expansive and luxurious houses in Pompeii; the free-born Vettius family, and the inhabitants of the House of the Dioscuri, with their likely connection to Alleius Nigidius Maius, cannot have failed to notice the women's insalubrious presence. The prostitutes' clothes declared their availability quite unambiguously: either diaphanous garments that would have been disgracefully provocative on the back of any other woman or else, by a strange irony, a version of the *toga praetexta* that was otherwise reserved for prominent men.

Another group had its turf around a street corner between the forum brothel and the inn owned by a man called Phoebus that ran a sideline in sex: perhaps they hoped to pick up trade from drinkers on their way home from one or other of these establishments by offering knockdown deals and a flexible service. Euplia was not an uncommon name in these parts, but perhaps the prostitute by that name, who flattered her clientele with claims she had been there 'with thousands of good-looking men', was not averse to making house calls too, for a consideration. A Euplia certainly 'sucked it for five *asses*' – a steep price – in a house just on the other side of the via di Stabia. There is no record of what she charged to make the longer trip to the House of the Floral Cubiculum half a dozen blocks away, where her client might have observed their sport in a fine obsidian mirror set into the wall, just to the right of which, perhaps in a moment of post-coital languor, he described her as being 'loose and clitorious'.[20] For those who were looking for something between a knee-trembler and the full bordello experience, a number of minute rooms set into the walls of back streets provided a halfway house: a flimsy curtain would have afforded a little privacy and a quick and easy exit.

Prices could vary greatly, dependent presumably on some combination of the age and beauty of the prostitute, the look of the client, the services required, and the location. All prostitutes were required to register with the junior magistrates and were charged a tax, though how it was calculated is an imponderable. For an additional fee, the magistrate leased out space around public buildings such as the amphitheatre, under the arches of which satisfied clients have scratched their testimony to the delights enjoyed there. But the most miserable of all venues were the *necropoleis*, where those older prostitutes who had survived the many risks to their health from disease and pregnancy finally washed up. Tombs that by day offered seats and shade to passing travellers, at night provided makeshift shelter for those bold or desperate enough to venture out into the realm of witches and werewolves in search of dirt-cheap sex.[21]

Among the hundreds of inhabitants of Herculaneum who died in the eruption, the pelvic bones of two fifty-year-old women show, in exaggerated form, the kind of abnormalities that are habitually found in present-day prostitutes in North America. Victims of the inadequacies of ancient contraception, it is not hard to imagine them failing to scrape a good enough living outside the Nucerian Gate to support any unlucky survivors of the five or more children they had borne. Their skin was scraggy, their mouths ruined, their undernourished bones brittle and their joints would have creaked painfully through the long, cold January nights. But in AD 61, they were still barely out of their prime and we cannot even be sure whether their lives had yet taken the downward turn into prostitution.

Male slaves were undoubtedly subject to the same sexual exploitation as their female counterparts; and if freed, it remained their duty to make themselves sexually available to their patron when called upon. Trimalchio manages to excuse the indignities he suffered in the sexual service of both his master and his mistress. 'What the master orders is not shameful,' he insists and, whilst he can hardly be considered a reliable character witness on his own behalf, other writers agree that different standards did apply. The kind of receptive sexual role that was unacceptable for the free-born was recognised as a simple necessity for the slave – an involuntary peccadillo that could easily be overlooked in his later incarnation as a respectable freedman.[22] It would still be interesting to know whether the pressure for such indulgent amnesia came more from the slaves' masters or their masters' wives, who might have been relieved to see their husbands find an alternative outlet for their sexual needs than starry-eyed girls. Unlike slave girls, who blossomed into childbearing fecundity, when an adolescent slave boy's voice broke and they ceased to resemble the Greek ideal of the smooth-limbed catamite, their appeal – and with it any continuing threat to the mistress's position – quickly faded.

Sex between men, however, did not begin and end with members of the same household. Older men could take their pick of lovers as long as they were in the penetrating role, while younger men – if discreet – could allow themselves to be penetrated with relative impunity, as long as they had not yet completed the rites of passage to manhood. And for those whose tastes ran to such boys of a better class and who were not afraid for their preferences to become public knowledge, or for young men who revelled in their own effeminacy and enjoyed the attention of their elders, or simply for those who liked to admire the physique of the oiled African attendants, the more outré public baths were the place to go.

The Sarno Baths were the epitome of a cultured leisure facility, tucked away in a highly desirable residential area of the city, which was both central yet secluded from the bustle of the forum. Perched on the edge of the escarpment, with several storeys cut into the cliff-face, its location responds in many particulars to a building in which Seneca stayed once on a visit to Campania – one of his closest friends lived in Pompeii – and his account of the interruptions he suffered as he tried to study vividly evoke the life of the place. Above the baths were fine apartments where some of the city's young bloods and older bachelors could have taken lodgings, while alongside stood an exercise hall that was decorated with fine images of wrestlers and body-builders. Here *otium* was promoted in its noblest and most rigorous form: simply time spent away from public affairs and business negotiations, on the legitimate exercise, cleansing and refining of the body. Indeed, the daily ritual of bathing as practised here had come to stand almost as the defining symbol of Roman civilisation, in contrast to the Greeks, who persisted in shunning regular washing and instead doused themselves with perfume.

There may have been a separate door in the Sarno complex available for use by the tenants of the apartments and honoured bathers, but this did not detract from the symbolic importance of baths like these. Everyone could attend and partake of the same forms of relaxation and purification, making this a binding force in civic life. Architecture, hydraulics and the decorative arts came together in the baths to exhibit Rome's technical skill, and donations of bath buildings or fittings were a much-appreciated form of munificence. And yet from the first century until the fourth, Rome's moralistic writers inveighed against the baths in thunderous terms. So what was it about these places that so pricked moral sensibilities? Was it simply that, whilst thought of as representing what was best about Rome, in reality they fell far short of the ideal? Or was there something about them that was more acutely unsettling?

One obvious source of distaste lay in the burgeoning commercialism of what had once been a purely functional and rather austere environment. With a captive clientele, bath-owners were now exploiting to the full the monopoly they enjoyed and feeding their visitors' appetites for everything from food and wine to the services of beauticians, masseurs and personal trainers. Here again, Seneca's testimony concerning the distractions he faced when trying to philosophise is invaluable: vendors of sausages, cakes and sweet-meats hawked their wares, pimps and prostitutes tried to drum up trade, hooligans who had overindulged in wine splashed and screamed in the water, and unwanted hangers-on angled noisily for dinner invitations. Cash flowed as fast as the water but the result was a raucousness that was all but unbearable to sensitive natures. Yet even this cannot fully account for the level of moralistic disapproval that was expressed.

In mosaics from the private homes and public baths of Pompeii alike, the figure of a black swimmer or bath attendant appears repeatedly: four are found in the House of Caesius Blandus, three around the small private bathing suite of the House of Menander, others in that of the *praedia* of Julia Felix. They carry jars of water, or *strigils* to scrape off the oil in which the bathers' bodies were smeared to ease away the dirt, or else they are furnace-stokers with shovels, as befitted 'Ethiopians', whom the Romans thought had been burned to that colour by the sun. And, except where they are naked, their uniform is a short, white kilt from beneath which an impressively sized, usually erect penis protrudes. An ethnic stereotype, to be sure, but intended to serve a similar function to all the other phallic imagery that is ubiquitous in Pompeii, from the carved phalluses set into pavements and walls, to the small protective charms carried by individuals, and encompassing the paintings and statues of Priapus himself.

Like the ribald mimes who performed in the theatre with their gigantic prosthetic penises, it was laughter that was meant to be evinced by these images, since laughter was a potent magic in subverting malign influences: thwarting the Evil Eye and warding off *invidia*, or envy. But perhaps this was not the only currency of these phalluses.

The aesthetic ideal in the classical world dictated that penises should be small and childish, as they appear on Pompeian statuary. The literature of the first century paints a different picture, however, of at least certain groups of men, who would spontaneously crowd around at the bathhouse to admire and applaud penises of especially generous proportions.[23] If Simplex and Petrinus – the two slave attendants bought by Dicidia Margaris from Poppaea for use in the Sarno Baths – were granted such a reception, were their mighty members being praised for their efficacy at warding off the Evil Eye, or were they being coveted in some other, more corporeal sense? Would their audience have envied or desired them?[24]

Fortunately, the walls of Pompeii are not entirely silent on the subject. The apprehensive attitude that women might have felt towards their well-endowed lovers is seen in some frescoes and hinted at in graffiti, but it is the accounts by those who performed anal sex with other men that are most revealing. Secundus proclaimed that he had 'buggered boys who wailed', while Quintius, 'has here penetrated waggling buttocks and seen the pain it causes'. One bold seducer even had recourse to mythological allusion when trying to persuade a reluctant lover of his bull-like attributes: 'Let Damoetas surrender to me and he will be happier than Pasiphae. All this is written by Zosimus.' Yet despite Zosimus's boasting, it was men like him – corrupters of male youth – who were responsible for dragging the bathhouses into disrepute.[25]

The great anxiety surrounding the baths was that the pervasive atmosphere of sexual licence created by the presence of prostitutes, perfume-sellers and others of their ilk would erode all moral boundaries, so that young men approaching maturity risked falling prey to the lusts of their elders – in a public space – and would therefore lose their reputation for ever. It was an impression that at least one bathhouse in Pompeii did nothing to correct; quite the opposite, in fact. For the paintings in the changing rooms of the Suburban Baths – situated down the steep slope beyond the Marine Gate towards the harbour area – go out of their way to catalogue nearly every permutation of sexual debauchery that might have plagued the anxious fathers of adolescent sons.

Variously, in the series of panels (of which eight from an original sixteen survive), a woman on her hands and knees is skewered by a man at each end; another kneels to receive a man from behind who is himself taken anally by a second man; two women are shown in a lesbian embrace; and a reclining woman holds her legs to better enjoy cunnilingus from a male partner. All were seen as outrageous forms of sexual behaviour and would have elicited a tittering excitement from ancient viewers. But in almost all, it is the humiliation of a male participant, by one means or another, that provides the focal element.[26]

For real men, the only role to admit to in the orgiastic activities shown would have been that of the penetrating male, who can be seen, in the most complex of the scenes, punching the air in jubilation that he has evaded being cast in the submissive role. But through the example set by Nero himself, the AD 60s saw a very different male sexual persona gain recognition: one that was more closely embodied in another figure from the same series of paintings. Sandwiched between a male and female lover, this male character holds the hand of the man behind him in the only gesture of emotional intimacy in the entire series. A cheeky graffitist could still get a laugh out of writing 'Icarus buggers you' on a wall of the House of the Citharista, yet it is possible that not far away there could be found something like a community of men who espoused alternative values.

Columella, the expert on agricultural affairs, summed up the traditionalists' disapproval of the changed sexual mores that they encountered on a visit into town: 'I suppose that the old-fashioned and manly way of life is no longer agreeable in the face of today's glamorous luxury ... We watch in amazement the gestures of the effeminates who are abroad, as their womanly movements imitate what nature has denied to men, and so deceive all who gaze upon them.' His targets are specifically the *cinaedi*, a group whose deviancy Juvenal would describe in the AD 90s as 'spreading like a contagion', their name being derived from 'those who publicly shake their buttocks, that is to say, dancers or pantomime performers'. The implied slur is clearly that they were inviting anal penetration – it was said that their freedmen were called upon to service them – but what best identified them as a social set was their active embrace of precisely those symptoms of *mollitia*, or culpable softness, that normal men were supposed to disdain. And for a while, at least, their perceived weakness was no longer something to hide: in the *Satyricon*, a *cinaedus* sings a song inviting his associates to join the party he is attending.[27]

The dress of the *cinaedi* was brightly coloured and diaphanous, the preferred style of tunic having long, draping sleeves. Their hair was arranged into pretty curls; they bathed excessively and soused themselves in the sweet perfumes of balsam and cinnamon; and, most tellingly of all, they removed the hair from their bodies to make themselves more like women. Perhaps some of the small forceps found in the city were used for depilation by men rather than women, though eyebrows could always be shaved, as could buttocks, the latter to maintain an appearance of boyishness. Ants' eggs could be applied to boys' armpits, while dealers in slave boys used the blood of castrated lambs or of bats, or the gall of hedgehogs, to prevent the first growth of a beard.

In the newly designed baths of the mid-first century – of which Pompeii's Central Baths, whose construction was still some years off in AD 61, are a perfect example – the sternest moral critics saw effeminacy written into the fabric of the building. Where once the bracing wind had blown through narrow slits, now large windows poured in light. Here the fragrance of red-hot walnut shells being applied to hair would have drifted past the nostrils of bathers as Vesbinus, Caesonius Felix and their friends prinked and preened.[28] And if these Pompeians are only known to us as *cinaedi* through abusive graffiti, there are others who were quite happy to publicise their own sexual identity on the walls in the secluded street tucked in behind the basilica. Euplia's name appears nearby and it may be that Lattarius, Restitutus and Januarius were simply male prostitutes who used *cinaedus* as a marketable label. Intriguingly, though, the latter two names appear twice here: once as '*cinaedi*', once, boldly, as '*niironas*'. It is an association repeated elsewhere.[29] The Emperor's reputation, it seems, was spreading.

The last of the respectable bathers were already leaving by the time Rustus finally reached the baths. As usual he had brought with him only a single slave, Dexter, and even he was left to wait on the street outside until his master tired of taking his pleasures. Rustus could feel the disapproving but lustful gaze of his elders on him in the changing room, as they adjusted the folds of their togas with exaggerated propriety while he sloughed off his tunic and flexed his adolescent limbs provocatively before them; whatever their opinion of his behaviour, the decurions who came here would never dare tell his father.

Slaves, though, were a different matter, as he knew only too well. Even those who had their own reason to keep quiet about their master's appetites could become garrulous. Foolish of them; a whiff of scandal and they would be tortured for the full story without a second thought. Still, it was when gossip from the slave quarters in the Numisius household had reached the ears of his friend Gratus's father that the poor young man had been forced to take such drastic action. Drastic, of course, only in the minds of those who had not yet liberated themselves from convention: to anyone right-thinking it was only common sense.

Dexter had brought a few bottles of Rustus's own unguents to the baths, classy merchandise straight from Capua, but having to carry it from the changing room for himself seemed effortful to Rustus. In any case, he felt like splashing out on something new from the bathhouse's own stock. He deserved some serious pampering while he daydreamed how he might have dealt with finding himself in Gratus's position.

What was it that the boy's father had said to provoke him? 'Dripping with foreign perfumes, crippled by lust, walking more softly than a woman just to turn women on – and I can't say how many other things that show bad judgement.' If his old man had thrown the book at him like that, Rustus certainly wouldn't have drawn the line at a legal action for dementia. Parricide was such a lovely word. Hadn't their patron, Nero himself, shown how there could be virtue in ridding yourself of a parent who held back your potential?

On leaving the massage room, Rustus found his attention caught by a monkey that swung between the vaults, cackling knowingly. He threw a nut into its darting mouth. Who cared if the law stated that a man who killed his father should be whipped, then sewn up in a sack with a dog, a cockerel, a snake, and some Barbary ape for company and all of them drowned together in the sea? Times were changing and Rustus was protected by important friends – men like Gratus himself, but Claudius Verus and Popidius Ampliatus too. Now was the moment, if ever there was one, to cross some boundaries.

You could never have too many friends, he reflected; never too many people whose deepest secrets you shared. As Rustus shimmied past Veranius Hypsaeus, he could hear the older man's breathing deepen. Even through the haze of steam, Hypsaeus saw and appreciated the buttocks that Rustus kept perfectly smooth, the sheen on his arms where the hairs curled tight and golden. Perching on the edge of a marble bench, Rustus looked directly at his mark, straightened a single finger and lifted it to scratch his perfectly coiffed scalp in unmistakable invitation. Hypsaeus would not need asking twice.

—— VI ——

The poet Horace expressed what would be the refrain of pessimistic cultural observers for centuries to come when he wrote, 'What does not ruinous time degrade? The age of our parents, inferior to that of our grandparents, brought forth ourselves, who are more worthless still and destined to have children still more corrupt.'

With the emperor setting the moral tone for his subjects, the latter part of Nero's reign would be one of those moments in the history of imperial Rome when society's ongoing struggle between the demands of duty and delight, would bubble uncontrollably to the surface. During the AD 60s, those tensions would have permeated all aspects of personal, family and civic life in Pompeii.

It was not, in fact, until the beginning of the second millennium that the word 'decadence' first appeared, in medieval rather than classical Latin. Today, however, it still offers the closest we can come to a translation for those ideas of *vacillatio* and *inclinatio* that so vexed a Roman elite who were transfixed by fear of national decline. The nineteenth-century French poet Paul Verlaine, himself immersed in an epoch struggling to comprehend the intangibles of decadence, offered a personal testimony to the associations conjured by the word. 'All shimmering with purple and gold,' he wrote, 'it throws out the brilliance of flames and the gleam of precious stones. It is made up of carnal spirit and unhappy flesh and of all the violent splendours of the Lower Empire; it conjures up the paint of the courtesans, the sports of the circus ... the collapse among the flames of races exhausted by the power of feeling.'

Such would have been the miasmic atmosphere into which the close associates of Nero were drawn in the years that followed the murder of Agrippina: a *demi-monde* of unmitigated luxury, other-worldly artifice and hopeless self-delusion, where money was spent with abandon yet where the most dangerous kind of inflation was at work in the realm of desire. Tacitus was in no doubt that it was Nero's own plunge into degeneracy that led the way.

For an elite who still clung desperately to the past, AD 61 was a deeply unsettling year. In Rome, the City Prefect, Pedanius Secundus, was murdered by a slave from his own household. The senate, all too conscious of the need to reassert deference as the very cornerstone of society, and of the dangerous precedent that this crime might set, sentenced Secundus's entire household of four hundred slaves to death for failing to protect their master. Their crime was one of omission, but there was to be no mercy. When crowds armed with torches and stones, and composed largely of freedmen, took to the streets in sympathy, they had to be forced back by the ranks of Praetorian Guards.

It might seem a small matter by comparison, but in the fraught atmosphere of these days, graffiti from a large farming estate near Pompeii, asserting that the mother of Augustus had been mortal rather than divine, might have read like a revolutionary clarion call to the large barracks of restive agricultural slaves. After all, hadn't Spartacus himself, once a main attraction in arenas like Pompeii's own, fought and won a battle on the slopes of Vesuvius? And what of the freedmen who were never truly satisfied with their station in life, however much money they accumulated?

To compound the general disquiet, news arriving from abroad was far from reassuring. The province of Britannia was still in a state of open revolt: the newly built Roman city of Camulodunum had been burned to the ground, having been betrayed to Boudicca's rebel army by its *incolae*, the 'alien' residents whom Roman generosity had allowed to settle within its walls. Pompeii's households were staffed by slaves of Greek descent; the city's businesses were run largely by men with strong Greek or Egyptian sympathies; and slaves from the whole spectrum of conquered races lived alongside the Pompeians in their homes. The local aristocracy must have quaked at the number of potential fifth columnists in their own midst.

With such a weight of uncertainty bearing down, the consolations of reason proved no match for superstition, and the evil portents did not disappoint. In Rome, a vestal virgin who had been accused of being unchaste was buried alive, and a lightning strike on Nero's Hellenic gymnasium melted a statue of the Emperor into a lump of shapeless bronze. Not long before this, rumours had surfaced for the first time that a possible successor was plotting to usurp the purple, and a comet in the sky was seized upon as a sign that there would be an imminent change of ruler.

The discontented crowds in the capital certainly knew whom to blame for their unease. Popular demonstrations were staged against Poppaea Sabina and in support of Nero's first wife Octavia, the last remaining link by sacred blood between Augustus and the imperial succession. By this point, Octavia was already doomed to make way for the amber-haired temptress, and plans were under way to have her framed for infidelity and treason, exiled and then murdered. Yet still, statues of the usurping Poppaea were smashed in anger and frustration by the mob. Increasingly, the reaction of the Emperor to such manifestations of public discontent was one less of conciliation than of straightforward disdain, influenced by the semi-official sycophants who surrounded and increasingly insulated him from popular opinion.

The dangerous sports and theatrical displays that followed Agrippina's death had quickly gone far beyond mere celebration of the Emperor's survival, to become the defining feature of Nero's reign. The Roman moral universe was sent spinning. For the Emperor's alarmingly Hellenistic appetites not only shamed him but invited the flower of Rome's youth to follow suit. Inspired by older fraternities, whose interests had been more military than artistic, a new club called the Augustiani was founded, which at first drew its members from the young knights of Rome. Their role was to act as cheerleaders during Nero's appearances onstage. Organised into sections under group leaders, each was tasked with perfecting a particular style of clapping in emulation of an orchestrated team of Alexandrian claquers that Nero had once encountered while in Naples: the buzzing 'bees', whose method is obscure, the 'hollow tiles', whose cupped hands provided the base notes, and the 'flat tiles', with their palms meeting. With members taking pains to make sure that they removed any rings that might inhibit their performance, the sound they made would have reassured even the most nerve-wracked diva.

Unlike the organisations established by Augustus to channel the energies of the ambitious in society, the ethos of Nero's new club did not revolve around piety for the founding father and his message of obedience, conformity and respect for tradition. Indeed, its purpose was almost a travesty of these values: to promote the image of an emperor who saw himself more as gender-bending international pop star than the dependable *paterfamilias* of the nation. And its members were inspired not by the altruistic desire to contribute to public life, but by the promise of vertiginous riches with which some would be rewarded by the Emperor, along with the erotic thrill that came from feeling oneself so close to the aphrodisiac of the imperial purple.

Over the next few years, this exclusive cadre would throw open its doors to a far wider membership. And, as the Emperor's vanity grew, so too did the financial rewards for his neophytes, with millions of sesterces handed out to those who were in the right place at the right time. Before long, the effects of this very particular form of largesse would even flow over into Pompeian society, as Nero's sycophants became cheerleaders for the Emperor's cause beyond the confines of theatre.

In AD 61, the majority of Pompeians were more inclined than the Roman mob to forgive Poppaea, out of local loyalty; yet the sight of the first of these Neronian gauleiters strutting their undeserved wealth around the city and condescending to their betters must have roused fierce resentment in some quarters. As time passed, and the Emperor's credibility declined, such sentiments only grew. The signs of factionalism are subtle and elusive, but one cluster of graffiti points towards the punning mockery that may have been directed at the claquers behind their back. Close to some cocky pronouncements by the Augustiani themselves are found messages for or about the prostitutes Aphrodite, Ias, Timele and others in which they are called 'classy'. The original Latin is 'augustiana'.

For all their pride in being the classy favourites of the Emperor, in the eyes of others the members of the claque were nothing more than whores. But for the moment, it was the whores and *cinaedi* who ruled the roost.

CHAPTER 7

When Will our Fears Be at Rest?

February AD 62

Delayed by business in the city the previous afternoon, Fabius Secundus had only reached his vineyards as dusk was falling and had allowed himself the dubious luxury of staying overnight on the farm. His back now ached from the hard pallet and his head from the rough wine he had been served, but he was glad to have done it: on crisp mornings like this, walking through the fields and orchards, and along the country roads, he understood how fortunate he was to be a citizen of Pompeii. To be part of a rural world of honest toil, which Nature blessed, yet to live in a city of some sophistication in which to spend one's profits; all this under the wise governance of Rome and her emperor. What more could a man ask for?

Everywhere that Secundus looked on his way back to the Vesuvius Gate, he saw beauty and industry. High up on the steep mountainside, where his own land lay, the workers had been busy about their February tasks of hoeing, and tying back the vines that had come loose during the winter winds. Lower down, gangs of slaves laboured, thick on the ground and well marshalled by their vilici: *up to eighty to each* iugerum *of land, working in chained rows, they dug irrigation trenches or planted out sapling trees. Soon, they would have to turn their hands to sowing corn, for with the fifth of the month the window during which the seeds of the first harvest had to be in the ground was coming to a close.*

And the fifth of the month had arrived: it did not take the bustle of activity within the city walls to remind Secundus of that, though it explained why he had not lingered on Vesuvius. For 5 February was the anniversary of Augustus being named Father of the Nation, and, as though that were not enough cause for celebration, in Pompeii it was also des-ignated as the feast day in honour of the city's own guardian spirits. It

*would mean two sacrifices rather than one: those readying the sanctified
'salted grain' that would be sprinkled over the backs of the victims before
their ritual death would be twice as busy today.*

*Secundus had hoped to have a quiet word this morning with the freed-
man Venerius, who was responsible for so much of the smooth running of
the colony's administration – from the rental property that was let out to
citizens, to the organisation of the ceremonials. He should have guessed
that Venerius would be too busy to talk. There he was, fussing around,
desperately trying to ensure that all those citizens who wished to attend
the service were installed in the temple in a timely manner. Secundus
watched as the freedman chided Caecilius Jucundus for trying to get the
senior magistrate's signature on one last document for the day. He saw the
auctioneer leave for home in high dudgeon, while Claudius Verus hurriedly
donned his ceremonial garb and made his way through the crowd to the
altar, all the while swearing that he would never again witness another
deal for the infuriating man.*

*For lesser mortals, there was no longer room to squeeze into the temple
and Secundus hung back, listening but relishing the opportunity to gaze
out over the forum as it stood, empty and magnificent. What better memorial could there be to Augustus's memory than this fine spectacle? He had
turned Rome from a city of brick into one of marble and, while Pompeii
could not reach those levels, its forum was a fair attempt to emulate the
grandeur of the capital. Secundus scanned the vaulted portico that arced
around the southern end of the public space, two storeys high. To the
west lay the precinct of the old Temple of Apollo with its more recent
embellishments; to the south the three buildings of the civic administration
with the old basilica on either side; and to the east, the Augustan ensemble.*

*To think that he, Fabius Secundus, had first seen this place as a slave,
awed and terrified. Yet here he was now, a respected citizen of a flourishing
city, a wealthy merchant and an Augustalis. The thanks that he gave to
Augustus needed no sacrifices, so he headed for home.*

Unlike the rest of the forum, which was faced with porticos, the
narrow north side was instead dominated by a Capitoline temple
that was aligned with Vesuvius, and whose dedication to Jupiter
Optimus Maximus had been reconfirmed in AD 37. On either side
of its imposing bulk, two monumental arches completed the

encirclement of the forum in further emulation of Rome's grandeur.[1] And to complement the brilliant white of this centrepiece, the plaster in which the rest of the forum buildings were coated, to conceal their tufa construction, was decorated with a clever illusion of veined marble. The result was a source of enormous civic pride.

To the worshippers who gathered on the morning of 5 February AD 62, the physical proof of Augustus's determination to return Rome and her Empire to the straight path of *pietas* must have appeared capable of withstanding any assault. But the religious faith that the buildings were intended to embody might well have seemed more fragile. With his usual satirical brio, Juvenal would later write, 'Today not even children ... believe all that stuff about ghosts, or underground kingdoms and rivers, or black frogs croaking in the waters of the Styx, or thousands of dead men ferried across by one small skiff.' Juvenal was doing no more than echo the thoughts of many Roman intellectuals of the period who expressed equally rational views about the pantheon of gods and the catalogue of supernatural events associated with them. Cicero had been careful to articulate such views only in his letters while paying lip service in his public speeches to the strongly superstitious sensibilities of the popular mass. Ovid expressed his own wry cynicism with even more caution when he wrote, 'The existence of gods is convenient and, since it is convenient, let us assume it.' Nevertheless, if there were worshippers in the forum on that day who doubted the power of the gods, their atheism was shortly due to be shaken.

The morning of 5 February saw preparations for two sacrifices. Presiding over the ceremony was a magistrate, who combined in his person priestly, political and judicial functions: it was his technical dexterity that counted, rather than any supposed special gift of mediation with the divine. The gods had very precise and stringent expectations of what they would receive in return for fulfilling their side of the bargain by ensuring mankind's well-being: to disappoint them with shoddy service was to cross the most retributive of masters. Whilst the written accounts of religious rites from Rome are rare and somewhat opaque, paintings of animal sacrifice from the walls of the House of the Vettii and elsewhere in Pompeii, as well as the striking scene carved in bas relief on the marble altar of the temple itself, help in imagining how a typical ceremony might have begun (Plate 11).

Crowds would have gathered as the figure who was leading the rite, Lucretius Valens perhaps, or the fast-rising Claudius Verus, who was a senior magistrate at the time, raised a fold of his toga over his head to form a cowl out of respect for the deity and uttered the cry that initiated the proceedings: '*Procul, o procul este profani.*' All who are profane – by which was meant any who were not citizens and might wish to make malevolent magic during the rites – should leave. Attendants hovered, ready to proffer the bronze instruments of sacrifice or to pour water from jugs as required.[2]

As well as the presiding priest, there were others present who had reason to feel a certain stage fright. Central to events was the *haruspex*, whose duty it was to check the entrails of the animal once it had been slaughtered and to monitor the proper conduct of the rites throughout. Whilst any laxity in this supervisory role could prove disastrous, his greatest concern was probably that the quivering mass of entrails might slip from his grasp as he offered them up. Any mistakes or flaws in etiquette along the way and the sacrifice could be repeated, but an error at this last moment and the auspices could not be worse: ill fortune was bound to follow. A greater burden still fell on the shoulders of the other key participant in the ceremony: the man – by profession perhaps a butcher or blacksmith, but certainly someone strong and familiar with wielding a hammer – who would lead the sacrificial victim to the altar and dispatch it with his own hands.[3]

The contract was awarded by the council of *decurions* on what was probably a five-yearly term, and may also have involved the supply of an appropriate animal for each occasion. Rules governed each god's preference for sex, colour and especially species, which was often rooted in the personal interests of the diety in question: Bacchus, for example, had a vengeful taste for the flesh of the goats that ate his vines. On this occasion the stakes, should a mistake be made, were higher. The deified Augustus was due a castrated pig, but the *lares* of the city demanded nothing less than an ox, a beast of such value that even the accidental killing of one had until not long before incurred the same mandatory death penalty as murder.

Stripped to the waist and with the shaft of his great hammer slung over his shoulder, the contractor feigned nonchalance, but kept a firm grip as he led the horned bull forward by its nose. He knew that the sacrifice would be invalidated if one of the victims ran away, but even the slightest hint that the animals had not proceeded willingly to their deaths would be interpreted as a bad omen. Spectators liked to see slack in the rope between the beast and its guide, just as they liked their gladiators to meet their fates unflinchingly. Both the bull and its smaller companion, a hog, were already adorned with a ceremonial sash, and everyone would have been relieved to see the latter trotting ahead as though oblivious to the crowd; the contractor, especially so. It was not allowed for him to stun his charges before delivering a *coup de grâce* – only a single clean blow was deemed acceptable. With such precision required at every stage, there would surely have been great tension in the air.

When the first, barely perceptible pulse of energy rose from the depths of the earth, Pompeii was tranquil, the great crowd assembled in the forum attentive to the prayers offered to the statue that stood above the temple's altar, and to the wine that was poured over the ox's white head, trickling down its cheeks like tears of blood. The animals sensed it first: the crowd of pigeons that rose as one with great kerfuffle; the mule tethered to a hole in the pavement that now kicked out, snorted and snapped its teeth in the air; the placid pig in the temple, which squealed suddenly, then launched itself against the legs of those who sought to hold it, and bolted to a hiding place far under the altar.

In buildings across the city, disbelieving eyes watched as cracks opened in the walls around them and daylight shone through. Precious vases and phials jittered to the edge of shelves and crashed over; furniture rattled across the floor. Those caught in their homes tried to stand, but lost their balance and fell to the ground; those old enough to have lived through quakes before simply lay down until the worst had passed. In his house, where he had dallied to count his coins, the auctioneer Jucundus closed his eyes tight and pitied those in the forum.

Even before the bull began its unearthly lowing, the haruspex had seen the beaten bronze tray in his hands begin to quiver, its polished surface throwing off shards of light. He knew that, beside him, the magistrate Claudius Verus was speaking, but he could neither hear nor respond. At that moment, the strange silence of the forum was broken by a sound like the distant snapping of twigs, filling the air from every direction, then a rumble that rose until finally it was upon them in a terrible crescendo, shaking them from within. The ground itself became liquid and began its mad dance; the pavements rolled and some thought they saw the streets themselves become a flowing wave. Time and space stretched.

Then, in an instant, the fear that had frozen the crowd exploded and they scattered, crying out in despair. No longer was the butcher holding the bull's horns to control the animal but clinging to them for dear life, the worshippers around him tossed like mariners in a storm.

Even as the marble inscribed with the words 'Jupiter Optimus Maximus' sprang from its fixings and crashed to the ground, foolish instinct made some seek shelter indoors, while those within hauled their way hand over fist towards any door in sight. Minutes passed, but the noise and terror did not subside as men and buildings alike reached breaking point. The slave girl Pherusa watched as her hated master disappeared under the collapsing weight of a ceiling. Wallowing in the deserted baths, Hypsaeus would have sworn that the plunge pool split open and swallowed every drop of water before spewing it back out. From the harbour came the sound of splintering timbers as boats of all sizes were thrown against the harbour wall. Colonnades that had stood for centuries swayed and fell, walls tore apart like paper or coughed out great scoops of brick and stone into piles of rubble. Even the noblest buildings of the forum slumped sideways like drunkards, awaiting only a feather's blow to crumble entirely. To anyone with a head clear enough to take in what was happening it would have seemed that the whole city was collapsing in on itself.

Finally, the last juddering heave gave way to a queasy steadiness, and the clouds of dust began to settle. Only the sounds of human misery could be heard, punctuated by the occasional crump of buildings as they surrendered in their struggle to remain standing. At the south end of the forum, smoke billowed from the curia building; as Venerius turned to the north, a lintel above the entrance to a distant shop gave way. Those struggling to free Jucundus from the rubble leapt free, but the auctioneer himself was killed where he lay.

Amid the groans and wails of sobbing children, a chorus of calls began that was taken up by men and women from one side of the city to the other, each more desperate than the last to locate their loved ones among the debris. Already Magonianus the surgeon was seeking out those whose wounds he could treat. Working alone, though, he could give scant solace to those injured in body or mind. For many, time simply refused to restart.

Then, from far out in the bay, the first of a series of towering waves surged around the delta, towards the shore and upstream as far as the Sarno Bridge. Already weakened by the quake, when the third wave struck, the bridge's piers gave way, and it fell into the eddying waters below. Behind the port, the lower-lying warehouses were flattened and the rest inundated. As the waters retreated, dragging their plunder with them, those in the city looked down on the dry bed of the estuary for a few moments before the sea closed over it once more.

Fabius Secundus, trapped beneath the ruins of his home, heard the roar of water but could not see its effects. All that was visible to him, through a gap in the tumbled stones, was the wrecked Temple of Venus, whose statue had come to rest against a column. Now, jarred by the impact of the waves below, it slowly pivoted and toppled to the ground. As he drifted out of consciousness, Secundus vowed that in the unlikely event he survived, he would raise an image in her honour more glorious than the one that had been lost.

The earthquake that struck Pompeii and the surrounding region on 5 February AD 62, is thought to have measured over 7.5 on the Richter scale.[4] In all likelihood it was the result of an upward flow of magma within the earth's crust along the geological fault line that ran under Vesuvius: having vented its fury, it then subsided before finally forcing its way out in dramatic fashion seventeen years later. Seneca, at work on his book of *Natural Questions*, recorded a summary of its impact: 'Pompeii, the famous city in Campania, has been laid low by an earthquake which also disturbed all adjacent areas ... even the structures that are left standing are shaky,' he began. Whilst the region was known for its minor earth tremors, no one alive had experienced anything approaching the present catastrophe, which came as a particular shock since the earth was generally held to be dormant during the winter months. The disaster would be talked about far and wide. Although it was said at first that Naples had escaped with only light damage, it soon became clear that this meant only that no public buildings had collapsed, as the private housing stock had suffered considerably. And Naples was twenty miles away from the epicentre of the event.[5]

In the cities that bore the brunt of the devastation, Pompeii and Herculaneum, the archaeological evidence suggests that scarcely a single building was untouched. Temples lay shattered, houses crushed into a mess of rubble and the thick city walls and gatehouses, which had withstood siege engines on more than one occasion in the past, were breached. The immediate aftermath would have verged on chaos, as fires started by toppled oil lamps raged throughout the city. In the absence of any effective emergency measures, the population struggled to comprehend the human cost.

Those who abandoned their homes for a provisional life under canvas acted wisely, since during the following days and weeks further aftershocks were likely and even those buildings left standing would have been unsafe for habitation. Certainly that was how the majority of the inhabitants of Puteoli, modern-day Pozzuoli, reacted in 1980 when their city suffered a similar if somewhat less severe earthquake. It is common for those who have lived through the trauma of a quake to be reluctant to re-enter their homes even once they have been secured; in Pozzuoli's case, the camps around its perimeter were occupied for a full nine months or more, with the population only venturing into the city itself during daylight hours to conduct their business.

Much of the physical evidence of destruction in Pompeii has been obscured or erased by subsequent restoration work, while the chroniclers who touched on the events of AD 62 summarised only a handful of anecdotes from the great tome of personal testimony that would have been available. But tantalising indications of the conditions that prevailed after this first natural disaster have surfaced from the city that was buried half a generation later: a bas-relief of the moment the quake struck and its immediate effects, glimpses of dedicatory inscriptions that point to the most pressing restoration needs, hurriedly erected buttressing concealed behind later walls. And by drawing on analogies with more recent and more fully documented quakes it is possible to fill the lacunae in the ancient records.

Seismological events and mankind's response to them have changed little or not at all in the two thousand years that constitute less than the blink of an eye in geological time. From very recent earthquakes in Kashmir and Iran to those that afflicted Assisi and Pozzuoli in Italy within living memory, and back to the great catastrophes of San Francisco at the turn of the nineteenth century, and Lisbon a hundred and fifty years earlier, the psychological and physical impact is similar and quite comparable to that which would have prevailed in Pompeii during the days following the Festival of Augustus.

Tsunamis of varying scale and destructiveness are a well-attested side effect of earthquakes of comparable magnitude, in coastal areas, and the bridge over the River Sarno was indisputably destroyed at this time in one way or another. Similarly, Seneca's allusion to sheep dying in their hundreds during the earthquake, for example, seems to confirm the link between the earthquake and the eruption of Vesuvius seventeen years later, since there are many instances documented in Iceland where entire flocks have succumbed to the clouds of sulphurous gas belched out of volcanoes. If the earth on the hillsides where the flocks grazed had recently been watered by rain, then fissures would indeed have opened up, to discharge the fatal fumes.

Other stories might have had a less obvious source. The bather who believed that he had witnessed the ground open to swallow and regurgitate the water in which he sat could be accounted for by the hallucinations that are triggered by disturbances of the inner ear that regularly occur during severe quakes.[6] Reports of yawning chasms that open up in the street and appear ready to swallow the observer before closing again without a trace are familiar delusions from modern earthquakes, while all manner of other surreal occurrences with the same physiological cause are also well attested. In any case the psychological impact of the disaster and its toll on casualties would have been profound. Almost everyone would have been nursing physical injuries, cuts and bruises at the very least, and had the quake occurred today, around a third of the survivors would also have been diagnosed as suffering from post-traumatic stress disorder. For some it would become a long-term mental condition and for most it would be at least a year before the numbness and despair, the sudden outbursts of anger or panic or inconsolable grief, began to fade. Seneca's evocation of a city in which men and women wandered in madness was no exaggeration.

When the community within the ruined city sought for symbols of divine anger at some failure or disobedience, they could have found them on the floor of the *comitium*, in the mangled remains of the tablets on which Pompeii's laws were written. We know for sure that they had to be recast soon afterwards.

The death toll would have been huge. That the quake occurred in the early afternoon, when many people were out of doors, at least minimised the number of people who were vulnerable to falling masonry; one earthquake in Roman Italy was said to have cost the lives of twenty thousand when the theatre in which they were assembled collapsed. Nevertheless, in light of the extent of the physical damage to Pompeii, it seems inconceivable that the number of dead did not run into the high hundreds or low thousands at the very least. Quakes of a similar severity in modern times have resulted in large numbers of fatalities, especially where construction techniques still followed ancient principles or when measures to cushion the impact had not been implemented: thirty-five thousand died in Calabria in the nineteenth century, whilst as late as 1960 there were twelve thousand deaths when the Moroccan city of Agadir was destroyed.

Regrettably, there are no records of which Pompeians died on that terrible day or in its aftermath. Only in the case of Caecilius Jucundus does the evidence seem to suggest that he was probably a victim: the sequence of contracts negotiated by him and recorded in the archive wax tablets terminates abruptly a few days before 5 February AD 62. There is pathos in this sudden silence, and it is perhaps telling that the bas-reliefs that are so informative about the post-quake condition of buildings were sculpted for the altar in what had been his home (Plates 12 and 14). Perhaps they were commissioned by his heirs to commemorate the loss of the man who had laid down the foundations of family wealth on which they would build their political careers in years to come. But for the moment, such honouring of the dead was a long way off.

Amid the bewilderment, for hours and days there would have been little realistic sense of what the final death toll might be. Figures would have been provisional and poorly collated, with news slow to arrive from the outlying areas. Hope and helplessness would have fought for the upper hand as the survivors dug frantically, hampered by insufficient equipment and resources, to rescue those still trapped beneath the rubble. Pompeii could have expected little help from neighbouring cities. Herculaneum had been devastated and Nuceria had also been affected, and was probably unable to provide immediate assistance to its rival, even if it had been willing. With bridges down and the roads broken, the surest means of bringing aid to Pompeii would have been by ship, and the naval docks at Misenum were no more than a couple of hours away.

In some respects, it was perhaps fortunate that the earthquake struck outside the sailing season. It being February, most of the trireme and quadreme crews would have been assigned to land duty and available for redeployment, whilst the navy could supply the ropes, pulleys and grappling hooks needed for a concerted rescue operation. As a first-hand witness of the eruption of AD 79, Pliny the Younger would take great pains to glorify the selfless heroism of his uncle, the admiral of the fleet, in acting on his own initiative to launch an expedition to take refugees off the beaches that lay within range of the volcano's fire and toxic gases. Of course, there is no reason to suppose that such humanitarian missions did not constitute part of the fleet's standing orders. However, with the majority of its ships in dry dock and the naval personnel dispersed, it may have taken some time – days even – for the fleet to prepare and launch a relief operation.

In the meantime, anarchy ruled, and the unscrupulous benefited from it. Theft would generally have been rife in the ruins of the city and little attention would have been paid to the usual notices written up on house frontages asking for assistance in tracking down stolen items, as in the case of one copper pot that went missing from a poor family home. Even the undertakers who laid out the dead must have been tempted to take their chance with any jewellery and money that was left on corpses – the Roman legal digests make clear that their profession was habitually suspected of corrupt behaviour, even at the best of times. Popular opinion would also have taken little convincing that, more widely, the magpie instincts of all slaves were bound to come to the fore now that the old controls had been loosened. Amid all these other anxieties, as the freezing nights of early February closed in over the great mass of men, women and children, the most pressing need by far was for water, food and shelter.[7]

The bas-relief in Caecilius Jucundus's atrium shows the collapsed Vesuvius Gate and beside it the city's central 'water castle', which channelled the city's supply down a gentle slope. Whilst the water tower appears to have proved remarkably resilient – unsurprisingly, perhaps, for such a squat and functional box of reinforced brick – the same cannot be said of the infrastructure of plumbing and water tanks that fanned out from it. The aqueduct itself would have been highly vulnerable to disruption, but until remedial action was taken, whatever water did continue to reach Pompeii would either have bubbled up uselessly from severed water pipes or else dribbled from the decapitated columns atop which the storage tanks had been situated to ensure that pressure was maintained. In the great vestibule of the forum's basilica stood an open well from which water could be drawn by means of a hydraulic wheel. It was a practical resource, certainly, but also a symbolic reminder of the archaic basis for urban life. Yet even as the people of Pompeii rediscovered the value of wells such as this, and of the cisterns in which they gathered rainwater and which may have been only lightly fractured, for most of the homeless there would have been little alternative but to scoop up the liquid from the ordure-ridden depressions where it pooled and make the best use of it they could. As always in such circumstances, even with organised emergency relief, disease threatened to rapidly overtake injury as the major cause of death: typhus and dysentery would have been only too ready to seize their chance.

The law tablets of Roman cities included specific measures to deal with food shortages, outlawing the hoarding of grain and the monopolistic control of prices in times of need. Considering that agricultural production rested mainly in the hands of the Pompeian elite, with most of the surplus of recent harvests stored in granaries on their estates or in the warehouses operated by their freedmen, it was a strikingly egalitarian solution to the problem. Yet even tapping into the grain reserves and rationing the distribution of bread from the city's bakeries would have been unlikely to meet the nutritional needs of the population for very long. With the sowing of the spring crop interrupted by the quake, the city would have had to plan for up to six or seven months before another full harvest poured in. It may have adopted the same radical solution as Rome had during the grain shortage of AD 6. Then, in order to reduce the number of mouths that needed feeding to a manageable level, all but essential slaves were expelled to a hundred miles from the city. The fortunate ones would have been shipped out to the estates of their owners, but the vast majority were left to forage for themselves.[8]

Such a policy may have benefited the city in one way, but by depriving it of the majority of its manual labour at a time of such need, it would have hampered rebuilding and repair work severely. It would have taken only a cursory inspection of the city blocks situated between the forum and the city walls to the north, where many large aristocratic homes were to be found but which also housed a cross-section of the population, to reveal the scale of the challenge. Along what we now call the Street of Mercury, hardly a building had escaped damage: in its vicinity, the houses known as the Anchor, the Dioscuri and the Centaur were all in need of very substantial repairs. The style of masonry employed in the Herculaneum Gate, next along the wall to the Vesuvius Gate in an anticlockwise direction, indicates that it too would have had to be rebuilt from the ground up.

At night, during the weeks and months that followed, animals were free to enter the city and wander the streets in search of food, though competition from the human population for any scraps would have been intense. For those of a nervous or superstitious disposition, it also meant one less barrier between them and the spirits of the dead whose numbers were swelling by the hour and against whom only the *pomerium* now stood as protection. Confronted with so many demands on their attention, whatever magistrates or civic leaders had survived, and were mobile and competent, would have been hard-pressed to manage the provision of even the citizens' basic physical needs, let alone worry about their psychic security.

With the makeshift mortuaries full and those responsible for treating the injured unable to cope with the demands made of them, some thoughts would have turned to the question of burial and how the traditional rites of death could possibly be maintained. The prospect of wild animals scavenging the bodies of the dead or near-dead meant there would have been no let-up in the search for bodies or survivors. But eventually, as the pleading voices began to fade, the prospect of loved ones suffering the indignity of mass burial or cremation would have edged the fierce determination that had sustained the rescue efforts towards bitter anger.

Once the hope of finding survivors had faded, the citizens of Pompeii would have turned their attention to restoring what they could of the city. The situation in the area to the north of the forum was repeated everywhere, with the blocks around the amphitheatre to the south-east perhaps worst affected; in due course this area would be cleared completely and given over to crop-growing. In the north-east, one large block of housing was so completely destroyed that no one in later years could bring themselves to replace it, and public baths would take its place.

It is possible for archaeologists to trace a pattern of damage and repair in the walls of Pompeii where the replaced plaster has fallen from the ruins of the post-eruption city to expose the stone beneath. One characteristic is the unmistakable 'scoop' effect, where the corners of buildings remained self-supporting but the walls crumbled in the middle and needed reconstruction, using more makeshift materials. The type of damage shown in the Jucundus relief, however, is more dramatic still and the naïve style of the carving has led many to dismiss its version of entire walls and buildings skewed to a forty-five degree angle. But comparison with photographs of the immediate aftermath of the 1904 San Francisco quake in particular suggests that, improbable as it may appear, entire walls constructed of stone and mortar really could lean so precipitously, yet remain standing.

No one in their right mind, of course, could have imagined that it was possible for buildings in this state to be simply pushed upright and become viable again, but as the seismic aftershocks continued to tweak the nerves of the people of Pompeii, sanity would have been in short supply. Men who, an hour before, had owned property worth hundreds of thousands of sesterces would now have been found staring in disbelief at buildings on the verge of collapse. Destitution threatened. Insurance in the Roman world began and ended with the emperor's limited guarantee to make good any losses to shipping that carried grain; household cover was unheard of. Even today, in predominantly secular societies, policies are carefully worded to exclude 'acts of God'.[9]

In the cities of Italy, it was normally necessary to consult the council of *decurions* and receive their approval before any demolition work took place. But, in such circumstances, with many of the elite dead, injured or fled, would it have been possible even to convene the council? And if so, would its deliberations not have ground to a standstill beneath the torrent of urgent appeals? Even the authority of the magistrates, and their ability to maintain basic order, would have been sorely tested. There was little incentive for the citizens of Pompeii to act with the communal good in mind as long as there remained even a shadow of a chance to salvage their own property. With so many demands on them, how would magistrates have monitored the fair distribution of supplies or medical care that, in normal circumstances, were provided on the basis of ability to pay. Disputes are likely to have flared up everywhere.

Perhaps it was with this in mind that the incumbent senior magistrate, Claudius Verus, announced that a festival of games was to be staged, less than a month after the earthquake. It amounted to an audacious attempt to raise the spirits of what remained of the population with a show of normality – as normal as could be, since large sections of the amphitheatre seating had collapsed and the ban on gladiators was still in force. Where the games were staged and who performed is not recorded, though we do know that a distribution of money was planned, but only 'if time allows'. Such moves were no more than placebos; there were to be no easy answers.

Still, it is tempting to imagine the friends who formed Verus's political clique rallying round in his moment of need. Like him, most of them were the descendants of imperial freedmen. Whether by dint of their contacts or the sheer determination that such a background bred into them, they would become mainstays of the community in the difficult years ahead – years through which it would take strong nerves to stay in Pompeii, but during which there would be great opportunities for the bold to flourish.[10] As the first of Admiral Anicetus's boats finally nosed their way through the flotsam into the harbour of the stricken town, on perhaps 7 or 8 February, many in Pompeii would have felt that they were already too late.

It seemed to Diogenes that Pompeii had become one vast mine. Everywhere a scintilla of hope remained, men were delving – levering stones and burrowing down. In the fields to the north of the walls, the off-duty marines were digging trenches for a camp, while round by the Vesuvius Gate, his own men were digging a pit for the speedy disposal of the bodies of slaves and paupers. The ranks of the city's paupers had swelled in the last four days. The strain on the resources of the burial clubs was such that many could no longer pay for their members to have a proper place and plaque in a columbarium. *And where there were no men digging, scavenging dogs took their place, foraging beneath fallen buildings with a ravening hunger for whatever flesh they could find.*

Over the years, Diogenes had acquired a hard stomach, but even he had taken to holding a scented cloth to his mouth and nose when he entered the city. What sickened him the most, though, was that in the midst of all this death they still demanded that he add to the toll in his sideline as city executioner. After the first forty-eight hours of anarchy, the following two days had seen half a dozen slaves sent to him by their owners and as many others by the interim authorities, who needed to demonstrate their ruthless resolve. One of his apprentices had been among the convicts, caught relieving corpses of their jewellery. Diogenes only wished someone could tell him what he was supposed to use to mount the crucifixions: there was so little wood coming into town that they even had to build the pyres from salvage.

Not that crime would be stopped that way, in any case. Everyone was at it, bending the rules at the very least. In a couple of days it would be the Festival of Feralia and it wouldn't surprise him to see the mourners snaffle the cinnamon and frankincense from the pyres. Even in such straightened circumstances there would be offerings left to nourish the ancestors: food on a platter beside the tomb, wine poured down the pipe to dampen the ashes, maybe a bunch of violets to brighten the afterlife. Perhaps this year the elite would make their gifts less indecently lavish, but the starving would have few scruples about feeding themselves with what was only being wasted on the dead. With a shanty town being erected across the pomerium, *nothing was sacrosanct.*

The sight of smoke rising from the campfires of the clumsily erected dwellings made Diogenes consider how he too might exploit the current situation. It broke his heart to think that so many fine houses now stood deserted inside the city walls, where he was so unfairly forbidden to live. With the owners of these properties dead, the heirs were often men who never came to Pompeii and they would be unlikely to start now. Such houses would be sold for a song. And now that death was everywhere, what was to stop him living within the pomerium? After all, the authorities needed him: usually, they scarcely acknowledged his existence; now let them show their appreciation.

It had been backbreaking work, but he'd done the family of Vestorius Priscus proud. Diogenes watched as they filed past the young aedile and paid their last respects: he had laid out the boy's broken frame in such a manner as to cause the least possible distress. Priscus's name was spoken once by each mourner in final greeting and handfuls of earth thrown onto his corpse. Already Diogenes had snipped a sliver of flesh off his crushed thigh to be buried apart from what would soon be his ashes. Now he removed the coins that covered the late aedile's eyes and eased open the lids so that he could gaze sightlessly up into the grey sky as the flames lapped around him. Passers-by looked on with mild resentment: this vision of normality had obviously required special dispensation.

From where he stood, Diogenes could hear the hammers ringing out on stone and the calls of the marine rescue teams as they dug out even more corpses, a fair proportion of which would be claimed by families who considered themselves no less worthy of a decent funeral than the Vestorii.

There were unlikely to be many more cases like Fabius Secundus, the miracle man who had been hauled out earlier this morning from amidst the worst destruction in the city, close to the Temple of Venus, where a leak from a water tank had sustained him for days. But in any case Diogenes could read the signs around him. Even when the last of the earthquake dead had been taken care of, disease would continue to provide him with an overwhelming supply of work. The time was fast approaching when he would strike with his demands.

— VII —

According to the Roman code of military ethics, the conqueror of an enemy city was expected to show mercy to the vanquished. There was no guarantee that its inhabitants would all escape enslavement, though some might even be offered Roman citizenship; but the fabric of their homes and in particular their temples should be respected. Any failure to observe the code risked incurring the wrath of the gods. The ill-fated journeys of Odysseus and the other Homeric heroes on their way back home to Greece was accounted for by the lack of mercy and discrimination they had shown when Troy fell. Similarly, the younger Scipio had brought down long-lasting misfortune on Rome by his merciless sack of Carthage. It was to that moment of impiety that later critics dated the beginning of Rome's moral decline.

To pass the plough over ground where once a city had stood was an almost unimaginable act of erasure – a travesty that no one in AD 62 could have countenanced for a city like Pompeii. Yet her temples lay in ruins, damaged beyond the ingenuity of even the cruellest general. Some areas within the city walls had suffered such complete annihilation that there was little will to rebuild on the part of their owners, and the cleared plots would eventually be ploughed up for cultivation.

The great Augustus had recognised the responsibility that was incumbent upon central government to provide support to communities stricken by earthquakes and is on record as having staged relief efforts at Paphos. Similarly, a handsome brass coin was struck in Rome in AD 22 to commemorate the compassion that Tiberius had shown to Sardis and eleven other Asian cities, granting them ten million sesterces and the five-year suspension of all payment of taxes to Rome. There is nothing, however, to suggest that such assistance to Pompeii was forthcoming from Nero. If Pompeians had hoped that the growing influence Poppaea exercised over the Emperor, now that she was his wife, would induce him to come to the aid of her home town, they were disappointed. The Emperor had other problems to occupy him. Indeed, it must have seemed to many observers in the early AD 60s that it was preferable to be a British city overrun and burn d to the ground by rebellious natives, or a Parthian outpost in Armenia viciously destroyed after a siege by the Roman general Corbulo, than a loyal Campanian colony. The former, at least, were certain to rise again, while Pompeii languished in uncertainty.

It cannot be disputed that there was good reason for the Emperor to be distracted at this time. Aside from campaigns abroad, the previous three years had seen many changes at the imperial court and, by AD 62, the removal and replacement of nearly all those who had been closest to Nero since the beginning of his reign were almost complete. A new generation of ambitious courtiers, who sought personal advantage through their uncritical and unprincipled backing of the Emperor, were challenging the supremacy of advisors such as Seneca and Burrus. Matters came to a head over the question of what was to be done with Nero's unwanted wife Octavia. Poppaea was impatient to see Octavia officially ousted so that she could assume her place on the throne beside Nero; yet, as the daughter of Claudius, Octavia provided Nero with his last remaining link to real legitimacy as emperor.

Of the Emperor's two wily old counsellors, Burrus had always been the more outspoken, yet on this occasion the Praetorian Prefect was forthright even by his own uncompromising standards. Whether weary of demeaning himself in the role of sycophant, or finally exasperated by the persistent foolishness of his young charge, Burrus had been incautiously direct: if Nero divorced his wife, then he should be decent enough to resign the Empire that came as her dowry. It was a step too far. To a twenty-five-year-old emperor who was beginning to embrace delusions of divinity, such a suggestion sounded close to blasphemy and closer still to treachery.

Nero did not need to overexert himself in search of a solution to the problem Burrus presented: Claudius and Brittanicus both provided precedents for poisoning and Nero was always said to have been quite shameless in praising the virtues of mushrooms, with a knowing wink. Yet the precise method of murder chosen on this occasion showed a characteristically Neronian combination of ruthless flair and guilty equivocation that served only to make it all the more distasteful: the fatal dose was contained in a throat medicine delivered to the old man along with heartfelt expressions of concern for his health. Burrus knew his ward only too well, and one can imagine how he must have gagged when swallowing the deadly, gift-wrapped tincture.

Seneca's position was equally threatened and he saw the signs all too clearly, quoting an old proverb in a letter to a friend: 'To the swordsman's acute gaze, a look on the face, a twist of the wrist, a certain inclination of the body are enough to give him warning of his enemies intentions.' Unfortunately, his petition to Nero, asking that he be allowed to retire from his position as the 'first friend' of the Emperor, fell on deaf ears. Nevertheless, the wily old politician and sharp-eyed businessman became insistently reclusive, turning callers away from his morning *salutatio* and spending ever more time away from Rome.

With Burrus gone and Seneca increasingly absent, the divorce from Octavia was speedily accomplished, thanks in part to the good offices of Ofonius Tigellinus, the rising star at court, who had inherited one of the two positions of Prefect of Praetorians that had previously been combined under Burrus. Success in this delicate matter was a further step in Tigellinus's rise to notoriety and he insinuated his way still deeper into Nero's trust and affection, first by orchestrating the suppression of the popular demonstrations that came onto the streets in protest at the mistreatment of Octavia, and then by getting rid of the Empress altogether. Accused of planning a *coup d'état* in conspiracy with the same Anicetus who had plotted Agrippina's murder with Nero, she was put to death for treason. Tacitus would later reflect, 'As the ills of the state grew worse, the forces of good were declining.'

Writing in didactic vein during the earlier, sunny years of Nero's reign, Seneca had attempted to define for his pupil the single quality that distinguished a good ruler from a tyrant. His answer was *clementia*, the same virtue that saw defeated cities left standing. It was a matter of self-discipline. '*Clementia*', Seneca wrote, 'means restraining the mind from vengeance when it has the power to take it, or the leniency of a superior towards an inferior.' But as the wrath of General Corbulo was let loose against the cities he besieged and conquered in the course of his campaign against Parthia, and the machinery of a primitive police state made its presence felt in Rome and elsewhere, '*clementia*' was in short supply.

Nero's new guide, his 'conspirator in crime', led the Emperor deeper into depravity. Tyranny in all its manifestations was on the rise and the atmosphere of fear became increasingly pervasive. In the process, the Emperor was engulfed by the very paranoia that his own actions were propagating. It was the same vicious circle as so many of his predecessors had manoeuvred in vain to escape. Wearied of the constant anxieties of government, Tiberius had retired from Rome entirely, isolating himself in his palace on the seaward side of the isle of Capri, to indulge his more outré tastes in sexual voyeurism, and leaving Sejanus, then the Prefect of the Praetorian Guard, to misrule in his place. The plots and counter-plots that swirled around Sejanus's caretaker government led to bloodbaths that consumed most of the imperial family. Later emperors would defensively assert, 'No one believes there are plots, until the emperor is dead.' It was certainly the paranoiac's maxim by which Caligula had ruled. Acclaimed as emperor by the Praetorians when still in his youth, he had witnessed most of his family being picked off around him by political vultures. His response had been to channel his energies into a witch-hunt that saw great swathes of the senate killed or cruelly humiliated before their tolerance finally ran out and Caligula was murdered. Between Caligula's reign and Nero's own lay that of Claudius, and his life too had probably ended in murder. Was Nero now destined for a similar end?

For a ruler constantly troubled by dark imaginings of assassination, any potential prophylactic was to be seized upon. The drug *theriaca* was a sophisticated cure-all with particular efficacy as a pre-emptive antidote to poisoning. Originally created to the specifications of King Mithridates VI of Pontus in the first century BC, its ingredients and preparation were a closely guarded secret. Pliny recounts how, in the chaotic wake of his victory over King Pontus, Pompey had made it his priority to capture the defeated ruler's medical treatises and gain possession of the secret compound of fifty-four ingredients, many of them toxins administered in small doses in order to develop the patient's resistance. The danger posed by everything from poisoned arrows, insect stings and snake bites, to the symptoms of haemorrhaging and dysentery, was supposedly mitigated by regular use. By the latter part of the first century AD, poets were recommending their readers to 'Take a dose, before meals, of the stuff that saves kings – and fathers.' But by the strange calculus of paranoia, as the medicine's exclusivity was eroded, so its placebo effect was diminished.

As ever, Nero's response was to up the ante, and he instructed his private physician Andromachus to enhance the recipe to suit his unique needs by adding viper meat. That Nero survived for fourteen years as an emperor famed for his good health, and was finally killed by cold steel rather than poison, may testify to the mysterious properties of this drug. Yet those who suffered from the vicious purges of his later years might have been surprised to learn that the most powerful active ingredients in the mixture were both relaxants: *cannabis sativa*, with its mildly hallucinogenic properties, and *papaver somniferum*, which was rich in morphine. After centuries of speculation, the ancient formula has now been discovered through analysis of a jar of the medicine that was found just outside Pompeii. It contained material from forty-seven vegetable species and the powder of seven types of ground bones. Of viper flesh there was no evidence.

One year after the earthquake, Pompeii was also in desperate need of a cure, but neither opiates nor snake oil were what was required.

CHAPTER 8

Ashes of a Jawbone

July AD 63

The two men crouched in the scrub, holding themselves still and silent as they waited for a rabbit to trip one of the traps that they had set. Magonianus, the doctor, and his companion had set off from Pompeii in the darkness to walk the ten miles east of the city and up into the forests that clad the hillsides where the vineyards stopped. Not for them the pleasure of hunting as sport that their richer neighbours enjoyed, with packs of hounds and slaves on hand bearing refreshments, and a mosaic or wall painting at home to echo their triumphs; nor the professional trapping of animals for the arena that had provided a few countrymen with a good living until the ban on gladiators had come into force. Today was about the simple imperative of an empty stomach.

The hunters had not been short of company as they crossed the plain. The long road ahead was dotted with other city-dwellers, weary of bean stews and in search of something more substantial for the pot, while on either side farmers and farm workers offered them greetings from where they toiled in the fields. During the dog days of late July, once the star of Orion's hound Sirius had risen in the night sky, only in the cool hours at the very beginning and end of the day did anyone but a slave contemplate serious work. At these times, dykes and culverts were hurriedly dug to channel any dribbles of water that were available to where they were most needed for the crops, and foliage from trees and bushes was cut and collected whilst it still held a few precious drops of the night's moisture: scant sustenance for the cattle as they later suffered in the sun.

Although normally a day away from his patients would have been a pleasure to Magonianus – even if it was to be spent catching rabbits rather than in study – the previous months had left him weary and dispirited. He had been surrounded by death and madness for so long that he now saw nothing but illness in even the most limpid of summer mornings. Since June, the sick had been arriving in rapidly growing numbers. It was the same every year but this time round the winter had seen no slackening off.

Stories had been circulating of the deadly vapours that had poured from cracks in the hillside the previous year, engulfing the flocks but also spreading pestilence to the farms and into the city. Magonianus trusted in his own theories, though, and was glad when he and his companion had begun their climb through the vines and towards the thinner air of the mountains. He knew how the shepherds in their hilltop cabins lived to a ripe age while the dwellers on the plain and in the marshes died young and miserable. And he was relieved to be free for a while of the mosquitoes that swarmed down below, endlessly disturbing his sleep with the angry sound of their flight.

With two brace of rabbits and half a dozen partridges already strung up to be carried home, the huntsmen sat down to eat their bread in a better temper. Still, looking out over the plain towards Pompeii, the doctor could not rid himself of the feeling that the whole world was ailing. Pompeii was full of rumours. It was said that the subterranean cisterns that stored rainfall from the wet months were cracked and seeping, and the landowners unable to afford their repair. Water was scarce while wine was simply being poured away. Whether from death or sudden impoverishment, buyers were failing to collect their part-paid goods and so, as the law allowed, the vignerons were throwing out thousands of gallons to make space for the coming year's vintage. And this was only the beginning of the landowners' troubles.

Gazing down onto the broken city, its walls and gates still in ruins, Magonianus's mind drifted to the many stricken victims of the quake whom his ministrations had failed to save – their limbs twisted and bloody, their breath rasping and their clothes soiled from terror. He was too preoccupied to hear the dogs approaching; only just in time did he jump up to see a magnificent boar make its furious headlong charge into the clearing and be brought down by its faster pursuers. Soon after, the huntsmen emerged from the scrub to deliver the beast from the baying hounds. Among them, the doctor could see Julius Polybius, the son of Phillipus and a man on his way up, who strode forward to deliver the coup de grâce *with his spear; behind him stood old Macer of the Cornelii. One boar, Magonianus thought, and the leader of the chasing pack.*

Even eighteen months after the earthquake, Pompeii would have presented a pitiful sight to Magonianus, as he gazed down from the hillside above. Piles of rubble still sprawled where they had fallen. Whole sections of the city, most likely including the forum, would have been closed off while buildings were made safe and the salvaged material laboriously stored for reuse. The city would have been in chaos, and everywhere clearance and building work would have been under way, with men and resources spread too thinly to make much impression on the monumental task ahead.

Looking at the painting of a building site from the Villa San Marco, which was not far from Poppaea's villa at Oplontis, or at the scene showing the construction of Troy from the Pompeian home of Vedius Siricus – perhaps executed as a boastful reflection of his involvement in the local rebuilding programme – the cacophonous sounds of industry almost ring from the walls. Carpenters with saws and adzes dress the young trees that have been cut down for use as scaffolding, or prepare the timbers that will be used to create new superstructures for nearly every building: the heavy beams that will be hauled up to rest on columns and pilasters, the joists and planks for the floors. Masons dressed in short brown tunics rough out the stones to fit their assigned place, while the more skilled among them sculpt the relief design onto a section of marble revetment or the fluting onto an unfinished column like those that would later be abandoned in the great courtyard of the new bathing complex, still only half-finished when Vesuvius erupted. Initially, of course, money and time were short and only hasty and essential repairs could be undertaken. Grander projects had to wait.

The structural problems afflicting the public buildings were propped up with makeshift solutions, that were later hidden behind marble cladding. Archaeology enhances our impression of a scene in which hoards of labourers mixed cement and other perquisites in large amphorae from which the necks have been snapped off, before trowelling it into cracks and holes with cannibalised salvage of bricks, tufa rubble, limestone, mosaic *tesserae* and tiles. The results of their efforts were the walls created in what is known as *opus incertum*, an undistinguished hand-to-mouth technique whose presence in excavated buildings reveals a fairly reliable map of earthquake collapse and complements evidence of repair in walls that have suffered from the characteristic 'scoop' effect.

It seems that among the first public works to be undertaken were the rebuilding of the bridge over the Sarno and the relaying of the road that led into Nucerian territory. Speed would have been of the essence to provide a lifeline for supplies in the aftermath of the earthquake, and funds were provided by junior magistrates from two prominent families: Gaius Cornelius Fuscus and Marcus Antonius Tertius, who appear to have served as *aediles* immediately after the earthquake.[1] The gates into the city were another priority. No inscriptions have been found claiming credit for this undertaking and it is possible that they would have been self-funding. Fines of three thousand sesterces were payable to the *lares* of the gates by those who buried their dead in adjacent tomb enclosures without permission. At a time when people were vying over burial plots, the income reaped from fines for illegal burial may well have financed the early restoration of the Vesuvius Gate.[2]

But, from his hilltop vantage point, the doctor Magonianus would have looked with greatest anxiety at the damaged aqueduct. Without clean fresh water flowing into a city of this size, disease could never be brought under control. Crystalline water direct from Italy's mountain ranges was delivered to her cities by a fabulous series of aqueducts, which rank amongst the greatest achievements of Roman engineering. The water in Pompeii flowed from the Augusta Aqueduct that stretched across the Campanian landscape. Close to a century old, its main line extended for ninety-six miles from the Falls of Acquaro to the east, all the way to the furthest tip of the Bay of Naples and into the vast reservoir that had been constructed there to serve the Misenum fleet. Even the water-bearing channel that surmounted the spur leading off to Pompeii was more than six square metres in cross-section. It is highly likely that whole sections of the Augusta's tiered arcades had to be rebuilt after the earthquake, an undertaking that it would have been impossible for the citizens of Pompeii to afford without imperial help of some kind.

Magonianus may have reflected how like a giant broken body the city of Pompeii now looked, reminding him perhaps of the ancient analogy between human anatomy, the form of buildings and the functioning of cities that the architectural writer Vitruvius alluded to. At first glance, the circulation of people around the streets of the city, and in and out of its many gates, appeared normal; but looking more closely, the natural processes of life were disrupted everywhere. While builders flocked into the city together with the materials they needed for their work, many of its inhabitants had packed up and were busy leaving, some never to return. The wagons that carried their furniture risked collision with those bringing much needed supplies into the city, and where the traffic insisted on travelling in both directions, vehicles would have been forced to mount the high kerbs and squeeze through the narrowed streets at great hazard to pedestrians (Plate 14).

In order to resolve its congestion problems, Pompeii may well have had to resort to the solution adopted by Rome, where the density of housing made gridlock in the streets a very real danger. There, wagons were banned from moving within the city during daylight hours, with the exception of those employed in sacred processions, or in building or demolition work for temple and other public projects.[3] To the consternation of inhabitants kept awake through the night, the result was a capital city that never slept. The entire provisioning of the vast population had to be carried out under cover of darkness. Staples and luxuries alike were ingested via a constant stream of vehicles from the warehouses and outlying farms, while in the other direction wagons carried out the waste excreted by the population for disposal beyond the walls.

In the human body, ancient medicinal treatises particularly focused on any interruption to the circulation of the blood, as causing dangerous fluctuations in vital heat. In the same way, the embolisms that afflicted Pompeii at this time may have threatened the very health of society, for at each point of conflict, there was an opportunity for change in the status quo. For citizens anxious to see a return to the way things were, the destruction of the Temple of Venus was, symbolically at least, perhaps the most devastating blow of all.

A city should provide many things to support the physical and emotional needs of its population: defence and shelter, health, civic order and solid structures within which trade and industry can flourish. But whilst shortcomings in any of these areas may lead to inconvenience and hardship, the erasure of a city's identity is the most catastrophic of all. Those who had criticised the razing of Carthage in an earlier age had seen the destruction of the Temple to Juno, the north African city's protectress, as the most heinous atrocity. With Venus's temple in ruins, Pompeii was metaphorically decapitated.[4]

The house of Aulus Pumponius Magonianus lies close to the temple that was for long mistakenly ascribed to Jupiter Meilichios but is now thought to have been devoted to Aesculapius, the mythic son of Apollo and Coronis and the Roman god of healing, appropriated from the Greek Asclepius. His temple in Rome was founded in response to three successive years of epidemics; AD 63 would have been a good time for him to find a home in Pompeii.[5]

Along with architects, the medical profession was the other skilled trade that Cicero held in high regard and considered an honourable vocation for the able but lower-born members of society. After a period of training, during which dozens of student doctors shadowed expert practitioners, much to the alarm and chagrin of their patients, official registration was accorded. Even then, a doctor would have limited the extent of his interventions, seeking to establish his reputation through the cures he was confident he could affect. Doctors assigned to the legions chose to follow one of two specialisms – to be a 'bone man' or a 'wound man' – but for either, the dangers of surgery without anaesthetic or antibiotics was not to be underestimated. Whilst the limited number of scalpels and probes he owned indicate that Magonianus would probably have undertaken invasive surgery only as an occasional necessity, there were many ways aside from simple bone-setting in which he could have helped his patients.

Gynaecological instruments were found on his premises and there would, of course, have been a regular call on his obstetric skills. The pestles and mortars that sat alongside them, would have received more frequent use still. Investigations in the gardens of Pompeii, using plaster casts of the root forms to determine which species were grown, have revealed a remarkable range of plants with properties that would have been beneficial in remedying and even preventing many common ailments. But while responsibility for much healthcare was undertaken within the household – with the combination of herbs grown in the small garden of Julius Polybius suggesting a certain level of domestic knowledge about their use – the pharmaceutical expertise of Magonimus was essential in preparing the more complex and much-needed remedies described by the herbalist treatises of the period.

Although convalescents were sent from Rome to the slopes of Vesuvius to recuperate, skeletal remains from Pompeii and Herculaneum show that tuberculosis and malaria were endemic to the region. The coastal plane was a prime breeding ground for mosquitoes and from the swamps around Paestum, south of the Bay of Naples, to those around the River Volturnus to the north – which would eventually be abandoned by humans – malaria was rife. The brackish marshes of the Sarno were no better. Although mosquitoes are weak flyers, and avoid windy conditions or uphill flights, the pools of standing water from broken pipes and cisterns in Pompeii after the earthquake would undoubtedly have attracted them into the heart of the city – assuming, that is, they were not already there. Pompeii's homes were, in normal times, generously equipped with fountains and pools, and – contrary to expectation – research in Rome has shown death rates to be far higher in those richer areas of the city where there were such water gardens.

In addition to its direct effects on health, in those affected by malaria and a respiratory illness such as tuberculosis there was an increased risk of pneumonia, which was often fatal in itself. But a number of other chronic diseases were also rife. Nearly one in five bodies, from a large group who died while trying to flee the eruption, show the kind of vertebral lesions that indicate infection with brucellosis, or Malta fever. Contracted from contaminated milk products – with traces of the bacterium identified in the remains of some cheese from Pompeii – the onset of the disease was marked by flu-like symptoms of sweating and fatigue before a debilitating arthritis set in. With facilities for refrigeration all but non-existent, food-borne diseases were common in southern Italy throughout the summer months, when the death rates soared.

In one minor respect, however, the people of Pompeii could count themselves fortunate. Both Celsus and Dioscorides agreed on the palliative properties of one unexpected substance that was not in short supply. From dog bites to dysentery, sciatica to putre-fying ulcers, *garum* was considered among the best cures available.[6]

Observing the sick and injured who visited the temple of Aesculapius to ask the god for his help, or listening to those who came to buy his professional advice, Magonianus might have won-dered whether his task, demanding as it was, might not have been somewhat less challenging than that faced by Pompeii's civic leaders. Whilst there are numerous examples in the skeletons from Pompeii of broken bones that were badly set, there is also evidence of victims recovering fully from fractures in femurs that were already degraded by osteoporosis, and which, without adequate treatment, would have been expected to carry a high risk of mortality. Aesculapius's petitioners may have walked with a limp, but the doctor's care, and the ashes of an ass's jawbone with which their poultice would have been impregnated, somehow saw them through.

Ultimately, the physical damage to the city could also be repaired, along with the resulting disruption to the rightful balance of society; but Magonianus, as a student of Hippocrates and Celsus, would have known to consider questions of health more holistically. An imbalance of the four humours – blood, phlegm, black and yellow bile – lay at the root of all ailments. It was for this purpose that the doctor owned his bleeding pots. These he could place over incisions in the skin and heat with a flame to create a vacuum that would draw out the blood, so purging those afflicted with excess sanguinity. Whether the city council would be able to institute a similarly tough regimen to restore the health of Pompeii was open to question.

In AD 63 the *decurions* on the council were faced with a series of seemingly intractable problems. Their most urgent priorities were clear and must by now have been, to some extent, in hand. But when it came to initiating and managing the restoration of the city's key buildings and facilities, progress would have been hindered by a number of factors. The negotiation and conclusion of contracts for public building work normally fell to the senior magistrates on behalf of the council, but the ultimate voting of the necessary funds required a quorum of the council to meet and agree by a majority of two thirds of those present. With many *decurions* dead and others already gone from the city to their country estates, or no longer eligible for membership due to a collapse in their finances, it is highly unlikely that these requirements could have been met.

It would also have been extremely difficult to replenish member-ship of the council and raise the necessary funds for public building work when the dominant direction in which wealth was moving appeared to be out of Pompeii. So strong was the affinity between a family and its home that to leave was a wrench, but for the same reasons that impelled the aristocratic Roman to go on a regular *peregrinatio* around his country estates – hygiene, the rural con-centration of his wealth, the spiritual benefits of being in an aes-thetically pleasing location – many Pompeians now abandoned the city for good. Even those who were not driven by financial need to sell their town houses opted to escape. Some must have started to wonder what was left for them in Pompeii other than painful memories.

Of those who decided to get out, a proportion might have taken advantage of the temporary shortage of habitable property to offer rentals at inflated rates, or else perhaps left their slave or freedman bailiff to caretake their empty properties and oversee repairs in the expectation that they might one day return. Such was the case with the largest of several houses owned by members of the Cornelii, which stood in a prime location just beside the Arch of Holconius. Audiutor is the name of the last bailiff to preside there.

The exodus from the city was noticed in Rome, which must have looked on in concern at the power vacuum that might result. Seneca took it upon himself to deliver a reprimand to the people of Pompeii in their suffering: 'Let us cease listening to those who have turned their backs on Campania, and who have emigrated after this mis-fortune, and say that they will never go back to the region in future.' He went on to implore the elite of the city to show leadership and to set an example by remaining in their town houses. First he appealed to their sense of civic duty and then to their self-interest, arguing that since it was impossible to predict where something equally disastrous might happen next, there was no advantage in leaving one place for another.

For those aristocrats who listened to him, staying in Pompeii was a grim prospect. Many had had their homes destroyed and the sources of their wealth wiped out overnight. Whilst the Roman legal system almost inevitably favoured the wealthy, one exception to the rule was landowners who were liable for losses incurred by their tenants as a result of circumstances beyond their control. It was with them that the final responsibility rested for the defaulted payments on the vintage produced on their land, for the unsown seeds and crops that were not harvested owing to lack of labour. Some members of this group, who usually considered themselves distinguished by dint of having invested their money in land, yet did not belong to the very highest echelons of society and therefore could not call upon large cash reserves, were particularly vulnerable at this time. With revenue from their rentals drying up, stock dead and in need of replacement, and property and equipment in need of repair at the very least, no banking system existed to offer bridging loans.[7] Only by liquidating their assets could they hope to keep their heads above water. But aside from luxury goods whose resale value was limited, that meant selling property, the slaves who worked the land or the land itself, and once these were gone so too were the means to re-establish their fortunes and their positions in society. What was worse, in a buyers' market, where the desperation of the vendors was all too evident, prices were plummeting.

Had anyone present at these emergency meetings of the council dared to venture a quick reckoning of the rebuilding costs for only the most important public buildings in Pompeii, the sum arrived at would have startled even the most optimistic mind. Estimating today on the basis of costs mentioned in dedicatory inscriptions on ancient buildings around Italy, even the most modest scheme of renewal and replacement would have required every single member of the council to pledge up to nearly half of what they owned.

The restoration of each temple in the town would have cost at least sixty thousand sesterces and probably in excess of one hundred and fifty thousand, where the damage was extensive. Whilst the Temple of Venus was unusual in its size and grandeur, it was not wholly exceptional, and at least eight other temples would have needed significant attention. Another one hundred thousand plus loose change would have paid for the colonnades around the forum; a complete rebuilding of the entertainment facilities would have come in at around a quarter of a million, though for the more minimal repairs to arches and seating that are likely to have been needed, the cost would have been far less. But when it came to the city's bathing facilities and the crucial issue of water hygiene, whatever budget the city had in mind would have had to be torn up. The bill for repairs to the Stabian, Forum and Suburban Baths might have come in at not much more than sixty or eighty thousand sesterces each, but, in the years to come, the clamour for a huge new bathing complex would have been no cheap undertaking, to judge from the Baths of Neptune in Ostia, which are known to have cost a cool million. On top of that, the price of getting the spur from the Augusta Aqueduct that fed Pompeii back on line could have ranged from a couple of hundred thousand anywhere up to a million or more, though how much of this Pompeii itself would have been liable for we do not know.

At a minimum, then, the prospective cost of restoring public life would have been one million sesterces; more realistically, it was likely to have proved closer in the end to two million, taking into account the port, the city walls, roads, the internal water and sewage infrastructure, and any number of services and smaller buildings for which the city was responsible. Whatever half-measures the anxious *decurions* might have been prepared to settle for in AD 63, the architecture that they would see rise from the ruins in a few years' time would be far from modest. Had they followed the example of Rome in the aftermath of its crisis the following year, they would have insisted that no buildings could be pulled down unless those who did so were able to replace them.[8]

A rough calculation of the annual return on properties owned by the *decurions*, based on evidence from the Jucundus tablets and elsewhere, suggests a disposable income for each individual of between ten and forty thousand sesterces. With most houses needing repairs, only a small proportion of this sum would be available for expenditure on public works until several years into the future. The need for supplementary funds was not a matter for debate, only how to secure them.

Refusing to stand on his dignity, Maius had dressed that morning in a workman's tunic, ready to join with his fellow citizens. All had been summoned to attend the forum for the five days of civic service that they owed each year to the city. But never before had a holder of Pompeii's highest office been seen there in anything other than the customary snow-white toga. In the face of widespread shirking by other decurions, Maius had decided to set an example, and so it was that he now found himself lending his weight as they heaved the fallen columns of the portico into a pile.

As the sun beat down, his companions cursed those who had failed to turn up, and joked at the expense of a man who claimed he could not bring his yoke of oxen because they were ill. Everyone knew full well that he had hired them out to Cornelius Tages, the building contractor. Exempt from social duties because they might delay the essential construction projects on which he was engaged, Tages instead used his time to wheedle the loan of oxen and slaves from men who should be donating them free of charge to the city.

But Tages's patron and erstwhile master should have known better. It was Macer, after all, who had failed to teach his former slave the meaning of duty. Maius had remonstrated with his fellow decurion only the previous day, but while Macer had mouthed excuses and feigned embarrassment, he had still shirked his annual service and paid Tages to send a man to do it in his place. In the long term, it didn't even cost Macer anything: as a Junian Latin, everything Tages earned would return to the Cornelii coffers when he died.

His day's service over, even before he bathed Maius set off to pay a visit to his own freedman, Nigidius Vaccula, the bronze merchant, whom he had recently commissioned to recast the city's mangled law tablets. Newly installed in a fine house on the road that led north from the forum, Vaccula could count some of Pompeii's proudest families among his neighbours: in one direction Tages's master, Cornelius Macer, and the old Vettii in the other. Like those all around him, though, his house stood in need of major repair. There were too few builders in Pompeii capable of the work, and not many willing to move there until conditions had improved.

As Maius approached, he caught sight of Tages, standing on the street corner in heated discussion with a local homeowner. He slowed as he passed in the hope of eavesdropping. What struck him first was the tone of the two men: Tages jaunty in the knowledge that he could exact whatever price he pleased, the other pleading in a manner quite unbecoming in one of his station. Then he noticed that they were staring into a hole in the pavement where the water pipes lay exposed. At that moment they caught sight of him and lowered their voices.

It took Vaccula to explain to him the significance of what he had seen. The contractor was taking bribes to increase the size of the pipes that fed private homes and businesses. What was worse, enjoying the upper hand for the first time in his life, Tages was forcing the decurions to pay through the nose, while agreeing far more comfortable deals with his freedmen friends. Vesonius Phileros's laundry business, it seemed, was already back on line and making a mint. But – Vaccula shrugged – what could be done?

Until recent times, the first act of a revolution has always been to torch the public records office in which the documents that enshrined the perceived injustices of society were kept; even now only the seizure of broadcasting stations takes precedence. In Pompeii this insurrectionary feat was accomplished by purely natural causes. For those wily enough to take immediate advantage, the destruction of contracts and property deeds afforded them the opportunity to lay claim to goods and rights on a fraudulent basis. Subterfuge would have been especially effective where, for example, a neighbouring property was left temporarily undefended, its late owner being one of those stretched out in the mortuary and his heirs not residents of the city. Civic property was vulnerable too, since it was a safe bet that the town council would be so swamped with other problems that it would be incapable of paying much attention to minor infractions.[9]

Even when there were wills to refer to in the distribution of a dead man's estate, they were often meaningless because of the number of named beneficiaries who were also dead or because the property was now worthless. The usual practicalities of auctioning off the possessions was also made more complicated now by the deaths of those usually entrusted with the task.[10] Corruption would have been widespread. With such pressure on manpower and demand for skills, building contractors inevitably held huge power, knowing that they could simply down tools on essential repairs and instead attend to the less pressing needs of those who had the means to pay.[11]

This would have made it all the more urgent that the city council reassert its power as soon as possible – but where were its members to come from? Assuming that fewer than sixty-three *decurions* remained active in the council, it would have fallen to the elder of the two senior magistrates to choose replacements for those missing. Among those who spoke up for maintenance of rigorous standards in the selection of members, the voices of men such as the old Cuspius Pansa, who had been a senior magistrate four times over, and his son, who now served as the special Prefect dealing with the emergency, would have been prominent. Other members of the old guard, such as Postumius Modestus and Alleius Nigidius Maius would also have made their opinions felt. But even those families that had a vested interest in things staying as they were would have recognised the argument for opening up membership of the council a little. They would have remembered that every new member was required to pay a juicy fee of up to eight thousand sesterces on his admission, and might have predicted that those whose elevation came as an undreamt of honour would feel inspired to contribute something more out of gratitude.

It is interesting to wonder in which camp Julius Polybius would have placed himself in any debate on the question of accepting freedmen onto the town council. As the son of an imperial freedman, he may well have been open to the idea. But he might also have wished to protect his power, which was, at this time, growing. Polybius was involved in a complex network which would see his friends achieve political prominence alongside him. Their horse-trading was straightforward and seemingly transparent to popular scrutiny: 'I ask that you elect [. . .]. Elect him, Julius Phillipus and he will elect Polybius,' announced one message across the street from the Julii home.[12] Blunt it might have been, but this novel approach to political life did not deter Marcus Lucretius Fronto – a cousin of Nero's *flamen*, Valens – from partnering Polybius in the senior magistracy.[13] A few years later even Trebius Valens, the son of a powerful politician and census magistrate and at this time still an adolescent, would recognise the benefits of winning endorsements from the Polybius clique.

In the years to come, Polybius would attract also a dispro-portionately large number of admiring endorsements from the ladies of Pompeii. Although women did not enjoy the franchise, their opinions could still be influential, and Tacitus commented dismissively on the extent to which women's political preferences were swayed by good-looking candidates. With such natural advan-tages, it seems unlikely that Polybius needed to set much store by the bear's-tooth charm that was discovered in the remains of a cupboard in his peristyle. Polybius's political life was already charmed and he seems to have shown equal skill and judgement in his business dealings. For whilst in these difficult times it was the old elite who would have managed the flow of food from Pompeii's neighbours into the city, it seems likely that Julius Polybius and his friends exercised considerable influence over its distribution. Between the two, there can be no doubt whose contribution to the common good would have been more likely to catch the eye of a grateful public, and perhaps it was now that people truly appreciated the 'good bread' that Polybius was said to provide in the electoral postings.

If Polybius had always had an eye for the political advantages of distributing bread, post-earthquake Pompeii provided him with numerous opportunities to expand his interests. New businesses were opening up everywhere as tradesmen benefited from the rebuilding of properties either to incorporate shops and workshops into the periphery of domestic properties, or indeed to convert them entirely to commercial use. What motivated this activity was clear: it was the same eye for profit that had prompted Cicero to employ an architect to supervise the restoration of a block of dilapidated buildings he had inherited in Puteoli, with directions to ensure that the rental plots were subdivided. His canniness was rewarded with a gross income of eighty thousand sesterces in the first year, rising thereafter.[14]

Foremost among the businesses that took advantage of the new spaces available were the bakeries. The people of Pompeii liked their bread fresh. In the villas of the territory and in the larger workshops of the city, loaves were baked on the premises and served to the workers straight from the oven. Households would often make up their own dough, even sometimes grind the flour there, but then send the loaves out to be baked in professional ovens to produce a perfect crust. It would have been an especially popular option whilst domestic ovens were out of commission following the quake; take-out hot food was also carried on the heads of waiters from the inns to diners, even in the better houses.

The proximity of bakeries to the houses of the elite suggests either that the bakers were no respecters of status, or that they operated under the direction of precisely those families who were affected by their presence. The north-west of the city, where some of the finest and best-maintained townhouses of the post-quake period clustered, was no exception. Here, part of the great House of the Labyrinth, which tucked in discreetly behind the House of the Faun, was turned over wholesale to the bakers and equipped with millstones and bread ovens. The same occurred in the building next door to the House of the Bull, a house whose decor suggests that its owners prided themselves on their aesthetic sensibility and would have been vociferous in asserting their objections, had they had any. A few blocks to the east, the Stabian Road ran through the city on a northerly axis and it was particularly the area on either side of this strip that grew ever more dominant as a focus for bread-baking, with the support of half a dozen facilities in the artisanal zone that lay between its central stretch and the forum.

Close to where the Stabian Road intersected with the main street were the houses belonging to Julius Polybius and the freedman Popidius Secundus. Both properties appear to have had a relationship with a bakery. In the case of Popidius, the business nestled in so tight to the main body of his House of the Citharista that the ovens would have warmed him in the winter. The baker's workshop in which Polybius may have had a stake was slightly further away from his home, but all the evidence points to his involvement.

In the tradition of Roman patronage, a man should have one patron and yet two political notices posted by a man called Lollius pledge support for both Julius Polybius and his neighbour Popidius Secundus. It is, of course, possible that two different Lolliuses are concerned, but another man called Placidus was even more explicit in asserting that he was a client both of Polybius and of a relative of Popidius Secundus's called Ampliatus – he was probably Vetutius Placidus, who ran the bar opposite Polybius's house with his partner Ascula. What emerges quite clearly from these postings is that, in addition to their political co-operation, Polybius and the enormously wealthy Popidii freedmen were also bound together by shared networks of patronage and doubtless by shared business interests too.

With a wealthy business partner like Popidius Secundus, Polybius would have had the capital to invest in far larger enterprises. Who knows if he and Secundus didn't choose to fund whichever Lollius it was who, at this time, was making intriguing adjustments to a property close to both the Marine Gate and the forum. The House of the Sailor occupied the entire depth of a block and was unusual in having been laid out in two sections, with a front entrance leading into an elegant town house that extended back into a colonnaded garden, and a smaller rear street entrance from which a steep vaulted passageway sloped down into a complex of twenty-seven underground storerooms constructed beneath the colonnade. This warehousing space was floored in beaten earth and was therefore only suitable for the short-term storage of perishables and, in particular, grain. The building itself had been purpose-built decades before to accommodate a grain store – with skylights through which anyone in the garden could look down onto the scenes of industry below – but was now perhaps up for sale with vacant possession.

The initial injection of money from his patrons would have been more than enough for Lollius to buy the House of the Sailor and have the necessary repairs done to the collapsed entrance and west wall. The work was hasty and slapdash, the shortage of skilled workmen all too obvious, but Lollius was eager to install himself in his beautiful new home with its fine mosaics and only slightly cracked wall paintings; and when his patrons proposed that he should forego one of his two atria so that it could be converted into workers' quarters with a passageway to allow access straight through a second front door to the depot, it seemed ungrateful not to comply. After all, their commitment to the success of the business was ultimately to his advantage too, as they would soon demonstrate by using their influence in the council to have the road outside the rear entrance widened so that carts that clattered into town from the country granaries could unload and quickly return to collect another load. With concerns about the hoarding of grain paramount in the *decurions'* minds during the post-quake period, a scrupulous and reliable distributor had no difficulty securing approval.

A business such as Lollius's would have been destined for success and the area around his house must have echoed with the constant coming and going of workers and supplies. To facilitate the handling of goods a ramp was built up the pavement near the turning space so that sacks could be slung directly from the back of carts or pack-mules into the hands of waiting stevedores; the back doorway was wide enough for two men to pass with sacks over their shoulders. But even this was not enough to satisfy his investors, who wanted to maximise efficiency by providing meals for the workers on site. It might have taken some gentle arm-twisting to convince Lollius to accept the disruption involved, but the promise that his tiny bathhouse would benefit from the warm currents rising up from the oven below won the day. A donkey mill and a hand mill were installed, along with shelves on which the loaves could prove, while a kneading room was equipped with bowls. But the flues that were to warm the baths were clumsily cut into Lollius's prized mural of Galatea and Polyphemus and his patience was finally exhausted. Without any formal parting of the ways with his patrons, he used the money he had earned to assert his own authority, reclaiming the second atrium as part of his house. But thereafter, he could never afford to make good the damage to the decor.

The alterations that can be seen in the House of the Sailor were part of a far larger trend that points towards a new entrepreneurial attitude amongst Pompeii's elite and a new dynamism throughout society. Whereas, in the past, the production of profit had been merely desirable, in the economic climate of AD 63 it was indispensable. With endless private and public rebuilding to be financed, creditors were calling in their debts. Those with contacts outside the earthquake zone may have been able to sell their debt on, but for many others bankruptcy loomed. It was yet one more factor that played into the hands of the city's opportunists.

For those whose opportunism took the form of targeting a rich widow for marriage, the spring and summer of AD 63 would have been a time to step up their efforts.[15] Only with the express permission of the emperor could a woman remarry during the twelve months of mourning that she was expected to observe for her dead husband. But for suitors, who needed to prepare the ground, now was the time to strike. In some cases their attentions would not have been unwelcome. Women still in their childbearing years, with the added attraction of a dead husband's money to lure a good match, could afford to wait for the right man to come along and would have been interested in interviewing candidates. But older, less well-provided women would have feared a lonely old age: the example of the wealthy Ummidia Quadratilla, shut away in her Puteoli home with only the performances of her private theatrical troupe for company, was far from reassuring. But at least she had her money to console her: many middle-aged women faced impoverishment.[16]

The *captatores*, or legacy hunters, were among the most despised figures of the age. These charming sycophants, who wormed their way into the affection of those with money and then wheedled a healthy bequest from them in their wills, preyed on credulous old men and innocent youths with the same lack of compunction; as Juvenal commented wryly, 'If you have heirs, you are not invited out to dinner.' The easiest pickings were to be had from precisely those women of a certain age whom the rest of society overlooked yet who could not reconcile themselves to their new, invisible and undesirable state. Whatever it was that they needed, it was said, the attentive legacy hunter would provide: a massage, a lesson for the children, some advice about the house or on medical matters. As

Juvenal again joked, 'Tell him to fly – he's airborne.' It comes as no surprise that, for the satirical poet, this most despicable of creatures, who did not even draw the line at servicing old maids in their beds, was always a Greek – the archetypal filthy foreigner, fit to scapegoat for the faults of greed and amorality that bled through society as a whole.[17]

In post-earthquake Pompeii there may have been opportunities to take advantage of a family's wealth, even if an heir did exist. Although guardians were sometimes appointed in the terms of a will, children left without a father were otherwise taken under the wing of the most senior male relative, and where no obvious candidate existed, it fell to the town council to appoint one. In many respects it was an onerous task, which required an auditing of the estate on assuming the role, and imposed a duty to return the full value with benefits to the child when he or she came of age. Magistrates, army veterans and those over seventy could all claim exemption; in AD 63, doubtless many others would have pleaded to be excused on the legitimate grounds of poverty, ill health or madness, while the magistrate officiating in the case was expected to disqualify others whom he deemed to be of bad character. Yet with the prospect of a large fund to borrow from for one's own investments, and a long period of unaccountability, the role is likely to have appealed to the less scrupulous.

Ultimately, once all other alternatives had been exhausted, the duty would often have fallen to freedmen, who were doubly obliged by the continued *obsequium* that they were expected to show a patron's family even after his death. Some may have bemoaned their fate, but the more calculating would have embraced it. And even the tutor who started out with the most scrupulous intentions would have been hard pressed to resist asset-stripping their ward's estate to fund the odd flutter on the depressed Pompeian property market.

In the growing wealth of freedmen, the governing class of Pompeii saw a lifeline, distasteful as it may have been to them. One relatively painless means of tapping into this source of finance did already exist, and only required the elite to become slightly less circumspect in whom they agreed to admit to the priesthood of the Augustales.

An organisation composed primarily, though not exclusively, of freedmen, those elected to membership were expected to be of good standing in the community, but were also required to contribute a fixed fee to the civic treasury. At less than half the rate payable by a *decurion* on entering the council, the cash deposit made by a single new Augustalis was of negligible importance, but if the Pompeii lodge grew to anything like the size of that in the neighbouring city of Herculaneum, the total revenue would have been very welcome.

Among the few Augustales from Pompeii whose names we know there was a high proportion of wealthy and powerful men. But they would not have been easy people to manipulate: Vesonius Phileros, who would prove himself to be quite unforgiving when thwarted in his commercial dealings; Cerrinius Restitutus, whose son Vatia would rise to a magistracy on the back of his father's honourable position; and Conviva, one of the Vettii brothers, whose extravagantly decorated home remains a showcase for Pompeii's twenty-first century tour guides.

However, the strength of the ambition felt by the freedmen in the region devastated by the earthquake – their resilience and dynamism – is perhaps best demonstrated not by any evidence from Pompeii, but in a collection of wax tablets, relating mostly to legal cases, that was recovered from a row of houses in Herculaneum. There, a big shot called Cominius Primus, who owned tracts of local forest and bought slaves from Poppaea's own household, was attempting to get his business back on track without delay. The earthquake happened in early February; in early March he signed off on a transaction, and over the following months issued a number of promissory notes and receipts. But of greater interest still is the figure of Lucius Venidius Ennychus, Primus' neighbour who on 22 March – only six weeks after the town around him was, by all accounts, nearly destroyed – took probably the most important step of his life by making an application for full Roman citizenship.[18]

Venidius Ennychus belonged to the sub-category of freedman known as 'Junian Latin'. These were slaves who had been freed without the proper procedures being observed. Since AD 4, when Augustus had imposed legal restrictions on the overliberal release of slaves, freedom had only been officially available to slaves aged over thirty who had demonstrably done good service, or else those who were the illegitimate offspring of their master. For those who failed to fit these criteria, freedom came with all the usual benefits except the most crucial: nothing they achieved in their lifetime – neither their improved position in society, nor any money they had made – could be passed on to their heirs. Instead, except in very particular circumstances, their children would be classed as illegitimate and their personal fortune would revert directly to their one-time master, leaving their descendants destitute. Nor could they join the Augustales, for which citizenship was a prerequisite. Every possible loophole was carefully sealed, to leave a perfect mechanism by which the slave-owning classes could benefit from their slaves' entrepreneurialism, secure in the knowledge that their investments would ultimately be returned to them with profit.[19]

Any attempt by a Junian Latin to circumvent the law or have his status officially revised was hedged with difficulties. Regardless of whether a Junian's original master was dead or distant, only his personal testimony was deemed acceptable evidence that a Junian should be freed from the hopeless position in which he languished. Without such evidence, proof had to be produced that could satisfy a judicial panel containing a prominent figure such as a *praetor*, a provincial governor or the emperor himself. However, there was one alternative: to marry a citizen and profess before seven witnesses that the express purpose of the union was to beget children, then subsequently present the one-year old infant to the Praetor in Rome.

This appears to have been the strategy that Venidius Ennychus adopted. The earthquake took place almost exactly thirteen months after the recorded birth of his daughter, just at the time he was planning his application for citizenship. He must have hoped that, amidst the collective amnesia caused by the earthquake and the loss of the public archive, his case would be a simple one. To judge by events a decade later, when his eligibility to join the Augustales was still a matter of legal dispute, things did not go smoothly. But, according to the album of Herculaneum's lodge, he was eventually allowed to become a member.

Maybe Pompeii's town council did as Rome would shortly do

when faced with its own disaster: adopt the emergency measure of granting citizenship to any Junian Latin who invested one hundred thousand sesterces in rebuilding work. Their ex-masters, who probably saw the money as being ultimately their own, might have objected. But, with one eye on the soaring budget for civic rebuilding, the council would have paid little heed to their protests. And so another prop in the established hierarchy of Campanian society was removed.

It was perhaps in response to this erosion in deference that the Cuspius family made a strong statement through the public rebuilding project to which they chose to commit their private resources. The announcement that the repair of the amphitheatre was their preferred project doubtless surprised many. But their logic was sound. Practically, it was an entertainment venue that might help attract into Pompeii the labour that the city so urgently needed, even if it was temporarily banned from hosting gladiatorial fights. But symbolically, and more importantly in the eyes of its benefactors, it was in the tiered architecture of the arena that the traditional distinctions between society's different ranks were most immediately tangible. Restore the seating, as the Cuspii did, and there was no longer an excuse for the plebs to crowd together with their betters; rebuild the vaulted passageways and the magistrates could again enter in procession through their normal entrance, to the admiration of the crowds.[20]

However, for all the attempts to re-establish the past, things would never be the same in Pompeii. Many were gone, and others rose to take their places. A new hierarchy existed of those who had the courage to stay on in the perilous city, while those who fled were bitterly disparaged for their cowardice. Vibius Secundus, for example, who had been senior magistrate only five years earlier, was cruelly mocked for his ineffectuality in the wake of his departure. 'The Vibii,' lambasted one writer of graffiti, 'were once the wealthiest in Pompeii, but not for this did they hold in their hand a sceptre instead of a cock, doing what you do every day with your penis in your hand.' The backlash against these 'wankers', whose actions had undermined their credibility, was quite intractable. If such absentees had thought that by maintaining a property in Pompeii, and with it their right to sit in the council of decurions, they would still have an influential voice in local politics, they were very much mistaken.[21]

On the other hand, those who voluntarily joined the community, perhaps seeking their fortune, were warmly welcomed. Sextilius Rufus, who could boast a fine family pedigree in nearby Nola, appears to have made the journey in the opposite direction. On his arrival he befriended Julius Polybius, attracted the praise of another prominent citizen for having been 'good to everyone', and would serve as census magistrate before being celebrated, in death, on a tomb inscription back in his home town. It was men such as he who would provide the backbone of Pompeian society in the years ahead.

Since she had first entered Tages's house back in March, Julia's new guardian had spoken barely a word to her. It was a far cry from the tenderness he had pretended when she had first been brought to him, when his eyes had filled with tears as he pledged that he would care for her. How could all those important men have believed him? But at least here she was free to do as she wished, even if there were no friends to do it with. Now, as Tages lay face down on the bench, the light from the oil lamps glowing on his exposed skin, she knew that he did not care whether she was watching him or not.

Still, Julia stayed in the shadows. The kind doctor moved the flame to the pottery domes that dotted her guardian's flesh, while his patient twitched and cursed. But Tages's pain thrilled her; she watched, unmoving, as the blood was drawn up through the little cuts that the doctor had pricked into his back with his knife. Tages was so big and clumsy and boastful. And so crude in the way he spent his money, having never had it to spend before. See how he ordered the gentle doctor about. So different from what her father had been like.

Once, when their bailiff had broken his arm and the doctor had been called to set it, her father had joked that slaves always made the best patients: they were so used to pain that they didn't even flinch. But Tages had been a slave and look at him now. As he talked to distract himself – complaints, mainly, and ridicule of the fools he had to do business with – she could see only weakness and greed. Tomorrow, in the quiet of the morning, she would listen outside his bedroom for the rattle in his chest. It was already July and the season of new sicknesses was drawing to a close. But for those who were already ill, there were six more months to survive before the New Year brought a change of air.

Seeing the doctor's awkwardness as he took his payment, she felt a surge of hope. Perhaps he would not want to come back; perhaps Tages would sicken more without help. But as the kind man wrapped his instruments and left the room, he paused before her and from his sad smile she knew that her guardian would get better.

── VIII ──

With the humours of the city thrown dangerously out of kilter, the Emperor alone was seen as possessing the power to set matters right. Now was the moment when the people of Pompeii looked to their city's patrons to deliver on their promise of influence in Rome and persuade Nero to assist them in their time of need. Previously, only one imperial visit to Pompeii is recorded: most likely by Claudius on 24 May AD 50. But could the Emperor really now ignore the personal pleadings of an embassy from the stricken home town of his beloved Poppaea?

As always when a Roman city wished to send an embassy, it was up to the magistrates to present the suggestion to the town council, who would then give it careful consideration, before voting. Once the proposal had been accepted, Decimus Satrius Lucretius Valens probably volunteered, eager to celebrate the tenth anniversary of his appointment as *flamen* of Nero with a trip to the court in Rome. But there were others who had an equal claim. In such matters there was a protocol to follow: Pompeii must choose its representative by lot. When Julius Phillipus drew the winning pebble from the jar, there would have been general relief: who better to represent their case to Nero than a descendant of an imperial freedman with Greek manners?

Phillipus would have set off to seek an audience with the Emperor confident that he carried with him the hopes of his fellow towns-people and goodwill of Pompeii's most prominent citizens. In his absence, one freedman of the Cornelius family and a slave of the Cuspii Pansae would even visit Phillipus's house and inscribe a graffito, close to the small *lares* shrine, that expressed the feelings of the community: 'For the health, return, and victory of Gaius

Julius Phillipus, here, to his *lares*, Publius Cornelius Felix and Vitalis Cuspius make an offering.' Was this perhaps an official delegation?

Whatever authority might have been invested in them, the combination of names is resonant: Phillipus with his imperial connections; Cornelius, a descendant of the original colonists of Sulla; and Cuspius Pansa, who served as a Prefect during the state of emergency that followed the quake. It appears that the city was, in this initiative at least, united. But whilst Phillipus could be sure of the support he enjoyed, he would have been less certain of what he would encounter when he arrived in Rome.

In the face of a constant stream of ill tidings in recent years, Nero's news managers were still proving to be remarkably effective in pulling the wool over the eyes of the masses. The war with Parthia had reached stalemate, with a peace settlement that satisfied neither side and Corbulo ordered to withdraw his army to the near bank of the Euphrates, in present-day Iraq. The spinmeisters' response? To declare the war won, and shamelessly set up triumphal arches in celebration of Rome's victory over her greatest enemy. Then the entire grain fleet sank at anchor in the supposedly invulnerable harbour of Portus. Their answer? To stage a demonstration of confidence in the wheat supply by having Nero throw sacks of grain into the Tiber (and just hope that no eagle-eyed observer would notice that their contents were old and mouldy). Deep down, though, only the foolish could have failed to see that life under Nero was becoming increasingly uncertain.

Surrounded by sycophants, distracted by Poppaea, who was pregnant with their first child, and with his career on the stage consuming a large part of his energies, it is unlikely that the Emperor had a particularly clear impression, in AD 63, of the condition of the society he governed. Seneca may have tempered the Emperor's self-indulgence in the past (while doubtless turning a healthy profit on the five hundred matching tables with ivory legs that he provided for Nero's feasts), but for now he was heeding his own maxim: 'The wise man takes care to avoid the power that kills, avoiding, above all, that he appears to be avoiding it.' Without such wise counsel to act as a check on his megalomania, insulated from reality by his own propaganda machine, Nero's belief in both his brilliance as a performer and his divinity led him to identify ever more closely with the sun god, Apollo, with whom he shared a talent for the lyre, or *cithara*, and chariot driving (Plate 5d).

The Emperor's preferred medium was the tragic pantomime, an innovation, some decades previously, of a freedman actor who went by the name Pylades. Eschewing the ribaldry of the comic mime and pantomime, this was 'high art', and provided an ideal platform for virtuoso performance. Using material drawn from the Greek myths and tragedies – Aeschylus's *Orestes* and Sophocles' *Oedipus* were favourite departure points for Nero – a single actor would sing and dance a series of lyrical solos that told the story from beginning to end, accompanying himself on the *cithara*, and impersonating each of the characters in turn. Masks were worn by the actor and changed regularly, and a highly stylised gestural language, laid down by long convention, was used to express the emotional states of the characters. Even with a chorus providing narrative continuity, a full-length performance was a gruelling undertaking, and the critics could be exacting in their expectations, as Lucian reveals when he writes, 'The dancer should be perfect in every point, so as to be wholly rhythmical, graceful, symmetrical, consistent, unexception-able, impeccable, not wanting in any way, keen in his ideas, profound in his culture, and above all, human in his sentiments.'[1]

It was Apollo who was said to have presided over Augustus's victory at Actium in 31 BC, but for an emperor to extend his association with the god into the theatrical realm was a radical new departure. The theatre was the traditional venue where the plebs could express their discontent in the presence of their rulers; yet, by this time, any theatrical games Nero attended were tightly con-trolled. When he gave his first public performance in Naples – a supposedly friendly venue for the warm-up for his tour to Greece – soldiers were posted in the auditorium to ensure that the public showed the right level of appreciation for their Emperor's star turn. As always, though, it was the Emperor's own claque of Augustiani that could be relied upon to provide the most voluble support. He had not yet begun to perform publicly in the capital, but wherever else he appeared the local group of Augustiani, together with those who accompanied him, were ready to cheer him on.

By AD 63, the Augustiani had developed into a powerful political force in the Neronian cause. Their numbers, in Rome and around Italy, now topped five thousand and, with rewards of up to four hundred thousand sesterces given on whim to section leaders, it is hard not to believe that they were biddable to do whatever job was required. With only the acclaim of self-interested men like these to chasten him, Nero had little reason to doubt that his artistic talents were limitless, and so began to turn his attention to other spheres of creative activity. And for a man with a taste for the grandiose, where else to turn but to architecture? Like many other men of the Roman elite, who had picked up a smattering of knowledge from their reading of Vitruvius and infuriated their architects with their amateur interference, Nero felt himself perfectly well equipped to contribute his views in discussions with the professionals as they finalised plans for the long-mooted *grand projets*. His influence can perhaps be seen in the revisions of the brief for the great canal from Lake Avernus in Campania to Rome that had originally been intended to mitigate the loss of business to Puteoli caused by Portus. Now the design placed a greater emphasis on pleasure and luxury than mere practicality.

As though a hundred-mile-long canal that was wide and deep enough to accommodate ships with five banks of oars were not challenging enough, the linking section between Misenum and Lake Avernus was now to be roofed and colonnaded for its entire length and filled with healing water from the exclusive hot springs that bubbled up around Baiae. Had Nero personally invited his critics to draw parallels with Caligula he could not have done better: his uncle, however, had aspired only to create a bridge of boats across the Bay of Baiae and even that project had never come to fruition. To increase his own chances of mastering Nature, Nero decreed that all death sentences passed should henceforth be commuted to transportation to Campania, so that every prisoner from every part of the Empire could now be set to work. With little concern for the crippling cost of his visions, Nero pored over ground plans and elevations with his architects, and must have day-dreamed about what might be achieved if only old, crowded Rome could herself be remade.

Reports of goings-on in the capital at this time make clear that nothing was inconceivable any longer. Indulged by Nero, the Emperor's new Praetorian Prefect and general fixer, Tigellinus, was allowed to develop his own spectacular pet projects that would prove to be of a far more debauched nature than those of his master. In AD 64, they were to include an orgiastic floating extravaganza on the artificial lake that had been created by Agrippa in Rome for the staging of sea battles. Birds, beasts and marine animals were appearing in the harbours of Italy from every corner of the known world to be taken to Rome to dress the set. Lavish public banquets were to unfold across the capital, while on quays all along the water's edge, the wives of Rome's aristocracy could offer their services alongside the city's prostitutes in temporary brothels.

But the whoring of elite women that broke so many taboos was not limited to Rome. The inhabitants of Pompeii would have recalled hearing reports of similar scenes when the court had revelled in their barques off the coast of Campania during the previous spring.

In the meantime, Julius Phillipus's embassy had arrived in Rome at the most opportune time. Nero was planning a long performance tour to Greece, and then perhaps on to Alexandria. It was decided that his May journey from a warm-up gig in Naples down to the embarkation port of Brindisi would provide an ideal opportunity for a brief visit to Pompeii. After all, there was political capital to be made from being seen to extend a helping hand, however belatedly, to the struggling city.

CHAPTER 9

A Beryl for Venus

May AD 64

When the last of his morning callers had been sent on his way, Vettius Conviva remained seated in the tablinum of his new home, allowing himself a few rare moments of reflection. Five years ago, when they had been freed, no one would have believed that he and Restitutus would have set themselves up in such a fine house so soon. Yet here they were, in a prime location among the top people of Pompeii. With their flower business flourishing and the vineyards doing well, who was to say this wasn't just the beginning of their fortunes? If the Emperor's visit brought money flowing in, they'd be sure to claim their share, one way or another. And when they did, they would repaint the walls and boldly declare their slave origins to any visitor, without the slightest hint of shame.

Restitutus's voice drifted in from the peristyle. He was berating the plumber, as the workman painstakingly serviced each of their twelve fountain heads in turn, just in case any of the Emperor's entourage might decide to look in. Conviva could still remember the day when he had met the man he now called his brother. Even as small boys they had looked alike and it had pleased old Vettius, their master, to have them serve table together. The same height, they had shared a small pallet to sleep on, and that first night Restitutus had held him, calmed the fear he felt at being so far from home. And now listen to him! Scolding a man twice his age and three times his size for failing to squeeze out a stronger flow of water when the supply they enjoyed was already the envy of half the town council.

In the streets around them, between the Herculaneum and Vesuvius Gates, where the first sections of pipe leading out from the water castle had been repaired, the splash of water on stone could again be heard. But if that were little short of a miracle, how much more wondrous was it that *the boys of yesterday who had scuffed around those same streets in play during their scarce moments off duty – Restitutus, Conviva and their young friend Felix, the brilliant, reprobate son of Caprasia the innkeeper – should have come so far. Hard work and talent had brought them half the way, but if their master had not lost his son and wife and half his slaves in the quake, control of his wine and oil businesses would never have come the way of his freedmen, and Felix would never have been adopted by the man who had loved his low-born mother in secret for so long.*

But that was in the past; it was the future that now demanded Conviva's attention. Tomorrow would bring the inauguration of the Floralia festival and, while his stall-holders and agents had been selling blooms as fast as the carts could carry them in from the fields, there was still demand to be met. With Nero expected any day, anticipation was building. Even those cowards who had been hiding on their country estates and had not shown their faces in town for two years were turning up in numbers. And the city's own leading lights were vying to present the most impressive home.

He would have to slow down the deliveries, keep them hungry. Then when his customers thought it impossible that there could be flowers left to refresh their faded, wilting garlands, he would surprise them. Roses, lupins, violets and all manner of unseasonal beauties – all forced, all amazingly available. At whatever price he cared to name.

When Seneca reached for a metaphor to critique the depraved society in which he lived, it was to the world of horticulture that he turned. Such creatures as the young men around him who sought to retain their pre-pubescent sexual allure, he wrote, were like those 'who crave roses in winter, or seek to raise a spring flower in the snow'.[1] In the past, Pompeii's householders might have taken the arrival of the Floralia festival that spanned the last days of April and the first of May – with its bundles of flowers, fresh fragrances, comedies in the theatre and general air of levity – as marking the arrival of summer. By the mid-first century AD, though, the all-year-round availability of their favourite blooms, due to forcing techniques, lessened the festival's significance, just as in the twenty-first century daffodils before Christmas lessen the impact of spring.[2]

It was probably at around this time in AD 64 that Nero made his visit to Pompeii. The relatively short period between Julius

Phillipus's announcement that his mission had been a success and the arrival of the imperial party would have been full of frenzied preparations, as the inhabitants strove to give the Emperor a fitting welcome.

Was it perhaps in these brief months that Decimus Satrius Lucretius Valens – his home barely standing a short time earlier, with scarcely a doorway safe to pass through – had commissioned the great programme of redecoration that would see seven rooms transformed to showcase a series of fine mythological paintings in the newly fashionable style? If so, did he hope that the illusionistic perspectives of the stage decorations in which they appeared to be framed would impress an Emperor obsessed with the theatre? Or that the finely painted walls of his atrium would appear fittingly sumptuous to the prominent men from Rome whom he expected to receive there? Or that the great image of Venus – reclining on a vast scallop shell born on foaming waters – that covered the rear wall of the garden and could be seen from the atrium itself when the *tablinum* screens were pulled back would demonstrate to those who saw it the indivisible loyalty he owed to Nero and to Pompeii (Plate 16)?

Was this the moment, too, when the prospect of Nero's personal appearance prompted the Popidii freedmen to embellish the House of the Citharista with an array of Apollonian paraphernalia – the wall paintings, the bronze statues? If so, there was plenty of space to accommodate it, since they were busy buying up neighbouring properties to incorporate ever more rooms into their sprawling home. But perhaps a virtual palace with three atria was the minimum that would seem appropriate for a leading member of Nero's Augustiani.

It is even possible that it was in early AD 64 that the 'Murecine Inn' gave over the central area of its upper floor to the creation of a suite of three dining rooms with built-in couches and beautiful red walls to set off the figurative centrepiece: a painting of a lyre-playing youth with golden hair, dressed in diaphanous Greek clothing. A figure whose features bear such a striking resemblance to Nero's own that it may suggest that the building served, if only briefly, as a riverside lodge for the imperial party (Plate 23b).

Whatever the Murecine building's use, few would dispute that its walls have preserved a unique portrait of the central figure in the lives of Pompeii's last generation: a man on whom many still doted, despite the growing climate of fear. Along with the Augustiani club of claquers, another possible organisation of supporters is known only from graffiti on Pompeii's wall: the Neropoppaenses. They were clearly devoted to both the Emperor and his new wife, claimed freedmen members with families who held the magistracies, and appear to have been on good terms with the Augustiani.[3] Their existence would surely have bolstered Poppaea's relatives in the House of Menander and the House of the Golden Cupids, who already took enormous pride in their association. Both these properties benefited from a significant rearrangement or renovation of their rooms during Nero's reign, as well as redecoration that again featured designs inspired by the theatre. Nero's personal obsession had become the spirit of the age. But as the early summer heat built, these reminders of the aesthetic life would have done little to make the environment more comfortable. For that, the greatest enhancement possible was the cool sound of running water. And whilst walls could be rebuilt and repainted, restoring an entire water system whose pipes were buried deep beneath the pavements was a far greater challenge.

The great network of piping that until so recently had fed the thirty-nine or so public fountains that were such a focus for local life in Pompeii, and which carried water straight into any private house that could afford the tariff, remained out of order. Gone were the extravagant water gardens of the elite, complete with their tumbling cascades and myriad fountains, that sprang to life with the arrival of summer. Yet, even at the best of times, the water that flowed into Pompeii from the Augusta Aqueduct had to be carefully managed. There is every indication that the Pompeians would have had little difficulty in squandering the five hundred litres a day that could, in theory, have been delivered for each man, woman and child in the city. This meant that during the hot months from July through to September, when the flow of the aqueduct – as torrential as that of the River Sarno during the winter months – slowed to a trickle, careful rationing would have had to be imposed. In northern Italy there were melting glaciers to swell the headwaters; in Campania, by contrast, the waters that arrived were often still warm from their volcanic origins. With supply limited, at just the moment when demand was increasing, the junior magistrates' responsibility to ensure correct usage would have been onerous.[4]

Although Frontinus, the writer of the key text *De Aqueductis*, wisely asserted that fullers did not deserve to receive fresh water, an ancient law still protected their exclusive right, along with bath-houses, to channel their own water supplies. In some cases the two groups made common cause, locating their businesses close together to allow for the re-use of bathwater by a fullers' workshop slightly downhill of the bathhouse. Often, though, they were in direct competition with innumerable others who could always benefit from an extra gallon or two. With so many water outlets and so many potential ways of defrauding the system, the illegal tapping of water was a constant challenge to the law.

Sadly, we do not possess the plans by which the *aediles* and their assistants were able to maintain and manage the system. Without them, the routes taken by the pipes that snaked across the city remain as mysterious as the means by which the precision-fitting valves that are strategically placed to control flow were manu-factured.[5] We do know that the process began at the main *castellum aquae*, or water castle, at the highest point of the city, just inside the Vesuvius Gate, where the aqueduct's waters entered. Inside its squat brick walls, the arriving water was split into three channels which led into pipes of varying size that then disappear off into the unknown. The inference is that water to different parts of the city – or to different grades of recipient – was controlled by means of the sluices used to block one or more of the pipes. In subsidiary res-ervoirs, often constructed against or into the exterior walls of private houses or public buildings, further junction points were situated, and there were smaller water tanks too, placed high on towers around the city to maintain water pressure. Innumerable taps and stopcocks controlled the flow locally.

Even with a highly motivated workforce, it would have taken many months to check and mend all the pipes in Pompeii, replacing ruptured sections with new castings made of lead from Britain. It is likely that the first to benefit from repairs would have been the homes closest to the main water castle, since the stopcocks doubtless allowed leaks further down the line to be isolated, preventing further wastage. Also this area accounted for a large proportion of the city's rich whose homes inevitably would be most on show during the imperial visit.

Certainly this was the area that appears to have recovered most effectively after the earthquake, with the most widespread improvements to buildings involving lavish redecoration and the addition of large dining rooms as well as more straightforward repairs. Unlike in other parts of the city, luxury remained in fashion here. Not far from the House of the Vettii, two homes in particular relished the return of water and would take further measures to protect themselves against its loss in the years to come when further earth tremors again threatened supply. Over towards the Herculaneum Gate, the House of the Vestals already boasted a swimming pool in its larger peristyle and, throughout its double suite of public rooms, water spouted melodiously from fountains. The original investment involved in installing these charming embellishments had been considerable: throughout the house floors had been relaid at different heights to facilitate water flow, which in turn necessitated the replacement of all the mosaics. Post-earthquake, the cost of having an entire room at the top end of the house waterproofed up to a height of several feet in order to ensure sufficient pressure for the more elaborate fountains would have been negligible in comparison.

Even this expense pales when set beside the water displays of the House of the Bull that stands next to the House of Caecilius Jucundus. On entering, the visitor was immediately confronted with a magical army of sparkling fountains. In the extreme distance, at the back of a leafy half-courtyard, or pseudo-peristyle, water gushed from the three niches of the nymphaeum; in the main atrium, daylight shone down from a skylight onto the shallow marble pool, which glistened with spouts of water that poured from each corner before draining away into the cistern beneath. At the centre of the pool stood a bronze statue of a bull, from whose mouth water spurted in a scintillating arc. Elsewhere the house was graced with other water features, including a single vertical jet of a kind rare in Pompeii. But it was the bull itself that might have been purposefully designed to please Nero: an echo of sights that the Emperor could expect to see on his forthcoming trip to the Aegean.[6]

With only days remaining before the imperial train swept into Pompeii, the main repairs to the piping were finally complete. In a flurry of activity, couches would have been carried from the winter dining rooms – whose walls were often painted black to disguise the stains caused from the oil lamps – into the summer suites, with their filigree decoration of flowers. Canvas sunshades and awnings were taken out of mothballs; the formal beds planted with annuals from the city's nurseries, such as that to which the ground behind the House of the Ship Europa was given over following the quake. It was time too, perhaps, to put the finishing touches to the new paintings that graced the city's walls with their visions of bowls that overflowed with fruit; of plump birds strutting their worthiness for the dinner table; or of the whole abundance of the ocean poured out in a writhing mess of shiny-scaled fish and prickly crustacea (Plate 22). It was also time to transform what, for ninety-nine days out of a hundred, were only artistic representations of an ideal feast, into the real thing.

Fruit and vegetables were lifted from the straw in which they had been left to ripen. Lettuce, beets, artichokes, peas and beans, along with the onions and cabbages for which Pompeii was famed, were all harvested from kitchen gardens. Melons might also have been available, grown in greenhouses of the sort that the Emperor Tiberius had innovated on the isle of Capri only a few decades earlier. And the discovery in the House of the Ship Europa's garden of a number of earthenware pots with multiple holes punched in them, lined up against one of the walls, recalls Pliny's description of the method used by those who imported citron trees to Italy to allow their roots to breath. An awkward species to acclimatise, since they needed protection from frost, lemons would nevertheless have been a welcome addition to the feast.[7] In the specialist smallholdings of the territory, amphorae shaped with a spiral ramp inside were shaken to yield the nervously chattering dormice that, once honey-coated and roasted, would provide toothsome hors d'oeuvres.

The wealth of the bay itself was plundered too, as Pompeii's fishermen continued to cast their nets, hoping that they might land an especially fine specimen of the more prized species, and so make their fortune. Grey mullet – whose livers were considered an especial delicacy – fetched extortionate prices around feast days: one is said to have sold for six thousand sesterces in Rome, another to have cost three times the value of the slave chef who cooked it. Whereas in the past these fish had shoaled in large numbers around the rocky headlands of Italy, by the end of the first century, overfishing had resulted in the beginnings of an import trade from Corsica and prices becoming even more inflated. In AD 64, however, a Pompeian fisherman could still have hoped to strike gold. If unlucky with the mullet, other species could command a premium: lampreys, bass and bream were all favourites of the elite Roman diner.

Whilst the lack of refrigeration meant that fish that had breathed their last on the decks of the boats had to be sold quickly, a fish that was landed alive had a far longer shelf life. Placed first in the shaded pool in the middle of the *macellum* it could then be sold to some rich homeowner, who would transfer it to the brackish waters of his own pool, into the sides of which amphorae and specially shaped pottery tubes were set to provide the fish with shade from the sun, and where it could be admired by visitors until the next dinner party required its presence at table. This was common practice in the city's better homes, whose inhabitants may even have copied the aristocratic dilettantes who treated their fish as pets, decorating them with jewellery and buying them expensive treats when other food was in short supply.[8]

For fishermen, the life of the sea was hard and took a heavy physical toll. The skeletal remains of one sixteen-year-old who would die in the eruption of AD 79 show the effects of handling the hooks, lead weights and nets found around the harbour area of Pompeii: an upper body whose strength and muscle tone was astonishing even in comparison to that of modern fishermen, with teeth on the right side of his mouth worn down to nothing by gripping the taut lines on which his catch struggled. It was men like these whose interests were cared for by the *collegium* of fishermen that left its endorsements on the walls of Pompeii, though their collective bargaining power cannot have been any match for the professional fish-farmers of the region. In the previous century, an obscure Roman businessman who became known as Sergius Orata had made a vast fortune by speculating on the farming of gilt-headed bream – *sparus auratus*, from which he took his name – before branching out into property development and the oyster business.[9] Those who followed in his entrepreneurial footsteps would have provided the local fishermen with stiff competition.

In the midst of all these preparations, the news brought back from Naples by Pompeians who had travelled to see the Emperor's performance there – Lucius Popidius Secundus and the other Augustiani doubtless among them – may have caused some to worry that Nero was about to cancel his visit. Even as the new Apollo had sung and played, another earth tremor had shaken the theatre – of far lesser magnitude than that which had struck Pompeii two years earlier, certainly, but enough to give everyone a bad fright and do serious, if limited, damage. The Emperor, though, was not to be distracted. Even as the shock waves rolled in from the quake's epicentre under the island of Ischia a few miles offshore, Nero carried on undaunted, completing his programme with barely a quaver in his voice. Only after he had left the theatre and the audience had safely departed did its walls collapse. Or so, at least, the story went.[10]

As Nero recuperated after the traumatic event – perhaps weighing up whether a ruined theatre signified divine displeasure or the overexuberant acclaim of the gods (and doubtless coming down on the side of the latter) – he could at least feel assured of a doubly warm reception in Pompeii. Word had been sent on ahead that the Emperor would use his visit to revoke the ban on the gladiatorial games that had been imposed following the riot. It was crowd-pleasing news, with Alleius Nigidius Maius already planning to stage an event in celebration of the arena's reopening for its proper purpose. And now, when Nero extended his sympathy to the city for its suffering at the hands of the earth-shaking giants, his own first-hand experiences of the terrors of a quake would lend credibility to his words.[11]

Perhaps it was at his wife's villa in Oplontis that Nero rested before continuing his journey; perhaps it was even in the company of Poppaea herself and their first child, a girl born the previous year. Here they would have been surrounded by calm and beauty: the breeze whispering in the ornamental hedges of boxwood, the fine statues presenting a compelling case for the virtues of a life of cultured leisure. Baiae and Puteoli are known to have been distribution centres for the best of Greek workmanship – art worthy of imperial connoisseurs – and the parkland here in Oplontis could boast an Athena in the style of the great Praxiteles and the head of an Amazon that may even have been carved by Polyclitus's own hands.

It was here too, of course, that the statues stood of the boy prince and his older, amber-headed lady, the age difference between them no longer so pronounced in real life as it had appeared a few years earlier. Whether the dynamics of their relationship – between the egotistical younger man and the petulant older woman – had really changed so much is open to question. It is easy to imagine the imperial couple bickering beside the great pool of the Oplontis villa in May AD 64, the cause of their disagreement perhaps to be found in Poppaea's reluctance to accompany her husband on his jaunt. Neither would have relished the prospect of having their bones shaken over the dusty roads of Campania in some rustic local carriage like the one which was found in a villa only a mile outside Pompeii, an arched leather awning offering only the most rudimentary and inelegant shelter against the sun. But if Poppaea's obstinacy enraged Nero, whose visit to the Campanian backwater was probably in large part a favour to her, at least this time he refrained from physical violence: the suggestion that he was a wife-beater might have been the one thing that gave his Pompeian supporters pause for thought.[12]

It was many years since Satrius Rufus had visited the city of his birth and now here he was, accompanying the Emperor through Pompeii's Vesuvius Gate. Crowds thronged the road around them, slowing their progress, but it was not their presence that caused the Emperor to hesitate, but the shocking sight of the ruination that stretched out on every side. The destruction presented a vision of human frailty to unsettle even a living god. Turning to his master, Satrius Rufus watched the tears swell in Nero's eyes and knew them to be sincere. But he knew, too, that his master's pity would quickly pass.

In the years that he had served Nero as secretary and keeper of his notebooks, Rufus had learned the hard way to predict the twists and turns of his master's fickle nature. Today he had an advantage: he had seen the itinerary they were to follow and was familiar with the house where they were to be formally welcomed. There had been no argument in Pompeii's council when the Satrii had proposed that their great home with the faun statue in its atrium should have the honour of receiving Nero: few homes could match its grandeur and none its venerable history. But Rufus also knew that one of the treasures it housed was sure to distract the Emperor from his sorrow.

Now, as the doors swung closed behind them, a cool quiet descended. Blinking to adjust their eyes to the shadiness of the atrium, Nero and his attendants were shepherded across the patterned floor of the tablinum and on into the first peristyle. Spread before the Emperor across the mosaic floor of a side room was the rousing vision of Alexander astride his foaming steed, struggling but not quite able to reach his mortal enemy Darius through the melee of armed men that ebbed and flowed around them. At that instant, as Rufus had foreseen, all semblance of concern for the fate of those around him departed Nero's face, to be replaced by the smouldering of ambition.

Nero was transported. A minute passed, then another, as the Emperor gazed upon the one mortal he longed to emulate. Rufus knew his master's temperament well enough to feel no alarm, but he sensed the unease of the reception committee on either side of him as they shifted on their feet, unwilling to break the Emperor's reverie yet afraid that their seeming inattention might cause displeasure. Then suddenly, as unexpectedly as he had fallen silent, Nero swivelled back to his hosts to bathe them in a smile of such inhuman rapture that they fumbled to offer their carefully rehearsed greetings.

That Nero possessed a certain charisma is not in doubt, but to those Pompeians who had never before seen their Emperor in the flesh, and knew him only from coins, statues and paintings, his physical appearance may have come as something of a disappointment (Plate 5a). His face was most generously described as handsome, but other contemporaries insist that it was neither attractive nor charming; his eyes were a watery blue and his hair a tawny blonde. Jowly by nature, and spindly legged, by AD 64 he was growing distinctly fat, with a bulging waistline and thick, yet unmanly, neck: rather far from the 'golden Apollo' for which he wished to be taken. To the traditionally inclined, his slovenliness would have been a greater affront, while the long tresses into which his hair was allowed to grow during his performance tours, bound with a handkerchief, were a sure sign of his effete, precious manner. It was an impression that was compounded by the voice master who, following him everywhere, encouraged him to save his voice by whispering, or by holding a cloth in front of his mouth when conversing with his public. Despite all this, the simple appearance of power blinded many.

Even a minor Roman aristocrat could expect to be accompanied on his travels by a multitude of staff. Nero, like his stepfather Claudius, would have brought with him a vast retinue of soldiers, personal assistants and courtiers, along with such domestic functionaries as cooks, bakers and even meat-carvers to ensure that the Emperor's palate was adequately supplied. Most likely, on this occasion, there were architects as well, to offer their advice on Pompeii's rebuilding. All would have needed somewhere to stay and there would have been no shortage of offers from those eager to welcome the Emperor's men into their homes.

When it came to Pompeii's women, such offers were sometimes extended with open arms. When Valerius Venustus of the first praetorian cohort announced himself 'the greatest of fuckers', and a comrade-in-arms expressed regret that he had seduced only half a dozen local girls during his stay, their complacent tone was that of men who understood only too well the aphrodisiac effects of their proximity to power.[13]

Nero's entourage brought a level of glamour to Pompeii with which its inhabitants were simply not familiar. The adulation expressed on the walls by actors' fan clubs when their favourite troupes were playing was as nothing compared to the frenzy of excitement evinced by an occasion such as this. That little evidence of such outpourings has remained to posterity is best explained by the change in the political climate by the end of the decade, when association with the late Emperor had become more a source of shame than of pride, and any embarrassing references had been whitewashed away. But what has been preserved to the present day is the words of some of those who travelled with Nero and were billeted on families across the city.[14] Satrius Rufus, the imperial secretary, enjoyed his homecoming so much that he would later retire to the city and put up the only nameplate of its kind ever discovered; and Poliaeus Marsus, records his gratitude in the kind of gushing terms one would expect of Nero's bedroom attendant: 'Here and everywhere health to the most holy colony, and to the Pompeian people everywhere health.'[15]

Particularly dense clusters of such graffiti appear around the homes of prominent supporters of Nero and underline the preferential treatment received by those who were boldest in declaring their loyalty. They basked in the reflected glory of the new Apollo, a source of especial glee to those who until shortly before could never in their wildest dreams have imagined themselves being so favoured. Their excitable mood is perfectly captured in a single graffiti: 'Callistus, Augustinianus, to Vedius Ceratus, Neropoppaensis.' Whatever the subtle differences between the two groups of Nero supporters to which they belonged, this pair of freedmen appear to have relished the devotion that they shared and believed that a declaration of friendship would benefit them both. That Ceratus was the freedman of Vedius Siricus, a Neropoppaensis and a magistrate, underlines the strength of Neronian allegiances that existed across all levels of society.[16]

To bolster their confidence in the face of such glamorous house guests, the people of Pompeii could have been forgiven if they felt the need to don their finest clothes, though in doing so they risked misjudging the tenor of the times. The right to wear purple had always been the jealously guarded privilege of those who could claim a certain social status. Only the elected magistrates of the city and the local officials of the *vici*, along with the most promising young men who had not yet reached full adulthood, were entitled to wear the *toga praetexta*, its purple trim singling them out as the most honoured of their peers. But it was also the Emperors' colour, and, faced with the mid-century fashion for all things purple, Nero had felt the need to clamp down and institute strict rules about its use.

It must have amused the Emperor's entourage when their Pompeian hosts sought to ingratiate themselves by flaunting what, in Rome, was known to be such a dangerous colour. Even the type of purple dye used could determine the severity of the offence: officially, Amthystina and Tyrian purple, the former made from precious stones, the latter from *murex*, could now only be supplied to members of the imperial court, and any merchant who persisted in importing them for other customers risked having his business closed down. The use of purple dyes squeezed from roots or lichens, more muted in colour, was less troublesome. If Nero's strange and feared wardrobe mistress, Calvia Crispinilla, accompanied him to Pompeii, she would have been able to pick out infractions at a glance: in Rome, one such transgression had led to a respectable matron being stripped naked in public for her insolence by the Praetorian Guard.[17]

On being escorted to their respective lodgings to rest and refresh themselves prior to the evening's festivities, the members of the imperial retinue found themselves in a world of gardens that may have been somewhat smaller than those to which they were accustomed, but were equally charming. Here were spaces saturated in the atmosphere of an Arcadian past, in which glimpses of satyrs and woodland fauna, painted on walls or modelled in bronze or marble, peeped out from the abundant greenery of early summer. Rosemary bushes, beds of thyme and squadrons of other sweet-smelling herbs perfumed the warm air, while more sophisticated scents accosted any who passed a statue drenched in essence of rose or violet, or who stooped to admire the jewel-bedecked fish that swam in perfumed streams.

Having bathed and washed, there was little left for the guests of these households to do but savour the song of the birds that swooped beneath the umbrella pines and look forward to the pleasures of the long evening ahead. The concept of *otium* – the enjoyment of one's leisure time once the official issues of *negotium* had been resolved for the day – was not in itself freighted with any dubious moral connotations and, if kept in balance with the rest of life, could be positively virtuous. But when *otium* was combined with the designation 'Greek', there was no mistaking that the balance had tipped towards the evils of luxury. The leisure enjoyed by Nero's party in Pompeii would have been Greek in every sense, and they would surely have had it no other way.

By mid-afternoon, the sun still high in the sky, the wait would have been nearly over and the banquets about to begin. In some places a vine-covered pergola provided the necessary shade; in others canvas sails were now hoisted over the dining areas, great triangles of fabric slung between a high tree and a tall post like some giant hammock, or else awnings cut to fit the architecture and attached to metal rings set high into columns, such as can still be seen in the portico of the House of Meleager. Hearing the whip-crack of canvas in the light wind, appetites across the city would have sharpened.

However, not everyone was invited to the private feasts. Even with the domestic kitchens of Pompeii working at full capacity, there was a place at the banquets for only a tiny proportion of those who had spent the previous weeks angling for an invitation. The rest of Pompeii's citizens found their entertainment at the parties held by the various *collegia*, or else amidst the conviviality of the city's bars. On normal days, it was usually around the fourth or fifth hour that these *cauponae* began to open and receive deliveries of food and wine, though with the prospect of a late night ahead, and the spectacle of Nero's arrival too great a temptation to resist, on this one day at least the time of opening may have slipped. First the slats that closed the front counter off from the street had to be slid back over one another; then the preparation of the food begun in those establishments that offered it; finally the incense – which one inn has noted down on its shopping list as being in need of replenishment – would be lit as the evening drew in, to mellow the mood of the drinkers.

By the time the elite set off for their respective dinners, the inns would already have been full of merriment: drinkers spending freely in the hope of a distribution of money during the Emperor's visit, while innkeepers wondered just how long such carousing could continue before matters got seriously out of hand. For the moment, though, only Nero's prohibition on the serving of snacks could marr their enjoyment. Nero was encouraging vegetarianism and deemed pea soup the only fitting food to be consumed in bars. Since the inns were notorious for sourcing much of their meat from the remnants of temple sacrifices and since food-poisoning bacteria were rife, the Emperor's edicts were issued partly with hygiene in mind. However, the greater fear was probably that anything that tempted diners to linger at table increased the risk of conspiratorial activity.

While the elite dinner guests milled about in the atria and public areas of the grander town houses, waiting for the last of their fellow diners to be announced and admitted, they could amuse themselves by looking at the works of art and the records of the resident family's history. Only once all were gathered would the party begin its leisurely progress towards the dining area, pausing perhaps to observe as a slave of the household poured out libations onto the ceremonial hearth and offered samples of food to the gods of the *larariun*. Before sitting down to dine, guests would have removed their shoes for the dust of the dry streets to be washed off their hands and feet, as stipulated in a list of recommendations for visiting diners from the House of the Moralist. Having completed their ablutions, the venue for dinner was close at hand. In some cases, indoor rooms would have been used, but at least a quarter of Pompeii's larger private houses were furnished with a fixed summer *triclinium* that allowed dining on cushioned couches in the midst of the garden. Of these, ten were arranged to allow water to flow between the couches, so that rather than picking a morsel of food from the small dining table that was usually placed in the centre of the horseshoe of couches, guests could reach for delicacies from plates perched on the side of the pool or else floating upon it. To those ambling towards the torch-lit scene, the prospect of an evening of such luxury and in such elevated company must have been a happy one.

Taking advantage of their fellow guests' distraction, the ambitious may have slipped a bribe to the *vocator*, the most powerful of all the army of slaves involved in the dinner and the man responsible for the order in which the guests were placed on the couches.[18] With guests supposedly positioned in ascending order of rank in an anti-clockwise direction, the walls of the indoor *triclinia* were in some cases painted to echo this hierarchy with images that referenced the status of the diners who reclined in front of them.

Once all the guests were settled, chilled wine was brought – the connoisseur insisting that it be somewhat diluted, and sweetened with resin or honey – and the first delicacies were served. Seafood would have figured prominently in every home, always accompanied by a selection of aromatic sauces. In some cases, surely, oysters made an appearance, probably the fashionable bivalves that were lifted from their beds near Brindisi and transported across Italy to mature in the Lucrine Lake of Campania. It was the kind of extravagant pleasure that would have tickled the Emperor, and even Pliny appreciated how 'the resulting blend of two piquant flavours more than compensated for the effort.'[19]

Next, to stimulate conversation once the salty morsels had been gulped down whole, the paraphernalia for the first entertainment of the evening may have appeared: a sloshing vessel of water from which a flapping surmullet was lifted, placed on a polished surface, and then covered by a glass dome, which rapidly starved it of air while ensuring that its death-throes remained visible to all. For it is the curse and wonder of the surmullet that, as it asphyxiates, its scales pass through a whole spectrum of subtle colours to signal its passage from life. And for what nobler purpose could a fish die than to elicit the hollering, mocking delight of a Neronian diner?[20]

Although most of the slave household were busily employed behind the scenes, the sedate start to the night's drinking gave the wine waiters an opportunity to reflect upon the spectacle they had witnessed and the cruel and capricious appetites of their masters. Standing slightly apart from the diners, watching anxiously for the moment when the cup of their master or assigned guest might need refilling, the fate of the surmullet was a warning to these pretty young men – and the occasional older one who was forced to maintain a semblance of youth – to steel themselves for what lay ahead.[21] Smooth-skinned and long haired, some only recently acquired at market to add erotic lustre to this special evening, wine-waiters were often viewed as little more than sexual playthings. Long before they were required to drape the slack arm of an inebriated guest over their shoulder and drag him to his bed – a squalid scene that is depicted in one Pompeian painting – they would have had to submit to endless verbal abuse, humiliation, and drunken violence along with all manner of lascivious petting and predation. Seneca remarked of these beautiful unfortunates that, 'their slightest murmur is repressed by the rod; they pay a huge penalty for the smallest breach of silence; all night long they have to stand around, hungry and dumb.'[22]

The physical qualities that were favoured in wine waiters – meant that exotic imports from the East were hotly competed for at auction, with a beautiful Indian boy the ultimate accessory. But whilst there may have been some homogeneity amongst the slaves who waited at table, the physical differences in the bustling back rooms and slave quarters would have been pronounced: a Briton of the period was on average a full nine centimetres taller than his Pompeian owners, whilst other conquered races were smaller. Only in their shared condition of powerlessness would the slaves of a household have discovered some solidarity, and the cramped conditions under which they operated on occasions such as this would have tested its durability.

Even in a house such as the House of the Vestals, which was redesigned with entertaining in mind, or the House of Meleager, where the vast indoor dining area is positioned to facilitate the invisible movement of slaves, the amount of space given over to the kitchen and service areas was negligible. Yet it was in spaces such as these that gastronomic dishes were prepared for Nero's courtiers, probably to recipes along the lines of those recorded by Apicius: honey-roast fowl, broad beans cooked with cumin and coriander, and *porcellum hortolamun* – a pig whose bones had been extracted through its mouth before its carcass was stuffed with sausage meat, snails, dates, and the delicate flesh of thrushes and other songbirds. As local chefs worked alongside those from the imperial household,

whose elevated notions of culinary refinement left them unim-
pressed by dishes over which locals swooned, the temperature
doubtless rose. But with good ingredients – slices of precious beef,
perhaps, like those sold by the specialist butcher's shop in Rome
that nestled between a goldsmith's and a perfumery on the via
Sacra – it was hard for them to go wrong.

Wheeling out of the heat and chaos of the kitchen, the food
waiters balanced plates piled with the tops and green shoots of
purple carrots and beetroots – the Romans removed and discarded
the tuber as inedible – or with ice cream made from a base of snow
somehow transported from distant mountains. With other slaves
racing back in towards the concealed spaces of the house laden with
empty dishes, it took the combined skill of a ballet dancer and an
actor for those serving to keep their balance while maintaining the
servile expression that was expected when entering a public space.
There was little room for error and the slaves in the House of
Menander had cause to be grateful that some considerate soul had
seen to it that the decisive corner between one world and the other
was rounded off to ease the human flow.

*Half a dozen times, as he darted between the legs of slaves in the narrow
corridors, it was only the boy's nimbleness that saved him from being
caught. Instead, as curses rained down on him from every side, he skipped
out through the back entrance and onto the pitch-dark street. Since he had
crept away from the grand dinner his father was hosting for his fellow
Augustales priests, Cerrinius Vatia had scarcely stopped moving as he
travelled from feast to feast. On a night like this, even the staff in the most
self-regarding of houses were too busy to notice a twelve-year-old boy, small
for his age, as he slipped in where at any other time he would have been
unwelcome.*

*So much had he seen that the experiences of the night were already
becoming a blur. He had witnessed meat being sliced in time to the beat of
an orchestra, as though the carver were participating in some exhibition
of gladiatorial arts, and cakes that spurted saffron liquor. He had seen the
innkeeper Caprasia, whose shocking anecdotes of Tiberius's debauchery on
Capri he listened to avidly when playing near her bar, mixing with the
best of them and matching their cynicism, sneer for sneer – happy to do it,*

if that's what it took to win favour for Felix, her son. And only now he had nearly been swept away by the onrush of slaves as they scrambled towards the room vacated by the diners to launch themselves upon the remnants of the food. But for all these wonders, he was sure that nothing could touch what lay ahead.

In the distance, a rowdy group passed the end of the street with a lantern that swung on its pole, moths dancing around it. Vatia hid in the swaying shadows until they had gone. From all around, the sound of revelry in taverns and houses was rising, as the diners turned to the serious business of drinking. But Vatia was not to be distracted. For now he was on his way to one of the houses of the Poppaei, since it was there, he hoped, that Nero himself might be found.

When he reached the house of Poppaeus Habitus, Vatia readied himself to face the fiercest defences of all, but the guards posted outside barely noticed him. Within, the oil lamps were turned so low and the conversations so hushed that for a moment he wondered whether he hadn't arrived too late. But the chimes of music drew him through into the peristyle, its columns hung with terracotta masks whose features flickered in the lamp light. Suddenly, Vatia caught his breath. He had heard stories of ceilings in Rome that changed colour over the heads of party-goers, but he had never heard of anything like this.

On a small raised stage a scene was being played out, not by human actors but by a mechanical cast – a circle of dancing bacchants, a grandiloquently gesturing Dionysus – who moved in perfect harmony and animated the world around them into plumes of fire and fountains of milk. Even the most jaded in the audience gawped open-mouthed at these new wonders wrought by the ingenuity of Heron of Alexandria. Only the Emperor looked weary and paid little attention. Vatia was downcast at the sight of his idol's lack of interest. He might carry the weight of the world on his shoulders, but surely there could be no more diverting entertainment than this?

If Pompeii's cooks had strained to meet the gastronomic standards expected by the Emperor, Nero's hosts would have had to be still more inventive in the after-dinner entertainment they laid on. Once the guests at a Roman dinner had removed themselves from the dining area and settled into the drinking stage of the evening – the *symposium*, or *epidipnis* – it was not unusual for a spectacle of some kind to begin. But while the richer Pompeian families may have retained private theatrical troupes or hired itinerant players such as those led by 'Little Parsley', or Anicetus's Castrensis, their traditional fare would have been unlikely to impress Nero's courtiers, with their ceaseless craving for novelty.[23] Acrobats were a possible alternative – climbing ladders into the air, tightrope walking and eating fire – but Nero had seen all this before, and had even witnessed a fatal accident when a falling 'Icarus' had splashed him with blood. What else, then, might have tickled the Emperor's fancy?

The first and most obvious answer to have sprung to the minds of his Pompeian hosts would have been a sex show: after all, it would have been a natural progression from the erotic mood created by the prized paintings on the walls of many houses that Nero might have visited that day. At one end of the spectrum, it would have been possible simply to introduce some sexual element into the more traditional entertainments; orchestras comprising naked female musicians, or mimes who crossed the usual boundaries of obscenity would have raised few eyebrows. If the organisers had wanted inspiration, they need have looked no further than the local inns, where acrobats on parallel ropes balanced drinks while having sex, the famed dancing girls of Cadiz gave their all, and belly dancers gyrated in the manner that inspired Martial to write that it was 'enough to make Hippolytus himself masturbate'.[24]

Regardless of the likely presence of the Emperor's in-laws, Tigellinus's showmanship had recently whetted his master's appetite for more serious debauchery: 'The slave', we read of recent or impending entertainments, 'was given free reign with the mistress in the presence of the master, and the gladiator violated the noble girl before the eyes of her father.' So much then for the Pompeian house-rule that advised guests to 'Keep your lascivious looks and bedroom eyes away from another man's wife. Maintain a semblance of decency on your face.' Both Tigellinus and Petronius may have been on hand to advise on the evening's proceedings, as well as to talent-spot for future events. If so, their eyes are likely to have been scanning the crowd for contenders of both sexes, and the spectacles would have needed to contain at least a dash of homoerotic relish in order to fix the wandering attention of Nero, whose tastes increasingly involved transgression in this area. One of his favourite diversions is said to have involved donning the pelts of wild animals and ravishing young men and women tied to posts. Such behaviour might have been too much for a provincial city to stomach, but his appetites were not to be thwarted. Before much more of AD 64 had passed, and presumably with Poppaea's tight-lipped acquiescence, the Emperor would don a bride's veil to celebrate his 'marriage' to the freedman Pythagoras, with all the wedding night activity that entailed.[25] If there is one image from Pompeii that represents the characteristics of the *cinaedi*, those men who assumed female attributes, it is surely that of Nero himself, posed as a diaphanously robed Apollo, in the Murecine building (Plate 23b).

Perhaps, though, the prospect of trying to top the pleasures that Rome could offer was simply too daunting for the Emperor's hosts, and they looked instead to a strategy not of indulging his lusts, but of appealing to his more cultured nature and appreciation of all things Alexandrian. Once again, the scenes at Trimalcio's dinner party in the *Satyricon* may offer a clue as to what truly constituted a surprise, for amidst all the other excesses, the guests there suspected that at any moment some clockwork automaton might leap out at them.[26]

No remains of these complex mechanisms have survived, yet ever since Philon of Byzantium wrote his treatise on pneumatics, in the second century BC, the possibility of creating machines that could be programmed with a sequence of moves to imitate the interactions of living creatures had been a very real one. Philon's staging of a robotic serpent rising to threaten a nest of birds employed a system of levers, screws and gears to which an initial impulse was provided by the manual addition of water. Two hundred years later, Heron, the great proponent of automatism in Nero's day, was still using hydraulics to power his 'Drinking Eagle' or 'Owl and Birds' vignettes, though now he offered the additional attractions of interaction with an audience member and simulated birdsong. Although the Pompeii that hosted Nero would have been able to supply the running water necessary for such pieces, by the early AD 60s Heron had advanced beyond such needs to create a self-contained theatre that needed only an initial injection of energy from a falling sandbag to propel itself forward, fling open its doors and begin the performance.

Ultimately, the organisers of whatever entertainment was presented would have done well to remember that it was a mere sidelight to the radiant spectacle of Nero himself. In Rome, there were reports at this time of a *cithara* player who toured the inns of the city, claiming that one string of his instrument had been given to him by Nero as a reward for his musicianship and demanding money with menaces when he sang.[27] The logic of his threats? That failure to pay was a challenge to the Emperor's judgement and answerable as treason.

As the sun rose the next day, any of Pompeii's famous cabbages that had not ended up on the table the night before would have been called for to quieten the groans of the city's hungover guests. Surpassing all other medicines in promoting digestion and known for its laxative effects, cabbage would have figured prominently in the prescriptions that Magonianus the doctor made out for those suffering from their excesses: either eaten raw to cleanse the upper digestive tract, or blanched and macerated with cumin and salt to produce a vomiting of mucus and bile over several days of treatment. Whilst Nero's entourage had probably cultivated strong stomachs, the imperial slaves who accompanied them, and who were usually too busy climbing the career ladder to enjoy a drink or two, would have accepted whatever hangover cure was offered if it meant that they were fit to attend the important public events of the morning.[28]

Yet as they dragged themselves up, even those with more stamina felt homesick at the prospect of having to smile through a final day spent among provincial mediocrities dazzled by the imperial presence. 'Although we came here feeling eager, we are far more eager to get away, back to Rome and our own *lares*,' ran the formulaic complaint scratched into plaster by half a dozen of the visitors in their different lodgings.[29] Their hosts would have been foolish to expect anything else, and wrong to take their dissatisfaction as a personal slight: Lucretius, after all, writes of this period as one in which man's craving for change and novelty drove him to leave

Rome for the country at every opportunity, but made him desperate to return as soon as he arrived.

If one thing could be relied upon not to change, it was the oppressive atmosphere of imminent persecution in which those close to Nero existed. When the people of Pompeii gathered in their theatre for the first rites in the Emperor's honouring of Venus, for which Nero would have taken his customary seat at one side of the stage, they may have thought back to the visit of his own favourite actor, Paris, a few years earlier. Then Paris had been in disfavour with Agrippina, but now it was Nero, jealous of his talents, who was offended; and this time the actor would not escape with his life.

Later, standing amidst the rubble of the Temple of Venus for the culmination of the ceremony, Nero would have had nothing but the broken cult statue on which to focus his piety. Yet the moment when he offered his dedication to the goddess would have carried a great charge, both for him and for those watching. And it seems that the goddess did answer Pompeii's prayers, through the man who claimed descent from her – in spirit if not blood – via the great Augustus, whose title he now borrowed. 'When Caesar came to the most holy Venus – when, Augustus, your heavenly feet carried you – there were thousands of thousands of gold pieces,' records one message written in the fresh plaster paid for through Nero's benefi-cence. The goddess also received her due: 'Poppaea sent as gifts to the most holy Venus a beryl and a drop-shaped pearl; a large display pearl was included,' another graffito tells us. It is one story about Nero that Tacitus neglects to tell us, perhaps because it shows the Emperor in too benevolent a light.[30]

As dusk fell, Maius looked out from the steps of the ruined curia *as all around the forum the makeshift doors of temple buildings were closed to signal the beginning of the Festival of Lemuria. Then he turned his steps towards home, where his final duties awaited.*

It had been a long day since he had risen to wave the imperial party on their way, only to find that they had already quit the city whilst it was still night, but the sense of anticlimax lingered. The decorations along the streets already looked forlorn, the broken buildings on which they hung more hopeless than ever. And what new hope had the Emperor really given? To what did a few bags of gold, the promise of more, and a pair of supercilious architects with grand plans really amount? Maius hoped that the optimism he had seen brimming in the decurions would not colour their judgement.

Tired and anxious as he was, the hours until midnight crawled by; but he did not seek out company. It was the time once again when the restless, hungry ghosts of the city rose to reclaim the homes in which they had once dwelt; the first of the three nights when their approach must be thwarted. Maius thought of the many who had moved into these homes since the earthquake, imagined how they must shiver at the idea of the dead strangers' return; he counted himself lucky to have lived where he had for his entire life.

When at last he made his way to the atrium he was relieved to see that everything he needed had been laid out. Lifting his thumb to his forehead, he made the sign, then washed his hands in the basin of fresh water before taking the black beans in the palm of his hand. Their smooth lightness touched him. Could so little really tempt the dead back to their tombs?

Quickly he turned aside and threw the beans from him, scattering them over the mosaic floor like a brief and sudden fall of rain. 'With these I have cast, I redeem myself and mine.' Again and again, nine times he intoned the words, splashed his hands in the water and, crashing the small cymbals, ordered the ghosts from his home. The sound of ringing brass hung in the air, then slowly died to silence.

—— IX ——

Before Nero could continue to the port of Brindisi and embark for Greece, events intervened to force the cancellation of the performance tour for which he had prepared for so long. The pageant planned to celebrate his return to Rome was put on hold: the Emperor's glorious entry into the city in a chariot drawn by four trumpeting elephants from the imperial herd kept on a reserve at Laurentum. It was a spectacle, requiring sections of the capital's walls to be pulled down, that could have been inspired by the images of Venus on Pompeii's walls seen by Nero during his visit (Plate 5e). A coin of AD 55 had also represented such a spectacle, but then the occupants of the chariot had been the divine pair of Augustus and Claudius, and on the obverse was the head of Agrippina. Nero had come a long way since then.

Already that summer, in the Naples theatre, Nero had finally exorcised any remaining guilt for his mother's death through his acclaimed performance as Orestes – the son of Clytemnestra, who murdered her husband Agammemnon on his return from Troy – whose good reasons for matricide stood in for Nero's less noble ones. The other perceived crimes of his reign proved amenable to similar laundering, with Hercules and Creon both joining the Emperor's repertoire. And, to the surprise and dismay of those still nostalgic for the ideal of Rome's republican past, the closer Nero came to adopting the persona of a Greek king – a being as much from the world of myth as of men – the more the common people of the Empire seemed to rally to his cause.

The generosity of the gifts he bestowed doubtless quelled any doubts over his intentions, as did the general feeling of carefree affluence and luxury that burgeoned around him. That Nero should now declare any 'treasure trove' – buried gold and goods – the property of its discoverer rather than of the state, could be seen as emblematic of the prevalent sense that ancient rights of ownership counted for little, and that fate might hand anyone the chance to reshape their life.

Yet, as the years passed, no one who paused to look beneath the glittering surface could fail to notice that the paradoxes of Nero's reign had become ever more difficult to reconcile. In common with his main rival, Gaius Calpurnius Piso – a man, like Nero, of fine pedigree and artistic pretensions, who was said to preach against the evils of luxury while wallowing in their depths – the Emperor lacked self-knowledge. The various treasuries of the imperial administration were haemorrhaging their wealth, and the silver and gold of Rome's citizens flooded east with no controlling hand to staunch the flow. Fifty million sesterces found their way to India in one year, with merchants creaming off one hundred per cent profits at every stage of the journey. When the time came for Nero's successors to account for the losses caused by his absurd munificence, they would total in excess of twenty billion.[1] With a wife, in Poppaea, who demanded golden shoes for her mules and the milk of five hundred asses in which to bathe, the figures for Nero's expenditure seem quite plausible.

'The conquering Roman now held the whole world, sea and land and the course of the sun and moon. But still he was not satisfied.' The *Satyricon* hints at the megalomania that was rapidly poisoning Nero's rule. Already acclaimed a god by some, Nero would use Corbulo's most recent conquests in Armenia to reinforce the image of his divinity. For the first time in one hundred and eleven years the doors of the Temple of Janus finally closed to signify that war was completely banished from the Empire. But while peace was a noble aspiration, the lavish price of Nero's grandiose projects made war more necessary than ever before. Without it, the economic engine of the Empire was about to stall.

Fate intervened in the early hours of 19 July AD 64. Only a few days after Tigellinus's most lavish orgy, the capital was purged with a great fire that would finally topple the Empire's finances into the abyss. The Augustan regulations that limited the height of buildings had long since been abandoned; in the back streets of the city, timber-framed tenements rose to six or more storeys and were huddled together for support. Fires were common, but nothing like this had ever been seen. Spreading too quickly to be contained, it raged for six days, died down, before sparking up again, until more than a third of the city had been consumed. Nero was absent when the fire began, but hurried back to take control of the emergency. And, despite persistent rumours that its cause was arson committed on the Emperor's orders, he somehow emerged with his reputation enhanced.

Even in his decision to sing a lament for the fall of Troy as the city smouldered, Nero was seen to be articulating the grief of his people. Neither his judgement nor his piety could be faulted. The sacred Sybilline texts that Augustus had deposited in the Temple of Apollo were consulted; the supply of corn was assured by requisitioning from nearby towns; and scapegoats were found among a messianic Jewish sect who were notorious for their loathing of pleasure and obsession with death. Such was the righteous anger of the people, indeed, and so heinous the crime against the true gods whose temples had been destroyed, that the Emperor took it upon himself to search for a fitting punishment. For maximum publicity, it was in the gardens where the homeless were encamped that the victims were crucified in mockery of their late leader, Jesus, before being burned alive. This time it was Nero himself, dressed as Apollo, the charioteer of the sun, who lit the pyres, to the rapturous cheers of a crowd desperate to believe that they had the leader who could bring daylight back to their benighted city.

For some, Nero's spell would never be broken. For many, though, the first hint of disenchantment must have come when the charred rubble of Rome began to be cleared. There were undoubted advantages to a more regular scheme of urban planning to replace the chaos that had gone before, but now, instead of sweeping away the smouldering city to make way for new housing, an entire valley in the heart of the capital was left free for the realisation of the Emperor's cherished plans for a *domus aurea*, or 'golden house'. It may have been Nero's hope, as some have suggested, that his new home could somehow welcome the entire city into its embrace, encompassing the needs of its population and providing, in the planned baths and parkland, a desirable communal resource. But as a giant statue of Apollo-Nero began to grow from its vast base at one end of the Via Sacra in Rome, and the gold of the city's ruined temples were plundered and melted down to clad its thirty-five-metre height in gold plate, many would have feared the kind of despotic regime that such an egotistical ruler intended for the future.

When plague descended on the weakened city, word was put about that it was only thanks to a visitation from the goddess Vesta that Nero had decided to stay in Rome in order that he could be with his people in their time of need. This time few cared. The plague was horrendous: 'The houses were filled with lifeless bodies, the streets with funerals. Neither sex nor age gave immunity from danger; slaves and freeborn populace alike were cut down by the disease, amid the lament of wives and children, who had themselves become infected while mourning or tending the victims, were often burnt upon the same pyre.' In the face of disease, even Nero was powerless. The grandiloquence of his building plans only emphasised his all-too-human limitations, and slowly his credibility began to crumble.

It was now that the first plans for a coup against Nero were hatched. Among the ranks of the elite, enmity was growing. Senators whose wives and daughters Tigellinus had whored out and whose wealth he would increasingly be driven to appropriate began to conspire. But when the aristocratic Torquatus Silanus was accused and driven to suicide, the surprise was less that the ringleader was a relative of Augustus than that the core of his support came from freedmen. For freedmen were now at the heart of the regime: Phaon was Nero's spendthrift chancellor, Doryphoros clumsily mediated Rome's relationship with her provinces, while Polyclitus led the commission of enquiry to Britain after the revolt of Boudicca, and had, even then, attracted intense hatred for his lavish lifestyle on the long trip. Hate figures, to a man, for the resentful old Roman elite, but there could surely be no doubt that they were loyal to the Emperor, the only protector on whom they could rely. Or could they? Paranoia was swiftly gaining ground. No longer could anything be taken for granted.

As if to confirm the Emperor's worst fears, the portents were not good: again a comet presaged a change of ruler, double-headed embryos were discovered in sacrificial animals, and at Placentia a calf was born with a head sprouting from its leg. With lightning strikes more frequent than ever before, a further plot was being hatched by the end of the year; the only question was where the coup should be staged. Piso, a putative successor, procrastinated over the use of his Campanian home. Others were more resolute in their determination that, by the summer of AD 65, Nero should be gone.

CHAPTER 10

The Saturnalia Kings

December AD 64

Anyone who passed Vettius Conviva as he hurried across the city that chill winter afternoon thought twice before offering their greeting. With each fierce stride, a tiny fraction of the affront that seethed in him was pounded out onto the pavement. Most of the past week had been taken up with final negotiations for the wedding of his brother, a freed slave, to the second daughter of the Gavii. There were benefits for Restitutus, to be sure, in a match with such a well-connected girl. But for a family fallen on hard times, there were also advantages in the arrangement, as Conviva knew only too well.

Hadn't he agreed to slip them the dowry on the quiet, so that they could then repay it without public embarrassment? Hadn't he even offered to pick up the bill for the public sacrifices and the feast? And what thanks did he get? Only just now he had heard that the bride's aunt, of all people, had publicly insulted Restitutus when reading the omens for the couple's future. Was it any business of hers to comment that there were stormy times ahead, or that a freedman might struggle to weather them? What was it about these people that made it so hard for them to accept that things had changed for good?

Only on entering the Augustales' clubhouse did Conviva realise quite how late he was. The opening rites in honour of the Augustus and his successors were already being performed. A smattering of suitably deferential Junians hovered around the edges, along with the odd free-born local who had been smart enough to sense the tenor of the times and had scrambled onto the bandwagon. Mostly, though, the room was filled with freedmen like himself who had done well out of the last few years. There was Vesonius Phileros, elected to membership only last year. His normally confident face showed the strain of a failing business partnership. Orfellius Faustus, it was said, had been doing side-deals with Ululitremulus, their competitor, but he would regret it: now Phileros was an Augustalis he could depend on their support. And there was old Cerrinius Restitutus, his hair turning prematurely grey from worry over his tearaway boy, Vatia. He too was in need of a kind word. First, though, Conviva needed to offer his congratulations to Popidius Ampliatus, exuding pride at the birth of his new son, Celsinus.

Scarcely had Conviva concluded these pleasantries than the meeting settled down to business. There were hoots of laughter and the odd groan went up when it was announced that once again the Augustales were being asked to contribute to the city's rebuilding costs. Some straight away quibbled that local talent was losing out to big-name architects from Rome. Hadn't Decimus Cossutius, a Campanian, designed the Olympium in Athens? Hadn't Cocceius been good enough for the temples in Puteoli, or Artorius Primus when Pompeii had needed a new portico in the forum?

But all that was long ago, and everyone felt that the ambitious plans provided by Nero's own architects, Celer and Severus, were a challenge that should be embraced. It was an opportunity not to be missed for the city's freedmen to stake a true claim to respect. As each man counted his projected profits, and calculated what he could afford to give, the question on everyone's lips was simply, 'How much and how soon?'

For the less fortunate in society, the later part of December was a time to which they would have looked forward throughout the year: the Saturnalia. It was then alone that a brief reprieve was granted to slaves from their duties and the strict ordering of society overturned. Slaves and masters alike would dress down and don the felt cap that usually denoted freedman status, as a sign that they were freed from their normal roles. They would dine together, gifts would be exchanged, and excessive indulgence condoned for all. By the tenth winter of Nero's rule it seemed to many that the topsy-turvy world of Saturnalia had become the permanent condition of their existence. Indeed, Seneca could not resist commenting that, compared to everyday life under 'the most Saturnalian of princes', the Saturnalia itself seemed like a reprieve from excess.[1]

The Emperor's own behaviour only encouraged such an attitude.

The debasement of the elite that was such a key element in the orgiastic spectacles laid on by Tigellinus amounted to no more than an especially extreme example of the December revels. And as if in personal endorsement of this state of perpetual anarchy, Nero wore the banqueting outfit that was normally only seen at the Saturnalia every day to his audience with petitioners. In his actions and appearance, the Emperor was signalling his personal contempt for the conventions that stifled individual freedom while inviting others to follow his example.

The freedmen of Campania needed no such encouragement: their ascendancy already found potent expression in the flourishing priesthood of the Augustales, whose popularity had grown to embrace those beyond its original constituency. The extensive fragments of the album of the Augustales lodge from Herculaneum that have been preserved show that, in order to manage the influx, the organisation appears to have developed an internal structure, represented in the three columns of the document, which split the total membership into 'centuries' on the military model.[2] In one column, headed *Veneria*, were the true freedmen; in another, headed *Concordia*, the Junian Latins. But the third is occupied by the names of men who were free-born but of low status and who, seeing no stigma in being associated with freedmen, pressed hard for admission to this world of accelerated social climbing.

The only Augustalis from Pompeii whose home has been identified is Vettius Conviva who, we know from the tablets of Jucundus, had most likely been a member since the late AD 50s. The slightly ludicrous air of self-promotion that pervades his house points to its owner being very much the kind of man one might imagine Petronius's Trimalchio to be: ostentatiously proud of his achievements and rather vulgar in how he chose to demonstrate his wealth. Although situated in a good area of the city and surrounded by influential neighbours, the House of the Vettii stands on a relatively anonymous back street just opposite a bar. But past its unassuming entrance and into the atrium, everything declares an overwhelming confidence that fortune will continue to smile upon its occupants and their business interests.

Almost the first sight to confront the visitor is an almost life-size painting of a bearded figure dressed in the Phrygian felt cap of the freedman, who carries a set of scales in which he weighs a bag that is overflowing with coins, and whose vastly larger-than-life penis sprouts from under his tunic. When it comes to luck, the image says, what matters is the wealth it brings with it: and in this house we boast both luck and wealth in abundance. Having had an eyeful of the painting, no one need have questioned that the two money chests that were attached to the walls of the atrium and bore the names of Restitutus and Conviva, were filled with disposable wealth. And lest anyone think to test the strength of the bolts that held the chests to the wall, images of hermaphrodites were dotted around the house to ward off the Evil Eye of envy.

But the strange combination of hubristic assertion and twitchy superstition that so characterises the House of the Vettii does not end there. In one sequence of mythological paintings at the rear of the peristyle, the theme of transgression and punishment is encoded in stories of gods and men; in another, not far away, familiar mythic characters are represented at the moment when they prove their greatness. The Vettii, it seemed, liked to advertise how fine a line they trod between daring and overreaching, and how cleverly they trod it. That their chosen sphere of adventure was industry and commerce is strongly hinted at in the activities with which the chubby *putti*, or cherubs, are busy in the borders of the mythological paintings: wine and perfume production, and the growing and selling of flowers (Plate 7). Elsewhere, a picture of an owl might point to involvement in the small fullery a few doors down the street. Only the ubiquitous appearance of Fortuna and Mercury, the protective gods of commerce, betrays any anxiety that the Vettii might ever need divine help.

In AD 64 it was only eight years since the senate had debated what to do with the growing numbers of recalcitrant ex-slaves who refused to observe the implicit terms of their manumission. The problem was acute: 'Insolence grown harder with liberty had reached a point where freedmen were no longer content to be equal with their patrons, but mocked their tameness and actually raised their hands to strike, without punishment – or with a punishment suggested by themselves!' But even as the social contract that governed Roman slavery began to fray, the senate could not agree to return even the most notorious offenders to their bondage. As the satirists loved to point out, the only remaining option was to exile them beyond the hundredth milestone from Rome, with the result that Campania would have been home to more than its fair share of the capital's less tractable ex-slaves. Perhaps it is this, in part, that accounts for the range of 'tribes' from which the Augustales of Herculaneum were drawn, one third of whom are listed as not belonging to the local Menenia, hailing from further afield. If so, the sanction of exile surely proved counterproductive. The presence of outsiders simply opened up new possibilities for trading networks that could be operated beneath the radar of the freedmen's ex-masters.[3]

The Vettii freedmen were clearly from Pompeii: they and their patron lived only a few streets apart. Membership of the local Augustales lodge would have given Conviva access not only to colleagues from the Menenia – who might in any case have come from as far away as the Sorrento peninsula, with its prized vineyards – but also to those who had trading contacts elsewhere in Italy. But in all the lines of business that the cherubs in Conviva's paintings are seen to pursue, it was good relations with local producers and traders that were key, and nowhere more so than in the manufacture of perfume. For that, early December was one of the most crucial times of the year.

With a fortnight still to go until the beginning of the Saturnalia, when the god of seeds and sowing would be propitiated while the earth lay idle, Columella's advice was that no iron tool should be allowed to disturb the ground. However, there were plenty of other tasks for the freed-up labourers to perform: cherries, almonds, apples and quinces could all be grafted now and, more importantly for the Vettii, the best olives of the year – harvested in November – were ready to be sorted and processed. For a family that had a hand in both wine and perfume production, the cash flow from the sale of the previous year's vintage came at just the right moment for reinvestment in olives. Only the fresh green oil from this pressing was considered pure enough to be used as a base for floral essences and, as such, could command double the standard price, with the famed oils of Campania in particular demand.[4]

Growing and pressing one's own fruit was clearly the best way to ensure that standards were maintained. The owners of one charming perfume shop bought land close to Pompeii's amphitheatre that had been abandoned after the earthquake, creating a large garden that was irrigated for the cultivation of both flowers and olive trees. The garden even contained its own outdoor dining area, which may have been a remnant of what was there before, or merely an indication of the owner's taste for simple, graceful living. But whilst the existence of such establishments demonstrates that even the small-scale production of perfume was a viable industry in Pompeii, a far more developed operation would have been needed to support the refined lifestyle that the Vettii freedmen had come to expect.

The Campanian centre for perfume production was Capua – which lies some thirty miles inland and to the north of the Bay of Naples – and, in particular, its dependent town of Seplasia, which offered a scent made from local wild roses that were said to surpass any cultivated variety. Organised into a collective of workshops, the *unguentarii* of Seplasia were able to wield considerable power and the main perfume-making families could call upon influential patrons in Rome. At one point, a suit was brought by the entire district against a tax-collector accused of levying unlawful duties on the import of key exotic ingredients. Strings were pulled, and the case was handed all the way up to the consuls in Rome for judgement. In Cicero's day, a century or so earlier, it had been the Plotius family who were most prominent: one group trading with the East from Capua and another working in Puteoli. Their aristocratic patron, Lucius Plotius Plancus, was even betrayed by his strong perfume when in hiding from treason charges. But by the AD 60s, it was the Faenii who were in the ascendant, with tentacles that reached out to Rome, Puteoli, Ischia and even as far as the ancient city of Lugdunum, or Lyon.[5]

In AD 62, Lucius Faenius Rufus had served alongside Tigellinus as Prefect of the Praetorian Guard. With the clamour for luxuries from the imperial court growing by the year, and Tigellinus acting as impresario, Faenius Rufus's clients must have been overjoyed at the opportunities. But as demand soared to outpace supply, a monopoly would have been impossible to sustain and at least one other perfume dealer from Capua dedicates a tablet to the Emperor in gratitude for his custom. As much as the manufacturers themselves, the flower-growers too would have been under considerable pressure. A ready supply of fresh petals was needed to cover the surface of lakes during an entertainment or to strew upon the Emperor's bed. Second best was unacceptable: if even a single one of the petals was curled, Nero would complain of insomnia. And with the ceiling of the dining room in Nero's Golden House constructed from ivory panels that were designed to peel back to allow flowers and perfume to cascade down onto the guests, Pompeii's growers and perfumers would surely have been called upon to divert an increasing proportion of their exports towards Rome. Those with contacts, through patrons or associates in the Augustales for example, would have been well placed to profit.

And Pompeii was not without its natural advantages in this line of business. When listing the specialist tools and equipment that could be sourced from various Italian cities, Cato picks out Pompeii and Nola for the quality of their oil mills – even recommending a specific dealer, named Rufrius – and, at times, carts carrying the cumbersome blocks of finely hewn basalt blocked the roads north. In Pompeii itself, a dedicated workshop for the milling of olive oil was situated in the dense back streets of the commercial zone to the east of the forum and only a couple of minutes' walk from the House of the Vettii. Yet the Vettii's own standards were more exacting, at least if the scenes depicted in their wall paintings are to be believed. According to these, they eschewed any brutality in the treatment of the olive. Here, in place of a stone mill, stands an upright wooden frame into which baskets of olives that have been harvested before they are fully ripe, to avoid fermentation and the accompanying rise in acidity, are gently tipped. Then the frames' walls are slowly forced together by the insertion of wooden wedges, themselves knocked into place with tiny hammers. The oil tapped off from the base of specialised machines of this sort was unrivalled. But did the perfume made by the Vettii really use oil extracted by this time-consuming process, or did hard-nosed commercial sense drive them to adopt more industrial methods?

No wooden mills of this design have been discovered during recent excavations, but in light of the Vettii wall paintings, the function of a number of badly charred wood structures that were found previously is now being reconsidered. Certainly, any manufacturer of perfume who also grew their own flowers, as the Vettii appear to have done, would have been used to the care and effort required to squeeze out infinitesimal quantities of precious liquid. Dozens of cartloads piled high with flowers would have had to trundle in from the fields to provide the two hundred kilograms that were needed to fill a minute, five-ounce vial of essence. To then cut corners on the oil might have seemed a false economy; and for those ladies who were prepared to pay a fortune for one of the tiny bottles of unguent, the notion that every possible care had been taken in its production would have been reassuring.

At least we can be fairly sure that no effort was spared to make the sales operation as luxurious and as flattering to the customer as possible: another scene in the Vettii painting shows a woman seated on a chair with cushions provided for her feet, sniffing a sample that has been dabbed onto the back of her hand from a selection on display in an exquisite tiered cabinet. The atmosphere is like that of a highly exclusive jeweller's shop: all dark enamel and fawning assistants. And the prices charged would not have been so different either.

When the young bride-to-be of a perfume producer like Restitutus visited his shop to select her personal fragrance prior to her nuptial celebrations, the myriad scents that assailed her carried with them not only memories of wandering near the market gardens of the city, but suggestions of places far distant. But while the smell of costus tickled her nostrils, and Verax, the salesman, tried to hypnotise her with tales of the spiral flower that grew from this aromatic root in the foothills of the high Himalayas, even the mystique of the place names could not have taken the girl's mind off what lay ahead. And there was still plenty to dwell on as she sat at her toilet on the morning of her wedding, rubbing in the lomentum cream –

the last hope of preserving her youth – that had been 'sent by Verax to Gavia Severa' along with 'an amphora of thyme honey'.

Valens knew very well why he was there; how much his presence at the ceremony mattered to the Vettii brothers. Decimus Satrius Lucretius Valens, still the flamen of Nero, was lending his seal of approval to a match that at any other time would have raised more than the odd eyebrow. His unease was shared, he was sure, by Cuspius Pansa, the next most senior decurion present, whose strained expression he could see out of the corner of his eye. Both were committed to seeing their city through these difficult times, regardless of their personal feelings. But to see Gavia Severa married to a freedman did not sit easily with either of them.

The formality of the occasion came as no surprise. From the tunic fashioned on an upright loom and the yellow hairnet that Severa had worn to sleep in the previous night, to the six tresses into which her hair had been parted that morning by what Valens had no doubt was the spear-tip demanded by archaic convention, not a single one of the trappings of tradition was missing. Sticklers for detail in their business dealings, the Vettii were clearly determined that no lapse in etiquette by the Gavii should mar their moment of glory.

Valens had known Severa since she was a small child, and the pity he now felt for her parents was such that he half-wished his own son were old enough to have been in search of a wife. A husband had already been chosen for her five years earlier, a young man of good lineage, around the time her cousin had shared in the blame for the fight with the Nucerians. They had weathered that storm, but the earthquake had changed so much: with both families fallen on hard times, the agreement had floundered. Money talked and without a healthy dowry on offer to cover the cost of keeping a wife, the Gavii had found that their options were limited.

Watched over by an elderly matron – who could claim the requisite and, Valens wryly reflected, increasingly rare distinction of having been married only once – the couple joined their right hands and the contract of their marriage was confirmed. But as the celebrations erupted, Valens felt himself vertiginously poised above a pit of self-doubt. Had the Emperor to whom he had given his unquestioned loyalty for the last decade really made things better with his money? Wouldn't it take more than a mere handful of new buildings to cure Pompeii's sickness?

Around Severa's waist a belt of ewe's wool hung, loose over her narrow, childish hips. Its tight knot, in token of her chastity, would be a challenge for the groom's fumbling hands later on. Her reluctance as she was coaxed out of her mother's embrace had not been feigned. On either side of her stood a boy – bringers of luck, since their parents were still living – and each held one of the bride's hands in his own. A third boy lowered the torch he held to the fire that glowed in her birth family's hearth, the light of which he would carry before them to her new home.

Valens would not follow them. He knew too well the sights and rituals that lay at the parade's destination: the offer of fire and water from man to wife, the official marriage bed bedecked with flowers squatting in the atrium in promise, or threat, of their first night together. Instead, he stood and listened to the party, and as they disappeared from view, their obscene songs fading into the darkness, the flamen *of Nero prayed for change. Of what kind he was not sure. But the prayer frightened him.*

The legendary patron of builders and their guild was Daedalus, the man commissioned by the ancient King of Crete to create a labyrinthine prison on the island for the Minotaur, and whose daring escape with his son Icarus, on wings made from wax and feathers, had been such a tragically mixed success. Both father and son figure in one wall-painting from Pompeii that shows a procession of builders bearing Daedalus in a canopied seat on their shoulders, from where he gazes down in sorrow on the broken body of the boy who plummeted to his death after flying too close to the sun. The pleasure of a well-executed plan and the horror when an accident brought work to a halt would have been familiar to those who spent their days balanced on the scaffolding that still covered Pompeii's landmark buildings (Plate 21). But the senior magistrates, whose duty it was to negotiate with the building contractors on behalf of the city council, might well have asked themselves whether it was the overreaching Icarus rather than his ingenious father who might have been the more appropriate patron.[6]

Even with progress made on many fronts, and despite Nero's aid, Pompeii at the end of AD 64 would still have looked a sorry sight, and at times it must have seemed to the inhabitants that half of their city was a building site. With so many projects of such long duration,

15. The god Bacchus with his symbolic animal, the panther, and the peaked mountain of Vesuvius, at this time believed to be an inert volcano, from the House of the Centenary. Note the trellises for vines that stretch halfway up the mountainside. The serpent highlights Bacchic worshippers as a snake cult.

16. The new-born Venus emerging from a shell, from the House of the Marine Venus.

17. An illusionistic image of an ideal Roman garden, intended to create an impression of greater depth in a small townhouse courtyard. Bubbling fountains of this kind are found in numerous houses in Pompeii, most strikingly from Region VI to the north of the forum, where this painting was found. Note also the hanging theatre masks, examples of which were found in the House of the Golden Cupids.

18. Women at their toilet, from the famous "mysteries" sequence of paintings in the Villa of the Mysteries.

19. Daedalus demonstrates to Pasiphae the wooden heifer he has crafted to allow the queen's concealment and facilitate her coupling with Jupiter in his incarnation as a bull, from the House of the Vettii.

20. Two lovers in a relatively modest example of the erotica that was to be found throughout the city.

21. Construction labourers hard at work, and in a formal procession: sights that would have been familiar to the inhabitants of Pompeii after AD 62, as the city struggled to rebuild itself following the earthquake.

22. Still life of food in preparation, celebrating the abundance of nature in Campania.

23a. Detail of Nero as Apollo Citherista from the Murecine 'Inn'. A very intentional homage to a once popular emperor who visited the city in its time of need.

b. Nero as Apollo was the centrepiece of a suite of three adjacent dining rooms. The fantastical architectural framing of the painting very clearly alludes to theatrical set designs of the time.

24. Ceremony in a Sanctuary of Isis, depicted in a painting from Herculaneum. In a setting that strongly evokes the world of the exotic East, male and female choirs sing from opposite sides of the temple steps, whilst ibises strut before the burning altar in the foreground.

25. The façade of a house covered in graffiti and electoral notices, as most would have been along the main and lesser streets of the city.

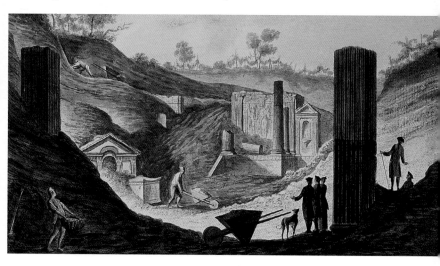

26. The excavation of the Temple of Isis in the mid-eighteenth century, showing a party of tourists observing the work. Painted to demonstrate the layering of the volcanic debris, for William Hamilton's publication *The Campi Flegrae* (sic).

27. Plaster casts of the dead, caught in flight, from the House of Fabius Rufus.

the failure of builders to meet contractual obligations would have been of great concern. It was to carry out an audit of false accounting for such projects that Pliny would be posted to Bithynia at the beginning of the second century AD. His contemporary Juvenal perfectly captured the sense of unease over 'sanitary engineers and municipal architects, men / Who by swearing that black is white land all the juicy contracts / Just like that – a new temple, swamp-drainage, harbour-works, / River-clearance, undertaking, the lot – then pocket the cash / And fraudulently file their petition in bank-ruptcy.'[7] The legal texts did make provision for such eventualities as a column being broken while being transported or raised, with the contractor who had been commissioned to undertake the job excused liability if he could demonstrate that he had taken all the precautions that could be expected of a 'very careful person'.[8] In most cases, though, the standard procedure was still that set out in an inscription from Puteoli, dated a century and a half earlier, where the contractor pledged land as surety for the satisfactory fulfilment of the job. In circumstances where land and property rights were still in turmoil as a consequence of lost records – as some must have been, with the fire in Rome perhaps destroying duplicates held there – such an arrangement may have offered little reassurance.

Of course, now that Rome itself was in need of major construction work, the demands on Nero's architects as well as on his cash flow would have escalated. But it does seem likely that he deployed some of this precious resource to Pompeii – the design of the one brand new temple in the forum, for example, is radical in conception, and reminiscent of aspects of Nero's Golden House itself. Architects were rarely mentioned in inscriptions unless they were the big names in the profession who focused their energies on the great temples and public buildings, but one architect does consistently appear to have operated on a more domestic scale in Pompeii.

There are almost sixty examples of the name 'Crescens' in graffiti and other lettering in the city, many of which might be accounted for by the popularity of a gladiator who went by this relatively common name. But at least two of the examples refer explicitly to a Crescens who was an '*architectus*' and whose commissions included work on houses at opposite ends of the city. In these cases, his name is converted, with real graphical flair, into the shape of a ship: the calligraphy stretches the ligatures of the letters into a bank of oars, while the final 's' curls up into a swan's neck prow. Elsewhere, the name figures prominently a handful of times on masonry that was put in place after the quake. Perhaps it was Crescens who restored the house of Albucius Celsus, now known as the House of the Silver Wedding, adding the bath suite and carrying out alterations throughout. Perhaps it was he, too, who went on to oversee the major rebuilding of the Sarno Baths. He certainly replaced the windows in one house near the forum and left his slick logo to prove it.[9]

Whatever the scale of the job, Crescens would have had to deal all too often with an elite who were infuriatingly confident in their views on architecture. Like Cicero critiquing a row of columns, the insensitive opinions would have flowed.[10] But an architect, whether a free citizen or a slave – as was surprisingly often the case – could always point to the professional training he had received in support of his own proposals. The educational tradition was largely Greek: that of the *tektones*, who were schooled in the use of scale models from which the dimensions of the final building could be read off using equivalence tables and specialist instruments. A proportional compass has been found in Pompeii and one interpreter of the city's remains has also seen evidence in geometrical shapes drawn on the walls in one section of the House of the Cornelii that it was used after the quake as a school for those working on the rebuilding projects in the nearby forum. Clearly there was no lack of these basic skills in Pompeii. But for Vitruvius, the most famous Roman theoretician of the architectural arts, there was a third area of expertise that was at least as essential as either construction methods or architecture. It was the art of making machines.[11]

Whilst machines were only a temporary presence alongside the rising facade of a temple or basilica, they were indispensable to the realisation of Roman civilisation's increasingly grand designs. Cranes constructed of two wooden legs bound together at a towering apex high above, and anchored to the ground by ropes, were employed to heave columns upright using a system of pulleys and counterweights. Towering derricks along the harbour side were rigged on revolving platforms to unload stones brought by sea: one ship that sank off Sicily contained a cargo of fifteen blocks amounting to over one hundred and seventy tonnes, a weight that would have been immovable without such mechanical assistance. Cranes, though, were among the least sophisticated examples of the advantages that mechanical science could provide.

Once again it was to Egypt – and in particular to the great museum of Alexandria and whatever remnants of the burned-out library it still housed – that each new generation of Roman technicians turned. For those students unable to make the trip in person, Heron's *Mechanica* – the same theoretician who had designed automatons such as the 'Drinking Eagle' – made the knowledge available in textbook form. Although it was the best part of a century earlier when Vitruvius had classified those machines that used either ladders, or wind, or traction, even then he had clearly believed that the architect's imagination was the only limit.

The arrival of building contractors in the kind of numbers required must have swelled the population of Pompeii significantly, and their needs must have changed the character of at least some parts of the city. One historian confidently asserts that it was in the zone to the south of the main street – where such grand homes as the House of Menander are found – that the majority of the itinerant labourers lodged, with commercial enterprises established to cater for them.[12] A case of a house nearby that was given over to use as a brothel lends weight to the theory, but other service industries too proliferated. Blacksmiths were needed to hone and service the tools of their trade – they are depicted on the builder's mark of 'Diogenes, your servant' that is inserted into a Pompeian wall – and for the time being, they could afford to sneer at their smaller clients. 'I hate the poor. Anybody who asks for something free is crazy; pay the price and get the goods,' wrote one. It was an attitude that this blacksmith would later have to reconsider, since he offered more emollient words in years to come.[13]

As the start of the Saturnalia approached, the people of Pompeii could, at least for a short time, forget about their woes, all the tasks that lay ahead and all the injustices of wealth and poverty, for with the festival came the prospect of a few days of unaccustomed pleasure. Feasting was at the heart of the festivities in individual homes, and a reversal of roles saw the master and his family supposedly serving their slaves, or at least taking their place alongside them at dinner, while a Saturnalia King was chosen from the underlings of the household and given licence to create mischief. Of course, if he were a wise man, this Lord of Misrule would make sure that his trouble-making left no lingering anger in his betters or resentment in his peers once order had returned. For, as Dionysus of Halicarnassus wrote, the real purpose of Saturnalia was as a safety valve to release the pressures that built up within a *familia* and to allow its members to begin the New Year afresh.[14] Its success in achieving this, even as the slave population burgeoned, can be seen in the creeping extension of the festival from merely a single day to almost an entire week by the time of Nero.

But while feasting was important, drinking was what really fuelled this period and unleashed all the boozy vices that were normally tightly policed. A few years later, Juvenal would write of the most notorious category of inns, the *popinae*, where it was possible to order a girl and a plate of stew along with your cup of wine: 'If you came across one of your slaves in such a den, wouldn't you pack him off for a spell of hard labour on your country estate? But blue blood has special licence, and gets away with behaviour that would shame a working man.' Come the Saturnalia, however, slaves could shame themselves to their hearts' content and compete with the most aristocratic young men in their debauchery: could drink themselves into oblivion, try their luck with 'waitresses' whom they couldn't afford, pick fights with one another, or gamble away their *peculium*, their hard-earned savings, on the throw of a dice. And no *aedile* would be sniffing around, ears pricked for the sound of the rattling dice box in the curtained-off back room.[15]

In some taverns during the winter of AD 64, the impression of a social levelling might have been especially pronounced. A side street just off the main road to the forum was home to a bar newly created within an old town house. The narrow entrance way was ripped open to create a hall where a serving counter was installed, and a hole knocked into a wall to allow customers to wander through into an adjoining property. Drinkers would have experienced the frisson of knowing that where their wine spilled, only recently the ancestor masks of an elite family might have stood; and that in the *cubiculum* to which they disappeared with the barmaid for a consideration of a couple of *asses*, the master himself might once have slept.

The inn walls around Pompeii communicate a vivid sense of the life they witnessed, the preoccupations of their regulars and the distinct character of the city's many establishments: from the respectability of the bar run by the ambitious Caprasia, quite possibly the mother of a rising political star of the time, to the seedy backroom of the neighbouring strip joint; and from the prim sobriety of the premises belonging to a married couple who were clients of Julius Polybius, to the coarse laughter that echoed from the muleteers' hang-out by the Vesuvius Gate.[16] But all too often the elite, who would never deign to enter such places, and the hard drinkers, who could never be persuaded to leave, were united in their criticism of the landlords. From one side the innkeeper was scorned as little better than a pimp and corrupter of public morals, while from the other he was railed at as a cheat who short-changed his customers and watered his wine. 'You deserve to pay for all your tricks, innkeeper. Selling us water and keeping the good wine for yourself!'[17] It was a serious charge, though at times the wine may have been watered down more as a tactic to maintain a certain level of sobriety. Even if found out and punished, innkeepers could take comfort from the story of Asiaticus, a slave from Puteoli who had recently been put in chains by the future Emperor Vitellius for selling such a mixture, but had been swiftly freed to become his pampered lover.[18]

If there was a legitimate case for watering wine, it lay perhaps in the official restrictions on serving food. Tiberius had banned even bread from being served, with drinkers cursing the Emperor the morning after for their unlined stomachs; Claudius had forbidden the boiling of meats, while confessing himself partial to an occasional snack. Now Nero was forcing pea soup on the drinking population. However, the rules were not necessarily strictly enforced. Pompeii's inns have pottery *dolia* sunk into their counters from which cold food could be ladled, and their walls show pictures of drinkers seated beneath hams and sausages that hung from hooks on the wall. One inn even markets its meals with the line, 'When ham is cooked and served to a guest, before he touches the meat he licks the pot and the dish.'

'If you're going to fight, get out!' exclaims one proprietor brusquely, ejecting two men who are caught up in an argument over dice. Any woman working in a bar would have needed to be even more ready to defend her corner. The law saw employment in such places as tantamount to an admission that one's body was for sale, with the women who worked there forced to waive their legal protection against charges of rape. Undoubtedly there were many inns where sexual services could be bought: one traveller's slightly ambiguous bar account actually lists the cost of a girl along with that of the bed she warmed and fodder for his mule. Some bars, though, adopted a different stance and offered written warnings that no one should presume the availability of the female staff, while others made the same point visually, for example in a painting of a woman with her hand clutched around the windpipe of a man who is advancing on her with an aggressive erection.[19]

The greatest pleasure to be derived from the saloon walls lies in the stories that they tell of identifiable individuals, of men and women who may even have passed this Saturnalia down at their local. A series of vignettes painted in the *caupona* of Salvius toys tantalisingly with the idea of a barmaid not as a passive object of lust but as a feisty coquette in full command of the situation. In one, the lips of two women touch in an experimental kiss, as though for the delight of onlookers. The caption nearby was censored by its excavators to read, 'I don't want to ... with Myrtalis.' In another, a waitress wards off the demands of two men for the flagon of wine she carries by drawing in a third, unseen figure with the offer, 'Come and drink, Oceanus.' It would have been a familiar name, as Oceanus was a gladiator, mentioned in another graffito next to sketches of his muscle-bound body, holding aloft the palm branch that was awarded for victory in the arena.

Salvius's inn stood on the far side of town from the amphitheatre. If Oceanus the gladiator were there, he would have been looking for a quiet drink. The idea captured in the wall painting is pure comedy: the moment before a true alpha male steps out of concealment, forcing the two leery customers to gulp down their pride and shuffle up the bench to make space for his magnificent bulk.

One instant the bar had been empty, Pherusa and the other girls killing time as the old regulars took small sips to justify their presence; the next it heaved with the back-slapping brawn of building workers, impatient for their orders to be brought.

There had been no work today. Instead the doors to the bathhouse had been thrown open early in celebration of the beginning of the Saturnalia, and it was from there that the crowd had just come, clad in laundered tunics and so fresh and clean-shaven that Pherusa had to scan their faces twice to be sure that Crescens was not among them. Then she remembered the long hours he put in and let herself hope that he might arrive later.

The expectation among the men was palpable as the waitresses arrived in convoy with brimming jugs. Their lip-smacking was not only for the wine. Later on the girls were to join them at table for the Saturnalia feast, with the slaves and servants and labourers, all so far from home and so friendless, transformed for the evening into a great surrogate family of equals.

Pherusa had been lucky in her new boss, who had bought her after her old master had been killed in the quake. Africanus had always been unusually strict in asking customers to show respect for his workers. Tonight, though, she feared he would be powerless.

As time passed, Pherusa repeatedly evaded the invitations pressed upon her to join the revellers in a drink. She was also careful to decline the offers from one man or another to sit down beside him for the feast. One by one, as the other waitresses succumbed and chose their places, her options were reduced and the prospect of a long and unpleasant night stretched out ahead of her.

The division in the room was clear. On one side sat the smaller group, the team of riggers drawn from the ship's crew of hoary old Tryphon who seemed to overwinter in Pompeii so often now that to many he scarcely seemed an Alexandrian any more. Under his tutelage they were a charming lot, pleased and amused in equal measure that Pompeii had seen fit to give them voting rights this year, and generous with their unexpected wealth. In the girls' eyes they were clearly the better bet, and the barmaids crowded around them with simpering smiles. On the opposite side of the room, the builders who worked under the foremanship of Vedius Turbo were packed in tight. Latin speakers mostly, puffed up Neropoppaenses, and riled at being bettered in love by foreigners. To console themselves they elected the Saturnalia King from among their number.

It was Tryphon who took the lead in attempting a rapprochement, challenging Turbo to a game of dice that he knew he would lose, and handing over the coins with good grace. He even found a tip for Pherusa, his innocent gesture eliciting a barrage of catcalls at just the moment when Crescens finally slipped in to take his seat.

When Pherusa noticed him, she momentarily dropped her guard and a hand snaked out to grope her. Crescens was quick to react but Africanus quicker, grabbing the man and hauling him away. The stand-off was over as quickly as it had begun.

Spotting Veranius Hypsaeus passing outside, the Saturnalia King ordered his cohorts into the street where they mocked the decurion with a cruelty that even the Saturnalia could not excuse. There was more to this than sport, and when Crescens stepped in to see Hypsaeus safely on his way, he knew that the danger was only postponed. The sweetened wine would continue to flow but the night had already soured.

Roman tastes in wine had changed over the course of the previous hundred and fifty years. Until the first century BC, Italy had been a net importer of wines from Greece, with the favourite brand being Coan, from the small island of Cos in the Aegean. But whilst it seems unlikely that the varieties of vine grown there were successfully transplanted, others that were more suited to the Campanian soil and climate did bear a grape of comparable quality, and provided the foundation for an export trade that saw amphorae making the long journey to the Red Sea as well as to regions with their own traditions of viticulture, such as Carthage on the north African coast. Although the Pompeian wines could not match some of those produced in neighbouring areas when judged by such connoisseurs as Pliny the Elder – who complained that they gained little from ageing and could be relied upon to give a cracking hangover – the contribution made by wine to the local economy, and equally to the local culture, should not be underestimated.[20]

In a famous painting from the House of the Centenary, the god Bacchus is shown standing on the lush slopes of mount Vesuvius, dressed in nothing but a giant bunch of plump black grapes on which the misty bloom is still visible (Plate 15). They might be of the Aminaea variety, that are known to have been grown in the area but produced only a hard wine (thanks probably to the sulphur levels in the ground), or else from the eponymous Pompeianum vine, that was originally known as Murgentina in Sicily, from where it had been imported.[21] If the latter, then the wine derived from them bore the name Holconii, thought by some to be among the best produced in Campania and named after the family who had pioneered its commercial production and grown rich enough on the proceeds to occupy a commanding position in the Pompeian hierarchy as magistrates and politicians.[22] That their unwise association with Caligula twenty or so years earlier had knocked their reputation was irrelevant. Most would have seen in them a model of enterprise, and few of the important or newly ambitious citizens of Pompeii in the AD 60s did not claim a stake in the same game.

The names that are found on amphorae, or on walls or artefacts found in premises involved with viticulture, or else in records of sales, are eminently familiar: the Vettii, Popidii, Fabii, Vedii and Gavii among many others. Lucius Popidius Ampliatus, the Augustianus from the House of the Citharista – and not to be mistaken with the Numerius Popidius Ampliatus who was also a key figure in Pompeii's last years – was a serious operator with multiple ties to the industry. The extended Fabius family owned wine shops as well as vineyards: Fabius Eupor, praised in graffiti as 'the prince of freedmen', operated on behalf of his patron Thelus, while Fabius Secundus did well enough out of the trade to make good on his promise to erect a statue in the Temple of Venus. Even Gavia Severa, the recipient of the perfume and honey delivery, was involved in dealing wine by AD 79.[23]

In all, almost two thirds of the villas that have been investigated in the Pompeian territory show evidence of wine production, as opposed to only a quarter where olives were processed. Quite what the relationship was between vine grower, wine producer and merchant is hard to fathom. Whilst there were good profits to be made from wine, the initial start-up costs were high: vines took five years to reach fruit-bearing maturity and only after that would they start to show a return on investment. Furthermore, the cost of the kind of machinery needed for processing the grapes was prohibitive for the small grower and so the use of shared, perhaps mobile facilities was one option, while the other was to collect the yield of a number of vineyards in a central location for co-operative pressing and cellaring. Everything points towards the desirability of a patron with a number of wine-growing clients, who could offer loans and economies of scale.

Even for major traders, the profit margins could be tight. The grapes grown on a hectare of land cost around four times as much to transport as the equivalent grain harvest, and a balance had to be struck between the ideal growing conditions, which were to be found on the slopes some distance from the town, and the erosion of profits that would be entailed in bringing the end product to town. That the land close to Pompeii and the Sarno was dense with vineyards perhaps points to a cautious emphasis on profit over quality. In a letter written later in his life, Pliny the Younger alludes to what appears to be overintensive farming on the expanding estates near his own villa in the north of the country. Pliny also remarks elsewhere, 'Campania, whether by means of careful cultivation or by luck, has lately increased its reputation.' Yet only seven kilometres from Pompeii, on a turning just off the main road to Nuceria, the remains have been discovered of what looks like a smaller farm that was subsequently swallowed up into an agro-industrial estate. Not only was the villa abandoned some years before the eruption, but some of its walls were even dismantled and the stone reclaimed for use elsewhere – a sad end for a place that would once have been fragrant with the smell of must, newly pressed from the ripe grapes, as it trickled along channels towards the *dolia* in which it would ferment for several months at least. The god Bacchus himself was said to die beneath the feet or wooden press that crushed the grapes, then rise once more in the froth and bubbles.

The solemn rites and less sober celebrations for the new wine took place in August, and while the households partied indoors for

December's Saturnalia, the wine was left to its long solitary task. In one of the working villas at Boscoreale, the presiding marble bust of Bacchus would have stared out from its niche at empty vineyards where the vines had been pruned back for winter, and only the pergolas or trees over which they grew were left to break the monotony of the view. When it came to the great *dolia* – left in cellarage that was open to the sky and whose walls were perforated with slits to allow the cooling wind to blow through – the vintners had finished their work. The recent discovery in a villa at Oplontis of over a ton of pomegranates, unripe at the time but carefully placed between layers of straw so as to ripen at the moment they were needed, provides evidence for one flavouring that could be added prior to fermentation. Straightforward sweetness was the most desirable characteristic, though, and whilst the addition of honey was one option, a syrup of lead acetate was cheaper. Its residual presence in the bones of drinkers has allowed studies of lead ingestion from the skeletons of Pompeii and Herculaneum to reach the unsurprising conclusion that men consumed considerably more wine than did women.

Pompeii's love of wine and the good things in life had found architectural expression from as long ago as the third century BC, when a sanctuary to Bacchus had first been established a few hundred yards outside the city, beyond where the amphitheatre was later built. For all the ferocity of the Senate's persecution of bacchants in 186 BC, during which hundreds of members of the supposedly subversive cult were executed, the savagery had clearly spent itself by the time it reached Campania. Indeed, the temple that was restored quickly after the earthquake had been built by the same city *aedile*, Maras Atinias, whose diligent law-keeping had reaped sufficient fines to fund the erection of a sundial in the Stabian Baths, while the family names that are set into the mosaic ramp of the temple were borne by two men who stood as magistrates in the AD 60s or 70s.[24]

Atinias was a scion of a famous wine-growing family, and although the original ownership of the great Villa of the Mysteries is unclear, it seems likely that its existence was always closely related to the wine trade in one way or another. Situated a short distance outside the Salt Gate on the way to Herculaneum, by the AD 60s or 70s, like many other properties, it had been partially converted to commercial use. Other rooms retained their original character – most notably, the dining room that contains a startlingly executed sequence of wall paintings of a young woman passing through a series of initiative rites – the 'mysteries' from which the villa takes its name (Plate 18). And while some have suggested that they offer a metaphor for the bride's transition into marriage, most are agreed that it is enlightenment through membership of the cult of Bacchus or Dionysus that is the reward enjoyed by the woman in the final, serene panel that marks the end of her journey.

As AD 64 drew to a close, Alleius Nigidius Maius may have felt that the entire world had espoused the values of the bacchants. He had tried hard to maintain both the morale and virtue of Pompeii through difficult times with his gift of new bronze tablets to enshrine the municipal laws, and gladiatorial games to celebrate their completion. Perhaps on seeing neither the letter nor the spirit of the law upheld in the wider world, even he now finally accepted defeat and embraced the retirement from public affairs that was his due. There would have been much that was hard to swallow as the unworthy grew rich on the confusion of the times: the freedmen, above all, who in Pliny's words, 'arrived with chalk on their feet, and returned with a retinue of lictors bearing fasces wreathed with laurel'. It was not only snobbery that drove the anger of the elite, but sometimes a righteous distaste for those who believed, as the mosaic from the house of the Neropoppaensis and senior magistrate Vedius Siricus put it, that 'Profit is Joy!' Yet what was there to do but make an offering at the Temple of Fortuna Augusta, on the corner of the street to the north of the forum, remembering how fortune's wheel could dash down men as fast as it had raised them?

Some may have been less quiescent. During the Saturnalia of AD 64, word might have reached the more receptive ears that a new and credible plot against Nero was taking shape in Rome, and closer to home as well. For those still undecided in their allegiance, the clinching argument might have been financial. The mechanism by which all new currency was introduced into circulation was through army pay or disbursements for public works. When the next stage of the imperial contribution for Pompeii's rebuilding arrived, squeezed out of a treasury preoccupied with Nero's Golden House, it would have been in the form of the new *dupondius* coin. Officially, it was worth two *asses*; but any experienced hand that grasped the bag of money would have known instantly that something was amiss: it was simply not heavy enough. A full eighth had been shaved off all gold and silver coins, or else replaced by bronze in an alloy.[25] It meant massive inflation at a stroke. Wise families hoarded their old coins, hurrying to bury them. And a shiver went through even those whom fortune had, until now, favoured.

There were only three of them there, a fourth expected. Nobody spoke. They knew what they were there to discuss but no one wanted to begin. In the smoky light of the single oil lamp, Alleius Nigidius Maius looked at the faces of the men who had joined him. They had left their families at home, made their excuses and crossed the town at night without a single slave for support. They were good, right-thinking men but seen now, half in shadow, their eyes smarting and bright, it was easy to believe them the most treacherous of conspirators. And in truth, wasn't that indeed what they were?

The sounds of revelry in the neighbourhood echoed along the corridors of his house as the minutes passed. Helvius shifted, only stretching his legs, though he half wanted to walk away. Much longer, Maius thought, and their nerve might break.

Then, outside, the loudest voices changed from laughter to anger. They were coming from the street. A fight? An ambush? Weren't they Veranius Hypsaeus's peevish tones? Only now they seemed to have assumed a commanding tenor. There was a scream of agony, another more prolonged, then a stunned silence until the sound of talk and laughter began again and rose quickly to its previous volume.

A moment later Hypsaeus himself entered. Never had they seen him so pleased with himself, so seemingly at ease – babbling through a smile about how wrong his old father had been; how only a fool would wait to punish a slave when the pleasure of acting on impulse was so great. But the spots of blood on his toga made everyone pause. Startlingly red, it ran down his hand and dripped onto his sleeve. And in his fingers he held something obscene and glistening.

Hypsaeus had taken his revenge. He had blinded the King of Saturnalia, Vedius Siricus's slave. But to harm a man's slave was to harm the man himself. If Nero survived, Vedius would not be easily placated.

— X —

Within the first few months of AD 65, the most dangerous plot of Nero's reign, intended to place Calpurnius Piso on the throne, had collapsed before it could even be sprung. Impatient with the lead conspirators in Rome, a woman called Epicharis took it upon herself to approach a naval officer from Misenum by the name of Volusius Proculus, who was known to be disaffected after his role in Agrippina's murder had gone unrewarded. He was well placed to oversee an assassination whilst accompanying Nero on a cruise around the Bay of Naples but, whether he saw greater advantage in loyalty or simply cracked in the pervasive climate of fear, Proculus divulged details of their plans to the authorities.

Retribution was brutal. A glut of executions or forced suicides ensued that were intended to purge the body politic with ruthless efficiency. But as, one by one, the guilty were arrested and interrogated, further names came to light, and with each revelation the scope of the enquiries broadened further until few were untouched by suspicion. The mere trace of a childhood friendship with one of those indicted could mark a man out, or at least provide a pretext for those who wished him ill. A period of terror and darkness was beginning in earnest that would last until Nero departed the throne.

It was inevitable that Nero would be disturbed by the revelation that the last remaining confidantes and advisors from the earlier part of his reign were implicated in the plot against him, though his reaction could not have been predicted. When Poppaea, heavily pregnant with their second child, nagged him once too often for arriving home late from yet another failed attempt to lose himself in pleasure, he lashed out. With a barrage of kicks to her swollen belly, Nero killed the unborn child and, with it, the beloved wife on whom he had so depended.

As guilt flooded over him, the last shreds of Nero's sanity and self-control seem to have washed away. Always convinced that lavish expenditure was the most reliable route to salvation, the faltering Emperor now tried to make amends by staging a funeral for Poppaea that would properly honour the full scale of the extravagance she had shown in life. The whole of Italy was scoured for each last drop of perfume and every final bloom, but such conspicuous mourning only played into the hands of his critics, who looked on sceptically as his regime edged ever closer to economic implosion.

His spending knew no limits. Spring AD 66 saw the arrival in Italy of Tiridates, the new King of Armenia, to receive his crown from Nero's own hands in what was little more than a ludicrously expensive piece of propaganda. Each day of the nine-month visit cost over two hundred thousand sesterces, yet Nero was convinced that the presence on the public stage of such a delightfully sycophantic Eastern prince was a sound investment. Flattered by Tiridates' references to him as Apollo, the sun god, he chose to overlook the puppet ruler's praise for the real hero of the war, Corbulo. Further emboldened, the claquers marched on ever more brazenly: 'We are the Augustiani and the soldiers of his triumph.'

From the moment that Tiridates' visit had been announced, the excitement it aroused offered the perfect cover for a draconian crackdown on recalcitrant senators, including those whose criticism had been only mild. Anyone who possessed either the lineage or independence of mind to challenge Nero was ousted from the senate, exiled or more summarily dispatched. In their place, fresh faces were recruited from outside the senatorial ranks, whose dependence on imperial patronage was such that their loyalty appeared to be guaranteed.

One such was Vespasian, who had survived both Caligula's dissatisfaction with the dirty streets for which he was then responsible as *aedile*, along with a severe reprimand for closing his eyes during one of Nero's theatrical performances, to become an estimable (if not yet quite top-ranking) military commander. The Emperor's elimination of senatorial rivals had included a large number of

Rome's most celebrated generals. Stepping into their shoes at this point, Vespasian was well placed to understand the extent to which the morale of the legions had been sapped, and to gauge the efficacy or otherwise of yet another vast imperial bribe to the troops, the third of Nero's reign.

The coins distributed were more propagandist than ever: stamped with visual references to Apollo, and also to the sun that had brought to light the Pisonian plotters (Plate 5d). The more astute soldiers would nevertheless have seen the lightweight bounty for what it was: a gesture of desperation. A handful of sesterces may have kept mutiny at bay for a while longer, but the metal for the newly minted coins had to come from somewhere. After the short-term successes of a liberal fiscal policy in the early years of Nero's reign, the realities of the economic hangover were beginning to bite, and with each new source of revenue that was tapped, popular resentment grew.

Tacitus claimed that by the mid-AD 60s, 'Italy had been laid waste for contributions of money.' Compulsory contributions of one kind or another were rocketing; freedmen, whose infractions of the social hierarchy had previously been overlooked, suddenly had the greater part of their wealth confiscated for relatively minor transgressions; the property of exiles was declared forfeit by the state; even Neronians who had in the past enjoyed the astonishing munificence of the Emperor were now being asked to pay an equally flabbergasting four million sesterces for an invitation to dinner. It was political fund-raising gone mad. The best solution to the gaping budget deficit that Nero could propose? Sending out teams of excavators to search for the buried treasure that the mythical Queen Dido had taken from Tyre to Carthage, and whose location had supposedly been revealed in a dream to one of the Emperor's favourites. The notion was both pitifully inadequate and ironically incompetent, coming as it did from the same Emperor as had only recently revised the law to allow private individuals to keep any treasure they found. But digging in order to fill the imperial coffers was nothing new.

The rapacity of Rome is most tangible today in a three-kilometre-wide scar on the Spanish landscape at Las Medulas. The largest open-cast mine in the world prior to the Industrial Revolution, it was there, at around this time, that Pliny the Elder was supervising the hydraulic processes used to extract gold from the ground, in his role as Procurator of Metals. In another Roman mining area, in what is now the Middle Eastern kingdom of Jordan, hundreds of thousands of tons of slag fill a rift valley where copper was mined down shafts that open into dozens of cavernous underground chambers. The most horrifying environmental costs of the operation are less obvious, though: even today the hair of goats, the snails and the local bread contain several hundred times the acceptable levels of lead and copper. Down the mineshafts themselves, the levels of radon to which the labourers were exposed would have left them dead from lung cancer within a few years. Yet even the fruits of their appalling hardship were insufficient to support Nero's expenditure. Balancing the books now needed a miracle.

On receiving the news that the inhabitants of Judaea had taken up arms in revolt against what they saw to be unfair taxation, those closest to Nero must have thought that their prayers had been answered – if the untold riches hoarded within the thick walls of the Temple in Jerusalem could be reached and looted quickly enough to save the economy. The quirk of fate in February AD 67 that saw Titus Flavius Vespasianus, at the age of fifty-eight, put in charge of the expedition to quell the Jews – and, in the process, handed the purse-strings of the one remaining source of easy money in the Empire – would have a profound impact on Roman history.

Vespasian sailed for Judaea as soon as the seas opened at the beginning of AD 67, having been appointed to the command following the catastrophic defeat inflicted on Rome's army by fanatical insurgents in the battle of Beth-Horon the previous November. There is no question that the posting went to the right man – for Rome at least, if not ultimately for Nero. Having already proved his credentials in the conquest of Britain, Vespasian's response to the threat of outright war in Judaea was straightforward: a crushing display of Roman military might. And unlike many who had risen through the ranks by virtue of their unthreatening mediocrity, Vespasian was also to prove a clever and subtle political operator.

With Vespasian's dominance in the field assured by early victories – to the satisfaction of the domestic audience in Rome – the road to Jerusalem lay open. Military logic suggests that he should immediately have pressed his strategic advantage and pushed on for the capital. But Vespasian understood well both how valuable an effective general and war hero can be to his political masters in times of need, and how expendable he becomes once his immediate usefulness is over: he had seen how even the great Corbulo had been forced to commit suicide on his recall to Italy. Vespasian was certainly playing a dangerous game. On the one hand his procrastinations served to sustain his own value, but on the other they starved Nero of the funds he urgently needed to buy the people's favour.

However, Vespasian was surely correct in believing that he was safer facing the zealots of Judaea than returning to face those of Rome, where Tigellinus was running amok. Lucan the poet was already dead, Seneca had finally committed suicide on the considerate advice of visiting Praetorian Guards, though it had taken the example of his wife's courage to persuade him to be stoical about it. Even Petronius, who had been so central to the debauched life of the Emperor, was forced to slit his own wrists – always one to squeeze the last drop of experience out of any situation, he had repeatedly opened his veins and bound them up to prolong with sensation of dying. Who would be next? And how many men would have to die before the hydra of conspiracy was prevented from sprouting another head, like that which planned to intercept Nero at Brindisi on his return from his latest tour of Greece?

Yet however strong the opposition, for Nero there could now be no turning back. When he paraded into Rome garlanded with the prizes he had won in Greece, some might have seen the four hermaphrodite mules that pulled his chariot as symbols of good luck. Most, though, would have recognised his flamboyant boast for what it was. And to hell with those who dared to question his morality. Accelerating towards his doom, shocked but undeterred by the revelation that Petronius had left behind a comprehensive account of his master's debauchery, the Emperor became ever more brazen in his behaviour. At every opportunity he flaunted his vanity and his sexual ambiguity along with it. Poppaea's place in the emperor's bed – her very identity – was swiftly assumed by an adolescent slave named Sporus, who bore a certain initial resemblance to the dead Empress and was castrated and then further surgically altered to make him more anatomically convincing. But while Nero still believed that he could reshape the world – even human flesh – to his liking, his past outrages were finally catching up with him.

'He has destroyed the Roman world ...' declared the governor of southern Gaul to his troops, firing the starting pistol on the race for the succession, '... he has destroyed the flower of the senate ... as for Nero's other outrages, it is barely possible to find the words for them ... I have seen that man in the orchestra of the theatre, lyre in hand and dressed like a strolling player ... I have heard him sing and act parts in tragedies ... Is such a man fit to be called Caesar? To be hailed as emperor and Augustus? Never! ... So, now, at last, rise against him! Save yourselves; save Rome; free the whole world!' One of the most famous prophecies of the age had suggested that apocalypse would come out of Gaul: for the self-obsessed Emperor, the prophecy was now coming true.

Nero received the news of Vindex's speech in Naples, and his stunned inaction was the response of a man who knew that the game was up, even if he was afraid to admit it. Not for him Caligula's attitude of, 'If I must fall, let me fall with the world shattered.' Instead, Nero seems to have focused on making his peace with those he had wronged, as best he could in the time left to him. Absorbed in overseeing the completion of the shrine to the wife he had killed – Poppaea Sabina, now deified as Sabina Venus – he fled reality in favour of the public stage, to rehearse the conclusion to his personal psychodrama. As his defences crumbled, they revealed a queasy mixture of bloated self-pity and pitiful self-awareness. Even the playbills for his last recitals were painfully ironic: *Orestes the Matricide*, *The Blind Oedipus*, *The Mad Hercules*. No longer did these tragic figures convince as dramatic alter egos: the more Nero himself drew the comparisons, the more the public saw through the absurdity of his mythic aspirations to the shivering, mortal man.

For years he had struggled to escape the ghosts of his ancestors. Now they crowded in on him, joined by the haunting memories of those whose deaths he had caused. His last performance was of

Oedipus in Exile, and his final, plaintive line, 'Wife, mother, father, all do urge my death.'

When his regime's collapse came, it came suddenly. The *coup de grâce* was delivered by a relatively low-ranking official, yet one who wielded enormous power. As the sailing season began, word arrived that Lucius Clodius Macer, the governor of Africa, had been assassinated, and that the Prefect of Egypt, Tiberius Alexander, was threatening to cut off the grain supplies to Rome and was urging the senate to consider its options. Cowed by Nero's power, and impressed by his surprisingly resilient popularity, the old senate had always felt impotent to act against him except by subterfuge, and since the purges its composition had supposedly become more Neronian than ever. But Roman oligarchy, although usually dormant, could be brutally responsive. As long as the plebs were fed and entertained, a ruler could feel secure; as soon as the city's collective stomach sent hunger signals to the political brain, anything was possible. For all the bonuses it had received, the mere possibility of delayed wages saw Nero's army desert him at a stroke; and with all its pent-up bitterness, the rump of the old senate convinced the newcomers to declare the Emperor an enemy of the people and strip him of his bodyguard. Almost overnight, the mightiest man on earth found himself alone and abandoned.

In headlong flight from his capital, Nero must have known that death could not be outrun. Even then, he lacked the courage to end his life by his own hand and turned to a doting slave for assistance. But if his final hours lacked tragic dignity, at least Nero achieved a kind of poetic symmetry at the very last, and perhaps a certain poignancy too, for he died on 9 June, the anniversary of his murder of his first wife, Octavia.

The Year of the Four Emperors

June AD 68–December AD 69

It was a close call when Papilio was accidentally jostled by a passer-by. High up on the rocking ladder, his partner Astylus threw out a hand to balance himself, the other still gripping his brush and pots of paint. Papilio shouted up his apologies from the pavement, but there was nothing that could be done to halt the stream of slaves leaving the house two doors down, who stumbled past bearing all manner of goods in their arms, bound for one or other of the auctions.

At that moment, Decimus Satrius Lucretius Valens felt every day of his forty-five years. Standing across the street from the signwriters, he stared at the name of his son – the same as his own – half-finished in red and black. Things were moving so fast. Even if the boy was elected as aedile *next March, Valens was unsure whether he could afford the costs. Who was to say where they would be a week from now, let alone a year? Who knew if he would even be in a position to settle with Astylus? Revolution was in the air; fortune's wheel was spinning. Those who only a few months previously had been at the zenith of their power now barely clung on; and those whom they had done down were looking for vengeance.*

Valens had been lucky so far. As flamen *of the late, unlamented Emperor, his position was awkward, to say the least. He had been circumspect in pushing Nero's agenda in recent years, but it was only the presence of powerful friends on the council that had saved him. Now old Galba had become emperor and had calculated the hole in the treasury's coffers at twenty-two hundred million sesterces. He was demanding that nine coins out of every ten be returned, and rumour had it that he was sending an inquisitor to Pompeii, like those who were busy scouring Rome for Nero's misspent monies. But those endless perks and gifts to Nero's favourites that had made their enemies so envious were all spent and unredeemable. Could the recipients now really be asked to cough up the feasts or rebottle the evanescent perfumes that had drifted up into the sky?*

There were reports from Herculaneum of houses being stoned by a mob. Vedius Siricus, the Neropoppaensis who had only recently been elected to oversee the census, was keeping his head down. The Popidii freedmen had closed their doors against those eyeing up future bargains. Others were rushing their goods to auction before prices fell, hoping that their haste might be taken for contrition. With the last of the construction workers pulling out, progress on the forum had come to a standstill and legal suits were being brought over the contracts that had diverted public funds into private pockets. Cornelius Tages, who had enjoyed his years in the sun, now found himself confronting bankruptcy. It was said he might even have to contemplate selling himself back into slavery.

What was Valens to do? Brazen it out as his wife insisted, arguing with him for additional funds to invest in their son's future? Her proposal was that they should buy more gladiators to stage yet another fight barely four months after the last, to show that the Decimi Lucretii were still a force to be reckoned with. But professional fighters were in short supply. There was better money to be made as a mercenary than in the arena: Valens himself had received a discreet approach about hiring out his own troupe. It seemed that things were going to get much worse before they got any better.

The death of Nero was a watershed. It marked the end of a dynasty that had ruled for more than a century. From this time on, the best man would be chosen on merit, or so everyone hoped. In the spring of AD 68, the elderly Galba had a lead on his rivals and was quickly proclaimed emperor but, as Tacitus wrote, the great secret of the Empire was out: an emperor did not need to be made in Rome. That revelation opened the floodgates to contenders, men who believed themselves qualified for the role, or were persuaded to claim the throne by others who saw personal advantage in being close to the purple. But whilst there was no shortage of self-belief in the ranks of the aristocracy, Nero's purges had removed all the most promising candidates and left behind a relative wasteland of talent. A period of blood-letting lasting nearly eighteen months would prove to be the only way to resolve the matter.

For much of this violent period, the people of Pompeii were little more than distant onlookers, struggling to pick up the pieces after Nero's divisive last years and to continue with the long and laborious task of rebuilding their city. As the fortunes of the various political factions who fought over the imperial throne in the north of the country ebbed and flowed, the levels of tension in Campania would rise and recede. But extraordinarily, we can get a startling view of the times through the eyes of two participants with strong links to Pompeii and her neighbour Nuceria. The older of the two was Alfenus Varus, for whom the auctioneer Caecilius Jucundus had travelled on slave-trading business a decade earlier, when he was still the *trecenarius augustus*, or first centurion of the Praetorian Guard. The other, who had not yet visited Pompeii but would later be of far greater significance to the city was following in his footsteps.[1]

In late AD 68, Suedius Clemens was a young and ambitious member of the Praetorian Guard, stationed just outside Rome on the Viminal Hill and watching the political events unfolding with great interest. Born to relatively humble parents, and too junior to have profited from the kind of sudden elevation that a man like Vespasian had enjoyed during Nero's purges, Clemens's attitude towards the situation was probably ambivalent. In an age of superficial values, which had not yet weaned itself off the flamboyance and charisma of Nero's reign, Galba's wizened features and miserly ways were deeply unattractive. But the Praetorians would have appreciated the summary justice meted out to the marines who, on Nero's whim, had been allowed to usurp the Praetorians' role as guard to the Emperor: decimation, with each tenth man to be stabbed to death by his comrades-in-arms. And they would have also appreciated the sight of the Batavian cavalry, recruited from the Netherlands, being dismissed and sent on the long trek north to their drizzly home, even if it was political folly to alienate such formidable fighters.

Such sport apart, there was little else for the Guard to look forward to from a seventy-one-year-old Emperor who refused to travel unless accompanied by a carriage holding a million sesterces, as reassurance against a rainy day. His austerity policy and the harsh measures he proposed to restore misappropriated property were precisely the antidote Rome needed to the spendthrift decade that had gone before, but Galba lacked both the personal authority and the political sensitivity to convince his patient to accept the cure. When the newly acclaimed Emperor refused to make an exception to his belt-tightening for the Praetorians, and neglected to pay over the bribe that was expected at moments when they were asked for their public support, he made a huge mistake. As long as Galba was the only act in town, men like Suedius Clemens would play along, idling their time away with jokes about his rumoured sexual appetite for adult men. But their pride had been wounded and any repeat of such a slight would prove fatal.[2]

The most attractive and conspicuous alternative to Galba was Marcus Salvius Otho, a Roman aristocrat whose name would have been familiar to Pompeians from the short time he had spent as the second husband of Poppaea Sabina, before she transferred her affections to his childhood friend Nero. Otho could rely on the support of the discontented loyalist troops of the late Emperor, who harboured a lingering affection for the good times and saw in Otho a symbol of continuity. Indeed, many saw him as the natural successor to the older man. But having toiled for ten years to establish his credibility as governor of Lusitania after a notoriously riotous youth, he had learnt the virtue of patience, and decided to wait for the right moment to strike.[3]

Otho's only demand was that Galba should recognise him as his heir, or at the very least refrain from naming someone else in his place. But for Galba, who was acutely aware that his advanced age was seen as a liability in such unstable times, the pressure to choose a successor was growing. When dispatches arrived from the army of Germania Inferior suggesting a planned *coup d'état*, the news impelled the obstinate Galba to make another, still more catastrophic error of political judgement. Rather than Otho, he named the youngest son of Marcus Crassus Frugi – Lucius Calpurnius Licinianus Piso – as his heir. Having nominated him, Galba then showed the unerring instinct of the gambler on a losing streak when he accompanied the young man up to the Viminal to receive the acclaim of the Praetorians, but once again failed to take with him even a modest bribe. The only surprise was that either of them walked away alive.[4]

Having eluded the assassins that Nero had sent to kill him while he was governor of Spain, and with at most only a few years of life ahead of him, perhaps Galba felt emboldened to brook no compromise in his campaign to set the world to rights. But the naïvety of his actions reduced those few years to a few short days. The great *haruspex* Umbricius Magnus was called upon to interpret the will of the gods. He read the entrails and quietly confided to Galba that the man who would overthrow him was already in the city. Unsurprisingly, word of the warning got out.

Realising the danger he was in, Otho seized the initiative. The mere signal of his readiness to make a stand was enough to bring the political divisions in the city out into the open. On one hand the common people converged on Galba's residence to plead with him for Otho's execution – perhaps more out of a desire for peace and order than as a sign of true support. On the other, supporters of Otho made imploring speeches across the capital. Emotions ran high until, imperceptibly, the mood in the crowd shifted, with support for Otho quickly gaining momentum. The mob suddenly understood its terrible power. As the sedan chair carrying Galba was forced forward by surging crowds and finally toppled to the ground, an eerie silence descended on the forum and spectators stood on tiptoe to get a better view of the sprawling old Emperor. Less than six months after he had been granted the title, a sword was laid across Galba's scrawny throat and pressed down by the force of a soldier's boot. By nightfall, Otho was installed in his place.[5]

But violence breeds violence. And AD 69 was only just beginning.

The message from the senate announcing that Otho had been installed in Galba's place reached the army in Germania too late, after it had already sworn allegiance to its recently appointed commander, Aulus Vitellius, a plump and pampered aristocrat, and no one's idea of what a Roman emperor should be. Perhaps, had the die not already been cast, the legions in Germany would have thought better of their decision at this point, and saved Italy from much bloodshed.⁶ For, as later writers would observe, Rome was about to be fought over by the two worst candidates imaginable. The last thing that the state needed was another Nero, yet both Vitellius and Otho were shaping up to fill his shoes quite plausibly.

Otho's sexual habits were the subject of much discussion and, in many people's view, he was even worse in this respect than Nero: not only was he effeminate, but the accusation was once again rolled out that he was a pimp, having married Poppaea solely to procure her for Nero. What was more, one of his first actions on acceding to the throne was to pledge a further fifty million sesterces of imaginary money to secure the completion of Nero's Golden House, the sprawling emblem of the late Emperor's despotism. He even went so far as to assume the name of 'Nero', and was hailed as such by the people of Rome. What Suedius Clemens saw in him we do not know, but force of circumstance made Otho the Praetorians' candidate in the war that lay ahead, and the possibilities of personal advancement were always foremost in Clemens's thoughts.⁷

Alfenus Varus's motivation for taking a prominent place in the ranks of Vitellius's officers was probably clearer. In the first place, he was at this time serving as Prefect of the Camps in Germany but, perhaps more importantly, he and Vitellius also shared a home town, though Nuceria ran stronger in Varus's blood than in that of his master. Fifty-two years old, Vitellius had actually been brought up on Capri, the infamous pleasure island where Tiberius used to enjoy luxuriating on a couch in a room of mirrors, from where he could observe the sexual antics of myriad young couples from any angle. Inevitably Vitellius was said to have acquired a taste for sexual depravity, with tales of penetration by older men the obligatory scandal. But it was for his gluttony that he would best be remembered. One dish that he had devised for his table was called the 'Shield of Minerva' and comprised delicacies from every corner of the Empire, including pike livers, pheasant and peacock brains, flamingo tongues and lampreys' spleens.

The appearance of a challenger for the throne with links to Nuceria could not have been more alarming to the people of Pompeii. Nero's reign might have disappointed them in many ways, but for the last ten years the majority of Pompeians had felt that 'their man' had sat on the throne. Now the city that had been their closest rival had usurped that privilege, at just the moment when Pompeii's influence as a political and administrative entity was being eroded, and its commercial dependence on Nuceria increasing. Already the second change of emperor in so short a time and in such an horrific manner would have jarred the nerves of those unsettled by the end of the Julio-Claudian dynasty. But when news of Vitellius's competitive claim to the throne followed, any debate over which way to lean would have briefly resolved: Otho would be their man.

In the imminent chaos, the other cities of Campania did not hesitate to choose sides. Puteoli favoured Otho, while Cumae went for Vitellius. The preferences of Stabiae and Herculaneum are not known, but perhaps in the face of civil war they too, like the people of Pompeii, harked back to the Social Wars of a century and a half earlier that had similarly divided the region. Then, whilst Nuceria had been an outpost of Rome against her allies, Pompeii had stood as one of the last strongholds in Campania after Stabiae and Herculaneum had fallen to Sulla.[8] Sulla's attack on Pompeii had been particularly vicious. To this day the walls between the Herculaneum and Vesuvius gates are still pockmarked from the impact of missiles from Sulla's siege engines, but recent excavations have revealed that the walls were less the target of the ballistas than the accidental victims of poor marksmanship. In one block of buildings, the destruction caused by the stone balls that were hurled into the city extends more than eighty metres back from the walls. Buildings were shattered to their foundations and the balls themselves, along with lead slingshot, have been found in rubble that was dispersed around the city. In AD 69, there was also good reason for Pompeii to be afraid.

No one recognised him. It had been nearly a decade since Grosphus's exile and he had aged under the beating sun of Africa. But he remembered every inch of the city that had witnessed his humiliation after the riot in the amphitheatre, and the face of every man who had shunned him.

When word had reached him of the earthquake, he had seen it as just punishment for his detractors and had hoped that the damage was severe. Now, though, walking up from the harbour in the crisp morning light and in under the arch of the Stabian Gate, he was taken aback to find how greatly the city was changed. With only a handful of old labourers to be seen at work, wedging ill-fitting blocks of stone into gaps in the wall beside the gatehouse, he wondered how such a transformation had been wrought.

Off to one side there was a bustle of activity. Accosting a man who was hurrying along with an armful of garlands, Grosphus discovered that they were destined for the inauguration of the new Temple of Isis. Its benefactor? A freedman of the Popidii named Ampliatus, the florist told him. With a sneer Grosphus guessed that this must be the same Neronian sycophant who had been on the make years ago. But no, he was quickly corrected. This man was from a different branch of the family altogether.

It was all most strange. Yet Grosphus liked this new city better than he had the old: it suited his style. Where, before, the main streets had been boulevards of elegantly spaced doorways through which you had to crane your neck to see the finer courtyards beyond, as often as not those entrances were now crammed between stalls and taverns. There was life and the scent of opportunity, even if there was little sign of joy. He almost felt that he could do business here. But Grosphus reminded himself that his stay was to be short: by the end of the afternoon he would be on his way to Nuceria, his new home.

Walking past the temple of Fortuna Augusta, he noticed his name, faded but still visible on the wall outside, and took it as a sign to enter. Who, after all, would have believed back then that his own memory would outlast that of Nero, whose name seemed to have been whitewashed out wherever it had previously been painted? For that, Fortune deserved a special offering. And with it, a prayer that she would ensure the rivalry between Pompeii and Nuceria remained as bitter as ever in the coming war, so that Grosphus could find a way to exact his revenge.

Despite setting out under terrible auspices, Otho cut a surprisingly martial figure at the head of his column of soldiers as they headed north from Rome. Vitellius, for his part, was marching south from the Alps with an army full of steely experience gained on the borders of the Empire. Even the most unsympathetic chroniclers could not deny that both men, buoyed up by the excitement of the moment, had roused themselves to unexpected heights of leadership. But by the time the impending confrontation was played out, one of them would have shown that he was capable of putting love of his countrymen before ambition.[9]

The armies converged along the Via Postumia and clashed in the wide valley of the River Po, not far from Cremona. In one part of the widespread battlefield, Vitellius's Twenty-First Rapax Legion engaged Otho's First Adiutrix; elsewhere the Fifth and the Thirteenth soon joined battle, with the five thousand men of the Praetorian cohorts deployed for Otho. But the crucial fight took place in the river itself, between men weighed down by armour and sodden tunics. Alfenus Varus, the man from Nuceria, had won the trust of the tall, streaming-haired Batavians a few weeks earlier, when he had quelled a mutiny by other troops irritated by the arrival of these boastful outsiders. Now they followed him with passionate enthusiasm against a corps of two thousand gladiators, under the command of Suedius Clemens, who had been promoted to the important rank of First Centurion. He too was appreciated by his soldiers, though for a different reason: in the face of catastrophic ill-discipline and mutiny on the long march from Gaul, he had allowed the troops under his command to rampage like an invading army, looting the farmsteads of honest Italians.

But there was no time for such laxity now. The fighting in the water was close and ferocious, a professional contest with pride at stake, as the gladiators boarded boats and the Batavians waded out to intercept and overturn them. It was a formidable military feat, but between men used to swordplay for show and those who would fight to the last for their comrades, the outcome was a foregone conclusion. As the Batavians hauled themselves up the reedy river bank and set off to join the main fray, they left behind them a bloody logjam of bodies, men whose courage in the amphitheatre might have won them mercy, but for whom war had proved a crueller game.[10]

The unexpected arrival of the northern giants on the battlefield – their adrenaline still pumping, the water spraying from their clothes – was decisive: their impact turned the flank of Otho's army. Before a messenger could reach Otho at his headquarters in the nearby city of Brixellum, the tattered remnants of his soldiers were already streaming back, carrying their own news. Unable to countenance being the cause of a massacre, Otho took his own life; as word spread, his troops quickly laid down their weapons or fled, lying low until the future became clearer.[11]

For Suedius Clemens, who must have cursed to see his star waning so soon after it had risen, Flavius Vespasianus – the general supervising the conduct of the war against the Judaean revolt – was now the only candidate who held any promise of prevailing against Vitellius. The east of the Empire had held firm for Otho, and there could be little doubt of Vespasian's reluctance to see Vitellius on the throne. Under Otho, Vespasian's brother Flavius Sabinus had been returned to the position of Prefect of the City of Rome that he had held under Nero. Now, for all Sabinus's oaths of loyalty and Vitellius's announcements of an amnesty, he was vulnerable, as was Vespasian's younger son, Domitian, who was also in Rome. It seemed to many that the general in the east would be forced to act.

Alfenus Varus, meanwhile, was riding high. When Vitellius entered Rome in triumph, Varus accompanied him as the new Prefect of the Praetorian Guard. It was not the old Praetorians he would lead, but a more makeshift force that had been newly recruited from the legions to replace those who might feel any residual loyalty to Otho. Such political moves were presented as part of a wider operation to show that Vitellius could be trusted to uphold the law. And when the hundred and twenty citizens who petitioned to be paid for their role in the assassination of Galba were rewarded not with gold but a death sentence, it was a strong statement that no ruler could condone regicide.[12]

By this stage of the struggle for the succession, however, the regular comings and goings of emperors had left the population of the capital inured even to shock tactics like these. Indeed many began to feel more like spectators at some numbingly extravagant piece of theatre, than witnesses to political turmoil. The debauchery of Vitellius's troops and the staging of gladiator games in any available public space confirmed the impression that the clock was now firmly turned back to Neronian days, and the sacrifices offered by the Augustales to Nero in the Campus Martius cemented the impression.

Events, however, took a decisive turn when, on 1 July AD 69, the Prefect of Egypt declared that instead of backing Vitellius or any of the senatorial insiders from Rome, he was adding his voice to the growing clamour for Vespasian to seize the imperial throne. His announcement provoked a groundswell of sympathetic opinion. That summer, Vespasian, accompanied by his eldest boy Titus, was still busy grinding out a victory in a vicious counter-insurgency operation against Jewish revolutionaries in Judaea. Up until then he had kept his powder dry, presenting the image of a man too preoccupied with the weightier matters of imperial defence to give much thought to self-interest. Suddenly, though, the balance of power had swung in his favour and he could no longer ignore his destiny. In later years, it would be to the date of the Prefect of Egypt's intervention that Vespasian ascribed the beginning of his reign.[13]

Initially, Vespasian remained personally aloof from the battle to make him emperor, doing no more than securing Egypt and thereby blocking the grain supply. The responsibility for advancing his cause back home fell mainly to the legions of the Danube and, initially, it looked as if their victory might be swift. A campaign of incitement spread like wildfire from legion to legion across the Empire. Looking up from his partying after a few months in power – during which he had managed to spend an additional nine billion sesterces to add to the deficit – Vitellius found himself confronted by a strong and well-organised enemy.

When the opposing sides in the civil war met again in battle near Bedriacum, modern Cremona, the standard of Vespasian's Flavians now fluttered over an army that included troops who had previously fought for Otho. In every other sense, though, the circumstances of the two forces were the exact opposite of what they had been earlier in the year. Sunk into easeful sloth, their morale sapped by commanders who secretly harboured Flavian sympathies, the army of Vitellius was now no match for the soldiers who charged them, fired with a fervour for revenge.[14] The Flavian side won a straight-forward victory and proceeded to vent their bloodlust on the unfortunate city of Cremona that stood nearby. Until this point, the battles of AD 69 had been played out against a backdrop of relative normality for most people. Certain towns might have expressed preferences for one emperor or another, but they had not come to blows. Suddenly, all that changed. The death toll when the victorious army went on to rampage through Cremona's streets, putting anyone in sight to the sword, was bolstered by the fair that happened to be in progress and many thousands of its townspeople and visitors died.[15]

For the inhabitants of Pompeii, however, Vespasian's victory must have come as a relief. First the marines from the fleet at Misenum went over to Vespasian, then the gladiator auxiliaries who were sent to suppress them defected. It seemed as though the blood spilled at Cremona might have saved the rest of Italy.

It was, it seemed, a walkover for Vespasian, *in absentia*. As the Flavian army marched through Umbria towards Rome, cohort after cohort of Vitellian troops laid down their weapons and welcomed them as brothers. As they entered the vast plain of Terni, the meagre Vitellian force of four hundred, who had been detailed to fight to the last man, folded after putting up only token resistance. Alfenus Varus, who was trying to hold the passes of the Apennines with a force of Praetorians, packed his kitbag in haste and hurried his remaining troops back towards Vitellius and Rome, the charges of cowardice ringing in his ears, never again to give him peace.[16]

But at almost the same moment, in an unexpected reversal that sent out waves of alarm as far as Vespasian in Alexandria, Vitellius's armies counter-attacked and won major victories on every front. Their successes south of Rome were especially striking, when the naval base at Terracina, not far up the coast from Misenum, was laid waste.[17] If the people of Pompeii thought they had escaped the war, they now had to reconsider.

Popidius Natalis had arrived early for the ceremony, though it was already growing dark. Since the new Temple of Isis had opened in the spring, he had been too busy to do more than attend the occasional afternoon service to bless the water of life; even at the Ship Festival, he had only caught up with the parade when it had already reached the waterside. But he had kept up his contributions to the maintenance of the new building and appreciated the thought of the sacrifices offered in his name. Now finally he could take a few moments to enjoy the craftsmanship of the paintings and statues as the other worshippers congregated.

The space itself was rather more elegant than it had been before, but there was enough that was familiar to make the longer-standing members feel at home: Isis herself in her diaphanous gown stood on the plinth outside the purgatorium, Bacchus and Venus in the temple itself. But on the walls of the precinct, wonderful new works glowed in the light of the low sun and oil lamps: the symbols of their faith, scenes of cult practice, of the bountiful Nile. And, here, a painting of triremes at sea, their myriad oars powering through the surf, their sailors safe in the knowledge that Isis looked over them.

Soon the choirs of men and women would appear on the steps, one lined up on either side, in a show of harmony. In their hymns and in the service that followed they would invoke the goddess's husband Osiris: dead and dismembered, scattered in a thousand pieces. Anubis, the dog-headed god of death, would run among the shaven-headed priests in mockery until they remembered how, at last, the love of Isis had restored him to life. And then the new initiates, half-starved and abstinent from sex for days, would descend into the purifying waters to be reborn.

Harmony, hope, rebirth. How odd to be celebrating ideals that seemed to be in such short supply. But that, he reminded himself, was half the point.

By the time the priests had performed their rites, and the concealed entrances and echo chambers of the new temple had sprung their mystical surprises, Natalis was surprised to find himself moved to tears of rapture. As the celebrations spilled out onto the streets, all troubles were forgotten in the laughter and embraces of the enlightened. Everything was as normal. Only this year, the twitchy lookouts on the city's gates declined the offer of a drink.

Popidius Ampliatus, his wife Celsa and their small son Celsinus were hugely generous in their donations to rebuild the precinct and temple of the goddess they worshipped (Plate 24). And not only was it rebuilt but it was expanded too; their names are set into the floor of the large room behind the temple that ate into the old

Samnite Gymnasium on the other side of the boundary wall. Father and son were also celebrated in a famous inscription above the entrance to the temple precinct: a rare example of commemoration for a freedman's munificence that also refers to the co-option of Ampliatus's six-year-old son to the city council in gratitude. Even Decimus Lucretius Valens had not made it until he was eight, and the way things were looking at the moment for the older Valens, *flamen* of the late Emperor Nero, the future prospects for Celsinus were a great deal brighter than for his son.[18]

By the time that the Festival of Osiris began on 12 November, negotiations were most likely under way between Vitellius and the representatives of Vespasian, who were keen to persuade Vitellius to step down from the imperial throne with the offer of safe passage to a secure palace on the Bay of Naples, where he could live out his days undisturbed. Whether he trusted them or not, it was an offer that Vitellius was more than prepared to accept. But nothing is predictable in civil war. Once the abdication had been agreed and orders issued by Flavius Sabinus that Vitellius's life was to be spared, renegade soldiers, who feared for their privileges if their master vacated the throne, turned on Sabinus. The Prefect of the City, who had always played the honest broker between his younger brother and Vitellius, was forced to barricade himself into the ancient Capitol building. It was not what Vitellius wanted, or so he said; yet when the Capitol was burned down and Sabinus captured and stabbed to death, he was powerless to prevent it. With tempers running so high, would Vespasian's son Domitian be next?

By December AD 69, the whole of the past eighteen months must have seemed like one long nightmare. It was said that those who had rejoiced at Nero's death a year and a half earlier had worn the distinctive Saturnalia caps; now they could be seen again, bobbing along the street as the real festival of midwinter got under way. Heads spun from drink, the world was topsy-turvy and nothing deserved to be treated too seriously – not even the men of Vespasian's Danubian legions who had entered the ill-defended capital and went about their business of settling bloody scores, while the revellers spectated as they might have any other sport.[19]

Now, as the new emperor's troops closed in and the soldiers and courtiers of Vitellius felt increasingly cornered, Domitian's life came under immediate threat. Held hostage under close supervision, there seemed to be no way out for him – until, that is, the priests of Isis disguised him as one of their own and miraculously spirited him out of the city to a safe house. That he remained alive and in place, ready to take the reins of government in his father's name, was thanks to them and to their goddess alone. It was a salvation that neither Vespasian nor Domitian would ever forget: the former built a chapel to Jupiter the Preserver where his son's place of refuge had stood, the latter a wondrous temple to Isis at Brindisi, surrounded by statues and obelisks. On one of them Domitian was named in hieroglyphs as 'beloved of Isis', and the cult would be looked on kindly throughout Domitian's otherwise cruel reign.[20]

When he was still a young man, Vitellius's own father had once pleaded with him not to inflict himself on the state in any public capacity; and on hearing that her son had been accorded the greatest honour in the Empire, his mother could only bemoan that, from that very moment, her son was a dead man walking. Having failed to heed his parents' advice, Vitellius was butchered on the steps of the rostra, close to where Galba had died less than a year earlier. Before delivering the fatal blow, his enemies had forced his head up to watch the statues he had erected toppling like dominos. His only lasting contribution to European civilisation was the pistachio nut, brought by him to Italy on his return from Syria some years earlier.

Unlike his fellow commander of the Praetorian Guard, who committed suicide in shame, 'Alfenus Varus', we learn from Tacitus, 'survived his own cowardice and infamy.' Perhaps he ended up back home in Nuceria.[21] Suedius Clemens, on the other hand, thrived under Vespasian. The service that he provided to the new Emperor in Pompeii, and for which he would be commemorated on an inscribed *stele* placed outside each of the city's main gates, was yet to come.[22]

XI

Vespasian spent the rest of the winter of AD 69 to AD 70 in Alexandria, holding court with men who, being less valuable to the state than he, were prepared to risk a stormy outward crossing. The new Emperor would await the reopening of the shipping routes in the spring. The delay must have been frustrating, but Domitian was in Rome with trusted supporters of his father to oversee affairs there, and at least this allowed time for the capital to reconcile itself to the idea of its new emperor. Far safer, in the meantime, to communicate by letters that 'spoke modestly about himself, and in admirable language about the state'. But his absence had the added benefit of keeping Vespasian out of the frame when it came to implementing the more unpopular aspects of the clean-up operation that was so urgently needed (Plate 5f).

The immediate problems facing his proxies were manifold. The treasury was transfixed by the chasm of debt it faced, and the senate squabbled over the cost of rebuilding the Capitol; as a necessary precaution, the Emperor's sternest lieutenants in Italy orchestrated the summary execution of anyone left with a claim to the throne and connections to the recently fallen regimes, including those who had acted as informers during the Neronian purges. But the most pressing problem of all was the habit of enmity that the civil war had engendered: in some places the violence was simply not yet quelled, while in others it threatened to spark up again.

Writing with the benefit of hindsight, Tacitus was able to remark of the period after Vitellius's death that 'the war appeared to have reached its end, the whole world being, so to speak, purged of guilt'. But in Campania, the cities were still in a state of unrest, 'more by enmities between themselves than by any opposition to their new

Emperor'. A detachment of light cavalry was dispatched and the smaller colonies, Pompeii presumably included, quickly saw reason: the restive elite of Capua required firmer treatment and the city was garrisoned until the spring. Meanwhile, in Gaul and on the borders, the unruliness that had been apparent the previous year had become endemic.

Roused by their leaders' speeches on how they had been exploited as cannon fodder in Rome's civil wars whilst at home their families remained second-class citizens, the soldiers of the northern provinces were in a state of open revolt. 'You are', the people of the Rhine had been told, 'a pure and untainted race; forgetting your past bondage, you will be the equals of all, or will even rule over others.' The rhetoric was persuasive and contagious, and with each month that passed, it became less fantastical to imagine that the entire Roman Empire really did stand on the brink of collapse.

For the moment, though, Vespasian's position was secure, which must have seemed incredible to the man himself. No son of a tax-collector, who had run a road-haulage business in his home town, had ever dreamt that he could become emperor. Vespasian's own qualifications for the post were practical in nature: the tactical acumen he had shown both on and off the battlefield, his living sons, his fiscal probity, an old-fashioned moral rectitude, and the absence of too many debts to political patrons that might alienate others in Rome. In desperate, pragmatic times, these attributes were enough, but would they still be so a few months or a few years down the line, when the appetite for hedonism reappeared and the longing for charismatic colour returned to the political scene?

During the long months spent in Alexandria, Vespasian actively sought reassurance from the Eastern deities and was endearingly credulous when the god Serapis offered him a sign. Yet when his advisors asked if he would cure the sick of Alexandria, he refused at first; only when they emphasised the public-relations angle did he spit in a blind man's eye and make him see. Such tricks were useful. Vespasian could not claim descent from Aeneas, but being able to perform miracles helped compensate. Some of the more tractable mystics of Palestine even co-operated with the Flavian agenda by back-dating a few prophecies so that they predicted the new Emperor's rise to greatness.

When Vespasian performed his next sleight of hand, it was on a truly gargantuan scale. Under the leadership of his son Titus, at long last the Roman legions successfully stormed the besieged city of Jerusalem and sacked the great Temple. Far more than simply the ancient centre of the Jewish religion, the Temple of Jerusalem was also the repository of untold treasures, and the heart of the entire economy of the Near East. Each year, all adult Jews paid a tax of half a shekel to its reserves, but it also held much greater sources of wealth: as a point of comparison, the Qumran scrolls indicate that the treasures of the Essene sect alone comprised an absolute minimum of eight thousand three hundred and sixty kilograms of silver, and two hundred and fifty of gold.[1]

The haul from Jerusalem would have been truly fabulous: that the value of precious metals in Syria plummeted to half of what it had been is some indication of how much wealth had entered the economy straight away. When it came to bolstering one's popularity, saving a man's sight was one thing; rescuing the entire Roman economy from freefall, quite another.

The sack of the Temple was an act of infamous brutality in the eyes of the Jews, tens of thousands of whom were killed or enslaved, but it provided a spectacular launch for an imperial dynasty. Vespasian had played his hand to perfection. Weeks earlier, while the seas were still storm-ridden, he had filled Alexandria's fastest ships with grain and sent them to Rome, where the floors of the storehouses were visible through the bare scattering of seeds that remained and the populace was facing severe shortages within ten days. It was a gesture that sent exactly the right message.

The wealth Titus plundered bought Vespasian the freedom he needed to see through the reforms and reclamations that Galba had attempted, and which had played a large part in his downfall. Rome had seen nothing like it since the defeat of Antony and Cleopatra at the Battle of Actium had delivered Egypt and its harvest into Roman hands. A tidal wave of money and slaves flowed across the Mediterranean. In the slave markets of Gaza, men, women and children were sold wholesale for deportation to the fatherland, close to a hundred thousand of them in total. With a continued Jewish insurgency to combat, and all the tithes that had gone to the Temple now payable to Jupiter, Titus would keep both slaves and money coming. The perfect means of redressing Neronian profligacy without frightening the horses had, it seemed, fallen into the new emperor's lap.[2]

But Vespasian's good fortune brought its own challenges, chief among them that of managing the widespread expectation that victory would guarantee grand expenditure for the pleasure of the plebs. To deal with the outstanding deficit, Vespasian felt compelled to implement strict fiscal measures, winning Vespasian a reputation for parsimony that the awareness of victory in Judaea can only have exacerbated. And although the influx of riches from Judaea significantly aided the task of restoring the economy, a profound shift in behaviour across society, towards more modest habits of consumption, was also required.

Nothing less than a cultural revolution was called for: 'A commission', we learn, 'was set up by lot to restore property stolen during the war, to determine and replace the bronze tablets of the laws that had fallen down from age; to purge the public records of the additions with which the flattery of the times had defiled them, and to check public expenses.' It was precisely for these reasons that Suedius Clemens was sent on his mission to Pompeii, probably around AD 75 or 76. By then, the initial shocks of the change in regime would already have been absorbed.

CHAPTER 12

A Feast of Beans

June AD 75

The time had come for these insufferable provincials to understand the true extent of the authority that he, Suedius Clemens, commanded as Vespasian's chosen judge. They were polite enough to his face. 'Venerable', 'Worshipful', 'Honoured', they called him. But all the fawning words meant nothing as long as the city's reprobates continued as they had before. Every time he initiated a line of enquiry, obstacles were placed in his path: doors were unexpectedly locked, keys lost, documents rendered conveniently illegible, evidence cunningly concealed. No matter how quickly he acted, it was always the same. Clemens had never counted subtlety and persistence among his strengths, but they were skills he was quickly learning. How else could he hope to root out the spy in his service?

When he had first arrived in Pompeii two months earlier, Clemens had been full of enthusiasm for the task in hand. He remembered how, as the reception committee had accompanied him into the forum with due pomp, his body had ached in every muscle from the shaking it had received, straight through the iron-shod wheels of his carriage over endless miles of stone flagged roads. But the fine team of four black mules that pulled it, symbols of his new status, had raised admiring heads in the fields through which he passed, and his mood was buoyant. No one could have imagined the trials to which this ill-fated part of happy Campania had been subjected in recent years: riots, earthquakes, whirlwinds, civil war had all taken their toll. The men who greeted him with garlands and warm words of praise were surely deserving of his help.

Little had Clemens realised the full scale of the task on which he was embarking. Superficially, the city had done a good job of concealing its Neronian past: he saw places where praise for the late Emperor had been whitewashed over, the letters too indistinct to embarrass those who had posted them in the first place. There was little sign either of the extravagant spending of past times: only the occasional appearance of a gilded Apollo betrayed a family's sympathies. And who was there, who had lived through those years, who could truly claim to be pure? Yet there was something deeper at work here, buried within the networks of allegiance that any outsider would always struggle to comprehend: a hidden hierarchy that kept its head down, and baulked at his interference.

At first, he had thought himself fortunate in those who lent him their support, and those who were recommended to assist in his task. No one could doubt that Alleius Nigidius Maius had done sterling service since being summoned from retirement to act as magistrate for the first Flavian census; Pompeii had much to thank him for, but now his time was past. And in Marcus Epidius Sabinus and Numerius Popidius Rufus, taken on after long consultation as the city's case pleaders, Pompeii seemed to have two able and promising young men.

Yet as Clemens's investigations dug deeper, he began to have his doubts. One or other of them was responsible for sabotaging his work.

Pompeii was not alone in receiving the attentions of an imperial judge, dispatched by Vespasian during the early AD 70s, whose primary task was to resolve disputes over the appropriation of public land and property by private individuals. Records of such missions have been found at Orange in southern France, and at Cirta and Apollonia in north Africa.[1] In Pompeii the cases Clemens faced might have dated back to the confusion following the earthquake. They probably arose either from careless rebuilding or the erection of unauthorised tombs in the areas outside the gates, whether intentional or inadvertent. Another area that would have been within his remit was land or property that had been gifted to supporters of Nero, free or at preferential rates, in a similar manner to the cash presents made to Augustiniani like Popidius Ampliatus. Vespasian certainly tried to reclaim from the Neronian colonies – of which Pompeii was one – the territory that had been set aside for distribution to veterans but never allocated, though he eventually had to climb down on these proposals in the face of opposition. Clemens's investigations might even have revealed that this too was tied in with Neronian corruption. The regulation of boundaries in particular seems to have been of widespread concern in Campania; there was ample scope for abuse in this area involving rental of pastures, fulleries and the like, on non-renewable five-yearly contracts, like those recorded in the Jucundus tablets. Finally, as with Pliny the Younger's mission to Prusa some years later, Clemens's role might have entailed holding to account those building contractors who had received payment for public projects that were still far from complete.[2]

Whatever the faults or crimes of the city, in other respects Pompeii had been quite assiduous in responding to Vespasian's assumption of the throne. Alleius Nigidius Maius's speedy appointment to the flaminate of the Flavian emperor was a bold statement, marking a clear breach with what had gone before. Maius had last held public office as *duovir quinquennalis* in AD 55–6, nearly twenty years earlier when Nero's reign was in its infancy, after which he had retired to a more private life. Whether from genuine affection or contrivance, he had maintained his public profile through occasional acts of generosity that reminded Pompeians of the traditional virtues and pleasures that they should cherish: through wall paintings of gladiator games during the ban, through the restoration of the bronze tablets of law after the earthquake, and by staging occasional celebratory games after the ban had been lifted. Now he could emerge as a man from a previous era, untarnished by the moral compromises or shame of Nero's reign. Such a notion of the veteran summoned from his farm to save his community had a powerful resonance in the Roman soul, and chimed with the self-created myth of Vespasian, a man older still than Maius's fifty or so years, who had reluctantly obeyed the call to the highest public service.

To celebrate his appointment, Maius had immediately organised gladiatorial games: 'In honour of the health of the Emperor Vespasian Caesar Augustus and his children and for the dedication of his altar, pairs of gladiators will fight at Pompeii without any delay, four days before the nones of July. There will be a hunt, sprinklings and an awning.'[3] Clearly, Maius and the city were in a hurry to assert their loyalty at the founding of what everyone must have hoped would be a long-lived dynasty. As a more permanent indication of allegiance, it appears that they might also have converted and cannibalised some public buildings: some have argued that a temple in the forum was rededicated to Vespasian and the altar that now stands there was moved, at this time, from the Temple of Fortuna Augusta.

As Suedius Clemens made his preliminary tour of Pompeii, he would still have been highly aware of the city's eagerness to shrug off its connections with Nero's failed regime. The late Emperor's statue appears to have been removed from public places and it is probable that a proportion of the coins from his reign had been stamped over with the face and name of Vespasian. Such behaviour was not usual in the case of the throne changing hands, but rather a response to the condemnation of Nero by the senate, just prior to his death, as a criminal against the state.

Damnatio memoriae would have been the harshest punishment imaginable for a man of Nero's aspirational nature. Usually reserved for traitors and those guilty of *maiestas*, or overambition, the practical effect of *damnatio memoriae* was erasure: not the complete removal of the criminal in question from the historical record, but the excision of his name on inscriptions and the removal of anything that recollected his image – just sufficient for the world to remember the punishment more than the rest of the man's life. A decree relating to the *damnatio memoriae* applied to a traitor earlier in the century is quite explicit that no funeral mask or other image of the guilty should be allowed to participate at funerals or wedding celebrations.[4] Recent research suggests that Nero may not, in fact, have had this very specific legal sentence imposed on him by the senate, but it is certainly true that the following centuries would see him confirmed in the popular imagination as a byword for decadence and despotism.[5]

The painting of the Emperor as Apollo in the Murecine building is probably the only representation of him to have survived in the whole city of Pompeii, and even that may only have been left undisturbed because it was in a room that had fallen into disuse. Graffiti conveying such sentiments as 'Hail, Nero and Poppea' remained visible in private homes, but the most ostentatious of

Nero's supporters, such as Popidius Ampliatus and the profit-loving Vedius Siricus would have been wise to keep a relatively low profile.

The civic-mindedness of certain political figures, even those who had served during the Neronian period, might have saved them from outright opprobrium: Julius Polybius, perhaps, whose voice appears still to have carried weight with his fellow citizens when it came to elections, or Bruttius Balbus, who had held a junior magistracy around AD 56 and the senior post ten or so years later. During his campaign, he garnered a surprising number of female endorsements, with that by Julia Primigenia demonstrating a degree of financial acumen in its suggestion that 'he preserved the economy'.[6] Her use of the word *munera* could imply that Balbus's provision of free gladiatorial games or his contribution to the city's rebuilding was merely a casual gesture. However, another posting not far away praises him in similar terms, and this time the word used is *aerarium*, which is closer in meaning to 'treasury' and which seems to indicate that Balbus's generosity helped the city more directly in what were unquestionably times of dire economic need.[7]

Balbus's town house was far from grand and may actually have been shared with a freedman called Titus Dentatius Panthera. In putting public service before his own advancement, was he one of those members of the elite who overstretched his resources and jeopardised the status of his descendants? If so, his sacrifice was at least appreciated and, during Pompeii's last years, his endorsement appears to have been much in demand by young and upcoming politicians. Perhaps it was a new sense of equity and justice dispensed by Suedius Clemens that encouraged popular acceptance of more selfless values that were so different from those espoused in Nero's reign.

Although the numbers remain relatively small, the messages written on Pompeii's walls in the final period of the city's existence – and in particular the electoral postings – show a very marked increase in the number of women's names. It is not clear whether this demonstrated the passionate and active engagement of women in political life, or that their opinions were becoming more tolerated, or simply that less time had elapsed in which to cover up postings that were deemed more insignificant and expendable than those by men. But it certainly appears as though these years saw the emergence of a number of powerful and independent women who were making their name in business.

At the bottom end of the spectrum, female loan sharks provided others with the possibility to borrow money. One money-lender – possibly the owner herself – operated out of Lusoria's tavern on the main road into town from the Vesuvius Gate, and in at least a couple of cases the borrowers too were women. Faustilla borrows the equivalent of sixty sesterces, pawning a cloak as security; Vettia asks for slightly more, but both loans were at an annual rate of interest that was set at around 40 per cent. The cost of borrowing was high but perhaps the mere presence of such a figure went some way to bolstering the financial independence of women and providing them with the means to strike out on their own.[8]

Of more interest to Suedius Clemens might have been Julia Felix, the daughter of a freedman of the imperial family who had presumably moved to Pompeii by around the AD mid-60s. At the time of Clemens's visit she had already embarked on the conversion of two entire blocks of the city into a lavish set of shops, apartments and entertainment facilities, all for rent.[9] Maybe she had started off her business life in circumstances not dissimilar to Faustilla or Vettia – borrowing a little to invest in a business and working hard to ensure that it paid dividends – but before long she graduated to a quite different level. Such business was a man's world, and although women could gain access through certain loopholes in social convention and law, they would be tolerated only for so long as they observed the fiction of having a male guardian sign on their behalf.

'To let, in the estate of Julia Felix, daughter of Spurius: elegant baths fit for the finest, shops with upper rooms, and apartments,'[10] reads an advertisement posted sometime late in Pompeii's life. To achieve this, two *insula* blocks had to be knocked together and the street between them built over. The loss was compensated for by the widening of the next street, which gained ground at the expense of the eastern side of Julia's estate. Nevertheless, such a radical change in the city's layout would have required the consent of the town council. That the lost street led almost directly from the city's main street to the amphitheatre must have prompted debate, and for Julia Felix to have won her case she must have had powerful supporters, or at least the means to buy them.

By the time the job was complete, Julia Felix had succeeded in creating a truly luxurious environment for her guests and tenants: from the dozen scenes of commercial life in the forum with which the main entrance of the building was decorated, to the garden with its elaborate long pool representing the Canopus canal in Egypt, and the row of dining rooms overlooking it replete with water cascades and wall paintings of Nilotic scenes (Plate 4). Whether such scenes were intended to add an exotic frisson, or to appeal to visiting Alexandrians such as the Ptolemy who is known to have sold linens in the market, or even more particularly to followers of Isis, nothing in the design was left to chance.[11] And to make the property work as a commercial whole, a less exclusive drinking and dining establishment was set up alongside the bathhouse, the latter accessible on one side straight from the street, and on the other from the gardens and apartments.

If Suedius Clemens had turned his beady eye on this exquisite but relatively bijou venture, he would surely also have felt a need to scope the vast new Central Baths, where construction was still under way. Although occupying a plot of land little larger than Julia Felix's, this undertaking did not entail the joining together of city blocks or the removal of a street, though it did cut into the thoroughfare at its rear. The scale of the architecture employed, however, was far more imposing and it is hard to imagine who might have been able to afford such a project. With its three great vaulted rooms and outdoor sports complex right in the heart of the city, this was a building whose financing and location might have intrigued the imperial judge.[12]

The creation of such large baths suggests that the city's water supply was more or less back to normal by this time, although there is strong evidence to suggest that the seismic activities that had caused the earthquake around Pompeii in AD 62 were felt on a number of occasions in the years that followed. But there was still plenty of opportunity for corruption in the fullery business, and Suedius Clemens may have taken a particular interest in this area, since at least one of Pompeii's main fulleries was rented out directly by the city's authorities. Avoidance of the tax imposed on fullers by Vespasian may have been an issue: 'All profit is good, no matter where it comes from,' the Emperor had told his son Titus, holding a coin to the battle-hardened general's nose when he complained that such a source of income was unsavoury. Interestingly, two of the women involved in offering electoral endorsements, in tandem with their male partners, were involved in the business: Ovia and Mustius ran the small fullery near the Vesuvius Gate, and Appuleia and Narcissus owned it.[13]

With the political undercurrents still strong in Pompeii, it is not surprising that disputes broke out between local business partners who had previously been close friends. The precise cause of the intense acrimony between Vesonius Phileros and his business partner, Orfellius Faustus, is unknown. The tomb constructed by Phileros, during his lifetime, to hold his own remains along with those of Faustus and his ex-mistress Vesonia, is eloquent in expressing his fury at the betrayal he has suffered rather than the details of its cause. Three statues stand side by side on the tomb, Vesonia in the centre; after his own name in the original inscription, Phileros has added the honorific title, 'Augustalis', but then there is another, far longer addition, in a less professional hand. 'Stranger,' it reads, 'delay a brief while if it is not troublesome, and learn what to avoid. This man whom I had hoped was my friend, I am forsaking: a case was maliciously brought against me; I was charged and legal proceedings were instituted; I give thanks to the gods and to my innocence, I was freed from all distress. May neither the household gods nor the gods below receive the one who misrepresented our affairs.'[14]

Cursing the dead was one form of vengeance, but the walls of the basilica suggest that others preferred to enjoy the suffering of their enemies while they were still alive. Of all the tibia bones analysed from the Pompeii and Herculaneum skeletons, the surfaces of more than one third are etched with the signs of an inflammation that is consistent with only a small number of medical conditions: leprosy, tuberculosis and syphilis. Further examination of the skeletons of these individuals revealed a number with lesions on the skull, where the syphilitic ulcers had healed. It was more than fourteen hundred years before the time when Colombus's crew supposedly carried the disease back to Europe from the Americas, yet a curse written by a certain Phyrrus on the walls of the basilica, not far from the *cinaedi* messages, revels in the details of a colleague's syphilitic misfortune: 'Oh Chius, I hope that your ulcerous pustules reopen and burn even more than they did before.' By the time Phyrrus wrote these words, the disease had probably already turned inwards to blister Chius's heart and lungs; Pyrrhus later added an unrepentant note recording Chius's death.

If these two examples were any indication of the kind of vitriol that Pompeii's citizens felt, it would have been doubly important for Suedius Clemens to have reliable local assistance that could help him see through the layers of infighting and malicious gossip. He appears to have believed that he had found this in the two men who were recruited to act as advocates in cases where wrongdoing was discovered. One was Popidius Rufus, the young representative of an old and vastly important Pompeian family that had been most prominent in the city's life during recent years through the actions of two of its freedmen, both called Ampliatus, though associated with two different branches of the family. Numerius Popidius Ampliatus was the individual who had paid for the rebuilding of the Temple of Isis, while Lucius Popidius Ampliatus had been a leading Augustianus and the guiding hand behind the grand remodelling of his home, the House of the Citharista, in honour of Nero.

Suedius Clemens's other case-pleader, Marcus Epidius Sabinus, had served as junior magistrate at the tail end of the late Emperor's reign, but appears to have escaped taint. Pompeian to their very roots, the name of the Epidii was Oscan in origin, and was said to derive from the family's deification by the ancient god of the River Sarno. The god's own name is not known for sure, but his heavily bearded face can be found in numerous paintings: surrounded by the flora and fauna of the nearby marshes as he is in the Murecine building, or else pouring the waters of the river from a jug into the *frigidarium* basin of the Suburban Baths.

Sabinus and his father, Epidius Rufus, are thought to have

occupied two houses that stand next to one another on the main street, opposite the House of the Citharista where the Popidii freedmen lived. Rufus's house was the larger and was built in monumental style. To any stranger who passed by, its frontage might well have appeared closer to that of a public than a private building. Steps up from the pavement led to a podium that ran the whole width of the house; in the centre a doorway opened into a small entrance hall with further doors that blocked any view through from the street; and once inside the atrium, sixteen vast doric columns rose to support the ceiling at a considerable height above. The altar to the family that was set up to one side of the atrium by two freedmen brothers perhaps testifies to its owners' sense of their own unassailable dignity.

It had been a good day and was going to be a better evening, Suedius Clemens reflected, as he was shown through the high-columned atrium to the dining suite of the Epidii. Although there was nothing to eat but the meagre fare of the Bean Kalends meal, the judge relished the contrast between the ceremony of frugality and the magisterial building in which the feast was being held. His host, Epidius Sabinus's father, was a canny old bird, and he led the conversation with an elegance that Clemens had not experienced for a long time.

As the diners scooped up the unseasoned mess of bacon, beans and spelt, there was more jollity than humility on show; only the case-pleader Popidius Rufus insisted upon taking each mouthful as though it was an act of penance. Clemens could hardly bear to look at him, so distasteful did he find his treachery. Yet he held his tongue as those present mulled over all that had been achieved since dawn, and tried to piece together what it all meant.

The crucial lead had come when Clemens's men had ransacked the public archives the previous afternoon, searching for any anomalies in the civic accounts that might previously have been overlooked. What they had found, hidden away, had led the judge to send out messages summoning his case-pleaders to join him in the countryside early the next morning.

They had gathered in a vineyard out towards the border with the Nucerian territory. It was part of what was supposed to be an eighty-iugerum plot, and the fields that bordered it were owned and rented out by the city. At first glance, there had been little to suggest impropriety: the records for the neighbouring property showed prompt payment by the city's tenant, a freedman by the name of Receptus. But a keen-eyed inspector had noticed the suspiciously low rate that was payable, less than it had been fifteen years earlier, and knew that something was amiss.

Their usual surveyor, Popidius Nicostratus, had set to work with a grand show of efficiency, measuring with his groma, pacing out and marking the ground of Receptus's land.

Clemens had watched from a distance, his case-pleaders by his side, Sabinus silent and observing, while Rufus maintained a constant stream of commentary. At that moment it had all become clear to the judge. How could he have failed to see until now the stranglehold that the Popidii family held in Pompeii's affairs? Even now Rufus continued to feign ignorance, when he must have realised that the judge knew full well that the vineyard belonged to his own freedman, Popidius Ampliatus.

The judge had waited until the surveyor had played his hand and signalled that all was correct before he set his own men to work, exposing the fraud. Methodically, they moved through the vineyard, probing the earth and occasionally digging down until, after only a short time, a triumphant shout went up to summon the judge. They had found what they were looking for: there, broken and half-buried, lay the line of boundary markers, deep inside the Popidii land.

The secret was out: they simply fixed the rental price on the city-owned fields so low that some poor dupe – in this case Receptus – thought they were getting a bargain, while all along half the rented land had been carved off to augment the Popidii holdings. The guests around the table shook their heads at the simple boldness of the crime. When the dinner was finished, Suedius Clemens would have his men humiliate Rufus, drag him away and throw him out onto the street.

But for now, the judge had business with Sabinus. Perhaps he would begin by recounting the tales of his fights with Alfenus Varus of Nuceria, during the civil wars – play with Sabinus a little before letting him know that he was now beyond suspicion. And then he would announce his plan to support Sabinus to become the city's next senior magistrate, and offer him his endorsement as its future leader. Rufus would be allowed to stay just long enough to hear Sabinus receive everything that he had just lost.

Like so many other walls in Pompeii, those in the House of the Epidii had needed extensive redecoration after the earthquake of AD 62, at just the moment when Nero's delusions of divinity were ballooning. One richly rewarded member of the Augustiani was a neighbour, and Ampliatus would have taken a perverse delight in reporting back on the willingness or otherwise of the city's elite to toe the Neronian line. But whilst they were not impervious to these pressures, the redecoration undertaken by the Epidii in their dining room perhaps offers a good example of how it was possible to weather the ideological storm.

The chosen scheme and subject of the paintings that the Epidii commissioned appeared to conform to Neronian preoccupations: theatrical in tone, the centrepiece depicted Apollo vanquishing the upstart Marsyas and all his other musical competitors in the Greek games, while Venus and the Muses looked on. But the Epidii were also wise enough to ensure that alternative meanings were encoded: Apollo could represent the cruel and capricious Nero, of course, but could equally be depersonalised to stand for the authority of the emperor and the state, to be wielded judiciously against the dangerous *libertas* of Marsyas and the people.[15] And the way that the muses surrounded Marsyas could have been interpreted as the stern and impartial judgement on an upstart's affront to the natural order.

In matters of aesthetic taste – in style as well as in content – Vespasian's rule marked a sharp break with what had gone before. Tacitus even went so far as to remark that the beginning of his reign had turned the clock back a hundred years, to the time of the Battle of Actium, before the Roman taste for luxury had burgeoned to the detriment of traditional values. It was an exaggeration, but one that succinctly expressed the *zeitgeist*, for in the modesty of his own existence, the ageing Emperor set an example of austerity that recalled that of Augustus, of whom Suetonius wrote: 'The simplicity of his furniture and household goods may be seen from couches and tables still in existence, many of which are scarcely fine enough for a private citizen.'

With Vespasian's moral revolution came a radical shift in Pompeian art, as householders commissioned work that harked back to the previous fashion for a less flamboyant and more true-to-life style of representation. The new painting of Concordia at the entrance to the House of the Vettii was certainly open to interpretation as a gesture of conciliation towards the new regime and to judge from the graffitists who would throw in casual references to art – 'Anyone who has not seen the Venus painted by Apelles should take a look at my girl: she is equally radiant' – such changes would not have passed unnoticed.[16] For artists like Lucius, who was unusual in signing his work, the process of relearning techniques that no customer had asked for in more than a decade would have been laborious. Still, they had plenty of opportunity to practise: two hundred paint pots have been found in the sites buried by Vesuvius and there was evidence of active redecoration in all areas of Pompeii.

Just off the main road to the forum, the workshop of a colour manufacturer called Numerius Fufidius Successus contained nine mortars in which colours were ground and in which later excavators found traces of pigments. Another block down, a second outlet stocked large blocks of orange ochre; three to the east, blocks of white calcium carbonate bear the imprint of the Attii, who presumably packaged them. The brown and orange of ochre were relatively inexpensive and used as the base for colour washes that were mixed in large containers. But it was in smaller vessels, such as those found at the artists' workshop not far from Successus's business, that the most specialised and expensive pigments were to be found: haematite and iron oxide for yellows and reds, blues and blue-greens made in Puteoli out of goethite, and many more that remain obscure. Pliny even describes the use of the ears and genitals of bulls in the manufacture of pigments, and as always the Eastern sea trade could be relied upon to bring in the most scintillating hues of all.

In the artists' workshop, alongside a cupboard containing numerous small pots, were the other tools of the trade: tiny mortars, together with pestles, spoons and spatulas, and the compasses and plumb lines used to transfer scaled sketches onto walls. Having a base like this was important for the teams, comprising half a dozen craftsmen or more, who would work together in close collaboration on each job, and travelled widely if their reputation was sufficient to bring in the work.

In the absence of signatures, give-away idiosyncracies of style – especially in the most intuitive brushstrokes used when painting eyes and noses – have been used as a fairly reliable guide to identifying different painters' work. The paintings of the Trojan War from the house of Vedius Siricus's son Nummianus, for example, were executed by the same person responsible for large parts of the Temple of Isis; to realise the mythological tableaux they wanted, the Vettii hired the artist whose work on the basilica in Herculaneum had made him a local celebrity. Occasionally, the huge task of completing an entire suite of rooms would be given to a single individual, as Lucius Cornelius Primogenis did in his home to the north of the forum, but it was more usual to hire a team with different specialisms, as his neighbour Nigidius Vaccula chose to do for the redecoration of his House of the Dioscuri.

Such is the coherence of many large-scale design schemes that it is clear that projects were overseen by a single, guiding hand, at least during the planning stage. First a coloured background wash was painted, then the figurative images and any more complicated aspects of the design were sketched out, often in yellow ochre. Usually, the plans would have been realised in sections back at the studio, for less skilled journeymen to implement on site. It seems almost certain that pattern books were referred to, not only for such elements as the recurring motifs that border many paintings, but also for the central vignettes, although sometimes intriguing variations were introduced and there was ample scope for individual genius to find expression. Such talent was rewarded. The *pictor imaginarius* who composed the central panels could command a daily rate of one hundred and fifty denarii, which was double that of the next most senior artist who worked on the decorative side panels. As well as an eye for colour and line, perhaps the most important skill that master painters had to acquire, as they worked their way up through the ranks, was speed. For the paintings were frescos, with the artist working alongside a plasterer – or sometimes doubling in both roles – to apply pigments that bonded into the fine skim coat of plaster and marble dust as it dried quickly to a solid surface in the southern Italian heat.

The process required a team to be working in perfect harmony, from the man who smoothed the medium with a float, to the boy who laid down the solid background colour, to the master himself, whose brush flew in delicate, deft strokes to bring the image to life. Balancing on ladders or scaffolding, everyone in the team knew their individual duties. Each in turn completed his task on a particular section of wall before moving down to begin the next. Rarely were they able to pause, stand back and ponder the whole. Carbonation incorporated the artwork into the wall, making the surface leathery, and the painting was ready to be polished to a luminous sheen, so that the colours would almost seem to be trapped in glass.[17]

Only the *pictor parientarius* might have had the leisure to contemplate the scene of balletic motion as his colleagues worked: his painting of the side panels or border ornamentation was done on a dry wall. In some cases the plaster was scratched out to allow for the addition of some fresh matrix, and when the design was geometrical in form, it often required the use of rules and compasses to trace the intricate patterns which were sketched in charcoal before applying the pigments. The *pictor parientarius*'s touch would often be meticulous, but there was still much that he could learn from the master craftsman. He would practise at night to free up his brush, embolden his stroke and perhaps, eventually, double his salary.[18]

Mythology was the staple theme of the majority of paintings in Pompeii, even in relatively humble dwellings; but whilst the stories were familiar from what was still a highly oral culture, the apparent familiarity with the detail of their narratives also underlines the relatively high levels of literacy in Pompeian society. Alongside these works, portraits and still lifes celebrated the cultured aspirations of its citizens. Portraits show men and women gazing out contemplatively with a stylus raised to their lips, as though pondering their next *bon mot*, rhymed couplet or shattering philosophical insight; and writing equipment – the ink pots, pens and wax tablets – was part of the furniture in graceful homes.

Whilst Nero had favoured the performing arts, Vespasian's preference was for reliable epic poetry, and in particular that of Augustus's laureate, Virgil. There was no line of descent from Virgil's hero Aeneas for Vespasian to boast, but the affinity he felt for the message of national rebirth and renewal seems to have been shared by those who wrote a wide selection of verses on the walls of Pompeii. In some it is almost possible to hear a conscious farewell to the bad old days: 'Now I have forgotten all my songs,' or else, 'Whoever you are, from now on forget the Greeks.'[19]

Before long, the national poet's tomb in Naples would be restored and people looked with new interest at the paintings of Aeneas's exploits on their walls.[20] But for the new regime there were more pressing priorities: to restore moral and civic order, while ensuring that the people were kept happy, or at least distracted. This was an especially hard task in Pompeii. Although work was forging ahead on the forum, the ongoing earth tremors must have been deeply unsettling. The *memento mori* motifs that figured in the city's mosaics – the skeletons drinking while the sun shone, the sundials across which the shadow of time glided, the fragile butterflies with their transient lives – took on a new intensity of meaning. And among the vast majority who stayed on in the city into the late AD 70s – for lack of anywhere else to go, or from an acquired taste for the intensity of life lived in a constant state of jeopardy – some appear to have been driven to superstition and the more obscure reaches of religion.

In her modest home, only two blocks away from Julia Felix's expansive complex, Biria and her father Onamastus had set up a private shrine dedicated to the mystery cult of the Thracian god Sabazius.[21] The paraphernalia of the cult of Herakles, or Hercules, were found in a nearby house a gem-cutter named Cerialis shared with his wife Cassia: the glass-lined terracotta cup with vine decoration and the bronze sacrificial knife may have been used on the premises, or taken to the small Hercules Temple that lay outside the city walls. For many, Sabazius was synonymous with Dionysus or Bacchus, to whom the mountain of Vesuvius was sacred; Hercules, of course, had been the saviour of the world in his battle with the restless giants of Campania. It seems as though the more anxious citizens of Pompeii may have had some inkling of where their doom might lie.

But if there was one other group in Pompeii who had at least as much reason to wonder whether there was not some element of divine retribution in the travails of the city, it was the Jews. 'Sodom and Gomorrah,' was the damning judgement on Pompeii that one graffitist familiar with the Old Testament stories painted onto a wall near the city's central crossroads. Whether placed there with prescience in the AD 70s, or immediately prior to the eruption, or even after it by the earliest looters, it was an understandably bitter response to the decadent world that the Jews must have longed to see swept away. No one had suffered more than they in the previous decade. Poppaea had been consistently supportive of the Jews of Italy, but her death had deprived them of their one protector, and in the last years of Nero's reign they risked being tarred with the same brush as the heretical sect of Christ-believers. Not only was the search on for scapegoats, but in Judaea, their homeland's bid for self-government had been subject to the most savage suppression, their nation scattered, and its bravest fighters made captive.

In Pompeii, a number of names in the graffiti have been identified as Jewish, though they may have been of Syrian or other Semitic origin: 'Maria' appears at least three times, along with 'Iesus', 'Ieshua' and 'Martha'. Abinnericus, the freedman of the Valerii, was a wine merchant who traded with Etruria, his name featuring on more than a hundred and fifty amphorae; Fabius Eupor and Felix Yudaikos, the most recognisable Judaean, were involved in the wine trade too. Many Jews living in Italy Latinised their names, and whilst Abinnicerus is a clear example of this process, names from Aster to Zosimus could perhaps have been adaptations. Of the graffiti most clearly attributed to Jews, all but one were found within a few streets of each other, towards the eastern end of the main street. It is near here, too, that the comfortable dwelling known as the House of the Hebrew stands – a possible gathering place for the Jewish community in Pompeii.

By the AD 70s, the beliefs of the Jewish sect devoted to the Nazarene Messiah had been filtered through Greek philosophy by Saint Paul to produce a religious package that would stand the test of time. In AD 75, Paul had been dead for almost ten years, probably executed during the persecution of Christians as scapegoats for the great fire of Rome. But as recently as AD 60 he had passed through Puteoli while under escort from Alexandria to Rome as a prisoner accused of sedition. That the centurion guarding him had allowed the accused a week's grace to stay with Christians in the port city suggests that he was persuaded by the prospect of comfortable accommodation during their sojourn: clearly the sect was not, then, an underground movement.[22]

By AD 75, however, it must have appeared to any Jew living in Rome or Campania as though the entire Jewish race had been criminalised. There had been twenty-five thousand seasoned militiamen in Jerusalem at the time of the siege, the cream of Judaea's fighting forces, and the order went out that all of those who escaped execution or the mines were to be kept for the arena. While still in the East, Titus mounted gladiatorial games to celebrate the birthdays of his father, Vespasian, and brother, Domitian, and hundreds of captives fought and died there; hundreds more did not survive the battle recreation that he staged on his journey back to Rome, and his triumphal reception there saw a further seven hundred of the finest specimens of Jewish manhood fight it out. The blood of a captive was cheap, and shedding it an effective way of distracting the Roman citizens from the belt-tightening that was demanded of them.

But if extravagant games were to be the means by which Vespasian won and kept the hearts of his people, then it was only right that they should take place in a fitting venue, one untainted by association with past Julio-Claudian regimes. In Puteoli, construction work began on a new amphitheatre, the prototype for an innovative design. But even that was soon to be dwarfed by Rome's own vast new arena: the Colosseum. The foundations were laid on a site close to where the gilded colossus of Nero-as-Apollo had stood. To complete the arena would take a decade and the labour of fifteen thousand Jewish slaves: for every minute that they worked, piling up stones as big as those that the Romans had hauled down when they razed the Jerusalem temple, they were tormented by the knowledge that the awful edifice was paid for out of the stolen wealth of their nation. As an inscription from the architrave of the original Colosseum read: 'The Emperor Titus Caesar Vespasian Augustus ordered the new amphitheatre to be constructed out of the spoils of war.'[23] They were rich spoils, indeed, but could they be made to stretch far enough?

The blood-sport spectacles that so pleased Roman citizens no longer had any meaningful link to their archaic, sacrificial origins, but had shifted into the realm of almost pure entertainment. Puteoli's new amphitheatre marked a generational leap in this process. At the inaugural games held there in the mid-AD 70s, the crowds would have witnessed agonising death raised to the level of sophisticated spectacle: the grandiose architecture of the building, as it reared out of the ground, offered the empty reassurance that there was something, however superficial, that was aesthetically refined about this site of constantly rehearsed brutality.

Gladiators from the troupes owned by Pompeians – Alleius Nigidius Maius, Decimus Satrius Lucretius Valens, and perhaps Claudius Verus – may well have been hired out to fight there. Those belonging to Suettius Certus and Suettius Verus certainly performed, in a unique recorded instance of games being staged by freedmen. A father-and-son team, in AD 75 the Suettii were in the process of planning their combined campaign for senior and junior magistracies and at some point invited Epidius Sabinus to become part of the ticket: Suedius Clemens's favoured candidate, together with the men who put on the best shows in town, must have seemed an unbeatable combination. There certainly appears to have been a gap to fill. Decimus Satrius Lucretius Valens had stopped staging games on his own behalf – or that of his son, who may not have survived this long – but the family still appear to have been involved in the business for profit. One transaction was noted in graffiti in the gladiator's training area behind the theatre: 'Sold to the wife of Decimus Lucretius Valens: Onustus, horseman, prime quality; Sagatus, Thracian murmillo, prime quality.'[24]

Pompeii's favourite fighters made their mark on the city's walls as well as its hearts: Oceanus, the barmaid's choice; Felix, the bear-fighter; Celadus, the Thracian; Crescens, the *retiarius*; Severus, who won fifty-five victories; Nascia, who won sixty; Albanus, a freedman of Scaurus, who won nineteen; and Petronius Octavius, who died in his thirty-fifth contest. Most were probably slaves, perhaps around a third were freedmen who fought from choice and for profit, while there was the occasional free-born pugilist who fancied his chances, and even the odd aristocrat, in it for the thrill. Some of those in the Suettii troupe were boldly announced as graduates of Nero's school in Capua: it turned out well-prepared fighters and most likely contributed a significant number of the gladiators who had served as auxiliaries in the civil war.

Six years on, though, few of the men commanded by Suedius Clemens and defeated by Alfenus Varus in the river near Cremona would still have been around: the chances of surviving a career in the arena were slim. The odds are impossible to calculate, but the death of Glauco, the winner of seven fights, at the age of twenty-three, provides a good guide to form.[25] A well-trained gladiator was an expensive commodity and worth preserving, but though the survival odds for any fighter who was disarmed and left to the mercy of the games' host, or *editor*, were roughly four in five, they fell sharply when the purpose of a games was to quench the spectators' thirst for blood. On these occasions, when the *editor* was feeling especially generous, even the victor of a contest could not be sure he would live to see the end of the day. As Seneca wrote, 'The spectators demand that those who have murdered confront, in turn, those who will murder; they reserve the victor of one bout for another round of slaughter. Death is the only issue for men who fight.'[26] In some Pompeian notices, precisely this kind of 'last man standing' contest is promised.

There could have been no complaints from the gladiators: no fighter was allowed into the arena until he had already sworn away his life, 'willingly and freely' undertaking to endure being burned, bound, whipped and killed by the sword, and renouncing all hope of a kinder fate.[27]

For long weeks now, Suedius Clemens had thought of nothing but the mountainous task that lay ahead: whilst he had been thorough and meticulous in his enquiries, he had seen little of the city beyond its corrupt shadows. Climbing ever higher, it had come as a surprise yesterday to realise that finally he had crested the last ridge, and that the summit now lay within easy reach. He was satisfied with his work. The old injustices had been exposed, and the city and its rights were again recognised as greater than those of any individual. A new mood of openness and optimism was tangible. All that was left now was for Clemens to ensure that fear was banished for good and that right-thinking men were strongly placed to lead the council.

The timing of his success was perfect. Today was the Vestalia, the occasion chosen by the noble Gnaeus Alleius Nigidius Maius for the last of the many gladiatorial games that he had staged over the years: to mark his final – and this time irreversible – retirement from public life. Ever since he had arrived in Pompeii, Clemens had intended to visit the gladiatorial barracks to seek out old acquaintances, although it was unlikely that he would recognise any faces there from those auxiliaries he had led in battle six years earlier.

The previous evening, too late to catch the gladiators' practice, Clemens had walked down towards the Nuceria Gate, past their favourite inn and the adoring fans outside, and had peered in to where the fighters had chosen to spend their last hours before risking death. But in the flickering light from the oil lamps, the faces of the men had been indistinct and their sorrows only too plain. The judge had understood what feelings lay beneath the sounds of jollity and bravado that charged the air before a battle, and had turned away.

He felt for them, too, as they stood before him now, saluting him and the magistrates who sat to his left and right. Crescens, the netter of virgins; Celadus, with his mighty cure for ladies in the night; Hilarus, Brebex and brave Oceanus. The crowd knew their names and chanted them.

With a flourish of his staff, the ringmaster traced a series of sweeping lines in the sand, a gladiator fixed behind each, staring his partner down until the signal for their combat to begin was given. Circling the arena, again and again the master of ceremonies swung his staff to release the paired gladiators from their posture of frozen defiance. Wary circling at first, a sweeping miss by a blade, then contact, as the sound of battle grew: the exaggerated grunts of professionals as they lunged and parried, the thudding blows of steel on soft bronze armour.

While those around him lost themselves in the sport, Clemens's mind *wandered, as he glanced from face to face. With men such as Epidius Sabinus, Pompeii's allegiance to Vespasian would be secure; but who would rise to the challenge alongside him? For three generations the Cuspii Pansae had never been far from the centre of power, and they could rely on that continuing. There was Bruttius Balbus, who was an honest man, but he was ageing and years of being ignored, even when a magistrate, had wearied him.*

Perhaps it was inevitable that the Neronian taint would fade and allow others back into the game. Julius Polybius had never lost his influence, and who would bet against the Popidii? Vedius Siricus would do well to stay out of the limelight, but he had a boy with obvious ambition. And then there was Cerrinius Vatia, the tearaway son of the esteemed Augustalis – see how he turns to wave at girls in the higher seats – surely he was a certainty for public office. And Helvius Sabinus, who was of lowlier origins, but had a growing following.

It took a moment before Clemens sensed the change around him: the crowd had stilled, the sounds of battle had grown fewer but more intense. Only two pairs were left standing, trading blows, picking their spot with ever greater precision. And then, suddenly, a man was down and only one pair left. A lunge, a parry. A scimitar reverberated on the murmillo's *shield, unbalancing him. A fall? A fall. And quickly the Thracian drove in to claim his prize, sword levelled at the beaten man's neck, his head raised to request the* editor's *decision.*

Clemens wondered if the vanquished fighter could hold himself still, without flinching. Would he prove himself a warrior, worth sparing? The whole amphitheatre watched intently until, suddenly, the defeated man's body crumpled in a barely perceptible sob. Death it must be.

After Suedius Clemens left Pompeii, a series of inscribed stones was set up commemorating his contribution to the city, outside the gates, and almost precisely one hundred metres from the city walls. The written reference was to returning public lands, but the implicit reference to the *pomerium* might also have carried a more symbolic weight. For the integrity and sanctity of the city itself had been compromised through years of impious opportunism.[28]

Vespasian's rule saw much that had gone awry in the Roman world set right, but in AD 75 he was already growing old. Some time in the first half of AD 79, the Emperor's declining health seems to have necessitated a convalescent sojourn in Herculaneum. Certainly the Emperor's personal physician Apollinaris was there at that time and it is unlikely that he would have travelled without his elderly patient: perhaps the unusual strength that year of the subterranean sulphuric gases on which the *sudatorium* – 'sweating rooms' – relied, promised the Emperor a quick cure. But they were not successful.

In July, as cities across Italy were managing the yearly transition of magistrates, and the common people heaved their possessions from one rental property to another, Vespasian's health worsened and he succumbed to severe bowel disturbances. The best cure that Galen proposed for acute diarrhoea was a soup made from lentils, beetroot and *garum*. Perhaps word was sent to Umbricius of Pompeii to provide his finest fish sauce – the 'flower of the flower' – for his Emperor. If so, the message must have arrived too late. True to form, back in Rome, Vespasian raised himself from the imperial latrine to utter his famous last words, 'A soldier should die standing.'

By then, Suedius Clemens's good work in Pompeii had earned him a posting to Egypt as Prefect of the Camps. It was there, in Alexandria, that he would receive the news of his Emperor's death and Titus's coronation; and there, too, that he would hear of the far greater upheaval that the natural world had long held in store.

The glass-bottomed Auto . . . . .

— XII —

*I beg you to elect Marcus Epidius
Sabinus senior magistrate with judicial
power, a most worthy young man. The
venerable council is electing him. Good
fortune to Clemens, venerable judge.*

**The phoenix is lucky,
may you be too.**

If honour is bestowed on a man who lives
modestly, a worthy honour should be given
to this young man, Cuspius Pansa.

**The gladiatorial troupe of Aulus
Suettius Certus will fight at
Pompeii on 31 May. There will
be a hunt and awnings.**

*Love dictates what I write
and Cupid guides my
hand: may I die if I wished
to be a god without you.*

I ask that you elect Lucius
Popidius Ampliatus and Lucius
Vedius Nummianus aediles.

**All the worshippers of Isis call for
Cn. Helvius Sabinus as aedile.**

> *If integrity in life is thought to be of
> any use, this man, Lucretius Fronto is
> worthy of great honour.*

The late drinkers ask you to elect Marcus Cerrinius
Vatia aedile. Florus ad Fructus wrote this.

All the deadbeats and Macerius
ask for Vatia as aedile.

> *Epidius with his household
> want and support Cn. Helvius
> Sabinus as aedile.*

**Marcus Cerrinius for aedile. Some people love him, some
are loved by him, I can't stand him. –** *Who loathes, loves.*

Valens, you're sleeping; you're asleep and
dreaming; wake up from your slumber
and make Helvius Sabinus aedile.

> *I admire you, wall, for not having
> collapsed at having to carry the tedious
> scribblings of so many writers.*

CHAPTER 13

Apocalypse

August AD 79

Nobody could claim that they had not been warned. Nero had fallen, civil war had flared and died away, and Vespasian's judge, Clemens, had come and gone since the first great earthquake had struck Pompeii. It was plain to anyone, though, that in AD 79 the overall fabric of the city was still in a worse condition than it had been twenty years earlier. The sections of the forum that had been rebuilt testified only to the civic spirit that saw the city through its difficult times, not a feeling that the danger had passed. A few hundred metres to the north-west, the construction team at work on the vast and as yet incomplete Central Baths had already been forced to repair and buttress the walls in places, where more recent quakes had taken their toll. And in the city's streets and houses, the rhythms of daily life were still disrupted by the endless attempts to repair and reinforce the water system: the current programme involved digging trenches to bury the lead pipes far deeper in the hope that this would limit future damage.

But whilst it was easy for those who dwelt within the walls to look only inwards, those who worked the territory would have found it harder to ignore the warnings from nature. As the strange summer of AD 79 crept on, the seasonal demands of the land provided plenty to keep the agricultural workers of Pompeii busy. From the beginning of August, attention turned to the preparation of equipment. Wine presses needed to be serviced, the great fermenting jars sealed with a treatment of pitch and then washed in sea water before being left to dry in the air for at least a fortnight. And once this was done, there was still the harrowing of the soil,

343

the weeding out of ferns and sedge, the cutting of corn stalks and the baling of the straw.

Most of this work would have taken place in the lower-lying areas of Pompeii's territory, where the arable farming was concentrated. There the talk would all have been of the inexplicable drought: of the wells and springs that had run dry despite a normal fall of rain in the preceding months, and of the blanched weeds and the dead fish that floated in the Sarno, whose low summer waters carried a poisonous level of sulphuric acid. But those who ventured up onto the slopes of Vesuvius to check the vines, or to graze their flocks, would have hurried back to tell of more worrying signs. For there the earth itself was changing: in places the ground swelled and wisps of smoke rose from newly formed fumeroles, wilting the vine leaves and wizening their fruit.

On 19 August, the first grapes of the year were ceremonially plucked during the festival of Vinalia Rustica and a lamb sacrificed to Jupiter, with prayers for a month of clement weather to follow before the main harvest began. By then many in Pompeii must finally have realised there was genuine cause for alarm.

Within at most a day or two, a series of earth tremors began, less serious than those the region had become accustomed to but of far greater, and increasing, frequency. Pliny the Younger is our witness, but modern vulcanologists confirm his observations by analogy with more recent eruptions and elaborate on his account with descriptions of the terrifying noises that would have sounded like thunderclaps coming from deep within the earth. The historian Cassius Dio may have been working from contemporary accounts when he recorded, a century later, the psychological impact of the disturbances around Vesuvius; the blurring of delusion and reality adds to the impression. 'Numbers of huge men appeared,' he wrote, 'of a superhuman size, such as the Giants are represented ... by day and night they were seen roaming the earth and wandering through the air ... People thought the Giants were rising in revolt, for now too their numerous phantom shapes appeared in the smoke, and a sound of war trumpets could be heard.'[1]

The geographer Strabo had taken delight in pointing out to his readers the geological evidence that, once upon a time,

Vesuvius had been a dangerous volcano – though he expressed not the faintest doubt that long before the first century BC it had become extinct. By August AD 79, with the proof of nature before their eyes, there could surely have been few who still believed him. With the symptoms of impending disaster multiplying by the day, the depths of resilience or resignation that led many – perhaps the vast majority – of Pompeii's population to persist in following their everyday routine is quite extraordinary. Was it overfamiliarity with the seismic hazards in Campania that blinded them to what was happening? Had the years since the earthquake, with their regular repetition of disquieting tremors, already rid the city of the risk-averse and left it populated by foolhardy souls who felt themselves invulnerable? Or was their obtuseness in the face of inevitable destruction merely the reflex reaction of the helpless – those who had too much to lose and nothing to live for outside Pompeii?

Finally, by 22 August, the message began to get through to at least some Pompeians. Those of a nervous disposition, or those blessed with a merely normal level of prescience, wasted no time in gathering their possessions ready for departure.

It was probably now, as people piled everything from silver plate to garden tools together and hastily sorted them to decide what to take and what to hide away, that the displacement of belongings occurred that has so mystified some contemporary interpreters of domestic life in Pompeii. There may even have been a run on cooking utensils by those who understood the demands of catering in emergency encampments, to explain the relative paucity of evidence for cooking in the city's houses. But for every one of those who set off along the roads that ran north or south around the bay, there would have been several others who looked on in disdain, mocking the refugees' cowardice or gloating over the profit that had been made out of their gullibility.

The inhabitants of the House of the Vestals continued to enjoy their water garden with no thought to the future, congratulating themselves for their decision to convert an entire room off the peristyle into a huge cistern, reinforced and sealed with waterproof plaster for the purpose. The water shortages that deprived nearly everyone else of the luxury had clearly vindicated their foresight. The Popidii probably grumbled about the slow progress on their own scheme to keep the Citharista's fountains running, not least since the holes in the pavement hindered access to the shops on which they now relied for extra income. A few blocks down the street, Julius Philippus stood dauntless and immovable with his family, including a pregnant daughter or daughter-in-law, while a few doors down Blaesia Prima looked forward to Pompeii's citizens confirming their solidarity at the theatrical games that were due to take place days later, and for which she had already bought tickets. Others were looking no further ahead than the following day's Festival of Vulcan, the god of fire and fertility.

Assuming that the Pompeian rites took the same form as those in Rome, then 23 August AD 79 would have seen the priests casting small fish onto the sacrificial fire and driving an assortment of other animals after them. It was an opportunity to assuage whatever affront had caused Vulcan to belch steam and smoke over the very fields for which he was supposed to care. It was quietly hoped, too, that the flesh of fish and beast would satisfy his appetite and prevent him coming after the worshippers. Those drawn to superstition, or those for whom one ceremony was not enough, may also have attended Biria's house, where the peristyle was substantial enough to hold large numbers for semi-public worship. The service was conducted on an altar at the far end of the garden, behind which the walls were painted yellow and into which closets were recessed that contained the sacred utensils of the cult, including the life-sized bronze 'magic hands of Sabazius', along with a gilded serpent that was passed underneath the clothing of initiates and across their chests as a key part of the mysteries.[2] And as if to reassure any who doubted Biria's credentials, the sacred space was even labelled on a wall as the '*antrum*', in specific reference to the holy place of the Cumaean Sybil that Virgil had described in the *Aeneid*.[3]

Whatever time was spent in worship that day, though, it was time wasted. As those businesses that were still staffed shut up shop, inserting the tall slats that passed for shutters into their grooves, the last moment was rapidly approaching when a family that set off to leave the city by road with a cart laden with possessions could be sure of reaching safety; and even for them there was the prospect of a long, hard journey through a moonlit night. For those procrastinators who finally saw sense and were prepared to leave with only hand luggage, there may still have been the odd boat available down in the harbour for hire or purchase at a vastly inflated price. If they fretted that their decision was rash, any second thoughts would have vanished as the moon's silvery light glinted off the floating bodies of dead fish far out at sea. And as they drifted out into the bay, they might have heard the sounds of another earthquake, quite identifiable even at this distance, as it rumbled across the countryside and shook the stones of the city.

Pliny the Younger described how 'There had been, for several days before, some shocks from earthquakes.'[4] As had probably become their habit, the inhabitants of Pompeii made for open spaces, away from any risk of falling masonry. But although the August nights were warm enough, and perhaps warmer that night than usual, few would have got much sleep, and it was tired men and women who arrived at work the next morning to assess the damage and set about providing a skeleton service. Somewhere in the city, though, there was a family who couldn't be moved. 'On Thursday 23rd', we read, 'the bear gave birth to cubs.'[5]

And so 24 August dawned. In the bakery of Popidius Priscus, a freedman of the owners of the House of the Citharista, the dust shaken from the ceiling would have had to be swept away before he could begin kneading the dough for the eight-sectioned loaves that his customers demanded. Even though Priscus dared to venture back to work while it was still night, it would have been late morning before the trays of proved dough were placed in the oven.

In the House of the Chaste Lovers, where extensive renovation was under way, the millstones in the bakery were out of use and the asses who usually turned them were braying uneasily in their stable. Perhaps the piglet and bird that were roasting in the oven were meant for the team of painters that was redecorating the house – a gesture by the homeowner to tempt them to stay at their job in spite of the despair they felt on discovering that the newly painted plaster had cracked. There was little point in restraint or small economies any longer, and who knows what other wild appetites might have been indulged around Pompeii in the hours that followed.

Among others remaining at their posts were the priests of Isis, who performed the morning service to welcome the return of the sun, and cooked eggs and fish in the small kitchen on one side of the precinct, either for their lunch or as an offering to the goddess. It was whilst they were doing so that the most shocking sound yet was heard: a sharp bang and prolonged roar of dispersing energy that reverberated from several miles away.

On the farther slopes of Vesuvius, in what is now a quarry near present-day Terzigno, the white-hot magma that had been pressing up through the earth's crust for years, causing the quakes and tremors and leaching sulphurous toxins out into the water supply, finally punched a hole through to the world of the living. The explosion disintegrated the plug and threw a dense cloud of fine ash into the air, which billowed out quite sedately until it had engulfed the mountainside in a grey haze. In the numerous villas nearby there was panic as, choking and stumbling, the inhabitants tried desperately to trace a path out of the darkness. In Pompeii, though, the consternation would have been only moderate. The optimistic may even have viewed the event as a noisy climax – an end rather than a beginning – while the more realistically inclined were still unsure whether to prepare for catastrophe or to sit back as spectators of a pyrotechnical display that now seemed likely to remain at a safe distance. Some, though, saw the need to act decisively.

It was still morning when the noblewoman Rectina dispatched a letter to the admiral of the fleet in his villa across the bay at Misenum: the distance to be travelled was nearly thirty-three kilometres and the letter arrived in the hand of Pliny the Elder between one and two o'clock in the afternoon. By then the drama of Vesuvius had moved on an act. While his instructions were executed to scramble the crews of the triremes that formed the backbone of the Misenum fleet, Pliny could only take the part of a spectator, knowing that by now it was a role that would have been denied to his correspondent.

At around midday, in another sudden and far larger explosion, the entire peak of the mountain had been blown away. A fiery column of pumice particles, most no larger than half a gram in weight, were thrust twenty-seven miles into the sky, where they blossomed out into what Pliny's nephew – Pliny the Younger, who was staying with him at the time – described as the shape of an umbrella pine tree, but is today more often known as a mushroom cloud. It was the beginning of a discharge of explosive power that over the following day or so would exceed one hundred thousand times that of the atomic bomb that destroyed Hiroshima. Vesuvius had finally revealed its true monstrosity.[6]

The Jewish prophets would have been gratified to learn, in due course, that the scale of the tragedy unfolding in Campania was truly apocalyptic. An eruption of such force occurs, on average, only once in a thousand years: there would have been no precedent in recorded history and mythology afforded the only point of reference. It is greatly to the credit of the Younger Pliny and his scientific training that, even while he watched his uncle set sail to his death, he was able to categorise his observations calmly enough to produce an exact report some time later. His account provided the textbook case of volcanic eruption for centuries to come. It is one that contemporary vulcanology, drawing on similar events, such as the eruption of Mount St Pelée in 1902, can in large part corroborate and, occasionally, correct and amplify. Indeed, the column of material of the type seen at midday on the 24 August is now known generically as 'Plinian'. Informed by the archaeological evidence, in particular the strata of debris left at different stages of the eruption and the position of bodies within it, the ancient and modern descriptions make it possible to reconstruct a very accurate picture of the experience of those in Pompeii during the course of the eruption.[7]

The sight of fire and stone roaring up to the heavens that Pliny witnessed from across the bay – 'thrusting ... bulging and uncoiling ... as if the hot entrails of the earth were being drawn out and dragged towards the heavens' – would have been massively more terrifying when seen from Pompeii. Although individually the pellets of pumice that showered down from a lofty height were relatively harmless, and a cushion or clothes held over the head provided considerable protection, their collective force was enough to cause those who were outdoors to cower and stumble, and the occasional larger stone caught up in the deluge could knock a person out cold. Presence of mind was called for, but with the heat radiating from Vesuvius, the hail of stones, and the infernal noise and light, disorientation and outright fear were more common. Where to head for? From where might help come? To flee, hoping to outrun the volcano's anger, or to stay and shelter in the hope of weathering the storm? Already those who had survived the earthquake of AD 62 would have seen the confusion of that day multiplied many times over.

Men, women and children, alone and in groups, poured towards the city's gates and out onto the roads or towards the river or the coastline. Here and there certain of them fell and struggled to continue, whether from concussion, exhaustion or some other injury: within minutes of the first *lapilli*, or hail of ash pebbles, hitting the ground, an unstable carpet several centimetres thick had formed and continued to deepen. One man who had screwed up his courage to leave town by the nearest gate, even though it meant heading directly towards Vesuvius, collapsed and died only a hundred feet beyond it, next to the commemorative stone *stele* that had been set up to Suedius Clemens. Another sprawled on the paving stones of the road that led out from the Nola Gate in the north-east of Pompeii. Although three different groups of people had taken shelter behind the nearby tomb of Aesquillia Pollia, no one attempted to drag him to what, for a while longer, could pass for safety. Perhaps the effort was beyond them: by now, every step was like wading through a perilous mixture of ball bearings and snow.

Whether by instinct or in the hope of rescue by sea, from this stage of the eruption onwards, those who were mobile tended to head south, towards the Sarno and Nuceria Gates, and away from the volcano.

As the Isis priests continued to pray to the merciful goddess for salvation, scores of desperate citizens would have passed the entrance to the precinct on their way to join the road down to the Stabian Gate. Their fear was contagious and eventually, after one of their number was struck by falling debris in the *ecclesiasterion* of the sacred enclosure, their nerve broke and the priests fled: one sought refuge in the service area, another fell in the street just outside. For a while, a third – who had been entrusted with a pair of silver beakers that were decorated with the cult's motifs – fared better, although even he would not make it out of the city. Perhaps, on seeing that there was no immediate sign of an evacuation fleet, he felt that the sturdy buildings within the city walls seemed to promise better shelter than the wharfs outside. Like many others, the Isis priest turned right before he reached the Stabian Gate and headed into the theatre complex.

Neither the main theatre, where the set-dressing for that afternoon's planned performance had been reduced to tatters by the bombardment, nor the smaller *odeon* next to it, provided any cover. But behind the main stage was the *palaestra*, where the gladiators could normally be found exercising and might be present, even now, to provide an example of courage in adversity. Mostly the *palaestra* was open to the sky, but at the far end of the large, colonnaded space stood a row of small rooms, hard by the city wall. It was there that the stragglers were making for, picking their way past the occasional body, eerily half-buried in the volcanic debris. The Isis priest followed them until suddenly he faltered, distracted perhaps by the screams that were emerging from one room where four slave fighters were still shackled into stocks, as the hail of *lapilli* had accumulated to the equivalent of their chest height. At that moment a heavier stone plummeted to earth, crushing the priest's skull.

In his home at the back of the servant's quarters in the House of Menander, the bailiff Poppaeus Eros tried in vain to comfort his seven-year-old daughter. Others remained in the main house, and the main doors were firmly closed and bolted; but Eros had concealed his absent master's silver dinner service in the bathhouse only a short time previously and knew that it was his duty to stay and protect it. Other homes were left entirely unguarded. Blaesia Prima's silver plate was discovered in the possession of one unfortunate who, whilst trying to escape town with it, briefly ducked into another elite house. Was he transporting it on Blaesia's instructions, emptying her property to prevent burglary, or was he the burglar and his fatal detour the compulsion of a man who couldn't resist trying his luck one more time?

With death all around, and the chances of survival minimal, it is hardly credible that looting was rife. But the hard experience of the past decade and more had taught the people of Pompeii to recognise an opportunity and seize it with both hands. Any compunction they might have felt would have quickly dissolved in a cup of the wine that was freely available from unattended counter-tops. The thief who left his assortment of swag in the inn on the last major crossroads before the Vesuvius Gate – beyond which the volcano raged – deserved the finest Falernian to steel his nerves. Did it make him too greedy and too confident? Did he roll out of there to raid another house nearby, never to return to claim his original spoils? Or did he simply ditch the least valuable items that he had snatched in order to facilitate his escape?

By late afternoon, the streets in the centre of the city were almost deserted. Some of the houses were empty; others still sheltered families who crouched, listening, as the roofs above them creaked and groaned with the pressure of the built-up pumice, imploring the gods that the worst would soon be over. But then, and not for the last time, Vesuvius dashed their hopes. With a roar mighty enough to make the thundering jet that had deafened and shaken them for the previous seven hours seem almost endurable, the column of ash surged and thickened, rising a further six kilometres and carrying with it into the heavens an endless mass of darker grey stones that were almost twice the size and weight of those that had fallen until then. Driven in a southerly direction by the wind, they tumbled onto Pompeii in a torrent, quickly obliterating the white drifts into which the previous *lapilli* had formed.

Modern building codes stipulate that heavy storage structures, such as reinforced concrete warehouses, should be capable of supporting a load of roughly two hundred and fifty pounds per square foot. The pumice that had so far collected to a depth of almost five feet already exceeded that allowance, yet still it kept falling. With most buildings constructed using timber beams, it was not long before the first roofs began to give way. Panic spread as those isolated indoors listened to the terrible noise of splintering and understood what was happening; but they could do nothing except huddle closer to the walls, or scuttle under staircases for the additional protection this might provide.

In the Murecine building, the Sulpicii businessmen's collection of wax tablets had long ago been buried, along with the hundreds of small marble plaques engraved with the letters 'SUL', with which one of their number – probably Faustus – had planned to personalise his property. There was no sign of any of the Sulpicii themselves, but a couple of women and their three children, the youngest of them only four years old, had moved to the upper storey to keep ahead of the build-up outside. When the sagging timbers above them finally gave way, the momentum of the falling debris carried away the floor on which they stood, and they died amidst the wreckage.

Not far from the forum, one man had remained in the House of the Sailor – the old Lollius Synhodus, perhaps, or his putative son Fuscus. He took up his place in the *tablinum*, where the patron would normally receive his visitors, and awaited the inevitable. It was a narrow room with solid walls on either side and thick beams above, and would have been amongst the most resilient spaces in the house. From here, seated beside his money chest, the house's owner could have watched his life's work and that of his father crumbling before his eyes: the finely painted atrium in one direction, the raised garden with its underground warren of storehouses and bakery facilities in the other. At last, though, the roof here also fell in, crushing the solitary, obstinate figure below.

The late Empress Poppaea's villa in Oplontis was worse afflicted than Pompeii. Of the magnificent statue collection that was kept there, by now hardly anything remained visible. The amber-haired beauty and her princely companion were submerged, and even the clumsy figure of Fortuna – on whose legs a sculptor had begun work only a few days earlier – would only just have poked her head above the sea of stone. A decade earlier, the mistress of the house would not have tolerated anything so crude as this, and the cack-handed artist might have felt secretly relieved that his efforts would never have to bear comparison with the masterpieces that stood all around.

The statue of another empress, Augustus's Livia, which stood in the Villa of the Mysteries, suffered the same fate at roughly the same moment. The area around the villa's peristyle, which had been converted for wine production, was inundated with *lapilli*, which had buried one woman and a child. A second woman had clawed and scrambled to stay on top of the vast and growing heap, rather than being smashed under the falling masonry of the villa. For hour after hour she won her fight, her hands scraped raw, her face and body constantly stung by the tiny missiles that fell from above and against which she could not protect herself. Her only thought was survival, her prayer surely that the rain of stones would cease.

At last, at around eleven o'clock on the night of 24 August, she was granted her wish. The deluge relented somewhat and the noise produced by the volcano modulated. A critical point had been reached: the matter hanging miles high in the air had become so dense that the upward force of the explosion was no longer sufficient to support it. Instead, for a brief period, the red-hot air issuing from the bowels of the earth at breakneck speed was being countered and pushed back, downwards and outwards, by the pressure of the gases and debris above.

Had the woman in the Villa of the Mysteries paused in her struggle for life and been able to look up towards Vesuvius, now all but hidden by flying debris, it might have seemed for a moment as though the mountain was about to suck all its sublime fury back into itself. But as the column collapsed downwards, it did not sink tidily back into the huge new crater where the mountain's peak had once been, but overflowed down the mountain's sides in all directions. Soon afterwards, stunned and exhausted, and with all hope gone, the unknown woman succumbed and was overwhelmed by the renewed hail of stones.

Among the last sounds she would have registered was a

turbulent wall of cloud hurtling towards Herculaneum a few miles away, thick with flying shrapnel and lit from within by fierce fires that had come straight from the earth's core. It was the first of six such pyroclastic flows and surges – the two distinguished by their relative ability to overcome obstacles posed by the relief of the landscape and the concentration of the debris that they leave behind – that would crash down on the landscape around Vesuvius over the next few hours. Travelling at a speed of over one hundred miles per hour, hugging the terrain and blasting even the largest stone blocks that lay in its searing path up to four metres from their original position, the first surge clipped the northern outskirts of Herculaneum. Rather cooler than those which were to follow, the temperature of the cloud was nevertheless hot enough to kill those it engulfed: skin burned and blistered, ash lined the trachea of the victim and death followed shortly from shock or asphyxiation. As the thinning cloud poured out over the sea and dispersed, it left sections of the town instantaneously carbonised – so burned out that they barely smouldered – and most of the rest consumed by flames.

It is possible, though by no means certain, that a group of citizens from Pompeii's neighbouring city survived this first major assault: if they did they would have been left only half-alive and trapped in hellish conditions. Not until 1982 was one of the most important discoveries of anatomical evidence from the Vesuvian sites made. Like Pompeii, Herculaneum was a coastal town, the bulk of which was situated several metres above sea level; since it was buried far deeper than Pompeii after the eruption, for reasons that will become apparent, it took many years of excavation to reach the lowest-lying areas along the shoreline. But it was there that fifty-one men, forty-nine women and thirty-nine children mustered, perhaps hoping to use the boats that were stored under the arches to make their escape. And it was there that they would meet their end.

Were Venedius Eutychus, Petronia Justa and Cominius Primus among them? If so, each had abandoned the baskets of legal tablets, by which we know their biographies, in their neighbouring apartments and rushed down the steep street outside, through the Sea

Gate to Herculaneum's beach-side bathhouse, before clambering down steps in the sea wall beyond.

Like all those who followed their primal instinct and hid from the sight of their awful pursuer, the sound of its approach – like a cavalry charge of giant demons – could hardly have been more terrible. There would have been just enough time for heightened senses to take in each discrete stage of its progress across woods and fields, the city walls and their homes, before it poured across the near precipice above them. But even if, by some cruel miracle, the pyroclastic flow somehow cascaded clean over them this first time – as a waterfall can leave those behind it dry – the heat radiated would have been far more than uncomfortable. The sea steamed and bubbled explosively while, above the city, the moisture in the earth itself was boiling and had begun to turn the soil viscous. Perhaps in an instant of relative peace, the uncanny sound of its gloopy movement would have sent a shiver through those nursing their burns.

Fortunately, the avalanche of boiling mud that drowned the whole of Herculaneum and left it mummified, up to twenty metres beneath the future ground level, did not reach the beach until after the second and far hotter pyroclastic surge had toppled the highest walls of the city. It saved the refugees from further suffering by inflicting instantaneous death at four hundred degrees Celsius. It also denied archaeologists access to what would have been an extraordinary archive of DNA, the structure of which breaks down beyond decipherment at slightly lower temperatures than this. But the combination of sudden death and almost immediate entombment has nevertheless preserved a unique snapshot of a population from the ancient world and allowed hugely informative analysis of the bones. One of the greatest frustrations consequent on the degradation of the skeletons' DNA is the impossibility of knowing for sure what kinship, if any, may have existed between individuals. But the quite recent excavation of the home of Julius Philippus in Pompeii has gone some way to redressing this gap as well as providing the unusually detailed record of the circumstances of his household.

*

As five o'clock on the morning of 25 August passed, it was more than sixteen hours since all preconceptions about Vesuvius had been blown sky-high, and at least eight since the extended family of Julius Philippus had found themselves trapped in two adjacent rooms near the back of the house. There were thirteen people in all – if we include the one who fell later from the upper storey – spanning a range of ages from three to nearly seventy.

Two men of around sixty were present, the younger of whom may have been Polybius himself, the other perhaps either a stalwart retainer or a relative: Julius Phillipus, we will assume, momentarily accepting the case for him being Polybius's elder brother rather than his father. Both of them suffered from osteoporosis, which may have contributed to their decision to stay where they were, though the condition of Polybius's eighteen-year-old daughter, who was eight months pregnant with her second child, would have quashed any debate. Both she and her mother, who was around forty years old and a prolific childbearer, were with them in the small room, together with the young woman's husband, who was in his late twenties, and three or four of her younger brothers, cousins or slaves.[8] That Polybius's eldest child was a daughter explains why no second generation of Julii had yet stood as *aedile*, but within a decade there might have been several vying for that first public honour. If all the younger people in the room are seen as the product of the same womb, then until eight years earlier Polybius's wife had been bearing children regularly, every third year.

Asserting his authority, Polybius would have tried to quieten his anxious dependents sufficiently to set about establishing contact with the other party nearby, whether by shouts or knocks on the wall. How they came to be separated was probably as much a mystery to Polybius as it is to us. Perhaps the key was the three-year-old boy, whose disobedience might have caused his selfless great-aunt to set off to retrieve him after he had scampered away to see what was going on outside; maybe, after a young male slave was sent after them, the hail of stone had intensified and all three ended up diving into the nearest available shelter. Whatever the scenario, it seems likely that an old, infirm man was separated from his wife and a pregnant young mother from her son. Their agonies would have been intense as, over and again, each enquired whether the other was still alive and waited for the reply over the surrounding sounds of cataclysm.

So long had it been dark – a dense blackness lit only by distant fires, which scarcely penetrated the volcanic material with which the air was thick – that it must have seemed as though an endless night had descended on the world. Dozens of people were still clinging on to life outside the northern walls of the city, caught there when the eruption began and unwilling since then to risk a dash for safety. Five or six were still alive, scattered around the Villa of the Mysteries, more than twenty in the Villa of Diomedes slightly nearer the city, and many more in or around the tombs of the Herculaneum Gate necropolis, perhaps wanting to be close to the ancestors whom they would soon join. It was a similar story outside the Vesuvius Gate, where some distance from the city a woman tried to control a slave whom, in her hysteria, she refused to release from the heavy metal ring around his ankle; on another highway an entire chain gang hobbled along. It is impossible to estimate how many hundreds of others were likewise on the roads and in the open fields, or else cowering in the villas that dotted the landscape towards the volcano, that are unlikely ever to be excavated. All must have been praying for a fresh, clear dawn to break – for the chaos around them to prove merely a nightmare.

The light of dawn that greeted them at five-thirty was of a different kind altogether. Then, for a third time, the rising column of debris blustered and roared and turned tail towards the ground. This time the pyroclastic flow that it generated swallowed up everything outside the city as far as Pompeii's outer defences.

For Julius Polybius and his family, for Poppaeus Eros and his daughter, for the gladiators and those crushed with them into the rooms around the exercise ground, the smell of sulphur and sudden swell of heat might, for an instant, have brought to mind the 'sweating rooms' that were the pride of Campania. Prescribed as a cure for respiratory illnesses, small flames burned in the enclosed space of the *sudatorium* to draw out the expectorant smoke from beneath the ground, which the patients gasped in as they panted against the effect of temperatures exceeding eighty degrees Celsius. Having paid their entrance fee, invalids and hypochondriacs alike could reel out into daylight feeling that they had received their money's worth of suffering. But from the great sweating room of August AD 79 there was no escape. Every entrance of every house in Pompeii was by now blocked with tonnes of *lapilli* and, in any case, the air outside was no fresher than that within.

Knowing that their end was near, Polybius appears to have become resigned and turned his attention to calming those around him. Perhaps he or Phillipus, who had made the embassy to Nero's court nearly twenty years before and may even have met Seneca there, was a Stoic: they behaved as such. A number of beds or couches were available in the space they occupied and as many as could fit on them were persuaded to lie down; others lay on the floor or awaited their fate standing. Last goodbyes and endearments having been shouted out, next door, Phillipus's elderly wife clasped the hand of the young man who was with her, and stilled her shaking to allow the infant whose head lay on her thigh to drift into an uneasy sleep.

Not all were so reconciled to their fate. In the fullery of Stephanus, the recriminations that had flowed for hours against the manager – who had kept his workers at their tasks until it was too late – had died down, as the desperate business of survival took over. Stephanus kept a tight hold on a bag of coins that must have represented many days' takings, but his workers clambered over one another to remain beneath the solid lintel of the entrance way that offered the surest protection. In the back areas of the House of the Faun, three stable boys and their overseer had long given up the fight to restrain the frightened, rearing horses and crazed oxen and instead let them bolt onto the street; and in the House of Menander, as in buildings across the city, a group who found themselves trapped or separated like the family of Julius Polybius, urgently applied whatever makeshift tools came to hand to break and jemmy their way through dividing walls in the hope of being freed or reunited.

After the blast of heat rushed over them at five-thirty that morning, they had only an hour of futile endeavour left. The fourth pyroclastic surge at six-thirty was the most deadly. Reaching up to one hundred and eighty miles per hour, it was not as hot as the surge that had finally destroyed Herculaneum, but lower in oxygen and richer in poisonous gases – a tornado of rock and urban debris that sliced through flesh and bone. The pyroclastic phenomenon is lethal in all aspects, but autopsies carried out on victims of the Mount St Helens eruption of 1980 showed that the cause of most deaths was asphyxiation. The more visible effects, some of which can still be seen in the posture of the bodies, was caused by the intense heat that baked flesh rather than burning it, mummifying hands and feet and shrinking internal organs. Thrown away from the volcano, prone onto the ground, their hands and forearms are clasped up to faces, their limbs flexed by tightened ligaments and their spines extended.

The inn of Mustius and Ovia would have felt the impact first, the house of the Vettii freedmen a second later, then the House of the Bull and the House of the Vestals, whose water reserves evaporated in an instant. The stable boys in the House of the Faun would not have been able to blink before they were hit; next the forum, where the terrible agonies awaiting two men who were perhaps praying on the steps of the Temple of Jupiter were curtailed when a column toppled onto them. Five people were killed in the house of Epidius Sabinus, one in that of Umbricius Scaurus, while four were found in the dining room of the House of Fabius Rufus, which overlooked the sea (Plate 27). Blaesia Prima died at home in her husband Postumius Modestus's house, the necklace of magic pendants around her neck and the tokens for admission to the previous day's theatrical show in a box beside her. The surge extinguished the lives of the thirteen people in Julius Polybius's house simultaneously.

The hundreds who had congregated so many hours earlier in the theatre and *palaestra* area, perhaps in search of some leadership, never got away. Decimus Satrius Lucretius Valens and his wife, if it was they, died beside their gladiators under the portico of the *palaestra*: after twenty-four hours of claustrophic terror, death might have come as a relief. The many others who had made it down to the harbour early enough, and who may have seen Pliny the Elder's evacuation ships from the Misenum fleet cross the Bay of Naples the previous day and land near Stabiae, never got the chance to board their own escape vessel. In what has become known as the Garden of the Fugitives, close by the Nuceria Gate and the road to the Sarno bridge, thirteen fell, including two children and three babies. Perhaps one of them was the child whose clumsy portrait had been sketched by a proud parent less than a month earlier on the wall of a small room in the heart of the city, beside the words, 'Iuvenilla is born on Saturday 4 August, in the second hour of the evening.'[9]

Within minutes of their deaths, the debris from this surge had settled on its victims' corpses. Almost immediately a fifth surge filled the site further, and at just after seven in the morning, half an hour after all life had been extinguished in Pompeii, a sixth and final surge sheered off much of the architecture that was left exposed and poured onwards as far as the beach where Pliny the Elder stood, filling his old lungs with dust and ash and suffocating him.

Since midnight, his nephew, Pliny the Younger, had watched from across the bay as lightning forked from the volcanic clouds. He experienced close-up the effect of the earthquakes that reverberated out and the tidal wave they created, until the distant landscape had become quite unrecognisable. With the plume of ash still towering above Vesuvius and threatening further violence, he gathered the books of Livy he had been reading and fled.

Several more days passed before the discharge of ash and *lapilli* from Vesuvius gradually petered out, to reveal a smoking crater barely half as high as the mountain that had stood there only a week or so earlier. But the changes did not end there. In total, a quarter of a cubic kilometre of rock had been macerated and dispersed by the eruption, the bulk of it falling within a radius of ten kilometres, although some pumice travelled eight times as far. The coastline had been pushed out by over four hundred metres and only the boldest relief of hills and valleys remained visible, smoothed out into a smoking moonscape of grey dunes. Even the highest buildings were buried a metre or so deep, with perhaps only the peak of an occasional temple roofline emerging, although Plutarch is more absolute still when he records how 'those who went there by daylight felt ignorance and uncertainty as to where these [cities] had been'.[10]

The terrain would have cooled quite quickly and by the time the first assessors arrived from Rome to stamp their feet on the *lapilli* and shake their heads in disbelief, it seems likely that looters and salvage experts – some of them presumably survivors who wanted to claim their own possessions – would already have begun tunnelling down to where they believed their homes, or the richest pickings, might lie. Amongst the ancient graffiti from Pompeii are undisputed examples of messages written after the destruction of the city: 'House tunnelled through', written in Greek – or some variant – was a favourite that suggests something like a co-ordinated operation, though it was probably a private rather than official initiative.[11] Digging down into small, loose stones was certainly a hazardous exercise, and it sometimes proved difficult for excavators in the earlier modern period to distinguish between the bodies of tunnellers who had been buried alive and the eruption's original victims.

Of a probable twenty to thirty thousand inhabitants of Pompeii and its surrounding lands the skeletons of only two thousand have so far been unearthed. The location of most of them, at the top of the pumice layer, confirms that they endured many hours of hopeless struggle before their final end. One third of the city within the walls, and the vast majority of the outlying areas, remain unexcavated and would doubtless contribute to the toll. However, the strong likelihood is that most of the remainder had left early enough to be on the roads some distance away by the time the catastrophe unfolded, although this does not mean that they all escaped. Not far beneath the ground for miles about, where modern housing has spread, many thousands of others may still lie.

Inhibitions about building again on the site of Pompeii only began to disappear in modern times. Whilst the new Emperor Titus, who had only succeeded to the throne less than two months before the disaster, acted speedily to ameliorate the suffering of survivors and reassure the population as a whole, there was no suggestion of re-founding the city. As a small proportion of the volcanic debris found its way into the atmosphere – travelling as far as Africa, where it settled as a film of black dust, and obscuring the sun for many months – Titus's priority was, unsurprisingly, to demonstrate to the Empire that the eruption was not a sign of divine disapproval for his reign, or for a past error such as the sack of the Temple of Jerusalem. Elaborate services were staged to propitiate the gods and pray for atonement: pairs of seats were laid out, each dedicated to one god and one goddess, on which symbols befitting their characters were placed; and, using the most effective mechanism available for distributing imperial propaganda, Titus had coins minted with representations of the pious actions he had performed. But, as Suetonius noted approvingly, his personal reaction was more humane – one of 'paternal affection' – and resulted in the appointment of a number of ex-consuls to oversee the restoration of Campania. The surviving cities were to receive the proceeds from the sale of the estates of those who had died without heirs, to help fund their own repairs, and the Emperor himself visited the disaster zone within the year, and replaced a sundial in Sorrento that had been damaged in the accompanying quakes as a symbol of his good faith.[12]

But of Pompeii itself, no specific mention was made. Perhaps its demise was so terrible that it was considered best to pass over it in silence. Campania as a whole certainly never quite regained its prestige as Rome's premier playground: the sense of death was simply too pervasive. In any case, the Flavians preferred to build their holiday villas in the Apennines; it was a self-conscious assertion of their honest, rustic ways and set a fashion that others followed. But within a few years, life of sorts did return to the land in the shadow of Vesuvius. The roads that had once passed through Pompeii now followed different routes, sweeping around the hill under which the city was buried and intersecting with the main road from Stabiae to Nuceria, and the fields newly fertilised with the rich volcanic phosphates proved difficult for farmers to resist. As the years passed and new generations were born and grew up, the history of the place passed into folklore: the stopping point at the

Sarno bridge became known simply as Sarnum, and whilst the name Pompeii continued to appear on maps until the ninth century, it was increasingly referred to merely as 'Civita', or 'the City'. Those who tilled the soil in latter years were all but oblivious to what lay beneath their feet: they asked few questions when a windfall of coins worked its way to the surface, and fewer still if it was a skull rather than gold that snagged their ploughshare.

Only a few simple tombs, dug into the *lapilli* and marked with tiles or an amphora, offered a physical memorial on the site. They appeared within a few years of the eruption and the remains buried in them seem likely to have been those of survivors who, when they died in the natural course of things, wished to be reunited with the family and friends whom they had lost to Vesuvius. The decision to be buried in such a wasteland entailed sacrifices, not only of the more elaborate tomb they might have built elsewhere, but of the cremation that was a usual part of the funerary rites: so complete had been the volcano's devastation of the area that there were simply no trees left nearby to supply tinder for a pyre, and their bodies had to be buried intact. But at least the dying would have known that deep below their graves lay fond memories: a tomb where the family had always celebrated their ancestor feasts, or a glade of fruit trees that had once swayed in the seemingly endless summer sun.[13]

No other record of those who succeeded in fleeing during August AD 79 has been found, except for one: the tomb of an army veteran who died and was buried in Spain some years later. 'To the shades of Numerius Popidius Celsinus, *decurion*, well-deserving. Quintus Cecilius his son set this up.'[14] Was he, as seems probable, the same Celsinus who had been granted his place on the city council of Pompeii at the age of six years old, as a reward for his father's rebuilding of the Isis Temple? Hardly could a more representative figure from the city's last years have lived to tell its tragic tale.

Behold Vesuvius, that was until lately covered with the green shade of vines, whose famous juice filled vats to overflowing. Bacchus cared more for these slopes than the hills of his own Nysa, and here Satyrs used to hold their dances. This was Venus' dwelling ... and the place where Hercules left his name. All now destroyed by flame and buried in ash. The gods themselves would rather this had not been in their power.[15]

Martial *Epigrams*

ACKNOWLEDGEMENTS

Our thanks to all those who assisted with this project extends back to before its inception as a book. The authors' collaboration began during a television programme produced by the production company Illuminations, and we owe a debt to everyone there; in particular to John Wyver, who initiated that project with characteristic vision and foresight. Thanks are due from that time to Seb Grant, Linda Zuck in London, and Nicole Leghessi-Mazdi and James Walker in Italy. At all times, before and since, Maria Pia Malvezzi and her colleagues at the British School in Rome have provided invaluable assistance in securing permits to visit the less accessible areas of the ruins, while Pietro Giovanni Guzzo and the staff of the Soprintendenza di Pompei have been unfailingly helpful. The staff of the Joint Library of the Hellenic and Roman Societies at the University of London, the British Library, and the London Library have guided us through the stacks and catalogues; the lengthy bibliography that follows recognises the work of generations of dedicated Pompeian scholars. However, specific mention should be made here of John Dobbins, Lisa Fentress, Renata Henneberg and Greg Rowe who have advised us on some specific queries.

At Weidenfeld and Nicolson, the enthusiasm of Richard Milner saw the writing process well launched, and our editor Kirsty Dunseath took up the reins with great authority: her forbearance has saved us from many errors in style and judgement, and her advocacy has been appreciated. We are grateful to our agent, Patrick Walsh, for his unflagging friendship, support and hospitality, along with that of the Conville and Walsh agency. Andy Beckett, Jerry Brotton, Sara Holloway, Mary Harlow, Rachel Holmes, Helen King, Ingrid

Laurence, Deborah Levy and Ruth Scurr have all offered timely encouragement and advice. Our young families have borne the absences of mind and body that authorship entails with bemused goodwill. Above all, thanks are due to Rebecca Carter, without whose constant and tireless help this book would not be half (but might have been double) what it is. The book's shortcomings are entirely our own responsibility.

For permission to reproduce the photographs in the plates sections, acknowledgement is due to the Society of Antiquaries in London (26), the Soprintendenza di Pompei (3, 23a, 27), the Heberden Coin Room of the Ashmolean Museum in Oxford (5, a to f), Fotografica Foglia in Naples (1, 2, 4, 6, 7, 8, 9, 10, 11, 12, 13, 14, 15, 16, 17, 18, 19, 20, 21, 22, 23b, 24) and the Instituto Poligrafico e Zecca dello Stato, Rome (25 – taken from *Pompei alla luce degli scavi nuovi di via dell'Abbondanza [anni 1910–1923]* by Vittorio Spinazzola). The copyright in these images remains with them.

NOTES

INTRODUCTION

1 The House of Goethe is now known as the House of the Faun.
2 In the House of the Sailor, where once the name of a slave called Mon-astatos was scratched into a wall, perhaps for Mozart to pass and note down for the Queen of the Night's henchman, now only bare stone remains.
3 *Corpus Inscriptionum Latinarum* (abbreviated hereafter to *CIL*), 3.33; 10.768, 791, 1018, 1059, 7203, 7579.
4 Compare Calpurnius Siculus, 1.42; Seneca, *Apocolycyntosis*, 4.1; *Carmina Einsidlensia*, 2.22.

CHAPTER 1, DEATH OF A ROMAN KNIGHT

1 The basis for the characterisation of Decimus Lucretius Valens comes from the inscription on his tomb found in a recent excavation outside Pompeii: Conticello de Spagnolis 1993–4.
2 Tacitus, *Annals* 12: 66.
3 The research into the archive material recording late nineteenth-century excavations allied with recent rescue excavations in the Scafati area has revealed the tomb and its associated villas. This research has been published by Conticello de Spagnolis 1993–4, 1994, 1995 and 2001.
4 Cicero, *Pro Sulla* 60–62. *CIL*, 10.844, 937, 997.
5 The nature of the evidence for these families is shaped by the survival and excavation of inscriptions. The decision to present Pompeii as a heritage site surrounded by walls caused excavators from the nineteenth century onwards to work inside the city. As a consequence, the cemeteries of Pompeii are only partially known. Further excavation of the cemeteries would shed new light onto the relationships of the families of the city. The election notices, or *programmata*, provide invaluable information, but by their nature tend to refer to relatively recent elections to AD 79. James Franklin (2001) struggles to find much material prior to the

Augustan Age. See also Henrik Mouritsen (1988) for discussion of the *programmata*.

6 Servius, *Commentary on the Aeneid*, 7.662. See also Isidore, *Etymologies*, 15.1.51.

7 *Diodorus*, 4.21.5–22.2.

8 Strabo, *Geography*, 5.4.3–13.

9 *Année Epigraphique*, 1971, no. 88. A document recording the contractual duties of one such undertaker, found in the port of Puteoli, hints at the kind of taboo that would have marked him and his associates out from the rest of society.

10 Naples Museum, room 97.

11 He is a witness in one of the wax tablets from the Jucundus archive.

12 For discussion of the tensions of freeing slaves, see Dionysius of Halicarnassus, 4.24.

13 The classic account of the Roman funeral is given by Polybius, *Histories*, 6.53–4; in addition a sculptural frieze from Amiternum provides a visual representation of the funeral procession with mourners and musicians.

14 Plautus opens his comedy the *Aulularia* ('*Pot of Gold*') by having the household god, or *lar*, speak in monologue that he has watched over the house for not only the current owner but for his father and grandfather, and of course it was the grandfather who buried a pot of gold under the hearth, unknown to his descendants. The ownership of a property over several generations could cause it, if sold to another person, to still keep its name as derived from the previous owners.

15 Andrew Wallace-Hadrill (1994) argues that the street forms a processional axis. It should be noted, though, that the junction with Via di Stabia was impassable to such processions and the route would have been diverted via the Triangular Forum and the theatres before returning to Via dell'Abbondanza.

16 *CIL*, 10.890.

I 300 BC–AD 56

1 Pliny, *Natural History*, 35.49.

2 Philo, *In Flaccum*, 26.

3 Reference to Vitruvius, *On Architecture*, 2.6; for example, in 179 BC Marcus Aemilius Lepidus built, on behalf of the Roman state, a harbour mole at Terracina (Livy, *History of Rome* 40.51); parts of this harbour can be seen today in the town.

Notes

CHAPTER 2, SEVEN WEEKS FROM EGYPT

1 *CIL*, 4.9867.
2 Excavations have not revealed a candidate for the temple's main statue of Venus, but a rudder of suitable scale to accompany an imposing statue of the goddess was discovered in a house close to the temple, to which it might have been removed during the renovation of her sanctuary in the years immediately prior to the eruption.
3 *CIL*, 4.1410.
4 Strabo, *Geography*, 5.4.8.
5 Valerie Maxfield provides a revealing synopsis of the evidence.
6 Recorded as wreck number 301, off Chiessi (Elba).
7 Petronius, *Satyricon*, 119.
8 So prominent was the trade there that the one non-specialist book by the medical writer Rufus of Ephesus is called *On the Purchase of Slaves*.
9 Berlin, Papyrus No. 27.
10 Pliny, *Natural History*, 3.61–2: the use of the verb *adluo* would suggest that Pliny was using a Greek source who regarded the Sarno as flowing or washing by Pompeii. Whether this implies the river flowed past the walls or through or over its territory remains uncertain.
11 J-P Descoeurdes, personal communication; N. Wood, personal communication.
12 The Canale Conte di Sarno, built in 1592 for the supply of water to the mills at Torre Annunziata, drew off water from the Sarno and also tunnelled through the southern portion of the buried city of Pompeii, running west to east, and can today be seen in Via di Nocera.
13 See Sogliano (1901), Della Corte (1928), and Fienga (1932–3) for excavation reports.
14 *CIL*, 10.814, 853, 942, 1027, 1042, 1074.
15 Our knowledge of the power of this man comes principally from the tomb inscription set up by his father: *CIL*, 10.1024. His house lay at Region VII Insula Occidentalis 12–15.
16 Cicero, *On Duties*, 3.58–60.
17 Giordano (1966) provides a full treatment of texts from this house.
18 Cicero, *On Duties*, 1.150–2.
19 Maius has a particular prominence in the painted notices of Pompeii: *CIL* IV.138, 499, 504, 512, 1177, 1179, 1180, 1493, 3453, 3785, 3883, 7690, 7980, 7989, 7990, 7991, 7993; *Notizie Degli Scavi* (1890): 333; and it also appears in the Jucundus tablets. Even so, our knowledge of this Pompeian is still limited.
20 The texts of the inscriptions are published in D'Ambrosio and De Caro (1983) as part of the description of the tomb 11OS.13.

21 He would still be active, recalled from retirement, twenty years later during the reign of Vespasian.

22 Pliny, *Natural History*, 31.95; Seneca, *Natural Questions* 3.17.

23 For an example of Oscan inscription see Vetter (1953), no. 23; Columella, 10.135–6 refers to the Pompeian marshes near which the salt pans of Hercules lay; and an electoral group called the Salienenses appear in the electoral *programmata* – *CIL*, 4.128.

24 Pliny, *Letters*, 7.3.2, 2.6.2; Seneca, *Letters*, 94.14. Each category of friendship demanded its own mode of behaviour.

25 Our knowledge today of the workings of this business depends on the delivery labels found on amphorae that mention the names of his freedmen and freedwomen who owned, managed or worked in the production of the fish sauce. Some 30 per cent of all such labels that can be read refer to Scaurus and his associates.

26 Cicero, *Letters to Friends*, 7.4. Marcus Marius also suffered from severe bouts of illness, probably gout.

27 On the children of freedmen, see Paul Weaver (1991).

28 *CIL*, 10.1403 for the list of Augustales from Herculaneum.

29 D'Ambrosio and De Caro (1983): 9ES, for the original tomb and its inscriptions; *CIL*, 10.1030, for the inscription from the second monument set up by Naevoleia Tyche.

30 Apuleius, *Metamorphoses*, 11.

31 Meyer (1970) provides the most extensive discussion of purple and its production in antiquity.

32 Pliny, *Natural History*, 32.6.21, 32.6.63.

II April AD 58

1 *CIL*, 4.8232, 8484, 8696, 8856, 8885, 8888a–c.

CHAPTER 3, SLAVES AND THE TERRITORY

1 Florus, *Epitome of Roman History*, 1.2.3–6; Pliny, *Natural History*, 3.60–65, 18.19; Strabo, *Geography*, 5.4.3–8. The excavations of rural villas and analysis of their soils and plant remains have confirmed these views. For all such archaeological evidence used in this chapter, see Wilhelmina Jashemski's *Gardens of Pompeii*.

2 Suetonius, *Life of Claudius*, 27.1, for an account of the accident.

3 Use of the Eumachia building for slave auctions: personal communication, Lisa Fentress.

4 The nature of sale is set out in *The Digest of Justinian*, Book 18, and for actions in relation to sale see Book 19, section 1.

5 Oxyrhynchus Papyrus, IV, 744, 'If it is a boy, rear it; if it is a girl, cast it out.'

6 Columella, *On Agriculture*, 1.8.19.

7 For advice on use of slaves and their supervisor, or *vilicus*, from antiquity: Columella, *On Agriculture*, 1.8–9; Cato, *On Agriculture*, 5; Varro, *On Agriculture*, 1.17–18. Plutarch, *Life of Cato*, 5, creates the image of a man kinder to his aged horses and old dogs than his slaves worn out through abuse.

8 Columella, *On Agriculture*, 1.4–9, gives a thorough guidance on how to set up a villa and farmstead.

9 Pliny, *Natural History*, 17.

10 Varro, *On Agriculture*, 3.17; Pliny, *Natural History*, 9.170.

11 A wall painting from house VII.3.30 shows a scene of the distribution of loaves of bread. The tomb built by Naevoleia Tyche features a scene of similar largesse.

12 Lucius Albucius's father was *duumvir* in AD 33–4, *CIL*, 10.901. There is no earlier evidence for their presence in Pompeii.

13 Cicero's speeches *Against Verres* set out the nature of a governor's asset-stripping and violation of individuals in Sicily. What is remarkable about Rome's Empire was that provincials could redress the balance in court, once the governorship was over, with the aid of powerful allies in the Roman senate.

14 Tacitus, *Annals*, 14.17. Frustratingly, the reason for the exile of Livineius was given in a book of the *Annals* for which no manuscript survives from antiquity.

15 The seals measure 1–2 cm. by 3–5 cm. Of the 90 found in Pompeii, the vast majority bear the names of slaves or freedmen. The seals might have been a means of identifying individual slaves' or freedmen's productive activity in a household owned by a member of the urban elite.

16 Lived in the house at IX.13.1–3. His candidature for the aedileship is attested from *CIL*, 4.429, 699, 1050, 3384, 7279, 7333, 7409, 7588, 7923, 7925, 7958.

17 His campaign for the duovirate is attested in *CIL*, 4.99, 108, 113, 121, 132, 133, 134, 146, 147, 271–2, 316, 348, 523, 875, 886, 909, 1034, 1053, 1060, 7136, 7167, 7189, 7204, 7232, 7264, 7277, 7345, 7841, 7864, 7867, 7872, 7888, 7941, 7956, 9831, 9837.

18 The text of the charter inscribed on bronze is published in Michael Crawford's edition *Roman Statutes* along with all other such charters surviving from the Roman world.

19 Jucundus tablet 81.

20 A figure based on a calculation to determine the percentage needing to be subtracted from all sales to arrive at a round figure.

21 Jucundus tablet 45.

III   Winter AD 58–AD 59

1 Herculaneum tablet 61.

CHAPTER 4, A WORTHY MAN, VOTE FOR HIM

1 Macrobius, *Saturnalia*, 2.3.11 reports Cicero's view.

2 *CIL*, 4.128, 470, 480, 783, 7676, 7706, 7747 for *programmata* related to these groups. For Poppaeenses: *CIL*, 4.6682, that becomes Nero Poppaeenses, or even Neroppaee(n)ses, *CIL*, 4.259, 1499, 2413i.

3 The texts of town charters from Urso and elsewhere are published with translation in Michael Crawford's *Roman Statutes*.

4 *Inscriptiones Latinae Selectae*, 5531.

5 *CIL*, 4.817.

6 Found on 15 November 1977, Inventory number OP 2789. *CIL*, 4.1064; Vetter, 8, for a similar inscription from pre-colonial Pompeii.

7 *Digest of Justinian*, Book 19, section 2.30.

8 Cassius Dio, 52.30.

9 *Digest of Justinian* devotes Book 50 to this topic.

10 On the timing of this ritual: Martial, *Epigrams*, 3.36, 4.8, 10.70; Horace, *Letters*, 2.1.104.

11 Vitruvius, *On Architecture*, 6.3–5 sets out an architectural description of the opulent house. The coincidence between this ideal and the houses of Pompeii remains a subject of debate. Compare Trimalchio's house in *Satyricon*, 28–30.

12 Juvenal, *Satires*, I.77–104.

13 Quintilian, *Institutes*, 1.3.14 and 6.3.25, 48 for beatings in later life as a stigma or a form of injury. *Hic ego cum veni futui deinde redei domi* – *CIL*, 4.2246, from the brothel at VII.12.18.

14 *CIL*, 4.451, 668, 3599.

15 Plutarch, *Life of Cato the Elder*, 20.4–7.

16 Pliny, *Natural History*, 7.16.

17 Strabo, *Geography*, 5.4.7.

18 *CIL*, 4.3302.

19 Macrobius, *Saturnalia*, 1.24.5.

20 Horace, *Art of Poetry*, 325–32.

21 Petronius, *Satyricon*, 29.4.

22 Cato, *On Agriculture*, 60.

23 The *Commentariolum Petitionis* gives an image of management of an election in Rome. The election referred to may have been Cicero's to the consulship in 64 BC.

24 The *programmata* published in *CIL*, 4, reveal the full range of the

vocabulary of elections. Occupational groups account for 6 per cent of all recommendations made, yet represent a large group of the electorate.

25 *CIL*, 4.423, 7525, 9831 = Astylus; *CIL*, 4. 480, 908, 1157, 3367, 7251, 7298, 7418, 7465, 7536, 9829a = Papilio. They may also have been associated with one larinus.

26 VB = *virum bonum*; DRP = *dignum rei publicae*; OVF = *oro/oramus/ orat/orant vos faciatis*.

CHAPTER 5, NO PLACE FOR IDLERS

1 *CIL*, 4.8863.

2 Details can be found in the Town Charters – see M. Crawford, *Roman Statutes*, for the relevant texts.

3 The contrast is summarised by Seneca, *On the Good Life*, 7.3.

4 *CIL*, 4.1768 and 1769.

5 Apuleius, *Metamorphoses*, 1.24–5.

6 Varro, *On the Latin Language*, 6.21. The predominantly oral culture of the *plebs* encouraged a facility for memorising.

7 Seneca, *On the Good Life*, 7.3.

8 Vetter, 23. Aeneas Tactitus, *On the Defence of Fortified Positions*, 1.1, for division of wall defences and use of muster points.

9 *CIL*, 10.1064.

10 Acts of the Apostles, 9:11.

11 *CIL*, 4.8356.

12 Compare the surviving street name in England: Grope Lane, which in the Medieval period carried its fuller name, Grope Cunt Lane.

13 Suetonius, *Life of Vespasian*, 5.3.

14 II.12.8: an amphora was found with anchovy bones in it from some eighty-two individual fish.

15 Tax on urine: Suetonius, *Life of Vespasian*, 23.

16 Columella, *On Agriculture*, 8.8.1 discusses breeding of wood pigeons; Varro, *On Agriculture*, 3.7 gives details of two types of birds and guidelines on building a dovecot.

17 Frontinus, *Stratagems*, 1.5.21.

18 Cicero, *Pro Sestio*, 34. Cicero, *De Domo Sua*, 54.

19 *CIL*, 4.60, dating to 47 or 46 BC, contains the only *album* of district officials to have survived in Pompeii and perhaps refers to a district stretching out northwards from this key crossroads. The wording is worn and fragmentary, with freedmen officials and three of the slave *ministri* who assisted them only just discernible and those of several other ministers entirely missing. But the identity of the *vici* in question is clear: the Urbulanenses.

20 Frontinus, *On Aqueducts*, 2.97.

21 Livy, *History of Rome*, 31.4.5.

22 Urso Charter: for text see M. Crawford, *Roman Statutes*; *Digest of Justinian*, 48.6 and 7, sets out the application of the *Lex Julia de Vis* in respect to gatherings armed or simply for intimidation.

23 Tacitus, *Annals*, 14.17.

24 Vitruvius, *On Architecture*, 5.1.

25 Small lead tiles found in Rome, and used as tickets for admission to the theatre, are labelled *Iuvenes Augustiani*, suggesting a fuller name for the famous Augustiani claquers of Nero, and a possible core for their equestrian membership.

26 *CIL*, 4.115 (IV V 1, 15).

27 Jucundus tablet 144, for new magistrates serving from 8 May AD 60.

28 *CIL*, 4.2508, 4286, 4287, 4291, 4302, 4309, 4325, 4361, 4374, 4384, 4405, 4413, 4870.

29 *CIL*, 4.1293.

v January AD 61

1 Ovid, *Fasti*, 1.46–310.

2 *CIL*, 4.671, 1074, 3225, 3726, 3625.

CHAPTER 6, YOURS FOR TWO COINS

1 Propertius, *Elegies*, 4.11.33; Lactantius, 2.4.13; Pliny, *Letters*, 5.16; Soranus, the *Gynaecology*, 1.33.

2 *CIL*, 4.1684, 1894; Propertius, *Elegies*, 4.5.45–62.

3 *CIL*, 4.8258, 8259.

4 Martial, *Epigrams*, 2.36; Seneca, *Letters*, 114.14; Ovid, *Art of Love*, 1.505–24; *CIL*, 4.1830.

5 *CIL*, 4.743.

6 Seneca, *Letters*, 95.20–21.

7 *CIL*, 4.1796.

8 *CIL*, 4.4200. *CIL*, 4.3999, 8940, 2400.

9 *Songs of Priapus*, 13, 22, 74.

10 The *Lex Julia on Punishing Adulteries* is set out in *Digest of Justinian*, 48.5.

11 Seneca, *Letters*, 95.20–21.

12 *CIL*, 4.4091.

13 *CIL*, 10.1059; *CIL*, 4.8820.

14 *CIL*, 4.8384.

15 *CIL*, 4.107.

16 Giordano, 34; *CIL*, 4.4185.

17 Horace, *Satires*, 1.2.114–19.

18 Petronius, *Satyricon*, 75.11; Columella, *On Agriculture*, 1.8, for slaves who served this purpose.
19 Cato, *On Agriculture*, 5; Plutarch, *Life of Cato*, 4, 5, 21; Cicero, *On the Republic*, 3.37; *CIL*, 4.6892.
20 *CIL*, 4.2310b, 5048, 10004.
21 Tacitus, *Annals*, 2.85; Suetonius, *Life of Tiberius*, 35; *Digest of Justinian*, 25.7.1.2; 48.5.11.2; Martial, *Epigrams*, 1.34, 3.82.
22 Petronius, *Satyricon*, 75; Juvenal, *Satires*, 9.43–6.
23 Martial, *Epigrams*, 9.3; Petronius, *Satyricon*, 27.
24 *CIL*, 4.3340.15. Notice the sale document reads: 'the slaves Simplex and Petrinus or whatever their names are'.
25 Martial, *Epigrams*, 11.43; *CIL*, 4.2048, 4977, 5007.
26 Ovid, *Art of Love*, 3.771–88; Martial, *Epigrams*, 12.43; Suetonius, *Life of Tiberius*, 44. The *Book of Elephantis* was perhaps the most famous of the first-century sex manuals but by no means the most adventurous. Martial – presenting himself as a reluctant reader – confides that it contained 'novel erotic possibilities such as only a desperate fornicator would countenance, what male prostitutes venture and keep quite about, in what combinations five people are linked, by what chain are held more than five, and what can go on when the lamp is out.'
27 Columella, *On Agriculture*, preface, 14–15; Juvenal, *Satires*, 2.51–115; 9.25–123; Petronius, *Satyricon*, 23.
28 'Vesbinus, you catamite, Vitalio has buggered you' – *CIL*, 4.2319b; 'Lucius Abonius hurts Caesonius Felix and makes him suck it' – *CIL*, 4.10232a.
29 *CIL*, 4.2310b, 2335, compare 2337, 2338, 2335, 2334, compare 2333.

CHAPTER 7, WHEN WILL OUR FEARS BE AT REST?

1 *CIL*, 10.794; 10.796.
2 During his tenure as priest, no instrument that was not crafted out of bronze could clip his hair, and it was a bronze knife too, of which examples have been found in Pompeii, that would have been ready for use on the sacrificial victim.
3 Cicero, *On the Nature of the Gods*, 2.10–12; for the actions of *haruspices* on Roman history: Livy, *History of Rome*, 5.15.4; 8.9; 41.14.7–15.4.
4 Personal comment, Stuart Black.
5 Seneca, *Natural Questions*, Book 6; Tacitus, *Annals*, 15.22.
6 Seneca reports this delusion being experienced in baths at Herculaneum.
7 *L'Année Epigraphique*, 1971: 88; *Digest of Justinian*, 47.2; 47.12.
8 *Digest of Justinian*, 47.9, 50.8; Cassius Dio, 55.26; Suetonius, *Life of Augustus*, 42.

9 Compare AD 17 earthquake in Asia Minor; Sardis received 10 million sesterces from the Emperor Tiberius and a five year remission of taxation: Tacitus, *Annals*, 2.47; Cassius Dio, 57.17.

10 *CIL*, 4.7989a, games held on 25–6 February in honour of the health of Nero.

CHAPTER 8, ASHES OF A JAWBONE

1 Inscription published in Conticello de' Spagnolis (1994): 48–50.

2 *Digest of Justinian*, 47.12.

3 Lex Heraclenensis, 56–61, text in M. Crawford, *Roman Statutes*.

4 Velleius Paterculus, *History of Rome*, 2.19.4; Appian, *Punica*, 81–9.

5 Livy, *History of Rome*, 10.47; Ovid, *Fasti*, 1.289–94.

6 Celsus, *On Medicine*, 2.29.2; Dioscorides, 2.34; also Pliny, *Natural History*, 20.55, 31.97, 32.90.

7 *Digest of Justinian*, 19.2.15.

8 It was also a legal principle in the Town Charter of Urso; *Digest of Justinian*, 1.8.6; 30.41.5, 9, 39.2.48, 39.2.72, 43.8.7.

9 Cassius Dio, 57.16, on the problems of lost city records.

10 Tacitus, *Annals*, 6.5; Petronius, *Satyricon*, 65; Cicero, *On Laws*, 2.22.55.

11 Pliny, *Letters*, 10.18.

12 *CIL*, 4.7316.

13 *CIL*, 4.973.

14 Cicero, *Letters to Atticus*, 14.9.

15 *Digest of Justinian*, Book 26.

16 Pliny, *Letters*, 7.24.

17 Juvenal, *Satires*, 3.72–8, 10.190–240; Pliny, *Letters*, 4.2.

18 Herculaneum tablets, 5 and 89. Gaius, *Institutes*, 1.28–34.

19 Gaius, *Institutes*, 1.22–4, 2.275–6, 3.56.

20 *CIL*, 10.758, 790, 788.

21 *CIL*, 4.1939.

VIII July AD 63–May AD 64

1 Lucian, *De Saltatione*.

CHAPTER 9, A BERYL FOR VENUS

1 Seneca, *Letters*, 122.8.

2 Ovid, *Fasti*, 4.943–51.

3 *CIL*, 4.2413.

4 Some estimates have put the number of houses to which piping was laid at no more than one hundred and thirty, scarcely more than the number of *decurions* on the council. So much for the trickle-down economy.

5 Hand or cast methods could not produce two surfaces that met so perfectly without leakage, but no evidence of suitable mechanical tools has ever been found.

6 Olympia was the origin of a spouting lion, dating from the seventh century BC, that is the oldest known example of such a piece.

7 Lemons would have been in particular demand for the Sukoth Festival celebrated by the city's Jewish population, when they were required as part of the bouquet made up of willow and palm fronds.

8 Varro, *On Agriculture*, 3.17.7.

9 Pliny, *Natural History*, 32.145; Columella, *On Agriculture*, 8.161–2; Varro, *On Agriculture*, 3.3.10.

10 Tacitus, *Annals*, 15.33–4.

11 *CIL*, 4.528, 670, 671, 820, 1074, 3525, 3726; Giordano, 5.

12 Giordano, 4, makes it clear Poppaea did not accompany Nero on the visit but sent gifts or *munera*. Suetonius, *Life of Nero*, 35, for violence and Poppaea.

13 *CIL*, 4.2145.

14 *CIL*, 4.8078a, 8065, 8066, 8075, 8092.

15 *CIL*, 4.7755.

16 *CIL*, 4.2413i.

17 Suetonius, *Life of Nero*, 32.

18 Suetonius, *Life of Caligula*, 39.

19 Pliny, *Natural History*, 9.169, 32.59–64; Horace, *Satires*, 2.4.33–4; Juvenal, *Satires*, 4.137–143.

20 Juvenal, *Satires*, 11.37–45; Pliny, *Natural History*, 9.64–7; Suetonius, *Life of Tiberius*, 34; Seneca, *Moral Letters*, 95.42.

21 Seneca, *Moral Letters*, 47.7.

22 Ibid.

23 *CIL*, 4.1679, 2290, 1661, 2180, 10236c. Letter preserved in Athenaeus written by a Hippolochus.

24 *CIL*, 4.1679, 10643, 5198; Martial, *Epigrams*, 1.34; Pliny, *Letters*, 7.24.

25 Lactantius, 1.20.10; Tacitus, *Annals*, 15.38; Cassius Dio, 62.28, 63.13; Suetonius, *Life of Nero*, 28–9.

26 Petronius, *Satyricon*, 54.4.

27 Philostratus, *Life of Apollonius*, 4.39.

28 Cato, *On Agriculture*, 156–8.

29 *CIL*, 4.8114.

30 Giordano, 4 and 5.

IX June AD 64–November AD 64

1 Pliny, *Natural History*, 12.84; ibid. 6.162.

CHAPTER 10, THE SATURNALIA KINGS

1 Seneca, *Apocolocyntosis*, 8 and 12.
2 Los (1995), (1996); Ostrow (1985).
3 Tacitus, *Annals*, 13.26–7.
4 Columella, *On Agriculture*, 11.2.93–6.
5 Pliny, *Natural History*, 3.40, 15.8, 18.111.
6 Pliny, *Natural History*, 7.198.
7 Juvenal, *Satires*, 3.29–33.
8 *Digest of Justinian*, 19.2.25.7–8.
9 *CIL*, 4.4755.
10 Cicero, *Letters to his Brother Quintus*, 3.1.
11 Vitruvius, *On Architecture*, Book 10.
12 Andreau, J., in 'Histoire des séismes et histoire économique', argues that the city's service-industry entrepreneurs responded to the new opportunities by expanding their provision, in much the same way as those of Lisbon did with alacrity after the quake there in the eighteenth century.
13 *CIL*, 10.868. Estimates of the number of brothels in Pompeii have varied by almost a thousand per cent; similarly, some have argued that there were hundreds of fullers run by virtual mobsters with a stranglehold over political life, while others say that only a fraction of the sites proposed in support of the thesis could have supported such an industry. The reality is probably somewhere in between.
14 Dionysus of Halicarnassus, *Roman Antiquities*, 14. 14.3–4.
15 Juvenal, *Satires*, 8.146–230.
16 *CIL*, 4.171, 207, 923.
17 *CIL*, 4.3948.
18 Suetonius, *Life of Vitellius*, 12.
19 *Digest of Justinian*, 23.2.43; *CIL*, 9.2689.
20 Pliny, *Natural History*, Book 14, examines a wide variety of wines.
21 Pliny, *Natural History*, 14.21.
22 Pliny, *Natural History*, 14.34–5.
23 *CIL*, 10.801, *CIL*, 4.5742, 5842, 5744, 5737, 5731.
24 Vetter, 11, 12; Poccetti, 107. Ovius Epidius and Trebius Mettius were the names of the other two *aediles*.
25 The aureus was reduced from 7.98 grams to 7.3 grams, the denarius from 3.89 grams to 3.41 grams with up to 10 per cent of the silver replaced by bronze.

CHAPTER 11, THE YEAR OF THE FOUR EMPERORS

1 Career of Alfenus Varus: Jucundus tablet 45; Tacitus, *Histories*, 2.29, 2.43,

3.36, 3.55, 3.61, 4.11. Career of Suedius Clemens: Tacitus, *Histories*, 1.87, 2.12; *CIL*, 3.33, 10.768, 791, 1018, 1059, 7203, 7579.

2 Tacitus, *Histories*, 1.6–7; Suetonius, *Life of Galba*, 14–17.

3 Suetonius, *Life of Otho*.

4 Tacitus, *Histories*, 1.14, 1.48.

5 Suetonius, *Life of Galba*, 18–20.

6 Suetonius, *Life of Vitellius*, for characterisation and career of Vitellius.

7 Suetonius, *Life of Otho*, 10, reports his father's positive recollections of Otho as his commander.

8 Appian, *Civil Wars*, 1.39, 1.50; Velleius Paterculus, *History of Rome*, 2.16; Orosius, *Histories against the Pagans*, 5.18.22.

9 Suedius Clemens and Alfenus Varus both stuggled during these weeks to suppress insubordination: Clemens succeeded by giving in to his troops worst instincts and allowed looting on Italian territory; Varus used a much more calculated ploy of denying his rebels the usual routines of camp life, until they were so unnerved that they fell into line. Tacitus, *Histories*, 2.29; Tacitus, *Agricola*, 7.

10 Tacitus, *Histories*, 2.43.

11 Tacitus, *Histories*, 2.46–50 on this heroic suicide.

12 Tacitus, *Histories*, 3.36.

13 Tacitus, *Histories*, 2.79–81.

14 Tacitus, *Histories*, 3.15–21.

15 Tacitus, *Histories*, 32–4; Cassius Dio, 54.15.

16 Tacitus, *Histories*, 3.55; Tacitus, *Histories*, 3.61.

17 Tacitus, *Histories*, 3.76.

18 *CIL*, 10.846.

19 Tacitus, *Histories*, 3.32–35.

20 Suetonius, *Life of Domitian*.

21 Tacitus, *Histories*, 4.11.

22 *CIL*, 3.33, 10.768, 791, 1018, 1059, 7203, 7579.

XI July AD 69–June AD 75

1 Stegeman, H., 1994. *Die Essener, Qumran, Johannes der Taufer und Jesus*, Freiburg-Basle-Vienna: Herder.

2 From this time on, monies traditionally paid as a tithe by Jews from across the Empire to the Temple were now paid to Jupiter.

CHAPTER 12, A FEAST OF BEANS

1 Intriguingly, several tablets from Herculaneum (Herculaneum tablets 77, 78, 80, 53, 92) record a legal interrogation of L. Appuleius Proculus by Cominius Primus, as to whether he had received boundary markers from

a third-party depository in keeping with an arbiter's previous ruling. It is dated 26 January AD 69. On 10 July AD 70 or 72, Primus's doors were stoned by a mob.

2 Pliny, *Letters*, 10.17a and 10.17b.

3 *CIL*, 4.1180.

4 The classic case of condemnation is found in bronze tablets relating to the condemnation of Gnaeus Piso; the law of condemnation clearly circulated to all cities in the Empire – since the tablet was discovered in Spain.

5 Edward Champlin (2003) makes a thorough critique of the modern invention of *damnatio memoriae* in his book *Nero*.

6 *CIL*, 4.3373.

7 *CIL*, 4.3773, 3702.

8 *CIL*, 4.4528.

9 *CIL*, 4.1136.

10 *CIL*, 4.1136.

11 *CIL*, 4.3340. 100; 1011; *CIL*, 10.796 records the dedication by the Alexandrian Gaius Julius Hephaistion to Jupiter Frigio on 23 April 3 BC in fulfilment of a vow.

12 Probably during the purges of Nero's latter years, a Crassus Frugi, who was related to the plotter Piso, had bought a bathhouse somewhere on the seashore, perhaps seeking an income-generating bolt-hole from Rome. A notice singing the praises of its sweet and salt water pools was found in the Villa of Diomedes outside the Herculaneum Gate.

13 *CIL*, 4.3528, 3529.

14 On Tomb 23OS in Nuceria necropolis. The presence within the tomb of some debris from the earthquake has been used to suggest an earlier date, but with recurring earthquakes and the explicit erection of the tomb during the life of those it was to contain, such dating is unreliable.

15 For full description and analysis of the paintings see A. Gallo (2000), 'I quadri perduti del triclinio della casa di M. Epidio Rufo (IX.1.20) Una lettura politico-sociale', *Rivista di Studi Pompeiani*, 11: 87–100.

16 *CIL*, 4.6842.

17 The process has been studied particularly in the House of the Chaste Lovers, which is still undergoing conservation, and where the remnants of the painter's work is clear to see.

18 Prices are from Diocletian's Price edict.

19 *CIL*, 4.10085a, 1841.

20 In the *Silvae* of Statius.

21 *CIL*, IV 9885.

22 The distinct mark of the cross in plaster that early excavators of Herculaneum were excited to find in the apartment of Petronia Justa would

not only have been iconographically anachronistic but has now been shown to have been left by a shelf unit that had become detached from the wall.

23 Reconstructed, in its abbreviated form, from fragments, over which a further inscription had been placed several centuries later. Alfody (1995), *Eine Bauinschrift aus dem Colosseum, ZPE* 109, 19–226.

24 *CIL*, 4.8590.

25 *CIL*, 5.3466 – his wife Aurelia set the tomb monument up to her 'well-deserving husband'. It has been suggested that the graffiti recording victories and defeats of gladiators were in effect advertising their form and might provide a guide to betting.

26 Seneca, *Letters*, 7.4.

27 Petronius, *Satyricon*, 117; Seneca, *Letters*, 71.23.

28 *CIL*, 10.1018.

XII August AD 79

1 *CIL*, 4.7579, 9850, 1189, 3549, 6626, 576, 7201, 575, 7708, 2993t, 1904.

CHAPTER 13, APOCALYPSE

1 Dio Cassius, 66.21–3 for full account.

2 Demosthenes, 18.259–60.

3 *Aeneid*, 3.446. Lines from the poem are also quoted on neighbouring facades, as though to drive the allusion home; *CIL*, 4.10085a, 10086a.

4 Pliny, *Letters*, 6.20.

5 *CIL*, 4.8820. It is possible that the graffito refers to a woman called Ursa bearing a child, rather than a female bear – *ursa* – giving birth.

6 It is Pliny's *Letters*, (6.16 and 6.20) to the historian Tacitus that provide us with the full eyewitness account of the eruption sequences.

7 Haraldur Sigurdsson and Steven Carey (2002) have produced the most plausible reconstruction of the sequences of the eruption and their studies are drawn on extensively in this chapter.

8 Studies of skulls from the Vesuvian cities has found evidence for *hyperstosis frontalis interna* (HFI), which is consonant with the post-menopause, in 10 per cent of the total sample studied. This is proportionate to the general population and is one further piece of evidence that gives the statistical lie to the myth that it was mainly the elderly, disabled and very young who were left behind in the city.

9 *CIL*, 4.294.

10 Plutarch, *Moralia*, 398E.

11 *CIL*, 4.2311.

12 *Sibylline Oracle*, 4.130–6; Suetonius, *Life of Titus*, 8; Dio Cassius, 66.24.

13 It is the tomb of the Decii family, from pre-eruption times, that directly underlies one amphora burial.

14 *CIL*, 10 846.

15 Martial, *Epigrams*, 4.44.

BIBLIOGRAPHY

PRIMARY SOURCES

For those readers who are new to Pompeii and wish to pursue the themes of the book further, we draw their attention to a number of works here. Alison Cooley and Melvin Cooley have recently provided a selection of texts in translation: *Pompeii: A Sourcebook* (Routledge, 2004). Throughout the book we make reference to texts of major classical writers: the Loeb series provides texts and translations. The major publication of the inscriptions on stone can be found as part of *Corpus Inscriptionum Latinarum*, volume 10, and the *programmata*, grafitti and all other painted materials, as well as the Jucundus tablets are published in *Corpus Inscriptionum Latinarum*, volume 4. Other inscriptions referred to can be found in *L'Année Epigraphique*. The following collections of inscriptions and other writing from Pompeii are essential:

D'Ambrosio, A. & De Caro, S. (1983), *Un impegno per Pompei: fotopiano e documentazione della necropolis di Porta Nocera*, Milan.

Camodeca, G. (1999), *Tabulae Pompeianae Sulpicorum: Edizione critica dell'archivio puteolano di Sulpicii*, Rome: Quasar.

Funari, P. P. A. (1991), *La cultura popular en la antiguādad clasica*, Ecija.

Giordano, C. (1966), 'Le iscrizioni della Casa di M. Fabio Rufo', *Rendiconti dell'Accademia di Archeologia, Lettere e Belle Arti, Napoli*, 41: 73–89.

Giordano, C. (1974), 'Iscrizioni graffite e dipinte nella Casa di C. Iulio Polibio', *Rendiconti dell'Accademia di Archeologia, Lettere e Belle Arti, Napoli*, 49: 21–8.

Giordano, C. & Casale, A. (1991), 'Iscrizioni pompeiane inedite scoperte tra gli anni 1954–1978', *Atti dell'Accademia Pontaniana*, 39: 273–378.

Kockel, V. (1983), *Die Grabbauten vor den Herkulaner Tor in Pompeji*, Mainz.

Langner, M. (2001), *Antike Graffitizeichnungen: Motive, Gestaltung und Bodeutung*, Wiesbaden.

Maulucci Vivolo, F. P. (1993), *Pompei: i grafitti figurati*, Foggia.

Pompeii

Sabbatini Tumolesi, P. (1980), *Gladiatorum paria: Annunci di spettacoli gladiatorii a Pompei*, Rome.

Vetter, E. (1953), *Handbuch der Italischen Dialekte*, volume 1, Heidelberg.

MODERN AUTHORS

The excavations of Pompeii remain poorly published, scholarly access to even those of the House of the Chaste Lovers remain preliminary reports. In contrast the work by Wilhelmina Jashemski on the gardens and natural environment of the city is well documented in her books *The Gardens of Pompeii* and *The Natural History of Pompeii* with Frederick Meyer. The interpretation of the *programmata* continues to provoke controversy: Paavo Castrén, James Franklin and Henrik Mouritsen have all provided guides to the evidence and their own personal interpretation of what remains. Jean Andreau's study of the tablets of Caecilius Jucundus and interpretation of the Sulpicii archive from the Murecine has become the basis for our understanding of credit and debt in Roman antiquity. Wim Jongman has followed through with a study of Pompeii's economy and its relationship to the city's social structure. Paul Zanker's interpretation of city and artistic development is fundamental, as is Andrew Wallace-Hadrill's contribution to our knowledge of house form and social institutions. John Dobbins has revolutionised our understanding of the fabric of the city in the years between the great earthquake and the eruption. John Clarke's study of Roman sexuality illuminates much about the artistic environment of the city. Ray Laurence pulls together the strands that made up the structure of urban form in an earlier book.

A.A.V.V. (1990), *Rediscovering Pompeii*, Rome.

Alfody (1995); *Eine Bauinschrift aus dem Colosseum*, ZPE 109, 19–226

Allison, P. M. (1992), 'Artefact Assemblages: Not the Pompeian Premise', in E. Herring, R. Whitehouse & J. Wilkins, *Papers of the Fourth Conference of Italian Archaeology*, volume 3: 49–56.

—— (1995), 'On-Going Seismic Activity and its Effects on Living Conditions in Pompeii in the Last Decades', in T. Fröhlich & L. Jacobelli, *Archäologie und Seismologie*, Munich: 183–9.

Andersson, E. B. (1990), 'Fountains and the Roman Dwelling: Casa del Torello in Pompeii', *Jahrbruch des Deutsches Archaelogia Instituut*, 105: 207–36.

Andreau, J. (1973), 'Histoire des séismes et histoire économique. Le tremblement de terre de Pompei (62 ap. J-C)', *Annales ESC*, 28: 369–95.

—— (1974), *Les affaires de Monsieur Jucundus*, Rome: L'Ecole Française.

—— (1980), 'Pompéi: mais où sont les veterans de Scylla?', *Revue des Etudes Anciennes*, 82: 183–99.

—— (1984), 'Il terremoto del 62', in F. Zevi, *Raccolta per il Decimo Centennario dell'Eruzione Vesuviana*, Naples.

—— (1999), *Banking and Business in the Roman World*, Cambridge.

Bagnani, G. (1954), 'The House of Trimalchio', *American Journal of Philology*, 75: 16–39.

Barbet, A., Tuffreau-Libre, M. & Coupry, C. (1999), 'Un Ensemble de Pots à Peinture à Pompéi', *Rivista di Studi Pompeianne*, 10: 71–81.

Beacham, J. R. C. (1991), *The Roman Theatre and Its Audience*, London.

Beard, M., North, J. & Price, S. (1998), *The Religions of Rome*, Cambridge.

Bergmann, B. (1991), 'Painted Perspectives of a Villa Visit: Landscape as Status and Metaphor', in E. K. Gazda, *Roman Art in the Private Sphere*, Ann Arbor: 49–70.

—— (1994), 'The Roman House as Memory Theater: The House of the Tragic Poet in Pompeii', *Art Bulletin*, 76: 225–56.

Bernstein, F. (1988) 'Pompeian Women and the *Programmata*', in R. I. Curtis, *Studia Pompieana et Classica in Honor of Wilhelmina F. Jashemski*, New York: 1–17.

Berry, J. (1997), 'The Conditions of Domestic Life in Pompeii in AD 79: A Case-Study of Houses 11 and 12, Insula 9, Region I', *Papers of the British School at Rome*, 65: 103–25.

—— (1997), 'Household Artefacts: Towards a Reinterpretation of Roman Domestic Space', in R. Laurence & A. Wallace-Hadrill, *Domestic Space in the Roman World: Pompeii and Beyond* (Journal of Roman Archaeology Supplement 22): 183–95.

—— (1998), *Unpeeling Pompeii. Studies in Region I of Pompeii*, Milan.

Berry, P. (1995), *The Christian Inscription at Pompeii*, London.

Bisel, S. C. & Bisel, J. (2003), 'Health and Nutrition at Herculaneum: An Examination of Human Skeletal Remains', in W. F. Jashemski & F. G. Meyer, *The Natural History of Pompeii*, Cambridge: 451–75.

Bonifacio, R. (1997), *Ritratti Romani da Pompeii*, Rome.

Bradley, K. R. (1984), *Slaves and Masters in the Roman Empire*, Brussels.

—— (1991), *Discovering the Roman Family*, Oxford.

—— (1994), *Slavery and Society at Rome*, Cambridge.

Camodeca, G. (1999), *Tabulae Pompeianae Sulpicorum: Edizione critica dell'archivio puteolano di Sulpicii*, Rome.

—— (2003), 'Il Credito negli Archivi Campani: Il Caso di Puteoli e Herculaneum', in E. Lo Cascio, *Credito e Moneta nel Mondo Romano*, Bari: 69–98.

Carandini, A. (1977), *L'Instrumentum Domesticum di Ercolano e Pompei nella Prima Età Imperiale*, Rome.

Carp, T. (1980), '*Puer senex* in Roman and Medieval Thought', *Latomus*, 39: 736–9.

Caspers, D. (1981), 'The Indian Ivory figurine from Pompeii – A Reconsideration of its Functional Use', *South-East Asian Archaeology*, 1979: 341–53.

Castiglione Morelli, N. (1983), 'Le Lucerne della Casa di Giulio Polibio a Pompei', *Bollettino dell'Associazione Internazionale Amici di Pompei*, 1: 213–58.

Castren, P. (1975), *Ordo Populusque Pompeianus. Polity and Society in Roman Pompeii*, Rome.

Cerulli Irelli, G. (1997), 'Officina di Lucerne Fittili a Pompei', in A. Carandini, *L'Instrumentum Domesticum di Ercolano e Pompei*, Rome.

Champlin, E. (1991), *Final Judgements: Duty and Emotion in Roman Wills 200 BC–AD 250*, Berkeley.

—— (2003), *Nero*, Harvard.

Chiaramonte Treré, C. (1986), *Nuovi Contributi sulle Fortificazioni Pompeiane*, Milan.

Ciarallo, A. (2000), 'About an Ancient Mixture Found in Pompeii', in *Homo Faber*, Rome.

—— (2001), *The Gardens of Pompeii*, Rome.

Cicerelli, C. (1995), 'Effetti Seismici sugli Insediamenti Abitativi di Terzigno Estremo Suburbia Nord di Pompei', in T. Fröhlich & L. Jacobelli, *Archäologie und Seismologie*, Munich: 211–19.

Clarke, J. R. (1991), *The Houses of Roman Italy 100 BC–AD 250: Ritual, Space and Decoration*, Berkeley.

—— (1998), *Looking at Lovemaking. Constructions of Sexuality in Roman Art 100 BC–AD 250*, Berkeley.

—— (1998/1999), 'Look Who's Laughing: Humor in Tavern Painting as Index of Class and Acculturation', *Memoirs of the American Academy at Rome*, 43/44: 27–48.

Coarelli, F. (1996), 'Fregellae, Arpinuim, Aquinum: Lana e Fullonicae nel Lazio Meridionale', in M. Cébeillac-Gervasoni, *Les Elites Municipales de l'Italie Péninsulae des Gracques à Néron*, Rome: 199–205.

Cohen, A. (1997), *The Alexander Mosaic: Stories of Defeat and Victory*, Cambridge.

Coleman, K. M. (1990), 'Fatal Charades: Roman Executions Staged as Mythological Reenactments', *Journal of Roman Studies*, 80: 44–73.

Conticello de' Spagnolis, M. (1993–4), 'Di Due Ville Rustiche Rinvenute a Scafati (SA) in Via Spinelli ed in Via Poggiomarino', *Rivista di Studi Pompeiani*, 6: 137–46.

—— (1994), *Il Pons Sarni di Scafati e la Via Nuceria-Pompeios*, Rome.

—— (1995), 'Osservazioni sulle Fase Edilizie di Alcune Ville Rustiche di

Scafati, Suburbio Orientale di Pompei Seppellite dall'Eruzione del 79 d.C., in T. Fröhlich & L. Jacobelli, *Archäologie und Seismologie*, Munich: 93–103.

—— (2001), *Pompei e la Valle del Sarno in Epoca Preromana: la Cultura delle Tomba a Fossa*, Rome.

Cooley, A. E. (2003), *Pompeii*, London.

Cooley, A. E. & Cooley, M. G. L. (2004), *Pompeii: A Sourcebook*, London.

Coralini, A. (2001), *Hercules Domesticus. Immagini di Ercole nelle Case della Regione Vesuviana*, Naples.

Crawford, Michael H., ed. (1996), *Roman Statutes* (2 vol.), London

Curbs, R. I. (1979), 'The Garum Shop of Pompeii (I. 12.8), *Cronache Pompeiane* 5: 5–23.

—— (1984), 'A Personalised Floor Mosaic from Pompeii', *American Journal of Archaeology*, 88: 557–66.

—— (1988), 'A. Umbricius Scaurus', in R. I. Curtis, *Studia Pompeiana et Classica in Honor of Wilhelmina Jashemski*, New York: 19–49.

—— (1991), *Garum et Salsamenta: Production and Commerce in Materia Medica*, Leiden.

—— (1997), 'Food Technology in the Ancient Urban Context', paper delivered at the Archaeological Institute of America Conference.

Dapato, P. (1987), 'Circolazione Monetale a Pompeii', *Rivista di Studi Pompeiani*, 1: 107–10.

Dalby, A. F. (1972), *Small Buildings in Earthquake Areas*, Watford.

D'Ambrosio, A. & De Caro, S. (1983), 'La Necropoli di Porta Nocera', in *Un Impegno per Pompei*, Milan: 23–42.

D'Ambrosio, A., Guzzo, P. & Mastroberto, M. (2003), *Storie da Un'Eruzione: Pompeii, Ercolano, Oplontis*, Milan.

D'Arms, J. H. (1970), *Romans on the Bay of Naples. A Social and Cultural Study of the Villas and Their Owners from 150 BC to AD 400*, Cambridge, Mass.

—— (1981), *Commerce and Social Standing in Ancient Rome*, Cambridge.

—— (1988), 'Pompeii and Rome in the Augustan Age and Beyond: The Eminence of the *Gens Holconia*', in R. I. Curtis, *Studia Pompieana et Classica in Honor of Wilhelmina F. Jashemski*, New York: 51–69.

—— (1991), 'Slaves at the Roman *Conviva*', in W. J. Slater, *Dining in a Classical Context*, Ann Arbor.

Day, J. (1932), 'Agriculture in the Life of Pompeii', *Yale Classical Studies*, 3: 166–208.

De Caro, S. (1987), 'The Sculptures of the Villa of Poppaea at Oplontis: A preliminary Report', in E. B. MacDougall, *Ancient Roman Villa Gardens*, Washington, D.C.: 79–133.

De Carolis, E., Patricelli, G. & Ciarallo, A. (1998), 'Rinvenimenti di corpi umani nell'area urbana di Pompei', *Rivista di Studi Pompeiani*, 9: 75–123.

De Franciscis, A. (1976), 'Sepolcro di M. Obellius Firmus', *Cronache Pompeiana*, 2: 246–8.

Della Corte, M. (1913), 'Il *Pomerium* di Pompei', *Rendiconti Lincei*, 22: 261–2.

—— (1928), 'Pompei – Borgo Marinario', *Notizie degli Scavi*, 1928: 369–72.

—— (1965), *Casa ed Abitanti di Pompei*, Naples.

De Ruyt, C. (1983), *Macellum. Marché Alimentaire des Romains*, Louvain.

De Simone, A. (1995), 'I Terremoti Precedenti l'Eruzione: Nuove Attestazione da Recenti Scavi', in T. Fröhlich & L. Jacobelli, *Archäologie und Seismologie*, Munich: 37–43.

Dixon, S. (1992), *The Roman Family*, Baltimore.

Dobbins, J. J. (1994), 'Problems of chronology, decoration, and urban design in the Forum at Pompeii', *American Journal of Archaeology* 98: 629–94.

—— (1997), 'The Pompeii Forum Project 1994–95' in: S. E. Bon & R. Jones, (eds) *Sequence and Space in Pompeii*, Oxford: 73–87.

Duncan Jones, R. P. (1982), *The Economy of the Roman Empire: Quantitative Studies*, Cambridge.

—— (1990), *Structure and Scale in the Roman Economy*, Cambridge.

—— (2003), 'Roman Coin Circulation and the Cities of Vesuvius', in E. Lo Cascio, *Credito e Moneta nel Mondo Romano*, Bari, 161–80.

Dunbabin, K. M. D. (2003), *The Roman Banquet: Images of Conviviality*, Cambridge.

Dwyer, E. (1991), 'The Pompeian Atrium House in Theory and Practice', in E. K. Gazda, *Roman Art in the Private Sphere*, Ann Arbor: 25–48.

Edwards, C. (1993), *The Politics of Immorality in Ancient Rome*, Cambridge.

Elefante, M. (1988), 'Testimonianze epigrafiche relative alla gens Crassia', *Rivista di Studi Pompeianne*, 2: 99–102.

Engels, D. (1980), 'The Problem of Female Infanticide in the Greco-Roman World', *Classical Philology*, 75: 112–20.

Eyben, E. (1993), *Restless Youth in Ancient Rome*, London.

Faulkner, N. (2002), *Apocalypse, The Great Jewish Revolt against Rome, AD 66–73*, Stroud.

Fienga, F. (1932–3), 'Esplorazione del Pago Marittimo Pompeiana', in *Atti dell'III Congresso Nazionale di Studi Romani*, II: 172–6.

Fiorelli, G. (1875), *Descrizione di Pompei*, Naples.

Flower, H. (1996), *Ancestor Masks and Aristocratic Power in Roman Culture*, Oxford.

Foss, P. (1997), 'Watchful Lares: Roman Household Organization and the Rituals of Cooking and Eating', in R. Laurence & A. Wallace-Hadrill, *Domestic Space in the Roman World: Pompeii and Beyond*.

Franklin, J. L. (1980), *Pompeii: The Electoral Programmata, Campaigns and Politics AD 71–79*, Rome.

—— (1987), 'Pantomimists at Pompeii: Actius Anicetus and His Troupe', *American Journal of Philology*, 108: 95–107.

—— (1990), *Pompeii: The Casa del Marinaio and Its History*, Rome.

—— (1997), 'Cn. Alleius Nigidius Maius and the Amphitheatre *Munera* and a Distinguished Career at Ancient Pompeii', *Historia*, 46: 434–47.

—— (2001), *Pompeis Difficile Est. Studies in the Political Life of Imperial Pompeii*, Ann Arbor.

Frayn, J. M. (1979), *Subsistence Farming in Roman Italy*, London.

—— (1984), *Sheep Rearing and the Wool Trade in Italy during the Roman Period*, Liverpool.

—— (1993), *Markets and Fairs in Roman Italy*, Oxford.

Frederiksen, M. W. (1980/81), 'Puteoli e il Commercio del Grano in Epoca Romana', *Puteoli*, 4/5: 5–27.

—— (1984), *Campania*, London.

Frier, B. W. (1994), 'Natural Fertility and Family Limitation in Roman Marriage', *Classical Philology*, 89: 318–33.

Fröhlich, T. (1991), *Lararien und Fussadenbilder in den Vesuvstädten: Unterscuchungen zur Volkstümlichen pompejanischen Malerei*, Mainz.

—— (1995), 'La Porta di Ercolano a Pompei e i Cronologia dell'Opus Vittatum Mixtum', in T. Fröhlich & L. Jacobelli, *Archäologie und Seismologie*, Munich: 153–9.

Fulford, M. & Wallace-Hadrill, A. (1999), 'Towards a History of pre-Roman Pompeii: Excavations beneath the House of Amarantus (I.9.11–12), *Papers of the British School at Rome*: 37–144.

Funari, P. P. A. (1993), 'Graphic Caricature and the Ethos of Ordinary People at Pompeii', *Journal of European Archaeology*, 1: 133–50.

Gallo, A. (2000), 'I Quadri Perduti del Triclinio della Casa M. Epidio Rufo (IX.1.20). Una Lettura Politico-Sociale', *Rivista di Studi Pompeiani*, 11: 87– 100.

Gardner, J. F. (1986), *Women in Roman Law and Society*, London: Routledge.

Garnsey, P. (1970), *Social Status and Legal Privilege in the Roman Empire*, Oxford.

—— (1981), 'Independent Freedmen and the Economy of Roman Italy under the Principate', *Klio*, 63: 359–71.

—— (1988), *Famine and the Food Supply in the Greco-Roman World*, Cambridge.

—— (1991), *Child Rearing in Ancient Italy*, in D. I. Kertzer & R. P. Saller, *The Family in Italy from Antiquity to the Present*, New Haven: 48–65.

—— (1999), *Food and Society in Classical Antiquity*, Cambridge.

Gazda, E. K. (2000), *The Villa of the Mysteries in Pompeii: Ancient Ritual – Modern Muse*, Ann Arbor.

Gigante, M. (1995), *Philodemus in Italy. The Books from Herculaneum*, Ann Arbor.

Gilman, R. (1979), *Decadence, The Strange Life of an Epithet*, London.

Giordano, C. (1966), 'Le iscrizioni della Casa di M. Fabio Rufo', *Rendiconti dell'Accademia di Napoli*, 41: 73–89.

Gordon, M. L. (1927), 'The Ordo of Pompeii', *Journal of Roman Studies*, 17: 165–83.

——(1931), 'The Freedman's Son in Municipal Life', *Journal of Roman Studies*, 21: 65–77.

Gradel, I. (1992), 'Mamia's Dedication: Emperor and Genius. The Imperial Cult in Italy and the Genius Coloniae in Pompeii', *Analecta Romana Instituti Danici*, 20: 41–57.

——(2002), *Emperor Worship and Roman Religion*, Oxford.

Griffin, M. (1984), *Nero: The End of a Dynasty*, London.

Guadagno, G. (1995), 'Documenti Epigrafici Ercolanesi Relativi ad Un Terremoto', in T. Fröhlich & L. Jacobelli, *Archäologie und Seismologie*, Munich: 119–35.

Guidoboni, E. (1989), *I Terremoti Prima del Mille in Italia e nell'Area Mediterranea*, Bologna.

Hallett, J. (1984), *Fathers and Daughters in Elite Roman Society*, Princeton.

Hallett, J. & Skinner, M. (1997), *Roman Sexualities*, Princeton.

Harlow, M. & Laurence, R. (2002), *Growing Up and Growing Old in Ancient Rome: A Life Course Approach*, London.

Harris, W. V. (1980), 'Roman Terracotta Lamps: The Organisation of an Industry', *Journal of Roman Studies*, 70: 126–45.

Harris, W. V. (1980), 'Towards a Study of the Roman Slave Trade', *Memoirs of the American Academy at Rome*, 36: 117–40.

——(1982), 'The Theoretical Possibility of Extensive Infanticide in the Greco-Roman World', *Classical Quarterly*, 32: 114–16.

——(1994), 'Child Exposure in the Roman Empire', *Journal of Roman Studies*, 84: 1–22.

Henneberg, M. and Henneberg, R. J. (2000), 'Reconstructing Medical Knowledge in Ancient Pompeii from the Hard Evidence of Bones and Teeth', *Homo Faber*, Rome.

Heres, T. L. (1992–3), 'The Structures Related to the Water Supply of Pompeii: Building Materials and Technology', *Mededelingen van het Nederlands Instituut te Rome*, 51: 42–61.

Higginbotham, J. (1997), *Piscinae: Artificial Fishponds in Roman Italy*, Chapel Hill.

Hopkins, K. (1965), 'The Age of Roman Girls at Marriage', *Population Studies*, 20: 309–27.

—— (1966), 'On the Probable Age Structure of the Roman Population', *Population Studies*, 20: 245–64.

—— (1978), *Conquerors and Slaves*, Cambridge.

—— (1983), *Death and Renewal*, Cambridge.

Hori, Y. (1993), 'The Upper Floors in Regio VII Insula 12', *Opuscula Pompeiana*, 3: 1–24.

Horden, P. & Purcell, N. (2000), *The Corrupting Sea: A Study in Mediterranean History*, Oxford.

Horsfall, N. (2003), *The Culture of the Roman Plebs*, London.

Houston, G. W. (1980), 'The Administration of Italian Seaports during the First Three Centuries of the Roman Empire', *Memoirs of the American Academy at Rome*, 36: 157–71.

—— (1988), 'Ports in Perspective: Some Comparative Materials on Roman Merchant Ships and Ports', *American Journal of Archaeology*, 92: 553–64.

Iaccobelli, I. (1987), 'Lo Scavo delle Terme Suburbane: Notizie Preliminari', *Rivista di Studi Pompeiani*, 1: 151–3.

—— (1988), 'Terme Suburbane: Stato Attuale delle Conoscenze', *Rivista di Studi Pompeiani*, 2: 202–8.

—— (1995), *Le Pitture Erotiche delle Terme Suburbane di Pompei*, Rome.

Ioppolo, G. (1992), *Le Terme del Sarno a Pompei*, Rome.

Jackson, R. (1988), *Doctors and Diseases in the Roman Empire*, London.

Jansen, G. C. M. (1991), 'Water Systems and Sanitation in the Houses of Herculaneum', *Mededlingen van het Nederlands Instituut te Rome*, 50: 145–63.

Jashemski, W. F. (1964), 'A Pompeian Copa', *Classical Journal*, 59: 337–49.

—— (1974), 'The Discovery of a Market-Garden at Pompeii. The Garden of the "House of the Ship Europa"', *American Journal of Archaeology*, 78: 391–404.

—— (1979 & 1993), *The Gardens of Pompeii*, volumes 1 and 2, New York.

—— (1999), *A Pompeian Herbal: Ancient and Modern Medicinal Plants*, Austin.

Jashemski, W. F. & Meyer, F. G. (2002), *The Natural History of Pompeii*, Cambridge.

Jongman, W. (1988), *The Economy and Society of Pompeii*, Amsterdam.

Keppie, L. (1984), 'Colonisation and Veteran Settlement in Italy in the First Century AD', *Papers of the British School at Rome*, 52: 77–115.

Kilmer, M. F. (1982), 'Genital Phobia and Depilation', *Journal of Hellenic Studies*, 102: 104–12.

Pompeii

Kleberg, T. (1957), *Hôtels, Restaurants et Cabarets dans l'Antiquité Romaine*, Uppsala.
Koloski-Ostrow, A. O. (1997), 'Violent Stages in Two Pompeian Houses. Imperial Taste, Aristocratic Response and Messages of Male Control', in A. O. Koloski-Ostrow & C. L. Lyons, *Naked Truths. Women, Sexuality and Gender in Classical Art and Architecture*, London: Routledge.

La Rocca, E., de Vos, M. & de Vos, A. (2002), *Pompei: Guide Archeologiche*, 3rd edn, Milan.
La Torre, G. F. (1988), 'Gli Impianti Commerciali ed Artigianali nel Tessuto Urbano di Pompei', in L. Franchi dell'Orto & A. Varrone, *Rediscovering Pompeii*, Rome.
Laurence, R. (1994), *Roman Pompeii: Space and Society*, London.
——(1999), *The Roads of Roman Italy: Mobility and Cultural Change*, London.
Laurence, R. & Wallace-Hadrill, A. (1997), *Domestic Space in the Roman World: Pompeii and Beyond* (Journal of Roman Archaeology Supplement 22).
Leach, E. W. (1988), *The Rhetoric of Space. Literary and Artistic Representations of Landscape in Republican and Augustan Rome*, Princeton.
——(1997), 'Money, Class and Decorative Taste in Flavian Pompeii', paper delivered at the Archaeological Institute of America Conference.
——(2004), *The Social Life of Painting in Ancient Rome and on the Bay of Naples*, Cambridge.
Leppmann, W. (1968), *Pompeii in Fact and Fiction*, London.
Levick, B. (1999), *Vespasian*, London.
Ling, R. (1990), 'A Stranger in Town: Finding the Way in an Ancient City', *Greece and Rome*, 37: 204–14.
——(1990), 'Street Plaques in Pompeii', in M. Henig, *Architecture and Architectural Sculpture in the Roman Empire* (Oxford University Committee for Archaeology Monograph 29): 51–66.
——(1995), 'Earthquake Damage in Pompeii I.10: One Earthquake or Two?', in T. Fröhlich & L. Jacobelli, *Archäologie und Seismologie*, Munich: 201–9.
——(1997), *The Insula of the Menander at Pompeii, Volume I: The Structures*, Oxford.
Littlewood, A. R. (1987), 'Ancient Literary Evidence for the Pleasure Gardens of Roman Country Villas', in E. B. Macdougall, *Ancient Roman Villa Gardens*, Washington, D.C.: 7–30.
Los, A. (1995), 'La Condition Sociale des Affranchis Privées au Ier Siecle après J.-C.', *Annales HSS*, 90: 1011–44.
——(1996), 'Les Fils d'Afranchis dans l'Ordo Pompeianus', in M. Cébeillac-Gervasoni, *Les Elites Municipales de l'Italie Péninsulae des Gracques à Néron*, Rome: 145–52.

394

Bibliography

Macmullen, R. (1970), 'Market Days in the Roman Empire', *Phoenix*, 24: 333–41.

Maiuri, A. (1942), *l'Ultima Fase di Pompei*, Rome.

Marchis, V. and Scalva, G. (2000), 'The Engine Lost: Hydraulic Technologies in Pompeii', in *Homo Faber*, Rome.

Marturano, A. & Rinaldis, V. (1995), 'Il Terremoto Vesuviano del 62 d.C. Evento Carico Responsibilità', in T. Fröhlich & L. Jacobelli, *Archäologie und Seismologie*, Munich, 131–5.

Mattingly, D. J. (1990), 'Paintings, Presses and Perfume Production at Pompeii', *Oxford Journal of Archaeology*, 9: 71–90.

Mau, A. (1899), *Pompeii: Its Life and Art*, Washington, D.C.

Maulucci Vivolo, F. P. M. (1990), *E l'Acqua Zampillera dal Deserto (Testimonianze Giudaiche e Cristiane a Pompei prima del 79)*, Pompeii.

Mayeske, B. J. B. (1972), 'Bakeries and Bread at Pompeii: A Study in Social and economic History', PhD thesis, University of Maryland.

McGinn, T. (1999), 'Widows, Orphans and Social History', *Journal of Roman Archaeology*, 12: 617–32.

Mckenzie, J. (2003), 'Glimpsing Alexandria from Archaeological Evidence', *Journal of Roman Archaeology*, 16: 35–61.

Meiggs, R. (1980), 'Sea-Borne Timber Supplies to Rome', *Memoirs of the American Academy at Rome* 36: 185–96.

Meyer, M. (1970), *History of Purple as a Status Symbol in Antiquity*, Brussels.

Moeller, W. O. (1970), 'The Riot of AD 59 at Pompeii', *Historia*, 19: 84–95.

—— (1973), 'Gnaeus Alleius Nigidius Maius Princeps Coloniae', *Latomus*, 32: 515–20.

—— (1976), *The Wool Trade of Ancient Pompeii*, Leiden.

Mouritsen, H. (1988), *Elections, Magistrates and Municipal Elite: Studies in Pompeian Epigraphy (Analecta Romana Instituti Danici Suplementum 15)*.

—— (1990), 'A Note on Pompeian Epigraphy and Social Structure', *Classica et Mediaevalia*, 41: 131–49.

—— (1996), 'Order and Disorder in Late Pompeian Politics', in M. Cébeillac-Gervasoni, *Les Elites Municipales de l'Italie Péninsulae des Gracques à Néron*, Rome: 139–44.

—— (1998), 'The Album from Canusium and the Town Councils of Roman Italy', *Chiron*, 28: 229–54.

Mouritsen, H & Gradel, I. (1991), 'Nero in Pompeian Politics. Edicta Munera and the Imperial Flaminate in Late Pompeii, *ZPE*, 87: 145–55.

Mourques J.-L. (1988), 'Les Augustians et l'espérience théâtrale Néronienne', *Revue des Etudes Latines*, 66: 156–81.

Nappo, S. C. (1988), 'Regio I, Insula 20', *Rivista di Studi Pompeiani*, 2: 186–92.

Nappo, S. C. (1989), 'Fregio Dipinti dal "Praedium" di Giulia Felix con rapresentazione del Foro di Pompei', *Rivista di Studi Pompeiani*, 3: 79–96.

——(1995), 'Evidenze di Danni Structurali, Restauri e Rifacimenti nelle Insulae Gravitanti su Via Bocera a Pompei', in T. Fröhlich & L. Jacobelli, *Archäologie und Seismologie*, Munich: 45–56.

Ostrow, A. K. (1990), *The Sarno Bath Complex*, Rome.

Ostrow, S. E. (1985), '*Augustales* along the Bay of Naples: A Case for Their Early Growth', *Historia*, 34: 64–101.

Packer, J. E. (1975), 'Middle and Lower Class Housing in Pompeii and Herculaneum: A Preliminary Survey', in B. Andreae & H. Kyrieleius, *Neue Forschungen in Pompeji*, Recklinghaussen: 133–42.

——(1978), 'Inns at Pompeii: A Short Survey', *Cronache Pompeiane*, 4: 5–53.

Painter, K. S. (2001), *The Insula of the Menander at Pompeii Volume IV: The Silver Treasure*, Oxford.

Parkins, H. (1997), 'The "Consumer City" Domesticated? The Roman City in Elite Economic Strategies', in H. Parkins, *Roman Urbanism: Beyond the Consumer City*, London: 83–111.

Parslow, C. (1998), 'Documents illustrating the excavations of the Praedia Julia Felix', *Rivista di Studi Pompeiani*, 2: 37–48.

Paterson, J. (1998), 'Trade and Traders in the Roman World: Scale, Structure and Organisation', in H. Parkins & C. Smith, *Trade, Traders and the Ancient City*, London, 149–67.

Peacock, D. P. S. (1977), *Pottery and Early Commerce. Characterisation and Trade in Roman and Later Ceramics*, London.

——(1989), 'The Mills of Pompeii', *Antiquity*, 63: 205–14.

Peacock, D. P. S. & Williams, D. F. (1986), *Amphorae in the Roman Economy*, London.

Popplow, M. (2000), 'The Concept of *Machina* in the Roman Period', in *Homo Faber*, Rome.

Pucci, G. (1976–7), 'Considerazioni sull'articolo di J. Andreau "Remarques sur la société Pompéienne (à propos des tablettes de L. Caecilius Jucundus)"', *Dialoghi di Archeologia*, 9–10: 631–47.

Raper, R. A. (1977), 'The Analysis of the Urban Structure of Pompeii: A Sociological Study of Land Use', in D. L. Clarke, *Spatial Archaeology*, London.

Rathbone, D. (2003), 'The Financing of Maritime Commerce in the Roman Empire, I–II AD', in E. Lo Cascio, *Credito e Moneta nel Mondo Romano*, Bari: 197–230.

Rawson, B. (1991), *Marriage, Divorce and Children in Ancient Rome*, Oxford.

Rawson, B. & Weaver, P. (1997), *The Roman Family: Status, Sentiment and Space*, Oxford.

Rawson, E. (1987), 'Discriminum Ordinum: Lex Julia Theatralis', *Papers of the British School at Rome*, 55: 83–114.

Richardson, L. (1978), 'Concordia and Concordia Augusta: Rome and Pompeii', *La Parola del Passato*, 33: 260–70.

Ricotti, E. S. P. (1987), 'The Importance of Water in Roman Garden Triclinia', in E. B. Macdougall, *Ancient Roman Villa Gardens*, Washington, D.C.: 135–84.

Riggsby, A. M. (1997), 'Public and Private in Roman Culture: The Case of the *Cubiculum*', *Journal of Roman Archaeology*, 10: 36–56.

Rossiter, J. J. & Haldenby, E. (1989), 'A Wine Making Plant in Pompeii Insula II.5', *Echos du Monde Classique*, 33: 229–39.

Rowe, G. (2001), 'The Archive of the Sulpicii at Murecine: A Family of Roman Businessmen Put Roman Law to Work', unpublished.

—— (2002), 'Law and Society in the Murecine Archive', unpublished.

Ruddell, S. M. (1964), 'The Inn, Restaurant and Tavern Business in Ancient Pompeii', MA thesis, University of Maryland.

Sallares, R. (2002), *Malaria and Rome. A History of Malaria in Ancient Italy*, Oxford.

Saller, R. P. (1982), *Personal Patronage under the Roman Empire*, Cambridge.

—— (1987), 'Men's Age at Marriage and Its Consequence for the Roman Family', *Classical Philology*, 86: 351–7.

—— (1994), *Patriarchy, Property and Death in the Roman Family*, Cambridge.

Saller, R. P. & Shaw, B. D. (1984), 'Roman Tombstones and Roman Family Relations in the Principate', *Journal of Roman Studies*, 74: 124–57.

Sabbatini Tumolesi, P. (1980), *Gladiatorum Paria: Annunci di Spettacoli Gladiatorii a Pompei*, Rome.

Scheid, J. (1992), 'The Religious Roles of Women', in P. Schmitt-Pantell, *A History of Women, Volume 1, from Ancient Goddesses to Christian Saints*, Cambridge, Mass.: 377–408.

Scullard, H. H. (1981), *Festivals and Ceremonies of the Roman Republic*, London.

Schurmann, A. (2000), 'Pneumatics on Stage in Pompeii: Ancient Automatic Devices and their Social Context', in *Homo Faber*, Rome.

Senatore, F. (1998), *Pompei, il Vesuvio e la Penisola Sorentina (Atti del primo ciclo di conferenze di geologia, storia e archeologia)*, Rome.

—— (1999), *Pompei, il Vesuvio e la Penisola Sorentina (Atti del secondo ciclo di conferenze di geologia, storia e archeologia)*, Rome.

Shaw, B. D. (1987), 'The Age of Roman Girls at Marriage: Some Reconsiderations', *Journal of Roman Studies*, 77: 30–46.

—— (1991), 'The Cultural Meaning of Death: Age and Gender in the Roman

Family', in D. I. Kertzer & R. P. Saller, *The Family in Italy from Antiquity to the Present*, New Haven.

Sigurdsson, H. (2002), 'Mount Vesuvius before the Disaster', in W. F. Jashemski, & F. G. Meyer (2002), *The Natural History of Pompeii*, Cambridge: 29–36.

Sigurdsson, H. & Carey, S. (2002), 'The Eruption of Vesuvius in AD 79', in W. F. Jashemski, & F. G. Meyer (2002), *The Natural History of Pompeii*, Cambridge: 37–64.

Sogliano, A. (1901), 'Il Borgo Marinaio presso Il Sarno', *Notizie degli Scavi*, 1901: 423–40.

Spinazzola, V. (1953), *Pompei alla Luce degli Scavi Nuove di Via dell'Abbondanza (Anni 1910–1923)*, Rome.

Sirks, B. (2001), 'Sailing in the Off Season with Reduced Financial Risk', in J.-J. Aubert & B. Sirks, *Speculum Iuris. Roman Law as a Reflection of Social and Economic Life in Antiquity*, Ann Arbor: 134–50.

Stefani, G. (2003), *Menander: La Casa del Menandro di Pompei*, Milan.

Stegerman, H. (1994), *Die Essener, Qumran, Johannes der Taufer und Jesus*, Freiburg-Basle-Vienna: Herder

Toynbee, J. M. C. (1971), *Death and Burial in the Roman World*, London.

Treggiari, S. (1969), *Roman Freedmen during the Late Republic*, Oxford.

—— (1991), *Roman Marriage*, Oxford.

Trevor Hodge, A. (1996), '*In Vitruvium Pompeianum*: Urban Water Distribution Reappraised', *American Journal of Archaeology*, 100: 261–76.

Tsujimura, S. (1991), 'Ruts in Pompeii. The Traffic System in the Roman City', *Opuscula Pompeiana*, 2: 58–86.

Tuffreau-Libre, M. (1999), 'Les Pots à Couleur de Pompéi: Premiers Résultats', *Rivista di Studi Pompeiani*, 10: 63–70.

Varrone, A. (1995), 'Più Terremoti a Pompei? I Nuovi Dati degli Scavi di Via dell'Abbondanza', in T. Fröhlich & L. Jacobelli, *Archäologie und Seismologie*, Munich: 29–35.

—— (2001), *Eroticism in Pompeii*, Rome.

—— (2002), *Erotica Pompeiana: Love Inscriptions on the Walls of Pompeii*, Rome.

Verney, P. (1979), *The Earthquake Handbook*, London.

Veyne, P. (1990), *Bread and Circuses*, London.

Wallace-Hadrill, A. F. (1989), *Patronage in Ancient Society*, London.

—— (1994), *Houses and Society in Pompeii and Herculaneum*, Princeton.

Weaver, P. R. C. (1991), 'Children of Freedmen (and Freedwomen)', in B. Rawson, *Marriage, Divorce and Children in Ancient Rome*, Oxford: 166–90.

Wiseman, T. P. (1977), 'Cicero, pro Sulla 60–1', *Liverpool Classical Monthly*, 2: 21–2.
—— (1979), 'Vesuvius: The Giants' Revenge', *History Today*, 29: 790–4.

Zanker, P. (1988), *The Power of Images in the Age of Augustus*, Ann Arbor.
—— (1998), *Pompeii: Public and Private Life*, Cambridge, Mass.
Zevi, F. (1984), *Pompei 79. Raccolta per il Decimo Centennario dell'Eruzione Vesuviana*, Naples.

INDEX